Golden Rules

Markets and Governments in Economic History
A series edited by Price Fishback

See also in the series:

Golden Rules

The Origins of California Water Law in the Gold Rush

MARK KANAZAWA

THE UNIVERSITY OF CHICAGO PRESS   CHICAGO AND LONDON

MARK KANAZAWA is professor of economics at Carleton College.

The University of Chicago Press, Chicago 60637
The University of Chicago Press, Ltd., London
© 2015 by The University of Chicago
All rights reserved. Published 2015.
Printed in the United States of America
24 23 22 21 20 19 18 17 16 15   1 2 3 4 5

ISBN-13: 978-0-226-25867-6 (cloth)
ISBN-13: 978-0-226-25870-6 (e-book)
DOI: 10.7208/chicago/9780226258706.001.0001

Library of Congress Cataloging-in-Publication Data

Kanazawa, Mark, author.
    Golden rules : the origins of California water law in the Gold Rush / Mark Kanazawa.
        pages ; cm. — (Markets and governments in economic history)
    Includes bibliographical references and index.
    ISBN 978-0-226-25867-6 (cloth : alk. paper) — ISBN 978-0-226-25870-6 (e-book)
1. Water rights—California—History—19th century.   2. Gold mines and mining—
California—Water-supply—History—19th century.   3. California—Gold discoveries.
1. Title.   II. Series: Markets and governments in economic history.
    KFC162.K36 2015
    346.79404′691—dc23

                                                                            2014041296

TO MY FATHER, TOORU KANAZAWA
I COULD ENVISION WHAT WAS POSSIBLE
THROUGH HIS SHINING EXAMPLE.

Contents

Acknowledgments

This book, which brings together two longstanding interests of mine—gold rushes and water—is the culmination of many diverse threads in my personal life and professional career. My grandfather, Matajiro Fuse, was a miner in the Klondike Gold Rush in the 1890s, and it is perhaps from him that I acquired a fascination with the idea that a shiny yellow metal, number seventy-nine in the periodic table, could exert an almost irresistible, hypnotic pull on the imagination of so many otherwise normal individuals. So irresistible, indeed, that these normal folks would willingly subject themselves to enormous physical and personal hardships in the mere off-chance that they might, just might, strike it rich. Like so many others, my grandfather was caught in the thrall of gold and in a different, academic, sense, so have I been for the past fifteen years.

My academic interest in water stems from my graduate school days at Stanford in California, where the arid climate reminded me on an almost daily basis how scarce and precious water was. I could not help but think about what to do about water shortages, water overuse, and the associated environmental impacts. My initial foray into these issues was largely about water policy. My advisors, Tim Bresnahan and Roger Noll, were not specialists in water issues, but they both actively encouraged my interest and provided me with invaluable guidance in how to think sensibly about water policy. At the same time, courses I was taking from Nathan Rosenberg and Gavin Wright were providing me with an appreciation for the importance of history in the development and performance of economies over time. I left graduate school with a firm belief in the importance of economics in guiding policy and the value of viewing economies within a longer-term historical context.

But it was not until a few years later, when I was pursuing a post-doctoral fellowship at UC-Berkeley, that I really began to appreciate the importance of institutions in influencing economic outcomes, and no-where did this seem to be truer than with respect to water. This real-ization led to a keen interest in water law and my training as an econo-mist naturally impelled me toward using economics to understand the currents in the law. The scholarly literatures in law-and-economics and the *New Institutional Economics* provided a coherent, comprehensive framework for understanding many of the features of the law from an economic standpoint. My training in economic history made me realize that historical events could play a key role in influencing the content of current institutions. And lastly, at Berkeley I was extremely fortunate to get to know and learn from Michael Hanemann and David Zilberman, who know as much about water as any economist alive. They strongly supported my interest in water institutions and were invaluable in shar-ing their expertise with me on a whole host of water issues.

The specific genesis of the ideas in this book came a few years later when I was becoming increasingly dissatisfied with merely poring over court rulings involving water disputes, which provided me with a good sense for the broad currents in the law but seemed impossible to convinc-ingly tie to economic factors. I attempted to forge this connection in my 1998 *Journal of Legal Studies* article on late nineteenth-century Califor-nia water law, and in the process of researching and writing that article, I became convinced of the importance of transaction costs in guiding the development of water law. However, I also became convinced that I was only scratching the surface in terms of really understanding the connec-tion between the content of water law and its underlying economic deter-minants. At that point, I decided that I needed to broaden my focus to examine a larger set of factors that seemed to be relevant, including the specific uses of water, externalities arising from use, the cost structure of water use and development, factor intensities, and technological change. I also believed there could be considerable advantages to examining a period in history, both for the insights into current institutions that it would generate and for the long-term perspective it would provide.

For many reasons that I will describe in great detail in the discussion to come, for my purposes the Gold Rush period and its aftermath proved to be an almost ideal subject of study. But the project turned out to be massive in scale and scope, requiring numerous visits to various repos-itories of information around the state, including the Bancroft Library at UC Berkeley; the California Room at the California State Library; the California State Archives; the Ahmanson Room at the Huntington Library; the Searls Library in Nevada City, Nevada County; the Placer County Court Archives in Auburn, Placer County; the Carlo de Ferrari Archive in Sonora, Tuolumne County; the State Historic Park Archives in Columbia, Tuolumne County; and the Tuolumne County Historical Society, in Sonora, Tuolumne County. A great many people gave generously of their time and energy to support my efforts in digging through their holdings to find the information I needed, but I wish to single out three special individuals: Carmel Barry-Schweyer at the Placer County Court Archives, Charlie Dyer at the Carlo de Ferrari Archive, and the late Ed Tyson at the Searls Library. Without their help, I would never have managed to successfully navigate their old, musty records, and I never would have been able to find the precious nuggets of information that form the empirical basis for this book.

I also wish to acknowledge a deep debt of gratitude to the National Science Foundation, the American Philosophical Society, and Carleton College. A perfect storm of support from these institutions occurred in 1999 and 2000, when I was awarded a major grant from the Economics Program at the NSF, a sabbatical fellowship grant from the American Philosophical Society, and a Hewlett grant from Carleton College. These grants freed me from my teaching responsibilities for over a year and supported numerous trips to California to collect data and other information on early disputes over water.

In the past several years, as my thoughts regarding early California water law have been coming together, I have presented some of the research for this book in numerous academic settings, which has provided me with much valuable feedback with which to polish and refine my argument. The forums where I have presented these ideas include the annual meetings of the International Society for the New Institutional Economics, the Economic History Association, the Western Economic Association, and the International Water Resource Economics Consortium. I have also received much useful feedback from participants in the Workshop in Political Theory at Indiana University; seminars at the Applied Economics Department at the University of Minnesota; the economics departments of Stanford University, UCLA, University of Arizona, Montana State, and Carleton College; and the Environmental Law and Economics seminar at the University of Arizona. I extend special thanks to Jenny Bourne, Karen Clay, Robert Glennon, Nathan Grawe,

P. J. Hill, Gary Libecap, Dean Lueck, Henry Smith, Kim Smith, George Vrtis, Gavin Wright, and Richard Zerbe for their insightful comments on various facets of the manuscript. I also wish to gratefully acknowledge the following former students of mine at Carleton, who have provided me over the years with able and enthusiastic research assistance: Aaron Swoboda, Justin Bauer, Alex Cook, and Barbara Marchevsky. None of the above individuals, of course, are to be implicated for any errors that remain.

I would also like to thank Price Fishback, who perceived sufficient value in my ideas and findings to encourage me to write the story that has become this book. Without that kick in the pants, this research may still not have seen the light of day. I also thank Joe Jackson, my editor at the University of Chicago Press, and Shenyun Wu and Jillian Tsui, who have helped me immensely in navigating all of the fine logistical details of actually putting this book together in its final form.

Last but not least, I am grateful to my sons Galen and Nick, for their support and for their patience with me when I was absent in California collecting all of the information that forms the basis for this book. And finally, I owe my deepest debt of gratitude to my wife, Kathy, who provided me with moral, emotional, and logistical support well above and beyond the call of duty while I worked on this manuscript. She is the unsung heroine in this endeavor.

Preface

As we move further into the twenty-first century, fresh water is scarce and growing scarcer. In all parts of the world, continuing economic and population growth place growing demands on available water supplies. At the same time, options for increasing fresh water supply sufficient to meet growing demands are appearing increasingly limited. It is becoming clear that we cannot rely solely, or even primarily, on technological solutions such as desalination and rainwater harvesting to "supply" our way out of growing scarcity. What is crucially needed is better management of what we have, toward making our available fresh water supplies go farther in meeting crucial human needs.

In moving forward, many management options present themselves, but much of the debate about what to do may be simply framed as centering on the question of how to treat private property rights in water. The economic approach to property rights to natural resources focuses on the way legal rights to ownership of resources are defined, with an eye toward the resulting incentives for how those resources are used. The way property rights are defined matters because it determines how those resources may be used by the owner in order to capture value. When it comes to improving management of water, we will have to rely heavily on changes in the behavior of water users and for this, incentives are crucial.

One entire set of strategies has centralized government regulation playing an important role in managing water, ostensibly in support of broader societal goals. In this case, whatever private property rights there are will be circumscribed, perhaps heavily so, by government policies. This need not mean any sort of command-and-control system. The policies could consist of, for example, clean water regulations, groundwater pumping taxes, wild-and-scenic rivers protection, or application of the public trust doctrine. The point is that under this set of strategies, individual right-holders are more or less restricted in how freely they can exercise their rights. Improved management comes about to the extent that government policies provide better incentives for rational water use. It can be a major challenge to improve our management of water, however, because those policies often inadequately reflect information available to the users themselves that influence their decision-making. There is the additional danger that policies may not embody larger social goals at all but rather may reflect political capture of government officials by vested interest groups, or that they will be vigorously resisted by groups who stand to lose if they are implemented.

A quite different set of strategies consists of assigning property rights to users that are largely, if not entirely, unconstrained by government policies, save that they are protected from involuntary seizure by third parties through an enforcement mechanism. As a result, these strategies assign much greater decentralized decision-making power to private parties. The property rights that are created are an attempt to capitalize on the information possessed by decision makers regarding their own preferences and local conditions, and depending upon how they are created, they may be much freer of political influences. Property rights of this form are implicitly assumed when policies are proposed to improve water allocation by relying more heavily on water markets. A common concern expressed about this latter strategy is that making water rights largely unconstrained may provide insufficient incentives for rights-holders to consider the effect of their use, including transfers of those rights to others, on third parties. Concerns about its distributional impact are also commonly heard, to the extent that it results in the denial of access to water to various, often underprivileged, segments of the citizenry.

These strategies are not, of course, necessarily mutually exclusive, as one can easily envision intermediate property rights systems containing elements of each strategy in different proportions. Water markets need not be completely unregulated, for example, and government policies may afford varying amounts of freedom of action for water developers and water users. How much of each system is desirable often comes down to how strongly one feels about servicing distributional goals or how concerned one is about third-party impacts. The question can then be phrased as not one-system-or-the-other but rather, the circumstances under which it is desirable to have property rights that are more conditional, and how conditional they should be. This is a crucial, often unstated, question underlying much of the current discussion on water management strategies.

Unfortunately, it is often the case that the economic rationale for specific features of water rights is not entirely clear. Part of the problem is the complexity of the water rights definitions that have emerged over time. It may not be clear, for example, whether it makes sense to base water rights in California largely, but not entirely, on the principle of *first-in-time is first-in-right*. Or why current water law in the state requires that water use be put to beneficial purposes, and exactly what this means. Or why it is that maintaining a water right requires that you use the water, the so-called *use-it-or-lose-it* provision. But without this understanding, it is difficult to know whether such provisions should be part of any new legal regime that wishes to improve water management.

A fundamental premise of this book is that we can gain insights into current issues regarding water right design by examining the emergence and operation of water rights in the past. Many of the issues we experience today in managing water have obviously been experienced before, and the experiences of the past may provide a number of useful lessons for today. The fundamental, unchanging physical nature of water provides a usable practical connection between different eras of water use. Technological advance notwithstanding, the fundamental methods used by societies to harness natural waters and apply them to achieving societal objectives has not changed fundamentally over the years: we still build dams, reservoirs, and diversion facilities. Nor has it changed much that water diversion and use can often inflict significant impacts on third parties. As a result, many of the same issues of property rights definition that we observe today have occurred in analogous form in the past. By understanding the development of water rights in previous settings, we have a better sense for the tradeoffs and challenges associated with adopting new property rights regimes in general.

The particular period that I have chosen to study is early California in the decade of the 1850s. This period is worth studying because it witnessed the confluence of the beginning of statehood itself and one of the most momentous events in California history, the California Gold Rush. The combination of these two events conferred upon the Gold Rush an enormous impact in influencing the subsequent development of the state's system of water law, because of the central role water played in the prosecution of mining. As we shall see, the Gold Rush generated a number of fundamental issues over how water rights were to be defined, which occurred right at the time when the resolution of those issues would have the most lasting influence: the formative beginning. It was during this period that many of the principles governing water rights in California were formed in the prosecution of mining, principles that exist to this day. Examining the circumstances under which many current principles were formed helps us understand how those principles came to be, and it reveals a great deal about what economic purpose they serve.

As this book will document, the development and use of water during that period was intimately connected to the prosecution of mining. This fact presents both a challenge and an opportunity. The challenge is to provide a consistent, coherent interpretation of the side-by-side development of the two sets of property rights. Both mining rights and water rights would have been influenced by the same economic currents operating in the California gold fields. Yet the very different physical properties of gold and water imply that the property rights that emerged for the two resources may well have been quite different in important ways. How we understand the differences in an economically coherent way is the challenge presented by the circumstances. The opportunity is that we can capitalize on a richer set of information to better understand the formation of property rights pertaining to each individual industry. As will be shown, this approach yields richer insights into the economic currents that molded the property rights of each.

The discussion to come will also speak to the fact that property rights may be generated by a number of different institutional mechanisms. In considering current options for management practices, for example, the rules governing water rights may be constitutionally mandated, legislated, created by courts, or chosen in a cooperative way by the users themselves. One question that might reasonably be asked is: What is the best institutional mechanism to rely upon? Answering this question is made more challenging by the fact that the different mechanisms may interact in a complex way. As we shall see, these issues arose in early California: the courts, legislature, and local mining camps were all sources of rules, and they interacted in a way that obscures easy interpretation.

Much of the story in early California is what happened in the mining camps and the rules created there. But the greater part of the story is what happened in the common-law courts, which created the official law of water and mining rights that survives to this day. Most studies treat the mining camps and courts as largely separate but as we shall see, they were also intimately connected. So just as when we study gold and water together, studying miners' codes and court rulings also provides richer insights into each. We gain insights into the dynamics of sources of different rules because the mining camps operated in a largely democratic fashion, whereas the courts created doctrine as largely impartial arbiters of disputes over mining claims and water. This, too, has ramifications for today, as we consider water rights created by official institutions such as courts alongside water rights that could be fashioned internally to commons as a result of collective action by the participants.

In sum, an in-depth examination of the circumstances of early California in the Gold Rush and its immediate aftermath may provide some important insights into the economic properties of different rules governing property rights. It may also help us better understand how to go about creating rules that promise better water management, by using the various institutional mechanisms at our disposal. And it may shed much light on how we got to where we are in the first place.

CHAPTER ONE

Introduction

I think that I may without vanity affirm that I have seen the elephant. —Louisa Clappe

1.1 Introduction

There is an age-old parable that goes something like this. An elephant wanders into a village in which there live some blind men. The blind men, who did not know what an elephant was, go to investigate, and each one touches a different part of the elephant. The one who touches one of the elephant's ears concludes that an elephant is like a fan. The one who touches the tail concludes that an elephant is like a rope. The one who touches the elephant's flank concludes that an elephant is like a wall. Each one draws a different conclusion on the nature of "elephantness."

The blind men were, of course, behaving kind of like social scientists. Each one was collecting evidence and drawing a conclusion based upon that evidence. The problem was that each one was basing his conclusion on extremely limited and selectively chosen evidence. And it comes as no surprise that they arrive at completely different conclusions.

For a book on water rights in Gold Rush California, this parable is appropriate for two reasons. The first is that there is a long tradition in Gold Rush history in which elephants figure prominently. When the gold seekers set out for California, many of them told their friends and family that they were going to "see the elephant." The expression came from a popular tale that circulated when traveling circuses commonly brought elephants with them to the towns where they performed. According to the tale, a farmer was on his way to town with a horse-drawn wagon full of vegetables and decided he wanted to go see the elephant. When he saw it, he thought it was a wondrous thing. His horse, however, was frightened out of his wits at the sight of the elephant and bolted, strewing the farmer's vegetables all over the ground. But when his friends commiserated over his misfortune, he replied: "I don't care, for I have seen the elephant." From that tale, "seeing the elephant" came to mean a once-in-a-lifetime experience that was, however, fraught with danger, hardships, and potential disaster. For many gold seekers, this seemed to describe perfectly the prospect of going to California to seek their fortunes.

The second reason I choose to tell this parable here has to do with the challenges of Gold Rush scholarship. It is hard and fraught with dangers because there is so much evidence available for scholars to consult and evaluate, including news stories, miner's diaries, government reports, state executive documents, court rulings, mining codes, county histories, statutes and their legislative histories, company records, and previous scholarship. The sources of information are many, and the information they provide is rich and detailed, almost an embarrassment of riches. But not all of the available evidence seems to be conveying the same message: indeed, sometimes different bits of evidence seem to be saying very different things. Like the blind men of the parable, every Gold Rush scholar runs the danger of drawing the wrong conclusions by sampling the wrong evidence. And just like touching a tail tells you something different than touching an ear, reading a mining code may tell you something different from reading a miner's journal. Reading one miner's journal might tell you something different from reading another miner's journal. To get the story straight, much evidence should be consulted and careful judgment exercised regarding the reliability of the evidence and once one is convinced, to make sure one is applying the correct interpretation.

There is a logical meta-question, which may not have occurred to the blind men: Why is it important to study the Gold Rush? The answer the blind men might have given is curiosity, pure and simple. As far as I can tell, nobody ever asked them why they wanted to know the nature of the elephant. They just did. But it turns out that there are good reasons to study the Gold Rush for someone like me, who has spent much of his professional career trying to understand the economic rationale for the rules governing water development and water use that have emerged in the American West. First and foremost, it turns out that the development and use of water was a central part of the story of how gold mining was done. This is because of the nature of the mining process itself and the way it evolved during the decade of the 1850s. From the very beginning, water was a virtually indispensable part of the process, and it became only more so over time. This meant that miners and ditch companies were continually and persistently engaged in efforts to define and clarify rights to available water supplies. Because of this, a clear and detailed picture emerges of the nature of the disputes that arose and the strategies adopted by competing claimants to water.

Second, the peculiar circumstances of the Gold Rush provide an unparalleled natural experiment in which to study the evolution of legal rules. The discovery of gold in California in 1848 set off a chain of events that can only be described as a massive exogenous shock to the California economy. Within two years, the nonnative population of the state had increased more than six -fold. Within five years, the state had undergone a major structural transformation from a largely pastoral economy to one in which gold production was the leading industry. And as water was integral to producing gold, the demand for water skyrocketed virtually overnight, along with its value. The result was predictable: numerous disputes over water that raised a whole host of issues that required resolution, and a sore need for ways to resolve those disputes quickly and consistently. The gold discovery and its aftermath generated enormous pressures for the creation of legal rules to accomplish these things. Very rarely do we have the opportunity to observe the process of rule creation where the connection to economic pressures is so rapid, strong, and obvious.

Third, the development of legal rules governing water development and use in early California had consequences going far beyond its own narrow slice of time and place in history. The basic precepts that emerged from the gold fields would comprise the fundamental principles of water law in California that continue to this day. To read the California water code of today is to catch a glimpse of the disputes over water that occurred in the gold fields in the 1850s. Because economic change typically occurs slowly, it is often difficult to discern the economic rationale for the water rights observed to exist, which are the end result of an evolutionary path-dependent legal process with roots in the past.[1] Examining in detail the economic currents that gave rise to those principles in their infancy helps to make economic sense of the laws in their current form.

1.2. Origins of California Water Law: 1849–1860

Prior to the discovery of gold in California in January of 1848, the California economy was a largely pastoral, heavily agriculture-based economy. A large number of Native American tribes occupied the region for some fifteen thousand years before the coming of the Spanish in the mid-sixteenth century. The Spanish gave way to Mexican rule in the early nineteenth century, which lasted for about twenty-five years until American takeover as spoils of the Mexican War in 1848. Under Mexican rule, large ranchos, commonly as large as tens of thousands of acres, dominated rural life, especially in the southern part of the region. Agriculture thrived, especially cattle production on the ranchos as well as irrigation-based production of wheat, barley, corn, fruits, and vegetables.[2]

The discovery of gold triggered a mass-migration of gold seekers to the region from all over the world, resulting in massive population growth within an extremely short period. Our best guess is that the non-native population of California increased from around 14,000 in mid-1848 to nearly 100,000 by the end of 1849, a figure that rose to one quarter million by the time a special census was taken in 1852.[3] The rise of the new gold mining industry generated a dramatic increase in demand for water as gold production rose and as water was used heavily in gold processing. Thus, the local value of water increased dramatically practically overnight, giving rise to strong pressures to create legal rules to define and enforce property rights to water. At the same time, the unique nature of water as a flowing resource created externalities resulting from its development and application to gold mining, which in turn gave rise to specific rules that established principles for resolving the disputes generated by those externalities.

As this book will document, water rights during this period were largely created in the courts, influenced by rules for self-governance written by the miners themselves in a network of extralegal mining camps that emerged spontaneously in the gold fields. These rules, set out in mining codes, originated in the basic social and cultural attitudes of miners as formed elsewhere and imported into the region when they emigrated to California. As a consequence, they partly embodied the collective interest of miners in allocative fairness.[4] However, they were mainly shaped by the economic realities of gold mining on the ground once they arrived, including the value of water in mining, which determined the propensity to invest in water development and use and the appropriate scale of individual mining operations. These factors in turn influenced the extent of division of labor and the adoption of water-using techniques.

The water rights that emerged from this period had certain distinctive features that would form the fundamental basis for the present-day doctrine of prior appropriation that governs surface water rights not only in California but in many other parts of the arid American West as well. Among these were several principles that will be an important focus of the analysis of this book. Perhaps the central principle defining appropriative rights is *first-in-time is first-in-right*, the rule that (senior) claimants who perfect their rights at a particular point in time enjoy rights that are superior to subsequent (junior) claimants. Another key principle is the ability of claimants to divert water for use at locations away from the river or stream in which it flowed, to which was later appended the rule that such use had to be *beneficial*. A third is the very nature of the right itself as a quantified use (*usufructuary*) right, as opposed to a right to ownership of the corpus of the water itself. A fourth is that claimants had to actually use the water that they claimed or risk forfeiting it, the principle of *use-it-or-lose-it*. By examining the manner in which these principles were laid down in the conditions of mining in early California, we can better understand the economic rationale for present-day water law.

1.3. Existing Interpretations of Early California Water Law

Though the basic facts regarding the origins of California water law in the demands of mining in the very first years of statehood are not in dispute, the specific drivers of this law have been the subject of a long-running and vigorous interpretive debate among historians, economists, and legal scholars. The oldest scholarly tradition ascribes the creation of appropriative rights largely to climate. Early in the twentieth century, such eminent legal scholars as Clesson Kinney and Samuel Wiel argued that it was the aridity of the west that necessitated the creation of new water rights.[5] This notion was popularized by Walter Prescott Webb in 1931 in his classic book *The Great Plains*, when he argued that

> The justification of the arid-region doctrine is found in the physical conditions of the country in which it has been adopted.[6]

As late as the 1980s, the aridity argument found its proponents in the writings of the eminent western historians Robert Dunbar and Gordon Bakken.[7]

In the 1980s, however, some historians began to question the basic aridity story. While not rejecting aridity as a central factor, they began to emphasize economic, social, and cultural factors in the creation of the new water rights. Scholars began to explore more deeply into human intentionality in devising water rights to meet their needs. In 1985, Donald Worster, drawing upon the previous work of Wittfogel and Morton Horwitz in other contexts, advanced the argument that appropriative rights were the result of an ascendant capitalist culture dedicated to dominance over nature. At around the same time, Donald Pisani advanced the very different notion that appropriative rights largely reflected a number of local factors associated with the complex circumstances surrounding the prosecution of mining in 1850s California. To Pisani, the early decisions creating appropriative rights were dominated by the immediacy of balancing competing needs for water under frontier conditions, leavened to some extent by early judges' sensitivity to charges of improperly ignoring precedent or judicial overreach. Douglas Littlefield echoed Pisani when he argued that judges' rulings, particularly at the local level, could be heavily swayed by public pressures.[8]

Early economic historians pursued the aridity story down a different path, emphasizing the importance of water value in determining the ultimate form assumed by property rights in water. In 1967, Harold Demsetz advanced the highly influential notion that property rights were endogenous to changes in economic conditions that increased the value of natural resources such as water or that resulted in uses that imposed additional external costs on others. According to Demsetz, changes in property rights would occur in the form of measures that permitted greater extraction of value or internalized these externalities. In 1975, Terry Anderson and P. J. Hill extended Demsetz's argument by emphasizing the importance of property rights enforcement in influencing the form taken by rights to natural resources. According to Anderson and Hill, we can expect to observe greater efforts made to enforce property rights in resources as either the benefits of enforcement increased, say, from increased value, and/or the costs of enforcement decreased. The creation of appropriative rights is then seen as the end-result of a process of redefining property rights to permit greater extraction of value.[9]

This basic dynamic that emphasizes value and enforcement costs in the creation of seemingly more-clearly defined water rights has been refined by Carol Rose, who does not view the creation of well-defined individual water rights as being the necessary end game of this process. Rose points to the emergence of riparian rights in the eastern United States as evidence of the feasibility of a stable legal regime based upon group-based rather than individual rights. In her view, the differences in eastern and western water rights that emerged over time occurred as a consequence of fundamental differences in the historical uses to which available waters have been put. In the early nineteenth century, when riparian rights were being defined in the eastern United States, surface water in that region was largely being used for powering water mills, a process that largely did not consume the water that was being used. Consequently, water use possessed important public good characteristics and it was sensible that the water rights that emerged would accrue to the group of users, as riparian rights did. However, in the western United States, the dominant uses, such as mining and irrigation, largely did consume the water, so that the water used by one claimant effectively deprived others of water. In this case, water assumed the features of private goods, and it is sensible that the emergent water rights would accrue to individuals. Thus, Rose speculated that the consumptiveness of use was an important determinant of the ultimate form taken by water rights.[10]

In emphasizing the internalization of externalities, the balancing of the costs and benefits of enforcement, and the private-good nature of western uses, Demsetz, Anderson and Hill, and Rose advance an interpretation that largely emphasizes the efficiency-enhancing properties of legal change. Under this view, the creation and development of water rights are largely driven by pressures to maximize the overall economic rents from available water resources. Law-and-economics scholars have, however, critiqued institutional regimes based upon first possession principles such as the first-in-time, first-in-right principle in appropriative law on the basis that they may give rise to a phenomenon known as *racing dissipation*. Racing dissipation occurs when claimants dissipate rents in the form of expenditures in a race to acquire the resource.[11] If rights to water were acquired under the first-in-time, first-in right regime, as they were under prior appropriation, this at least raises the possibility that racing dissipation may have occurred, resulting in loss of significant rents from the resulting race to capture the available water.

The efficiency interpretation of the origins of appropriative rights has recently been subjected to fundamental challenge by David Schorr on very different grounds. Schorr argues that the creation of appropriative rights was driven not by efficiency, but by considerations of fairness and distributive justice.[12] In examining the creation of appropriative rights in nineteenth-century Colorado, he argues that these rights were designed to distribute the benefits from available water resources as widely as possible across different miners, consistent with providing each miner enough water to successfully prosecute mining. Of direct relevance to the present argument, he also argues that the same dynamic was operating in early California in the period under examination here.[13] Indeed, numerous parallels between the legal rules that emerged in Colorado and California during this period are suggestive of a similar dynamic that shaped the creation of these rules. Schorr's interpretation, however, leaves open many questions regarding the role not only of fundamental water scarcity, but also of numerous other economic factors that may have affected the costs and benefits of different legal rules.

1.4. Institutions and Institutional Change

We are thus left with a persistent, as-yet unresolved interpretive question regarding how to understand the origins of appropriative water law in the prosecution of mining in early California. As I argued earlier, a major reason for the lack of scholarly consensus is the enormous amount of available evidence, in the form of court rulings, mining codes, news accounts, and miner's diaries and other contemporary accounts, plus the fact that these different sources of information do not always seem to be telling us the same thing. This means that support can be found for a number of different perspectives, depending upon what evidence one looks at and which pieces of evidence one emphasizes. What is needed is a careful, holistic examination of the evidence. At the same time, there is a need for a theoretical framework that permits sensible interpretation of the evidence in a coherent and consistent manner.

Water law is, of course, the set of legal institutions that govern the development, use, and allocation of water resources. In principle, these laws influence private behavior regarding water by shaping the incentives experienced by private users. Given the incentives provided by existing institutions such as legal rules or dispute resolution mechanisms, private agents optimize as best they can in their decisions to claim, develop, and use water.[14] When these rules are created by the courts in a common-law regime, or by some legislative body through a regime of statutory law, there will commonly be enforcement mechanisms created as part of that regime, in order to ensure compliance. The extent to which they are constrained and guided by these rules depends upon the perceived legitimacy of these rules and the process used to craft them, as well as the costs to authorities of enforcing the rules. In other contexts, however, users may cooperate to create self-governing rules, which may include enforcement mechanisms that are internal to the group.[15]

Legal rules, and institutions more generally, not only govern economic behavior, but also are subject to pressures to change exerted by the very actors governed by those rules. This is perhaps easiest to see within the context of a local community creating rules for local governance of water resources, where community members may participate in the rule creation process. Within a common-law regime, the courts create legal rules based upon the disputes over water resources brought before them. Thus, individual actors influence the rules by bringing cases to court, with rules evolving gradually over time, depending upon the particular issue at hand, how inclined judges are to adhere to precedent, and how rapidly economic conditions change. The cumulative outcome can be a body of law that evolves predictably over time in response to economic pressures and may tend toward efficiency.[16] When the legal rules consist of statutory law, individuals may engage in rent-seeking behavior to try to obtain favorable political outcomes, which may then be reflected in statutory provisions and mandates.[17] The ability of individual actors to secure such legislation depends upon their ability to organize into majority coalitions and to overcome free rider problems in order to bring to bear effective political pressures on behalf of their own interests.[18] Even constitution making can be subject to rent-seeking behavior, as individuals or groups attempt to secure constitutional provisions that promote their own interests.[19]

The content of water law, and its evolution over time, would seem to be a prime example of this reciprocal dynamic in operation. At any point in time, rules exist governing the development and allocation of water, as embodied in property rights definition, dispute resolution, and the regulation of various types of water development and use activity. These rules, which can exist in legislation, court rulings, constitutions, and informal norms and customs, influence the water-using behavior of economic agents, by both constraining and providing incentives for economic activity. For example, enforceable common-law rules that require water use to be reasonable or beneficial constrain users from engaging in certain types of activities; namely, ones that confer little benefit on the user or impose undue harm on other users.

At the same time, water development and use activities can lead to disputes that are brought to court, and the resulting rulings may create general principles that are applied to other similar disputes in future cases. That is, when courts make rulings on disputes over water, they are not only resolving the dispute at hand, they are creating new doctrinal principles, or reinforcing existing ones, that will govern future disputes with similar patterns of fact.[20] The entire body of doctrine that they create provides the common-law institutional framework that governs water development and water use activity, which incentivizes such activity and reduces uncertainty about what can and cannot be done, and about the consequences of taking action. So, for example, increasing water development along a river or stream can generate the impetus for new rules that require water use to be reasonable even where no such rules existed before.[21]

The courts themselves do not, however, exist within an institutional vacuum. Broadly speaking, judges themselves commonly operate within an institutional structure that guides and constrains their decision making. This structure can consist of constitutional principles, narrower legislative mandates, the philosophy and precedents of a common-law history, political pressures for certain types of rulings, and informal customs and traditions. Among formal institutions, constitutions provide the broadest level of guidance to courts, by setting forth constitutional principles that courts must abide by. In some cases, constitutions are relatively brief and operate at a level of broad generality, affording judges considerable leeway in laying out legal principles, including principles for water development, use, and allocation. In other cases, however, they are highly detailed and specific regarding what is constitutionally permissible. Article fifteen of the state constitution of Idaho, for example, contains seven sections governing a variety of aspects of water rights that are highly directive to both the courts and the state legislature. These include provisions that water is a public resource and therefore explicitly subject to regulation; that water rights are based on temporal priority; that in times of shortage domestic uses dominate agricultural uses, which dominate manufacturing uses; that agricultural uses are guaranteed to receive continuing flow once rights have been acquired; and that in times of shortage, the state legislature may impose "reasonable limitations" on water use.[22] These constitutional provisions can impose substantive and meaningful constraints on the types of water allocation principles that can be mandated by Idaho judges.

The interaction between courts and the legislature is more complex. Whereas courts are bound to operate within a constitutional framework, courts and legislatures can act as agenda-setters for each other. However, their influence tends to operate on different levels. Legislatures can enact statutes that direct courts in various ways, as long as issues of constitutionality are not involved. In this case, courts behave primarily as interpreters of legislative intent. However, courts are sometimes called upon to rule on the constitutionality of statutes. This has happened, for example, recently in California and Washington when state laws to impose fees on water rights holders and to strengthen the water rights of municipal utilities have been challenged on constitutional grounds.[23] Within constitutional boundaries, then, courts may operate within a narrower set of legislative boundaries that may effectively constrain them in terms of how they may rule. However, on certain issues the courts may challenge or even overturn legislative actions that stray outside constitutional mandates.

Within the English common-law tradition, judges are also constrained to some extent by doctrine established in previous rulings through the principle of *stare decisis*. Under this principle, previous rulings serve as precedent for subsequent cases involving similar facts or issues. When there is a rich set of precedents, the law may be considered to be settled on the matter at hand and judges will tend to be unwilling to deviate from the principles of that law. In this case, existing case law will have a good deal of explanatory power in predicting the content of new rulings. However, when economic conditions change, new issues and fact patterns tend to emerge, which can make existing precedent less relevant or persuasive to judges. The result can be the creation of new principles for resolving disputes, which in turn form the basis for future rulings under the new conditions.[24]

Most modern law-and-economics scholars have tended to model judges as largely insulated from political pressures to rule in certain ways, and I will largely follow a similar strategy. However, I will admit the possibility that under certain conditions, even nonelected judges may experience political pressures sufficient to influence their rulings. Within the context of the present study, I am thinking not so much of modern interest group politics but rather, a frontier setting in which local judges may know their neighbors, feel local pressures, and mistrust local law enforcement, and they may thus feel less than perfectly secure in handing down "objective" rulings that may incur local ire. We tend not to think of such factors nowadays, but I believe that they may well have been operant in the early days of California statehood.[25]

The point here is not merely that each of these factors can vary, with resulting different influences on judges' rulings. At any particular point in time, a judge can experience these different factors with quite different force. In certain institutional contexts, constitutional or legislative mandates may be salient in comparison with direct political pressures. In other cases, the opposite may be true. To the extent that there is a grey area in terms of what is constitutionally or legislatively acceptable, and judges have latitude in how they respond to these different, potentially conflicting forces, the rulings they hand down may well vary considerably depending upon the circumstances. Recognizing this fact will be important toward understanding the experience of California during the period studied here.

1.5. Some Currents in Gold Rush Historiography

Another contribution of this study is to shed light on various aspects of the California Gold Rush of the early 1850s and the subsequent development of the gold mining industry that dominated the state economy for the first fifteen years of statehood. There is an enormous scholarly literature that addresses various dimensions of the Gold Rush and its immediate aftermath, including its cultural, sociological, political, institutional, environmental, and economic aspects. The vastness of this literature reflects in part the grip that the episode continues to exert on our collective imagination. But it also reflects the sheer volume of evidence that we have at our disposal, including contemporaneous accounts, news articles, government reports, and numerous miner's journals and diaries. I will make no attempt to be exhaustive here in describing existing scholarship but rather, I will focus on those sources that speak to various components of my argument.

Gold Rush scholarship has undergone a distinct evolution over time, reflecting greatly increased sophistication in our thinking about the Gold Rush and the methods of analysis we have at our disposal. The early miners themselves left behind a great many records of their experiences in the form of journals, diaries, and letters home to their families. Many accounts need to be taken with a hefty serving of salt and a few were little more than frauds perpetrated on unsuspecting readers, but some of the better accounts by the more observant and insightful miners have enabled scholars to gain a good qualitative sense for what life in the gold fields was like. Needless to say, economic historians must be careful in drawing conclusions based on what is largely anecdotal evidence contained in these accounts. However, when combined with other sources of information, they are useful for obtaining a sense of what issues were important and how they were viewed by the participants in the Gold Rush and its aftermath. This study will rely in part on a number of these first-hand accounts.[26]

Two early histories published in the 1880s are worthy of note in helping us understand key institutional aspects of the Gold Rush era. One is *Mining Camps: A Study in American Frontier Government*, one of the first accounts written by an academically trained historian, Charles Shinn.[27] Though some of its interpretations have been subsequently called into question, this book remains a highly useful account of the origins of the mining camp system and its operation in California. The other notable history from this early period is Josiah Royce's *California from the Conquest in 1846 to the Second Vigilance Committee in San Francisco: A Study of American Character*, which examined the Gold Rush with a harshly critical eye and provides valuable commentary on the social impacts of mining. These two studies stand out in Gold Rush historiography as early attempts to provide reasonably objective analytical accounts of the Gold Rush, in sharp contrast to the largely romanticized depictions of the time. Shinn's account in particular will help inform some of the later discussion in chapters 5 and 6 of the mining camp system.

The modern study of the Gold Rush can be reasonably considered to date from roughly the time of the centennial of the original gold discovery. Around this time, two books appeared that would exert a major influence over subsequent accounts and interpretations of the Gold Rush. The first is *California Gold*, by Rodman Paul. For economic historians interested in the Gold Rush, it is difficult to overstate the importance of this book, which dispassionately treats numerous dimensions of the Gold Rush of interest to economists, including the great emigration; the mining technologies of the Gold Rush; the development of river mining and the ditch industry; the economic development of the state; the mining camp system; and the laws regulating mining. Though it cannot be considered to be a quantitative analysis of the Gold Rush, it is perhaps the first significant account that brings quantitative evidence to bear in support of its arguments, including data on gold production, miners' wages, ditch mileage, and the cost of ditch construction and operation of quartz mills.

The other important book that appeared about the time of the centennial was *Gold Is the Cornerstone*, by John Walton Caughey. Like Paul, Caughey treated a wide variety of aspects of the Gold Rush of interest to economic historians. Though not as scrupulous as Paul in providing quantitative evidence, Caughey's narrative is richer and even better documented, including heavier reliance on scholarly studies, government reports, and the eye-witness accounts of miners and overland emigrants. Together, the two books provide a rich and detailed picture of the circumstances of the Gold Rush.

Since Paul and Caughey, scholarly study of the Gold Rush era has flourished, as historians have taken their inquiries in a variety of directions, armed with new methods of analysis.[28] An important development here has been the growth of reliance on quantitative methods, in areas as varied as literary content analysis and the new social history. As regards the Gold Rush, these methods have been applied to better understand, for example, the incidence of violence and aggression, frontier opportunity, social mobility, and the growth of stable communities.[29] An excellent extensive example of the new social history is Ralph Mann's *After the Gold Rush*, a detailed look at two Gold Rush towns—Nevada City and Grass Valley—as they transitioned from the hurly-burly of the Gold Rush to become stable established communities. Mann's analysis is of interest for the picture it paints of the circumstances that permitted these two towns to survive beyond the rush days to become mature industrial towns, unlike many other Gold Rush towns. With liberal use of census data, Mann is able to document structural differences between the two towns, which led to the towns having somewhat different development experiences. He also documents many trends of interest and when they occurred, including a dramatic fall in the ratio of males to females, rising domesticity and orientation towards family life, and growing diversification of the local economies.

For their part, economic historians have also made substantive contributions to better our understanding of the Gold Rush era that have, broadly speaking, fallen into three areas of inquiry. The first has to do with characterizing the massive emigration to California and how the emigrants fared once they arrived. Importantly for our purposes, it is generally believed that on the whole, the emigrants tended to be relatively well educated and tended to come from higher social classes.[30] We will notice this later on when we consider the occupations of many of the miners, as well as the literacy of many of the sometimes sparkling narratives of miners in their letters, diaries, and journals. It will also come up as an important interpretive point when we consider how they searched for gold, how they interacted with each other, how they organized into mining teams, and how they operated their mining and ditch companies.

If there is a recurring theme of many Gold Rush histories, it is the bitter disappointment of many miners who came to California to strike it rich and came away empty-handed. At the same time, it is easy to find anecdotal evidence of rich strikes and individual miners doing quite well. One important finding of the economics literature is to largely confirm that on average, miners did not do particularly well when one considers their occupation alternatives, and controlling for differences in cost of living. At the same time, this did not necessarily mean that coming to California was a bad idea, as many who came ended up doing well in other occupations that supported the mining industry.[31]

The second important contribution of economic historians toward better understanding the Gold Rush is to document its impact on the California economy, especially on industrial structure, labor markets, and state and local public finances. The impact of the gold seekers on the California economy upon arrival is generally considered to be enormous, certainly in terms of aggregate economic growth. Perhaps equally important, however, were the structural changes to the economy that their arrival set in motion. This certainly includes the generalized move from agriculture to initially extraction-based industry, but also the transition to a more corporate business environment.[32] Furthermore, their arrival exerted a substantial, but temporary, effect on local labor markets, at least measured in terms of the effect on real wages, which rose to very high levels initially and then tapered off over time.[33] Their arrival also severely taxed the public finances of the state, by increasing the demand for public services while tax payments lagged behind.[34]

A third important contribution of economic historians directly connects to the subject of this book; namely, the study of Gold Rush institutions and institutional change. Studies in this vein really begin in the late 1970s with the work of John Umbeck. In his dissertation and a series of journal articles, Umbeck investigated the process of property rights creation during the Gold Rush and the determinants of the nature of those property rights. The special circumstances of the Gold Rush, with wholesale massive incursions into a region where effective controlling institutions were largely absent, provided Umbeck with a perhaps unique opportunity to view the creation of property rights from whole cloth. In Umbeck's words, he was interested in the emergence of property from an initial state of anarchy, or what he called the "original contract."[35] In a detailed examination of a number of miners' codes governing the definition of mining claims, Umbeck concluded that individualized, secure property rights can emerge as the solution to a noncooperative equilibrium when individuals possess roughly equivalent capacities to wield force.[36] These individual mining claims, to the extent that they conferred exclusive development rights on the right-holder, would have been largely efficiency-promoting.[37]

This view of property rights in mining claims held sway for the better part of twenty years, until economic historians began to take a closer, more nuanced look at the evidence. In 2005, Karen Clay and Gavin Wright issued a major challenge to the Umbeck thesis, arguing for a very different interpretation of the rules governing mining claims that were created by the miners. Rather than generating exclusive property rights in mining claims, Clay and Wright maintain that these rules are more reasonably interpreted as designed to facilitate turnover in claims, in order to maximize exploitation of the gold fields. They conclude that the gold fields were likely depleted too rapidly, compared with what would have been efficient.[38] To economists, the contrast between the Umbeck and Clay and Wright stories could not be more stark. Whereas Umbeck argues for a private property interpretation with attendant efficiency properties, Clay and Wright argue in essence that the gold fields much more closely resembled an open-access commons with free entry, implying potentially major inefficiencies associated with excessive depletion.

Umbeck's thesis has been challenged on different grounds by Richard Zerbe and Leigh Anderson. One feature of Umbeck's analysis was his useful fiction that there was an "institutional vacuum" in the gold fields, in which the miners operated largely unconstrained by governing forces. Zerbe and Anderson challenged this assumption by arguing that the gold seekers who emigrated to California during the early Gold Rush in fact brought informal institutions with them, in the form of shared customs and norms of fairness. According to Zerbe and Anderson, these shared customs and norms provided focal points that facilitated cooperation among miners in arriving at arrangements to allocate mining rights.[39] Acknowledging the importance of fairness helps to explain certain recorded situations where miners were not simply unceremoniously ejected from claims despite being hopelessly outnumbered by other miners. Zerbe and Anderson also suggest that it may help explain discrimination against foreign miners, to whom the norm of fairness was not extended, as they were not part of a shared tradition.

In some important ways, Zerbe and Anderson's argument is reminiscent of a series of studies by John Phillip Reid of emigrant behavior on the overland trail. Reid, who is probably the preeminent scholar on the overland emigration, argues that the Gold Rush emigrants who began to take the overland trail to California in 1849 were, for all intents and purposes, venturing "beyond the legal pale."[40] There were no sheriffs or civil authorities on the overland trail, and military posts and occasional military convoys were few and far between. Yet, Reid maintains, the emigrants on the overland trail were remarkably cooperative and nonaggressive in their dealings with each other. Much of the reason, he maintains, is the norms of comportment and respect for property that they had grown up with back east and brought with them on the trail. While out on the trail, in the vast majority of cases, overland emigrants honored their contracts, abided by decisions adopted by majority rule, and respected each other's person and property.[41] As Reid put it:

> When emigrants moved westward over the Oregon and California trails, they were not only bringing American civilization to the Pacific, they were carrying it with them as they went along.[42]

The notion that fairness may have been an important consideration for miners has also been developed by the legal scholar Andrea Mc-Dowell. In McDowell's view, miners may be best thought of as operating behind a Rawlsian veil of ignorance with regard to where the gold was likely to be found. This meant that they had an interest in formulating rules that would maximize turnover, as they never knew when they might find themselves in the position of going bust, as opposed to finding a rich strike.[43] McDowell may thus be interpreted as providing a self-interest story for why risk-averse miners might be interested in writing claiming rules that promote fair outcomes. Her story complements that of Clay and Wright, in emphasizing the tendencies for miners' codes to facilitate turnover of claims.

To summarize, the recent scholarship on the institutions of the Gold Rush has taken us a long way from Umbeck's seminal contribution. As opposed to the largely efficiency story told by Umbeck, the recent contributions suggest excessively rapid depletion due to commons-like conditions and miners' interest in procuring fair outcomes at the expense of efficiency.

In contrast to the contributions of Umbeck, Clay and Wright, Zerbe and Anderson, and McDowell, the main focus of this study is water rights, not mining rights. In this sense, my findings should be read as complementing and extending theirs in a different direction. However, the two industries were inextricably interwoven, so that conclusions that a person draws about one may be grossly incomplete without considering developments in the other. For example, technological advance that was occurring in placer mining had major implications for how both mining rights and water rights were defined. Part of the strategy pursued here is to consider developments in both industries simultaneously, which provides a richer set of evidence on which to draw conclusions about the sources and determinants of both kinds of rights.

As will be documented shortly, the decade of the 1850s was a time of tremendous growth and structural change in the mining industry. What is typically thought of as the Gold Rush was really only the first three years of the period, followed by an extended period of gradual consolidation, increasing corporatization, and continuing technological change. One of the central contentions of this book is that existing scholarship on Gold Rush institutions fails to adequately account for the fact that economic conditions were changing extremely rapidly within a very short period. Consequently, the nature of the economic pressures on institutions was changing rapidly as well, challenging the validity of coming up with one set of predictions regarding when and how the institutions would change. The most obvious change was, of course, the sheer magnitude of the horde of humanity that came flooding into California to look for gold. The effect was an enormous increase in congestion in the gold fields as miners competed for gold, with attendant impacts on the institutions governing gold production. The associated rapid depletion of the gold fields meant that actual rush conditions were over pretty quickly—probably lasting not much past 1851. This means that at the very least, it makes sense to distinguish the institutional developments prior to 1852 from the later institutional developments, as being governed by economic forces that were different in important ways.

Equally significant, however, were rapid technological changes in the way mining was prosecuted. As will be documented in chapter 3, placer mining moved from highly labor-intensive methods to highly capital- and water-intensive methods very quickly. This move had predictable effects not only on the use of different factor inputs, but also on the production scale of mining operations. As we shall see, these changes in turn had ramifications for what rules would be contained in the miners' codes, when they would be included, and how they should be interpreted. Similar implications apply to court rulings that resolved disputes over water and mining claims. Also associated with the technological changes were other important impacts, not the least of which was that mining came to generate significant negative externalities, which would lead to all sorts of other important changes in the rules governing mining. But again, in order to make sense of the rules that were generated, it is important to know when and where these changes occurred. Part of the strategy of this book will be to carefully document the pattern of technological advance, and then to trace out the temporal pattern of the creation of institutions, both within the mining camps and as promulgated in the court system.

1.6 Conclusions

We have come a long way since the earliest attempts to explain the origins of water rights in California. The story has become more sophisticated as various kinds of evidence have been considered and integrated into the picture. At the same time, we have made great conceptual strides in how to think sensibly about the economic determinants of institutional change: more specifically, as a reciprocal relationship between economic drivers and the content of the institutions themselves. The conceptual framework developed earlier in this chapter, though, provides only the broadest outline of fundamental concepts inherent in the theoretical approach of the book. Let us now turn to a more detailed examination of the concepts and tools that will be applied to help understand the development of the principles and content of water law in early California.

CHAPTER TWO

Economic Theory and the Evolution of Water Law

2.1. Introduction

Water is a scarce natural resource with many uses, and disputes over water can occur in a variety of ways when different parties try to tap the same water source, be it a flowing river, wetlands, artesian well, or groundwater aquifer. Water law, the rights to water use enjoyed by different parties, originates in societal responses to disputes, or the potential for disputes, over that water. In order to address the disputes that are likely to arise, the law needs to perform two related functions. First, it must define what a water right consists of. This can include all sorts of practically important issues, like how much water one has a right to and of what quality; when and where the right can be exercised, and for what purposes; and whether the water can be bought and sold. Second, it must provide principles for deciding the potential disputes among rightsholders that could occur. These principles would have to address the following: determining whether an actionable harm has occurred; assessing the amount of damages that have occurred to one or both parties; deciding whether the mere fact that an actionable harm has occurred is sufficient for a remedy, or whether intent or negligent behavior should also matter; and what remedy should be applied. These two functions are obviously related. For example, any legal limitations imposed on water use can be important in determining whether someone has caused an actionable harm to another if a dispute arises. However, for analytical purposes, it will be useful to treat them separately, which is what the law-and-economics literature has largely done, relegating the first func-

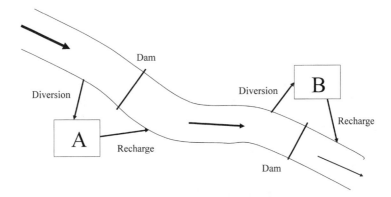

FIGURE 2.1 Potential for a surface water dispute: diversion, degradation, and dam failure

tion to the province of *property* and *contract* law and the second to the
province of *tort* law. In this chapter, I will largely follow their lead.

Much of the discussion will be of a general nature, applying to disputes over resources of all kinds, including land, hardrock minerals,
petroleum, fisheries, and wildlife. However, it is ultimately aimed at or-
ganizing our thoughts on the specific kinds of disputes that can arise
over surface water, and which in fact did arise in the gold fields of California. The essence of many surface water disputes is captured by the
stylized situation depicted in Figure 2.1. In Figure 2.1, a river flows from
its source past A, who uses it for his needs, and then past B, who is located downstream from A. In order to use the water, both A and B must
invest in damming the river and constructing diversion infrastructure to
transport the water to where it is used. Disputes can occur between A
and B for at least three distinct reasons: A's use of the water may reduce the amount available to flow down to B, it may degrade the quality
of water that flows down to B, or A's dam may burst, causing damage to
B's operation. All of these types of disputes were common in California
during the period examined in this book, and each one will be the subject of discussion and analysis later on.[1] Figure 2.1 is meant to convey a
sense of the practical connection between rights definition and dispute
resolution that will be useful for our purposes. No matter how the law
defines A's right, one can see that how A exercises it can potentially affect B in multiple ways.

2.2. What Is a Property Right?

The economist's typical starting point for defining what is meant by a property right focuses on the valuable uses that can be made of the resource. Specifically, a property right entitles a resource holder to a future stream of income from the use of that resource. It is this future stream of income that gives the resource value to the right-holder, and the present discounted value of that stream places a lower bound on what she would have to be offered to be willing to part with it. If the resource is in heavy demand by a number of potential buyers, the right-holder may be able to get more, perhaps much more, than the resource is worth to her. On the other hand, if there are many other resources out there similar to the one she is offering, this will tend to drive down the price that she will be able to get. Active competition on both sides of the market for homogeneous resources will tend to drive prices to the value of their income streams. Exogenous shocks that affect the size of the income stream should be reflected in the price of the resource.

The property law literature can be interpreted as drawing an analytical distinction between what I shall call *simple* resources and *complex* resources. The difference basically has to do with the number of economically meaningful attributes which different users can exploit to try to extract value from the resource. A simple resource has only a few attributes, as few as one, whereas a complex resource has many. Just about every resource we can imagine has multiple attributes, as illustrated by Yoram Barzel's orange example, in which attributes are things like juiciness, sweetness, and thickness of the peel. When one buys an orange, therefore, one is buying a bundle of attributes. As it turns out, the distinction between simple and complex resources will have important implications for our discussion, and we will return to the case of complex resources shortly. For now, the discussion will focus on simple resources, not because they are realistic or prevalent in the real world, but to provide a baseline for the discussion to come.[2]

A. Simple Resources

Consider, then, a simple resource with only one attribute. One might consider the resource to be an ounce of pure gold, which presents none, or at least fewer, of the conceptual challenges of Barzel's multifaceted

orange. I choose this example because it is easy to envision it being valuable. Because it is valuable, anyone lucky enough to own it will jealously
guard her right to keep it in hopes of selling it for a goodly sum, which
in this simple example comprises the future stream of income. If the cost
of guarding it until sale time is low, she will make the effort, be able
to maintain possession of the gold, and thus be able to realize the returns from selling it. How low does the cost need to be? At least as low
as the value of the gold minus any additional resources that must be expended for the transaction itself. If the cost is higher than this, it will
not be worth it for her to guard the gold, and she will leave it unguarded
and vulnerable for anyone to come along and nick it. Translating this account into economese, the higher are the costs of enforcing a property
right to a resource relative to its value, the more likely that resource will
be left in the public domain. In this case, a property right, in the sense
of a paper deed or a contract that someone else has signed on the dotted
line, is no property right at all, at least not in the economic sense of the
term. There is no income to be gotten, at least not once someone starts
coming along and coveting it. And that could happen at any time.

Enforcement costs and value, therefore, are two crucial determinants
of economic property rights. This was the basic point of the classic paper
of Terry Anderson and P. J. Hill, who argued forty years ago that economic property rights depend crucially on the cost of enforcing those
rights, relative to their value.[3] Conceptually, they represented this idea
with the simple diagram shown in Figure 2.2. In Figure 2.2, the extent
of enforcement activity is being measured on the horizontal axis, and

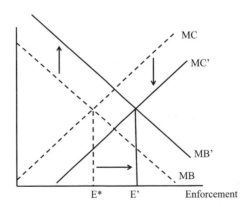

FIGURE 2.2. Creation of property rights

MC and MB represent the (private) marginal cost and (private) marginal benefit of enforcement. The maximizing individual will consider both of these schedules and select the amount of enforcement activity that equates MC to MB. To be clear, MB is directly related to the value of the resource: the more valuable is the resource, the greater are the benefits of enforcing rights to it. The higher is MB relative to MC, say if MC shifts down to MC' or MB shifts up to MB', the more property right enforcement will occur, and the less the resource will be left out in the public domain. In a real sense, the "more" private property there will be.

Returning for a moment to the ounce of gold example, the implicit assumption was being made there that nothing was keeping her from selling the gold to the highest bidder. Indeed, the privilege of being able to sell a resource commonly goes along with owning it, the so-called right of *alienation*. If alienation is possible and it is easy to buy and sell gold, notice an important implication of the example. Assuming that everyone who owns the gold could sell it for the same price, the greatest (net) value of owning it is enjoyed by whoever can most easily enforce her rights to it. Thus, under these circumstances, this means that resources will tend to end up in the hands of those with the lowest enforcement costs, all else equal, regardless of in whose hands those resources start out.

The other important point that needs to be made here is that when alienation is possible, the gold will flow to its highest value when both enforcement costs are low and it is easy to buy and sell gold. This is, of course, an implication of the famous Coase theorem, which states that it is only when transaction costs are positive that the initial assignment of rights matters for who ends up with the resource, and that outcome could well be inefficient if users who value it less get stuck with it. Thus, the possibility of alienation can be counted on to lead to efficient resource allocation only when transaction costs are low. I will define transaction costs very broadly here, as encompassing a wide variety of sources of costs that impede smooth transacting among interested parties. These include logistical considerations such as sitting down and negotiating terms, the enforcement of contracts, maintaining enforcement of rights over time, and measurement of goods and their various attributes. Also included are strategic considerations such as the possession of private information, which might lead to strategic gaming over the terms of a contract.[4]

Unlike an ounce of gold, it is the nature of many natural resources that possession and use to realize the stream of income from ownership can result in external impacts on others. Oil drillers tapping a common oil reservoir can reduce oil pressure within the reservoir, causing other drillers to expend more in pumping costs. Fishers who work a fishery can both reduce the fish take for others currently and diminish the stock available for others over time.[5] Groundwater pumpers tapping a common aquifer can lower the water table, increasing the energy costs incurred by others to bring the water to the surface. In all these cases, users inflict external costs, which may result in overly rapid depletion of the resource and inefficient dissipation of rents, to the extent that these costs are not internalized by the users. It is well known that efficient allocation will only occur when users fully internalize all external costs. In principle, this could be achieved through regulation; for example, quotas or taxes. However, efficient allocations could also be achieved by clear definition of property rights and then permitting voluntary exchanges of rights. The question is whether or not different users can negotiate over the externalities and contract to internalize them. The issue again is transaction costs. If transaction costs are low, then such negotiations should be easy, rent dissipation can be avoided, and efficient outcomes will be approximated. If not, then we would anticipate inefficient, overly rapid utilization of these resources.

An important question concerns the conditions under which transaction costs will be sufficiently low to permit effective negotiations to occur. In general, rent dissipation is thought likely to be most complete when exclusion is extremely costly (open access conditions); when users are roughly homogeneous; when rights are assigned when users render the resource to possession (a so-called *rule of capture*); and when users have no interaction with each other and cannot take effective steps to create local institutional arrangements for resource management. Under these conditions, a so-called *tragedy of the commons*, or near-complete rent dissipation, is likely to occur.[6] A useful metaphor to describe a potential tragedy of the commons outcome involves the notion of *roving bandits*, a term coined originally by Mancur Olson.[7] The term *roving bandit* describes a rapacious individual who swoops in on a valuable resource lacking any sort of effective governance structure, takes what he can, and then leaves before people know what hit them. Such an individual operates in stealth, completely out of communication with other users, and he is totally non-invested in the long-term health of the resource base. When all users behave like roving bandits, the conditions are ripe for a tragedy of the commons to occur.

The roving bandit metaphor is useful because it provides clues regarding when a tragedy of the commons is *not* likely to occur. It is generally recognized, for example, that complete rent dissipation associated with a rule of capture is predicted only under certain conditions having to do with the motivations and characteristics of the parties, and the ability to create institutional arrangements to manage the resource. Generally speaking, under open access conditions rents are predicted to be completely dissipated only when you have identical parties who are concerned solely with maximizing profits and it is infeasible for them to devise effective institutional arrangements to manage the resource. If parties take other objectives such as nonpecuniary rewards or altruistic concern for others into consideration; if they are heterogeneous in terms of ability, experience, or use of production technologies; and if they can meaningfully communicate and interact to design effective ongoing management institutions, then rent dissipation may be mitigated.[8]

One key difference between flowing surface water such as depicted in Figure 2.1 and many other common property resources is that the nature of the external impacts of a given party's use on other users is *unidirectional*. That is, the external impacts of use are generally inflicted only on downstream users, leaving upstream users unaffected. This unidirectional impact is obviously not the case with fisheries, underground oil pools, or groundwater aquifers. This special feature of surface water flows creates some unique issues in terms of characterizing the efficient use of the waterway. Importantly, the asymmetry in the positions of the upstream and downstream users will imply slightly different treatments of property rights allocation in order to maximize available rents from the water. As the same time, as we shall see, both the nature of their uses and the physical properties of the local hydrologic environment will also matter in determining their efficient allocations.

To see this, let us again consider Figure 2.1 and now, let us define some additional parameters for purposes of analysis. Suppose this river has a flow of X acre-feet (per time unit) at its headwaters and for simplicity, let us assume no flow additions occur downstream either through tributaries or precipitation, and no flow subtractions occur due to evaporation. Both A and B make an investment in water diversion, which creates the capacity to divert so much water from the river to its location. For simplicity, let us assume that the costs of diversion are all fixed costs that do not vary across users. Once applied to use, a portion of a given application of water returns to the river in recharge. For example, when a farmer taps an adjacent river to irrigate her crops, some portion of the water will percolate down and back into the river's water supply. Denote the amount of water diverted by A as D_A and the *fraction* of that water that returns to the river as R_A, where R_A takes on values between zero and one, and similarly for B. The presence of recharge creates a distinction between the amount of water *diverted* D and the amount of water *consumed* C, where $C = D(1-R)$. In words, when there is no recharge ($R = 0$), all of the water diverted is consumed in that none of it returns to the river after use. At the other extreme, all of the water diverted flows back into the river ($R = 1$), so that consumption has no effect on the amount of water in the river. In general, recharge of the river will be incomplete ($0 < R < 1$) so that when A diverts water, the amount of water in the river diminishes for B, but not to the entire extent of A's diversion. Specifically, after A takes her allotment, the amount of water in the river for B will equal:

(2.1) $$X_B = X - D_A(1-R_A)$$

For some added insight into the model, consider the extreme cases of $R = 0$ and $R = 1$. As we have seen, when $R_A = 0$, diversions by A subtract from the volume in the river by the entire diversion amount, since none of the diversion returns in recharge. In this case, in the terminology of the public goods literature A's diversion is *rivalrous* to B and may inflict an external cost on B to the extent that the volume in the river falls below B's privately maximizing diversion. On the other hand, when $R_A = 1$, diversions by A reduce the volume in the river not at all, in which case A's diversion is *non-rivalrous* to B and inflicts no cost on B.[9] Intermediate values of R reflect, of course, intermediate degrees of rivalrousness in consumption. To summarize, the recharge coefficient R reflects the extent to which water use takes on the characteristics of a public or a private good, the "publicness" of use increasing in R.

Efficient use of water requires maximization of the combined rents available to all claimants in this system, subject to the river flow constraint in equation (2.1). Let $f_i(W_i)$ denote the marginal revenue product of water, net of diversion costs, to user i. In the general case where there are N users, the combined rents available from the river may be expressed in the following Lagrangean function[10]:

(2.2) $$L = \text{Max} \sum_i \{\int_0^{D_i} [f_i(\theta_i)]d\theta\} + \lambda[X - \sum D_i(1 - R_i)]$$

In words, equation (2.2) represents the rents enjoyed by each user from their diversion D, summed over all N users, subject to the constraint on river flow. Optimizing over this expression yields the result that rent maximization requires equating the marginal value of consumptive use for each user:

(2.3) $$f_i/(1 - R_i) = f_j/(1 - R_j)$$

This outcome may be approached by specifying consumptive use $D(1 - R)$ as the legal basis for an appropriative right, and then allowing market transactions to achieve an efficient allocation, assuming zero transaction costs.[11] Intuitively, defining transfer rights only to the consumptive portion of one's diversion ensures that a transfer will not impose an externality on downstream users. Practically speaking, however, metering recharge is likely to be quite challenging and thus, transaction costs of defining rights to consumptive use are likely to be large. As a second-best solution given significant metering costs, therefore, one would thus expect courts in general to define rights based on diversion instead.

Consider, then, defining individual rights on the basis of diversion quantities. In general, this model says that such rights are unlikely to maximize rents within a river basin. One implication is that restrictions on transfers away from the river may be warranted, particularly on upstream users, to account for the fact that their diversions impose externalities on downstream users. Notice, however, that the desirability of transfer restrictions depends upon the value of the recharge coefficient. As we have seen, the smaller is the recharge coefficient, the more rivalrous is consumption and the more individual water use takes on the features of a private good. In the extreme case where $R = 0$, water consumption would be a pure private good and no restrictions on transfers would be warranted on the grounds of rent-maximization. In this case, the smaller are the transaction costs of exchange, the more likely it is that water rights based on diversion amounts will approximate rent-maximization.

We have covered a lot of ground, so at this point it might be useful to summarize the discussion so far. In general, resource value creates incentives for individual parties to enforce property rights to those resources. Enforcement activity, however, is tempered by the costs of enforcement. The greater these costs are, the less incentive there is to enforce rights and the more of those resources will be left out in the public domain. When alienation of resources is possible, resources tend to flow to parties both that value them the most and that incur the lowest enforcement costs. The extent to which this optimizing process occurs depends upon the magnitude of transaction costs. The lower the transaction costs, the more readily resources flow to their highest-value uses and the more efficient is the final outcome in terms of maximizing aggregate wealth.[12]

Transaction costs are crucial as well when resource use generates external effects on other users. Broadly speaking, efficient resource allocation requires that all external costs be internalized by users. The presence of transaction costs in negotiating over the generation of the externality limits the ability of users to internalize those costs, which encourages overuse of the resource and loss of available rents. In the case of flowing surface water, defining rights to consumptive use will tend to maximize rents from the available water. In this case, no restrictions on transfers of water from the basin are warranted, because transferring only the consumptive portion of one's use will inflict no external costs on downstream users. However, transaction costs will typically exist because it is difficult to accurately meter the recharge from users' diversions, making it prohibitively costly to define rights to consumptive use. If instead rights are defined to amounts diverted, restrictions on transfers of water from the basin may be warranted, especially on upstream users. This is because upstream users will not generally take into account the real costs of these diversions on downstream users.

B. Complex Resources

The entire discussion so far should be considered a baseline that is approximated when resources consist of only one economically important attribute. The picture is made somewhat more involved when one considers *complex* resources: resources with multiple attributes. In this case, the fact that there are a number of different attributes creates multiple margins along which others may try to expropriate resource value. A worker who is paid by the hour may have incentive to shirk on the job if it is difficult for her employer to monitor her intensity of effort. In this case, the resource in question is not just the number of hours spent on the job, but the quality of the work done while there. In Barzel's orange example, selling oranges by the pound gives the seller incentive to sell heavier, but less sweet and juicy, oranges, if it is difficult for consumers to distinguish. The problem is that it is often difficult to measure all of the attributes of a resource, meaning that some attributes are almost inevitably going to be left out in the public domain, vulnerable to expropriation. Alternatively put, the presence of *measurement costs* leads to incomplete, or imperfect, delineation of property rights.[13]

Measurement costs were not, of course, entirely absent from our discussion of simple resources. Regulation and management of fisheries is made considerably more challenging by the fact that fish can vary in age and size, which creates margins along which fishers can try to evade management arrangements. Even an ounce of gold can vary in terms of purity, shape, texture, and esthetic appearance. But none of the previous results are substantively affected by ignoring measurement costs, thus leaving our baseline scenario and implications intact. But now, explicit consideration of measurement costs in complex resources requires that we address certain additional issues, some of which have important implications for the creation and evolution of water institutions.

The significance of measurement costs is that they are an important component of transaction costs. Indeed, the existence of measurement costs in complex resources carries all sorts of important implications for various issues of interest to economists, such as the structure and content of contractual obligations, organization of firms, government regulation and antitrust policies, labor contracts, and the existence of brand names. Without measurement costs, for example, there might be no need for product warranties, professional certification, and occupational licensing requirements. The fact that they exist implies the possibility of private party responses in order to minimize costs. Indeed, though the specific implications of measurement costs across all of these different areas are quite varied, for our purposes they all come down to one thing: the incentive to exploit imperfectly measured margins, and the contractual and organizational responses designed to minimize the associated costs.

Barzel considers, for example, the existence of brand names and what purpose they serve. In Barzel's view, many consumer products are fraught with measurement cost issues. Because some attributes are costly to measure, the consumer is in part forced to rely upon the integrity of the seller. She knows full well, however, that it is probably costly for the seller to be completely straight with her, and the seller knows she knows this. To address the problem and encourage sales, the seller adopts a brand name, which is a signal of quality along various relevant attribute margins, to prospective buyers.[14]

This cost-minimizing dynamic occurs as well when one considers legal responses to the presence of measurement costs. When considering how to define a property right to a complex resource, the courts are confronted with all of the potential various attributes of the resource, which may vary greatly in terms of how costly they are to measure. What should the right consist of? One strategy might be to consider the attributes of the resource that are relatively easy to measure and simultaneously unlikely to cause disputes with other users, and to draw a clear-line boundary around those attributes. For example, since it is easy to measure land and since most of what happens on a tract of land commonly stays there, one might consider defining a simple unconditional right to do whatever one wants to with the tract of land. This, for example, characterizes the English common-law doctrine of *cujus est solum*, which governed groundwater law in California during the nineteenth century.[15] This particular definition of rights might well serve to minimize the sum of measurement costs and other components of transaction costs, which are small here as long as externalities are unimportant. Along with recent developments in the property law literature, I will call this unconditional right an *exclusion right*.[16]

Under an exclusion right as applied to a complex resource, certain attributes of the resource may well be left out in the public domain. However, depending upon the resource, the exclusion right should enable the right-holder to capture the vast majority of the value of the resource, as long as there are not some extremely valuable, hard-to-measure attributes. If the resource is transferable, then the resource owners should be able to realize most of the value upon sale. Once the basic exclusion right is established, the law may then turn to additional attributes of the resource, depending again on how hard they are to measure and the potential they raise for disputes with other users. If the measurement difficulties are not insuperable and the potential for disputes is large enough, the law may impose various targeted governance procedures on the exercise of rights, such as conditions for points of diversion and for purpose, time, and location of use and other attributes which are relatively easy to measure. The purpose of these additional restrictions would be to minimize transaction costs that might arise over resolution of the disputes. These restrictions I will term *governance* restrictions, again in line with recent developments in the property law literature.[17]

Thus, for complex resources, property rights are seen as driven by imperatives to minimize all components of transaction costs, including measurement costs. The form that they take, consisting of both an exclusion component and a governance component, reflect multiple attributes of varying measurement costs and varying degrees of impact on other users. Indeed, property rights to different complex resources may vary in how much they consist of exclusion as opposed to governance, which depends upon the relative magnitudes of these two components of costs. This fact will be important later when we turn specifically to property rights to water and how they are defined. The contrast to simple resources should be noted as well. Under the conception of resources as consisting of a single attribute, the definition of property rights came down to the question of the cost of enforcing one's right. This led to the not-terribly-informative prediction of "more" or "less" private rights. The broader notions of transaction costs and measurement costs provide considerably more substantive predictions on the form property rights are likely to take, and why.

2.3. The Evolution of Property Rights

Now that we are armed with a framework with which to understand property rights, let us turn to an extremely important question: How do we understand the evolution of property rights over time? The economist's approach is to treat this evolution as reflecting some sort of implicit cost-benefit calculus, in which new forms of property rights supersede existing ones when it is (net) beneficial for that to happen. The factors that could matter are legion, including technological change, changes in relative factor prices, growing capital investment, the opening of new markets, and the generation of externalities. But what it basically comes down to is this: devising ways to peaceably allocate rights to scarce resources. And the more valuable those resources are, the more urgent it becomes to do this.

The immediate question is how to test whether this is actually going on. Perhaps the most common strategy of economists has been to ex-

amine contexts in which resource scarcity has been demonstrably increasing, and observe what happens to property rights. The basic idea
in these studies is that growing scarcity leads to growing resource value,
which encourages the creation of private property rights in order to
support greater realization of that value. Examples of this strategy include studies of the Early Roman Empire, medieval European agriculture, fur trapping around eighteenth-century Quebec, silver mining in
the nineteenth-century Comstock region in Nevada, bison hunting in
the nineteenth-century American West, mining rights in the California Gold Rush, water rights in the nineteenth-century eastern United
States, and water law in imperial Japan.[18] It is fair to say that the evidence has been mixed. A number of studies have largely corroborated
the basic thesis regarding the importance of resource scarcity in shaping
the creation and evolution of individual property rights.[19] A number of
others, however, have been unable to confirm such a simple dynamic.[20]

One commonly proposed resolution to the mixed picture concerns
the effect of increased value on enforcement costs. This resolution may
be understood within the context of Figure 2.2, where an increase in
value causes a rightward shift of the MB schedule, as an increase in value
would in principle increase the benefits of property right protection.
This is the basic rationale for the theoretical connection between value
and private property rights, as modeled in the Anderson and Hill framework. However, some have argued that an increase in value can also result in a simultaneous upward (leftward) shift in the MC of enforcement
schedule, because increased value unleashes greater effort by others to
expropriate the value of a resource.[21] If so, the predicted effect of increased value on enforcement activity is ambiguous and could actually
be negative, if the effect on enforcement costs is sufficiently great. Consistent with this interpretation, Dean Lueck found that in the nineteenth-
century American West, the cost of excluding hunters from bison herds
was increasing at the same time that the benefits were increasing, which
partly explained why private property rights did not emerge.[22]

I would argue that the effect on enforcement is likely to be even
greater within the context of complex resources, where there are more
exploitable margins along which to extract value.[23] To see this, it is instructive to consider Harold Demsetz's 1967 paper.[24] In his famous example, expansion of the fur trade in the Americas in the eighteenth
century increased the value of furs, which encouraged more extensive
hunting by the Montagne Indians in the region around Quebec. The re-

sult was increased activity in traditional commonly-held hunting areas, which generated more extensive negative externalities. Demsetz argued that this encouraged the creation of exclusive hunting territories to mitigate external impacts and resulting rent dissipation, in order to permit greater appropriation of the increased value.

It should be noted that Demsetz was, for all intents and purposes, modeling beavers as simple resources, and exclusive hunting territories were thus interpreted as means of establishing "more" private property rights to these resources. His approach and conclusions have been criticized by John Umbeck for ignoring the complex resource nature of furs. Umbeck's criticism was two-fold: externalities could have been generated along various multiple margins, and the operation of some of these margins could easily lead to predictions at variance with those of Demsetz.[25] Though Umbeck's critiques are conceptual rather than evidence-based, his critiques are confirmed by a subsequent study by John McManus, who examined the actual operation of the fur trade and found little support for Demsetz's conclusions.[26] Of particular interest here is McManus' observation that exclusive hunting territories were established for furs *but not for meat*, and that it was the latter that resulted in dramatic reductions in beaver populations. Apparently, the opportunity to exploit the margin of a different attribute, not the one emphasized by Demsetz, was crucial in determining the overall resource outcome.

Given the complex multi-attribute nature of many resources, increasing enforcement costs in the face of increasing resource value may help explain why private property rights often do not emerge in response to growing resource scarcity in many contexts.[27] Indeed, we will provide an additional example later on in this book within the context of the gold fields. More generally, treating resources as complex resources with multiple attributes and therefore multiple margins along which value may be extracted may permit richer analyses of property rights law, which includes helping us understand some of the finer details of these laws. With this in mind, let us turn to some special issues related to property rights in water specifically.

2.4. The Evolution of Water Rights

In many ways, the development of surface water law in the United States seems predictable for economists and legal scholars who ascribe much explanatory power to scarcity. Much evidence suggests that water scarcity has heavily influenced the creation of specific water rights attributes, over both time and space. An important tradition in western US history, discussed in the last chapter, holds that aridity was a fundamental driving force in the development of a new species of surface water rights in the western states that was qualitatively different from rights prevailing in the eastern United States.[28] Eastern surface rights were historically riparian in nature—land ownership endowed private parties with the right to use unspecified amounts of water in adjacent rivers and streams on their lands. However, western states responded to generally reduced surface water availability by permitting diversions away from riparian lands, and quantity-based water use rights emerged to support investments in such diversions. Anderson and Hill cast this argument within the basic scarcity framework when they argued that increasing water scarcity attendant on economic and population growth "induce(d) individuals to devote more resources to the redefinition of property rights in water."[29] To economists who ascribe primacy to basic economic scarcity, the individualized, quantified surface rights that emerged in the nineteenth-century United States trace a sensible trajectory for western water law.[30]

The dichotomy between eastern riparian rights and western appropriative rights has turned out to be not entirely clear-cut, however. John Hart documents, for example, that for a time at least one eastern state (Delaware) adopted a system of individualized western-style rights to surface water.[31] Furthermore, a number of western states adopted hybrid systems under which surface rights were governed partly by riparian and partly by appropriative principles. Anderson and Hill argued that this pattern of surface rights adoption was not necessarily inconsistent with the scarcity thesis, since it was only the semi-arid Pacific coast and High Plains states that adopted the hybrid system, whereas the most arid mountain states abrogated riparian principles entirely. In sum, however, the fundamental connection between scarcity and water rights seems too imprecise not to consider other factors to be influential in shaping water rights.

An instructive 1990 study by Carol Rose provides some clues that help us go beyond and augment the basic scarcity account in the context of water law. Rose studied the evolution of riparian rights in the eastern United States in the nineteenth century, focusing on the adoption by the courts of the requirement that riparian use be reasonable given the demands of other riparian users. On the surface, this legal evolution seems to fly in the face of the scarcity story, as it seems to make water rights less specific and well-defined during a period when water was becoming increasingly scarce. She argued, however, that the application of reasonable use made economic sense, as it economized on transaction costs of resolving disputes during a time when eastern waterways were becoming increasingly congested.[32] Another study that corroborates the importance of transaction costs is my own 1998 study of nineteenth-century California water law, which invokes transaction costs minimization to help explain a pattern of judicial application of a rule of reason in disputes involving appropriators and riparians under their hybrid water rights system.[33]

In both Rose's and my study, growing transaction costs were associated with increasing congestion along surface waterways, resulting in growing negative externalities among competing users. Reasonableness provisions then came into existence because transaction costs became too high to permit users to negotiate over these externalities privately. Both stories are likely incomplete, however, as they focus only on a component of transaction costs; namely, the cost of negotiation over externalities. However, since water is a complex resource, measurement costs were likely important and thus, a complete story will have to account for these as well. The answer probably lies in the observation that both the eastern and western systems of water rights in the United States mix elements of exclusion rights and governance. In both systems, water rights begin as rights to exclude others from interfering with free exercise of the right by the rights-holder, and each then adds governance mechanisms that impose constraints on the free exercise of the right.[34] Under the eastern riparian system, initial exclusion is accomplished by the requirement that one needs to own land adjacent to the waterway to be entitled to use the water. Under the western system, exclusion is accomplished by mandating that temporal priority determines who enjoys the superior right in case of disputes. Thus, both Rose's and my study may be interpreted as consistent with a progression from what was initially only an exclusion right to one in which governance was superimposed on the basic exclusion right.

This progression—beginning with exclusion and moving to governance—is consistent with the view that exclusion and governance are two distinct yet complementary mechanisms for defining the scope of property rights. Under (initial) conditions of relative plenty and relatively little congestion to generate externalities, an exclusion right is a relatively low-cost way of defining a right that need not be defined with great precision, which has the added advantage of providing the right-holder with flexibility in the exercise of her right. Governance mechanisms, which are more costly to apply when great precision is not needed, come to dominate exclusion in terms of costs as resource value increases and users come into high-stakes conflict.[35] The governance mechanisms address the need to deal with various attributes of water use that impose impacts on other users. That is, the nature of water as a complex resource generates the need for legal provisions governing water to address the disputes over water that could arise.

2.5. Economics of Torts and Legal Remedies

The other dimension of water law we will consider in this book has to do with tort law, the set of principles applied by the courts to settle disputes over torts of various kinds. For torts, the courts have devised two basic types of remedies based on two distinct though related legal rules: *trespass* and *nuisance*.[36] Rules of trespass are rules that protect resource owners from being involuntarily deprived of their property rights to those resources. Under the trespass rule, neither lack of intent to injure nor claims of reasonable, or nonnegligent, behavior provides a defense: rather, a mere finding that a transgression has occurred is sufficient for a remedy, typically an injunction against future transgressions and an award of damages, if present. Under the rule of nuisance, on the other hand, the court will weigh both the magnitude of the damages and the reasonableness of the alleged transgressing behavior before deciding whether an actionable injury has occurred. Both rules have a long, rich history in common law, and both will appear as major actors in the evolution of early California water law.

An important insight provided by economists concerns the conditions under which we would expect to observe the application of a rule of trespass instead of a rule of nuisance, and vice versa. A key factor turns out to be the magnitude of transaction costs. When transaction costs are small, we would expect to observe the trespass rule, which awards clear property rights and paves the way for efficiency-promoting exchanges, if warranted. Large transaction costs, on the other hand, will tend to encourage application of the nuisance rule, under which the court weighs the relative costs and benefits to the parties and rules accordingly. The idea is that generally speaking, the market provides more accurate signals of resource value than do courts and thus, courts interested in promoting wealth creation tend to rely on them under conditions in which they are likely to function well.[37] This connection between transaction costs and choice of tort rule is widely recognized among law-and-economics scholars.

Transaction costs do not, however, fully explain which rule will be chosen by the courts. Thomas Merrill has observed that over the history of English common law, four factors seem to have been determinative of choice of tort rule: the location of the alleged tort; whether it resulted in direct, versus indirect, damages; whether it was a visible, and therefore salient, event; and the magnitude of the damages.[38] Courts have tended to apply a trespass rule when an intruder physically invaded another's property (rather than remaining on her own property and generating a nuisance that flowed onto someone else's property), and/or when these actions inflicted large, direct, visible damages on the other party. As Merrill noted, these factors map in the expected way to the magnitude of transaction costs only to varying degrees, suggesting that other factors may be operant in explaining application of the trespass rule.

Perhaps the most puzzling of the four factors to adherents of the pure transaction costs explanation is the fourth one, magnitude of the damages. The problem is that there does not seem to be an obvious reason why large damages should be associated with small transaction costs, as application of the trespass rule would suggest. Henry Smith has suggested that a resolution may lie in measurement costs and in particular, under circumstances when it is difficult to measure uses. Under his approach, trespass-like exclusion rules tend to emerge as ways of economizing on the cost of measuring uses that may inflict damages on others. However, if the damages to another's property are large, it is likely that the damages are large to all of the uses associated with enjoyment of that property. In Smith's view, this reduces the value of measuring damages in support of a more fine-tuned balancing instrument such as nuisance.[39]

It is important to point out a corollary to this argument: that the measurement cost perspective tends to blur the hard-line distinction historically drawn by legal scholars between the trespass and nuisance rules. Whereas the trespass rule bears close resemblance to a pure exclusion rule with few elements of governance, nuisance varies all over the map between exclusion and governance, depending upon the standard chosen to determine nuisance. In the case of large damages just discussed, for example, nuisance takes on much of the nature of exclusion.[40] Later on, this fluid nature of nuisance will help explain what would otherwise be puzzling treatments by the courts of surface water torts, especially within the context of disputes over damages to water quality.

An important type of dispute that could arise within the context of a river system as shown in Figure 2.1 is the collapse of an upstream dam, which would send water and debris flooding downstream, possibly inflicting significant damages on downstream users. Here, we seem to be squarely in the world of tort. Dam failures are commonly considered to be accidents, whereas nuisances like deliberately diverting water from your downstream neighbor, or sullying his water, are not. Conceptually, however, disputes over water quantity deprivation and quality degradation share much in common with disputes over dam failures. When a dam fails, it affects downstream parties who are often keenly cognizant of their cheek-to-jowl relationship with the upstream company. In this way, a dam failure feels more like the neighboring rancher/farmer example used by Coase and others than the classic tort of an automobile accident involving strangers. The analysis needs to be probabilistic, but in the commonly-assumed world of risk neutrality, there is not a huge difference between net benefit and expected net benefit calculations in support of efficient resource allocation.[41] Bargaining negotiations are at least in principle possible in a way that is not possible between two motorists.

All of this implies that nuisances like diverting or sullying the water that flows to your downstream neighbor and torts like your dam collapsing are largely subject to the same analytical principles that we have already seen. Yet the flavor of the theoretical analysis in this section will seem quite different from that in the previous section, because there will be much more of an emphasis on the capacity of parties to a tort to exercise precautionary behavior in their interactions with each other. This is partly attributable to the nature of dam failures, which are (mostly) accidental yet dependent upon the behavior of the dam builder. The discussion thus follows the lead of a sizable law-and-economics literature on accidental tort, in which the possibility of precautionary behavior plays a central role in interpreting the efficiency of different tort resolution rules and remedies.[42]

An important element of this perspective is to model liability standards such as strict liability and various forms of the negligence rule in terms of the relative ability of parties to a tort to exercise precaution. Rules are considered (economically) desirable to the extent that they minimize the total expected costs of harm plus the costs of precaution taken by both parties. In a situation such as depicted in Figure 2.1, both parties A and B are able to exercise precaution to avoid or reduce the damages from a dam failure. The upstream party A can, of course, build his dam more carefully to last longer and be less susceptible to collapse. What can the downstream party B do to exercise precaution in the shadow of the looming dam? There are in fact a number of possible strategies for B, including limiting the scale of operations, diversifying risk by working multiple diggings, moving away out of potential harm's way, or never moving to the downstream location in the first place. All of these would be ways in which B could limit the harm from, or even avoid being harmed by, a dam collapse.

Given all of these possible options for B, we thus find ourselves in a situation known in the law-and-economics literature as *bilateral precaution*, in which case there is a common normative presumption in favor of negligence rules, which hold A liable for damages to B only if he is shown not to have exercised sufficient care in constructing his dam. The primary alternatives to negligence—*no liability* and *strict liability*—fall short in the incentives for care that they provide to the two parties. If, for example, A was not liable for any damages to B, he would be given insufficient incentive to exercise care in building his dam. On the other hand, if A were liable for all damages regardless of how much care he had exercised (strict liability), B would be given insufficient incentive to exercise precaution in the various ways open to her. Given bilateral precaution, negligence rules are superior to both no liability and strict liability because they balance the incentives for care by both parties to a tort. It should be added that courts exercise discretion in setting standards of negligence as reflected, for example, in the "reasonable person" standard for what is considered negligent behavior. In situations where the parties to a tort differ in their ability to exercise precaution, courts may want to set tighter or looser negligence standards, imposing more of the onus of precaution on the party that can exercise it more readily (i.e., at lower cost).

It would be useful to point out an implicit assumption that is being made here; namely, that negotiations between the upstream and downstream companies over dam safety involve significant transaction costs.[43] If transaction costs were zero, then it would make sense to simply apply a trespass rule. Within the present context, this could be achieved by making the upstream company either strictly liable, or not liable at all, for damages and then relying upon private negotiations to achieve the efficient level of dam safety. However, if transaction costs are significant, this reduces the value of applying the trespass rule, as we saw earlier in the discussion of trespass vs. nuisance.

One might ask why we should expect transaction costs to be significant in a dam collapse dispute, especially in cases involving small numbers of parties. I think much of the answer comes down to the strategic costs of negotiating, in what economists call a *bilateral monopoly* situation. In this circumstance, the upstream and downstream companies are largely stuck with negotiating with each other, and private information possessed by one or the other party may make it difficult for them to come to an agreement. Here, the upstream company can take all sorts of actions in the design, construction, and operation of the dam that would make it more or less prone to collapse. These actions, which comprise attributes of dam safety, might be difficult to measure. Furthermore, the upstream company might have incentive to conceal its actions from the downstream company. For example, if it is costly to operate a dam safely, the upstream company might conceal that it is cutting corners to save money.[44] The fact that the upstream company possesses information that is difficult to measure and which it has incentive to conceal might well inhibit the ability of the parties to negotiate effectively on dam safety.[45]

The previous discussion has illustrated what some scholars refer to as the *contractarian* perspective: how the presence of transaction costs interferes with the ability of private parties to effectively negotiate contracts.[46] Indeed, much of the flavor of the first part of this chapter was obviously contractarian. The same issue might be usefully viewed from a different perspective, with the conclusions confirming our intuition: that transaction costs militate against application of a trespass rule. This alternative perspective is provided by what has been referred to as the *entitlement* perspective, which attempts to integrate the contractarian perspective and the tort perspective.[47] Under this approach, which originally derives from the famous "Cathedral" article of Guido Calabresi and Douglas Melamed, the question is the nature of entitlements and the economic determinants of the rules that will emerge governing these entitlements. Two basic types of rules are considered, what Calabresi and Melamed term *property* rules and *liability* rules. Property rules provide the holder with protection against being involuntarily deprived of her property, such as occurs under a rule of trespass. Liability rules, on the other hand, permit involuntary deprivation upon payment of compensation. The most important conclusion that Calabresi and Melamed draw is that transaction costs are central: when transaction costs are small, property rules will tend to emerge, as supportive of private exchanges of rights. When transaction costs are large, liability rules will tend to emerge, as court-ordered ways of reallocating rights to maximize overall wealth.[48]

It is fair to say that Calabresi and Melamed did not devote inordinate amounts of time to defining what is meant by transaction costs. Since "Cathedral" was published, subsequent scholars operating in the entitlement tradition have worked at refining the notion of transaction costs that would lead to a reliance on liability rules instead of property rules. Of particular interest here are the studies of Ayres and Talley, and Kaplow and Shavell. Ayres and Talley stress transaction costs that derive from private information in bargaining negotiations as a reason to prefer liability rules because compared with property rules, they reduce the scope for strategic holdup and other opportunistic behavior.[49] Kaplow and Shavell also like liability rules when there is private information but for a very different reason; namely, that liability rules help courts to economize on the costs of negotiating where the generator of a nuisance has incentive and opportunity to conceal information on his private valuation.[50] Both stress the importance of transaction costs arising from strategic bargaining, what Carol Rose has called Type II transaction costs.[51] The correspondence between what Calabresi and Melamed and successive scholars have termed liability rules and the nuisance rule of the tort literature is not exact, but the bottom line remains the same.[52] Lower transaction costs are predicted to be associated with more likely adoption of an exclusion rule of trespass.

2.7. Conclusions

This chapter has attempted to describe key elements of the economic approach to property, contract, and tort law in order to establish a framework for understanding legal developments in the gold fields with regard to mining and water rights. We have seen how economists view property rights for both simple and complex resources, as well as the various components of transaction costs that determine the efficiency of use under different assumptions about the existence and nature of externalities inflicted by those uses. Perhaps the central interpretive question concerns how, and the extent to which, the law promotes economic efficiency.

As a preview of things to come, we will view two contexts in which the concepts discussed here will play out in the development of legal rules. The first will be in the extralegal context of the mining camps, where miners self-organized to devise rules governing mining claims and water rights, largely absent any external controlling authorities. The framework employed here will largely center on concepts related to common-property resources. This will be the subject of chapters 5 and 6. The second will be in the courts, where judges heard cases involving disputes over water and promulgated official common-law doctrine. Here the focus will be on the content of those rules and how to interpret them normatively. This will be the subject of chapters 7 through 9. Before turning to those discussions, however, we will begin by describing key facts regarding the development of the mining and ditch industries to contextualize that later discussion. This will be the subject of the next two chapters.

CHAPTER THREE

Water and the Technologies of Mining

This day some kind of mettle was found in the tail of the race that looks like goald.—John Bigler, January 24, 1848

3.1. Introduction

The flakes of gold that were discovered by James Marshall at Sutter's Mill on the south fork of the American River on January 24, 1848, were there "in the tail of the race" because the action of water had taken the naturally occurring gold, washed it into the river, diverted it through the mill, and concentrated it in the tail race, the exit point for water flowing through the mill. But the importance of water did not stop there: from that point on, water was to figure prominently in the prosecution of placer mining throughout the Gold Rush period and through the remainder of the 1850s and beyond. Water figured prominently for two key reasons. First, it posed various technological challenges to miners by hindering access to gold deposits in the beds of rivers and in underground mines that were prone to fill with water. An important component of the story of water in the Gold Rush was the development of a thriving river mining industry, which reflected the ingenuity and perseverance exhibited by miners in the monumental task of diverting entire rivers to gain access to the gold in river beds.

Second, once the miners had gained access to the gold, water played a central role in separating it from the otherwise worthless soil and gravels in which it was found. Because water would turn out to be integral to the gold separation process, inadequate supplies of water in various localities posed major challenges to the successful prosecution of mining. Conversely, adequate water supplies dramatically increased gold production and because water was so integral to gold separation, miners proved to be highly ingenious in devising new ways to apply water in order to increase the productivity of their gold separation methods. Their efforts in this regard would comprise a major component of the story of rapid technological advances in placer mining that occurred during this period. The enormous resulting productivity gains would in turn dramatically increase the demand for water, setting in motion the developments in the law of water rights that are the subject of the later part of this book.

3.2. The Spread of Mining

Many people do not realize that prior to 1848, there had been a minor tradition of gold discovery and production in California. Perhaps the very first discoveries of gold in present-day California occurred in 1775, when gold deposits were found by Mexican miners in the far southeastern part of the state, near the Colorado River. This discovery was followed by a series of additional discoveries in present-day San Diego and Los Angeles counties beginning in 1828. One of these mines, at San Fernando, yielded some gold but the rest were not much worked for lack of water and because of their relatively minor nature. In 1842, the eminent mineralogist James Dwight Dana was perhaps the first to speculate that gold might exist in northern California when he conducted field studies as part of the famous Wilkes Expedition that explored the Pacific Ocean and Pacific coast from 1838 to 1842. Dana played down, however, the economic importance of whatever deposits might be found there.[1] On the eve of the discovery at Sutter's Mill, then, there was no real sign that a major gold discovery was about to occur.

The discovery of gold by Marshall in January 1848 was the first real inkling that gold might be present in the area that would come to be known as the Mother Lode. For the next month, however, news of the discovery was largely confined to a select few in the immediate vicinity of the mill, mostly men working for Marshall, who were not convinced that there was sufficient gold to warrant quitting their jobs working at the mill. However, Marshall shared his discovery with John Sutter, the

FIGURE 3.1. James Marshall at Sutter's mill, ca. 1850
Source: Library of Congress.

owner of the mill. Based on this information, Sutter went out and negotiated a lease of lands from local Indians. Then, in an ultimately unsuccessful attempt to secure official rights to the lands, Sutter dispatched a
messenger, Charles Bennett, to Monterey to try to procure official mining, milling, and pasturage privileges on the lands from Governor Mason. On the way to Monterey, Bennett stopped in San Francisco and
showed gold samples to a veteran of the earlier Georgia gold rush of the
1830s, Isaac Humphrey, who pronounced them to be genuine. Toward
the end of February, Humphrey accompanied Bennett back to the mill
and used his expertise as a former miner to take significant amounts of
gold out of the mill race. This was more than enough to convince the
workers that their time was not being well spent sawing lumber.[2]

It was not long before additional discoveries were made by Sutter's
men as they began to prospect the immediate vicinity. On March 2nd,
two men working for Sutter discovered what would turn out to be a very
rich strike downstream, not far from the confluence of the south fork
and the north fork of the American River, which became Mormon Dig-

FIGURE 3.2. John A. Sutter
Source: Library of Congress.

gings in April when seven Mormons left Sutter's employ to establish diggings there. Others left Sutter to comb nearby rivers and creeks for gold,
and three of Sutter's men soon discovered gold on Weber Creek, a tributary to the south fork. Soon afterwards, an Indian in their employ discovered what turned out to be extremely rich deposits of gold on Weber
Creek near present-day Placerville. The area around Placerville, then
known as Dry Diggings, was a center of major mining activity during the
summer of 1848 and would become a major destination of emigrants on
the overland route. According to Jacques Moerenhout, the French consul stationed at Monterey who traveled around the gold regions in summer of 1848, the gold was so rich in this area that miners often "gathered
up only the large pieces and used no other tools than a crowbar and a
knife."[3]

FIGURE 3.3.
James Marshall

Word of the discoveries began to spread to the coast in March when corroborating news accounts appeared in San Francisco newspapers. On March 15, the following item appeared in one of the two San Francisco newspapers, the *Californian*:

GOLD MINE FOUND.—In the newly made raceway of the Saw Mill recently erected by Captain Sutter, gold has been found in considerable quantities. One person brought thirty dollars worth to New Helvetia, gathered there in a short time. California, no doubt, is rich in mineral wealth; great chances here for scientific capitalists. Gold has been found in almost every part of the country.

Once this article appeared, word began to spread across the region. On May 12, a Mormon elder and businessman named Samuel Brannan ignited a local frenzy in San Francisco by waving around a bottle of gold

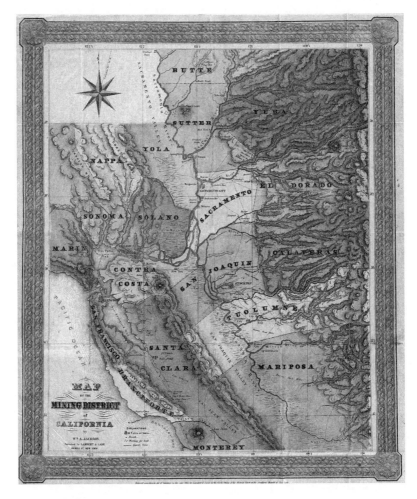

FIGURE 3.4. The cradle of the gold fields, 1851
Courtesy of the David Rumsey Map Collection

dust which he had brought from Sutter's Fort, after he had spent weeks buying up supplies that he knew miners would demand. Within days, the *Californian* was announcing that "many persons" had already left the coastal areas for the gold regions. By the end of May there was, in the words of one miner, a "great gold fever raging" in the city, with "half (of) San Francisco . . . already gone." On May 27, the following item appeared in the other San Francisco newspaper, the *California Star*:

Never within the last three years has the town [SF] presented a less lifelike, more barren appearance than at the present time, never so inactive, so void of stir as at present.

Stores are closed and places of business vacated, a large number of houses tenantless, various kinds of mechanical labor suspended or given up entirely, and nowhere the pleasant hum of industry salutes the ear as of late, but as if a curse had arrested our onward course of enterprise, every thing wears a desolate and somber look, every where, all is dull, monotonous, dead.

According to Walter Colton, alcalde of Monterey, word of the discovery reached Monterey on May 29 and after an initial period of disbelief, gold seekers began leaving the city for the gold fields in large numbers by the third week of June. The French consul in Monterey, Jacques Moerenhout, wrote on June 10 that there was not a single American left in the town of Santa Cruz. Cities in southern California including Los Angeles and Santa Barbara started experiencing a large exodus of residents to the gold fields the following month.[4]

During this time, word of the discoveries also began to filter outside California, with news reaching the Sandwich Islands by early June and Oregon and Mexico in July and August. According to Caughey, a "substantial exodus" began in mid-July. In early September, the *Californian* reported that two vessels had already arrived from the Sandwich Islands and that a vessel had already arrived from Oregon, with three more on the way. By autumn, significant numbers of gold seekers began arriving overland from Mexico, especially Sonora, and Oregon. By December, a number of Oregonians were digging successfully at Dry Diggings. At the same time gold seekers began to arrive from Chile and Peru by ship, which nations had by this time already established regular seafaring trading relations with California. Aside from additional small numbers of gold seekers from Australia and China, there is little evidence to suggest that gold seekers came to California in significant numbers from any other destination in 1848. In total, the nonnative population of California increased by some 6,000 in the latter half of 1848, a number that was to be dwarfed by the influx of the following year.[5]

The expansion of the gold regions outside of the American River watershed occurred in short order as miners began to explore the possibilities of the other rivers flowing westward out of the Sierras (see Figure 3.5). In March of 1848, John Bidwell, a close associate of Sutter,

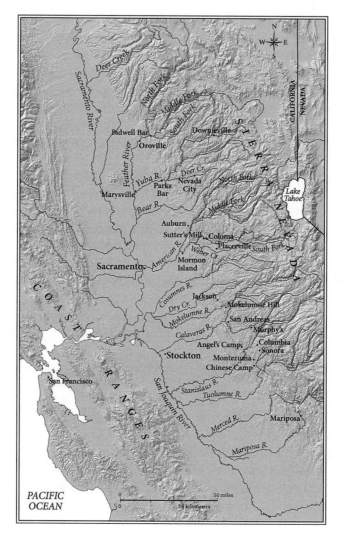

FIGURE 3.5. The gold fields

decided to go north and try his luck on the Feather River, where he discovered rich gold deposits and set up camp at what would be named
Bidwell Bar at the junction of the middle and north Forks. Owing to
the richness of gold in the area, Bidwell Bar flourished during the early
1850s, becoming a major population center for northern California and
county seat for Butte County until it lost the honor to Oroville in 1856.

The Feather River watershed became another rich early source of gold, with miners soon ranging "along the Feather and its tributaries in great numbers."[6]

The most important tributary of the Feather was the Yuba River, where a series of extremely rich discoveries were made beginning in spring of 1848. One of the richest was at Parks Bar, where gold was discovered in May, probably the first of a series of important early discoveries along the lower Yuba River. In September of 1850, the *Sacramento Transcript* reported that five men took 525 *pounds* of gold out of Parks' Bar in five days, which would have been worth roughly $134,000 at the time.[7] The Yuba River and its tributaries became perhaps the most important center of mining during the Gold Rush. One early town worthy of note was Downieville, located on the north fork of the Yuba, where gold was likely discovered in late 1848. According to Bancroft, Downieville grew rapidly to a recorded population of some five thousand in 1850, becoming the county seat in 1852 when Sierra County was established.[8] The deposits at Downieville were so rich that according to one eyewitness account, by spring of 1850, the town had fifteen hotels and gambling houses, and "every piece of ground was claimed and occupied."[9] The other important early discovery in the Yuba watershed occurred in autumn of 1849, when rich deposits were discovered at Deer Creek, a tributary of the south fork of the Yuba at what would become Nevada City, another extremely important mining center during the 1850s.[10]

All of the previously mentioned placer mining sites were situated in the northern and north-central Sacramento Valley, for which gold seekers coming from San Francisco would have traveled to Sacramento and then headed north and northeast. There were, however, also a number of important discoveries that occurred very early on in the southern mines, especially in present-day Tuolumne and Calaveras Counties, for which gold seekers from San Francisco would have headed almost due east to Stockton as the regional starting point. Perhaps the first discoveries in Calaveras County were made in fall of 1848 at Big Bar, along the Mokelumne River, by a party from Oregon.[11] The Mokelumne River and Calaveras River watersheds would become one of the richest centers of gold deposits in the southern mines, giving rise to especially rich gold discoveries at San Andreas, Jackson, Murphy's, and Mokelumne Hill.

The Gold Rush history of Tuolumne County begins with the discovery of gold at Wood's Creek, a tributary of the Tuolumne River in the southern part of the county, in early summer of 1848. In mid-1848, miners from Mexico prospecting up Wood's Creek made major discoveries at the site of Sonora, the most important early Mexican settlement, which Bancroft describes as the richest district in the southern mines. Extremely rich diggings were also discovered at Jackass Gulch, five miles north of Sonora, which one contemporary account described as "without doubt the richest (gulch) in the state" in 1848 and 1849. Numerous early discoveries were made in the area around Sonora, including at Montezuma and Chinese Camp, during which time the area "rapidly filled up" with gold seekers. Miners from Mexico mined in the area of present-day Columbia in 1849, and then major discoveries were made in March of 1850, which turned out to be so rich that six to eight thousand miners were mining in the area by the following month.[12]

3.3. The Location of Placer Mining

There's gold in them thar hills! —Unknown

The first miners who went off to the gold regions in 1848 were farmers, shopkeepers, soldiers, and the like who brought little by way of practical knowledge or experience to the business of mining. In the very beginning, of course, there was little need for any specialized expertise as many miners could literally pick up gold from the beds and bars of shallow streams or dig it out of banks and crevices using pick axes, shovels, spades, and knives.[13] However, this phase of extreme abundance did not last long and by all signs, it was over well before the end of the year. At that point, miners were presented with a greater challenge: where to look next.

Simple observation would have led the earliest miners to examine the bars of rivers, locations where sediment had been deposited by river flow that had the advantage of being shallow or dry, and the river banks, where seasonal variations in flow would have also resulted in deposition of sediment. This led to intensive mining of the bars and banks in the initial stages of the Gold Rush, especially in 1848, which was viewed as often being easier than mining the beds themselves, even though they sometimes involved having to dig down below the surface in shallow excavations. When Jacques Moerenhout toured the gold fields around the American River in July, he observed:

> The gold found here is taken principally from the banks on the sides of the river, where it is held in the clayey soil and caught in the crevices and fissures of the rocks. It is found also and perhaps in greater abundance in the soil carried down by the river and deposited on the turns, in the bends, on the little islands and other places that have been left dry. From one of these islands, only about an acre in size, called the Mormons' Diggings [Mormon Island], les exploitations des Mormons, and situated some distance below [Sutter's] mill, more than one hundred thousand dollars in gold has been taken out in a month, and this deposit is not yet exhausted.[14]

Another place they easily surmised gold was likely to be found was submerged in the beds of deeper streams and rivers, and the key issue here was how to get at it. This technological problem, and the measures taken by miners to solve it, gave rise to a booming river mining industry that lasted through the decade. Generally speaking, river mining required construction of a diversion dam in the river and a diversion ditch or flume, which ran parallel to the river, into which the water would be diverted at the dam site and turned back into the river some ways downstream. Miners would first select a stretch of a stream or river to be mined, and then build a ditch or flume of sufficient capacity into which all the water in the river could be channeled. John Sutter had in fact pursued a variant of this strategy when he constructed his famous sawmill, where he constructed a dam to divert part of the flow of the south fork of the American River into a diversion channel that fed his mill.

The very first diversion ditches were simple earthen channels, dug with pickaxe and shovel. It was not long, however, before miners began to fell trees and cut timbers to construct wooden flumes. Initially, dams were extremely crude affairs that miners constructed either by hauling trees and brush or rolling large boulders into a stream to form a wall, which would be supported and made water-tight using additional timber, clayey soil or sand, and/or canvas. Over time, however, they became more substantial and might be paired with the use of water- or steam-powered pumps to keep water out of the streambed. In some cases, a *wing dam* would be built, which entailed building a barrier of large boulders out part-way into a river and then perpendicularly downstream, which was then made water-tight. This did not expose as much of the river bed, but it was an attractive option for many miners because it rendered unnecessary the construction of a diversion ditch or flume.[15]

River mining spread quickly through the mining regions in the early years of the Gold Rush. As early as December of 1848, the *Star and Californian* reported that the "usual process" of extracting gold from the river bed of the Middle Fork of the American River was "throwing up dikes and turning the water from its channel, or draining portions of the river's bed."[16] By March of 1849, the *Alta Californian* was reporting that

> Companies are forming and making preparations to bring the hidden treasure within human grasp by devoting [*sic* diverting] the course of the stream in many places from their natural channels. It is supposed immense wealth will be realized from the rivers' beds.

Much of the initial river mining activity took place on the American and Feather rivers in the northern mines. According to J. S. Holliday, when William Swain came to the south fork of the Feather River in January of 1850, river mining had already been tried with "encouraging success" on both the Feather and American rivers the previous fall, and it had become "the ambition of most miners." By the summer of 1850, one miner reported that some forty miles of the Feather River had been dammed "whenever practicable." By August the *Alta Californian* was reporting that the American River was being turned at various places around Coloma. By July 1852, the *Calaveras Chronicle* reported that preparations were being made to flume almost the entire lengths of the Mokelumne and Calaveras Rivers, "between their sources and the plains."[17]

By this time as well, river mining was already spreading to rivers in the southern mines. In April 1850, the *Alta Californian* predicted that river mining would be undertaken that summer in a major way along several rivers in the southern mines:

> Daming [*sic*] operations will be carried off extensively this summer, on the Calaveras, Stanislaus and Tuolumne. At the pine log crossing, the Stanislaus will be turned, a distance of fifteen miles. For some time past, companies have been at work on the Tuolumne, digging canals, for the purpose of turning the river at many points.

Exactly a month later, in describing conditions on the Tuolumne River, it announced that:

> Companies have been organized along the whole extent of the river, and at every available point it will be dammed and turned, for the purpose of getting out the gold, which is known to lie in the bed. The work of cutting canals and races has been going on for the last six months. Immense ditches have been dug, and extensive beds of rock have been blasted away, during the winter.[18]

The very first river mining operations were relatively small-scale, probably in part because many were located on smaller streams where the gold was believed to be especially rich. In an early operation at Smith's Bar described by Buffum, it took five men "about two weeks" to dam off a space of "some thirty feet." Bayard Taylor describes two additional small-scale river mining operations along the Mokelumne River in fall of 1849:

> The first party we saw had just succeeded in cutting a new channel for the shrunken waters of the Mokelumne, and were commencing operations on about twenty yards of the river-bed, which they had laid bare. They were ten in number, and their only implements were shovels, a rude cradle for the top layer of earth, and flat wooden bowls for washing out the sands.
>
> A company of thirty, somewhat further down the (Mokelumne) river, had made a much larger dam, after a month's labor, and a hundred yards of the bed were clear. They commenced washing in the afternoon and obtained a very encouraging result.

Another miner, Daniel Woods, describes joining a river mining operation consisting of nineteen men near Salmon Falls on the south fork of the American River in August of 1849. Early on in the Gold Rush, river mining companies could consist of a handful of men engaged in exposing small stretches of river bed, and completing their task in relatively little time.[19]

At the same time, however, as early as the summer of 1849 miners were forming into much larger-scale river mining operations, in order to turn the larger rivers and lay bare longer stretches of river bed. In fall of 1849, forty miners comprising the Turner Company worked for

two months on a canal in order to drain five hundred feet of the Tuolumne River. An even larger company—the Mormon Island Mining Association—was formed in spring of 1849 to divert the American
River at Mormon Island, issuing shares in the company that were selling for $5000 apiece in October. To give some sense for the magnitude of
this price for a single share in this company, $5000 represented over ten
months of wages in California at the time. By another estimate, several
dams constructed on the south fork of the Feather River in fall of 1849
and summer of 1850 cost, "in labor and necessary expenditures, fifty to
eighty thousand dollars."[20]

The significant cost of river mining even as early as 1849 reflects the
fact that as river mining operations were increasing in size and scale,
technical requirements were increasing dramatically as well. Operations
could uncover not merely a few dozen feet, but hundreds and later thousands of feet, of riverbed, and stronger, sturdier dams and flumes were
needed when larger rivers were tapped. And no longer did river mining always entail merely digging a ditch or constructing a simple wooden
flume that ran in parallel to the river. With increasing frequency, river
mining companies had to cut through adjacent rocky terrain or blast their
way through hills in order to divert the water out of the river. In all likelihood, the increased technical requirements for river mining operations
were being driven by two separate factors: the need to tap larger, deeper
waterways, and the location of certain candidate stretches of river in
more rugged terrain. The earliest river mining companies quickly filled
up the smaller, most accessible river locations, leaving the more challenging locations for those who came after. It is important to note that
the technical ante was upped at what some might regard as surprisingly
early in the Gold Rush, as suggested by one miner in June of 1850:

> To dig a canal or race or to build a plank flume "requires much labor of the
> hardest kind . . . The general face of the country is such that digging a race is
> equivalent to blasting a channel through a ledge of flint and granite; and in
> order to make a flume, trees must first be felled, timber hewed, and boards
> sawed. Then the great spout is formed by patience and perseverance, all the
> while the miners living on Hope mixed with port and flour in sufficient quan-
> tities, trusting to the bed of the river to pay!"[21]

Around the same time, the miner Daniel Woods was elaborating on the
stupendous technical challenges facing his company:

We prosecuted both parts of our work at the same time. A part were employed in carrying the clay to the canal. An account was kept one day, and it was ascertained that each barrow was carried, during the day, fourteen miles. Since my last date I have carried such a barrow four hundred and twenty miles. . . . This was a most arduous undertaking. Sometimes [the canal] must pass through a solid ledge of solid asbestos rock, and then through deep holes in the river, where it has washed into the banks. In such a case, a heavy wall, filled with clay, must be made. When completed, the canal was six hundred and thirty-eight feet in length, and sixteen in width. Making the aqueduct to convey the water from the canal, which passed through Paine's Bar, above us, was the most difficult task. The logs, which were cut upon the mountain, were rolled to the pits, and then sawed by hand. Piers were constructed by making crates of logs, which were firmly pinned together, then sunk in their places / by being filled with large stones. Another large pier was made by rolling and carrying stones into the river a distance of thirty feet. The sleepers of the aqueduct were laid upon this and the laden crates. When it was finished, it was a handsome piece of workmanship, of which we were justly proud. It was one hundred and two feet in length, and twelve wide. This kind of labor—yielding no remuneration, only being preparatory to the more exciting, though laborious process of gold-digging, was prosecuted from July the 30th to this date, Sept. 24th.[22]

Note also the comments of the French miner Etienne Derbec on the massiveness of the undertaking that river mining had become by the summer of 1850:

It is unusual for a man to remain by himself; his isolation would render him powerless in the (face of such) heavy work. Therefore, the miners unite their strength to make their work more profitable; they join in small groups or form companies which sometimes count as many as several hundred men. These companies undertake gigantic tasks and change greatly the courses of the largest rivers, like the Merced for example, in the places which are considered the richest, in order to then dig in their very bed.[23]

Thus, within two years after river mining began to be used, miners were already facing the daunting prospect of hauling tons of clay; blasting through solid rock; and felling, hewing, and sawing timber to make a wooden flume, all for the uncertain prospect that there would be gold in the river bed. Yet many, apparently, were undaunted. Indeed, contemporary observers such as Buffum saw enormous economic potential in the prospect of extensive river mining.

> Here is an immense field for a combination of capital and labour. As yet no scientific apparatus has been introduced, and severe manual labour alone has produced such golden results. When steam and money are united for the purpose, I doubt not that the whole waters of the North and Middle Forks will be turned from their channels, and immense canals dug through the rugged mountains to bear them off.[24]

River mining would continue largely unabated for the remainder of the decade, as miners continued to be intrigued by the possibility of finding submerged gold, even in the deeper rivers. Rainfall was below average in 1855 and 1856, which provided added impetus for river mining in those years, both because the rivers were lower than usual and water was scarcer at the dry diggings. In addition, miners explored new, as-yet untapped river locations, such as the Kern and Merced Rivers in the southern mines. And when made economical by the local topogra-

FIGURE 3.6. Mining the bed of the American River, about 1859
Source: Vance, Robert H., *A Camera in the Gold Rush*. Courtesy of the Book Club of California.

phy, river mining operations became even longer and greater in scope as miners continued to tap the larger rivers such as the Feather, which required larger dams and longer flumes. By July 1856, the *Alta Californian* was reporting that one river mining company was in the process of building a flume 1,600 feet long on the Feather River, and that another one 3,000 feet long was being planned. And by September of that year, another flume had been completed that was capable of conveying the entire current of the Feather for a distance of 3,400 feet, and which the *Alta Californian* described as laying "the bottom of the river as bare and dry as a house floor."[25]

At the same time, however, miners were beginning to move away from the immediate vicinity of the streams and into the nearby ravines and gulches as the beds and banks became depleted. There they continued to find gold both on the surface in crevices and when they dug below the surface. On occasion, miners found pieces of quartz rock containing bits of gold, which encouraged them to pay closer attention to quartz outcroppings when they came upon them, where they sometimes found gold.[26] According to Moerenhout, by July 1848 many miners were aware that gold was to be found underground, as they learned by following veins of gold deposits into the hillsides. Moerenhout performed some of his own tests to convince himself of the presence of gold underground, also concluding that the gold may have originated in the hills and was then washed downward into the gulches, streams, and rivers:

> In several tests made with earth taken at a depth of two feet and at ten and fifteen feet from the gulches, I found more or less of gold everywhere. In six trials made with earth taken at the same depth but at one hundred and one hundred and fifty feet from the gulches and half way up the hills, I found gold in two places. It appears certain, therefore, that it is the hills themselves that are, if not the principal, at least the original depository and the source from whence all the gold has come; from whence, carried by the waters, it is deposited in the gulches between the hills, in the streams of the valleys, and in the rivers of the distant plains.

Some historians credit Cornish miners with suspecting the existence of underground gold, based upon their previous experiences with underground mining, and it is known that Cornish miners sank vertical shafts to deposits of gold in Nevada County in 1850, which were promptly dubbed "coyote holes" on the basis of their appearance. The earliest shaft operations involved digging vertically down to bedrock and excavating in various directions using crude wooden beams for support. A windlass (a cylindrical device turned by hand) was then erected at the top of the shaft and was used to haul bucket loads of dirt to the surface.[27]

Deep mining, or *drifting*, spread rapidly to various locations throughout the gold fields. In 1849, a rich outcrop of gold quartz was discovered in the southern mines, in the Mariposa grant claimed by John Fremont. Gold quartz was discovered the following year at Grass Valley, in Nevada County, which would become the center of a short-lived quartz boom in the early 1850s. By mid-1850, the *Alta Californian* reported that vertical shafts were being dug down to bedrock at claims near Columbia and Nevada City. By the following March, "about a thousand shafts" were reportedly being sunk at Gold Run, near Marysville. By that September, miners in the vicinity of Wet Hill in Nevada County were using horsepower not only to raise the earth, but to pump out water which tended to fill the shafts. By May 1852, so many shafts had been dug on the top of Gold Hill, near the town of Placer, that the hilltop was described as resembling a "pepper box." In October 1855, the *Iowa Hill News* reported the arrival of an elaborate steam engine to provide power for machinery used to dig shafts and pump water from them. However, use of the older technologies persisted throughout the 1850s. In mid-1856, horse power was reportedly being applied to old shaft claims near Oroville. Even in late 1857, both manual power and horsepower were being used in the shaft claims of a company of miners near San Andreas, in Calaveras County:

> The McCall Mining Company . . . has been at work over two months . . . They first sunk a shaft seventy feet deep, the water coming in about 35 feet below the surface in such quantities as to require constant bailing day and night, with two men at the windlass. They struck shelving rock, and started a horizontal drift, which they extended 50 feet from the main shaft, the water causing so much inconvenience, they were compelled to erect horse-power to bail it out. At the end of the drift, and 70 feet under ground, they erected a windlass and sunk a shaft 30 feet—making 100 feet in all, struck in the channel among wash boulder and gravel, where they received sufficient of a prospect to sink another shaft, which we learned they would start next week.[28]

When the gold was suspected to lie not under flats but inside sloped hillsides, miners would often dig tunnels, drifting laterally into the hills. Tunneling began to be undertaken extensively no later than late 1851 in Calaveras County, and was regulated by laws adopted by miners on Mokelumne Hill in late November. By the end of the next year, tunneling had spread to Downieville and Marmaluke Hill, near Georgetown. By November 1855, it was reported that a new, more powerful tunnel-boring machine had been brought to San Francisco from Massachusetts, where it had been used to bore the Hoosac Tunnel, a large public works project in western Massachusetts. Over time, these tunnel projects tended to increase in size. Figure 3.7 shows all observations on tunnel lengths reported in mining stories published in the *Alta Californian* from 1849 through 1859, and reflects a definite upward trend in the length of tunnels over this period. Tunnels also became more elaborate during this period, including both a main trunk tunnel and side drifts, as was the case in 1857 with several tunnels near Placerville.[29]

Miners also soon discovered that there were sometimes mutual advantages in sinking vertical shafts and boring lateral tunnels at the same claim. On the one hand, tunnel-boring presented the challenge that it was not always easy to drill at the correct depth. Miners would laterally tunnel some distance into a hillside, only to discover that they were at the wrong depth, resulting in a significant waste of time and resources. As a result, miners would sometimes perform a vertical bore prior to

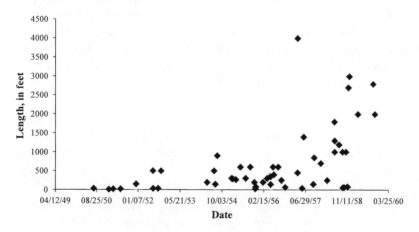

FIGURE 3.7. Tunnel length over time, Gold Fields. 1851–1859

tunneling, in order to determine the proper tunnel depth, as the Sonora Table Mountain Mining Company reportedly did in 1856. On the
other hand, in some claims a vertical shaft would quickly fill with water, in which case miners would dig a tunnel laterally to drain the shaft.[30]
The unfortunate experiences of one company of miners in 1857 illustrate
both these difficulties and the prodigious efforts of miners to cope with
them:

> The "Alabama Tunnel Company", opposite Six Mile Bar, last week, after get-
> ting through the rim rock, and some one hundred and twenty feet into the
> channel underneath the mountain, found themselves too high. They then
> sunk a shaft to the depth of forty-six feet, striking four feet of paying gravel,
> which prospects from six cents to a bit to the pan. [However,] It was impossi-
> ble to prospect the ridge, as the water prevented their doing so . . . The com-
> pany, not at all disheartened, have gone back and commenced another tunnel
> at the proper level, which it is thought, will take them a year at least to com-
> plete . . . The whole distance is through solid rock.[31]

This description of the movement away from the rivers to the dry diggings raises a question that merits some discussion: How did the miners
know where to look for gold? The earliest movement away from the rivers, as we have seen, occurred when miners pursued veins away from the
banks of rivers into the neighboring hills. This led to the deduction that
the hills might well be the source of much of the gold. But this deduction
alone would have provided only the vaguest of practical guidance. When
a miner wanted to know *specifically* where the gold was "in them thar
hills," how would he have gone about trying to find out? The answer to
this question, which speaks to the predictability of prospecting for gold,
will be important later when we consider how to interpret certain rules
that emerged to govern water development.

There is a strong, I might even say dominant, tradition in Gold Rush
historiography that emphasizes the random, hit-or-miss nature of mining for gold. Louisa Clappe provides an early, well-known example of
this view:

> Gold mining is Nature's great lottery scheme. A man may work in a claim
> for many months, and be poorer at the end of the time than when he com-
> menced; or he may "take out" thousands in a few hours. It is a mere matter
> of chance.[32]

Charles Shinn provides a similar expression of this position with regard to prospecting, in downplaying the value of expertise in favor of blind luck:

> The veriest greenhorn was as likely to uncover the richest mine on the gulch as was the wisest of ex-professors of geology.[33]

Such sentiments have been perpetuated by modern historians such as Brands, who has stated, albeit with rhetorical excess, that early miners "operated blindly, groping about the placers" for gold.[34] To the extent that these and other similar sentiments are accurate, new discoveries of gold would have been completely unpredictable, a mere matter of chance.[35]

I would be the last to suggest that there is no truth to these statements that emphasize the random nature of mining, particularly during the early 1850s. Various accounts attest to miners lacking good information about where to look for gold and succumbing to rumors of lakes of gold and folk theories of ancient exploding volcanoes spewing gold over the area.[36] Rodman Paul retells a humorous account of some clueless miners furtively trailing Marshall up into the mountains for days, convinced that he would lead them to gold:

> Like most gold-seekers, I for one was not satisfied and had the belief that if Marshall (the discoverer of gold) could be shadowed the fountain head would be found, forgetting that it was only by accident that he discovered it, in the tail-race while constructing Sutter's mills at Coloma. A party was made up of the various characters then predominant; old sea dogs (sailors on horseback) et al., and the writer, a boy in years.
>
> Knowledge having been gained of Marshall starting with a party between the north and middle forks of the American river, our party of about seven in number followed his, always keeping a sufficient distance in the rear to escape discovery by his party.
>
> It is forgotten how many days his party was trailed, but suddenly one day we came upon him having a siesta about noon. He had a good face, mild and somewhat attractive. He smiled and said that he knew nothing of where gold existed any more than we did. After a short halt our party moved on to hunt further for the precious metal.[37]—Pioneer

There is, however, also reason to believe that the characterization of finding gold as largely a matter of dumb luck does not fully capture the essence of the endeavor. For one thing, a considerable amount of practical useful folk knowledge made its way to the gold fields through miners from South America and Europe, and veterans of previous gold rushes, especially the Georgia and North Carolina gold rushes of the early 1800s. Experienced Cornish miners figure prominently in many accounts of the Gold Rush. It is also well known that many miners from Georgia and the Carolinas made their way to California after word of the discovery got out.[38] These miners would have brought much practical expertise in how to mine and how to look for gold, and this fact was recognized by other miners.[39]

Furthermore, it merits emphasis that American scientists in the early nineteenth century had devoted much effort to understanding the geology of gold deposits, toward trying to provide practical information concerning where it was likely to be found. In doing so, they were able to draw on a rich tradition of European scholarship, especially the sixteenth-century works of the medieval German mineralogist Agricola, whose work on the nature of ore deposits was centuries ahead of its time.[40] They were also able to capitalize on rich practical experience gained from the previous gold rushes. In 1833, for example, an article by a mining engineer appeared in the prestigious *American Journal of Science and Arts*, which discusses the geology of the Georgia gold rush and gives a good sense of the scientific understanding of gold deposition existing at the time. The article includes a detailed compositional analysis of the gold-bearing strata (especially quartz, gneiss, mica, and talcose slate), the importance of the action of water, and the likely slow evolutionary nature of the erosive process that produced the gold fragments(as opposed to volcanoes spewing gold everywhere).[41] Many of these principles would inform scientific understanding of the later California experience.

One of the leading geologists who contributed to the nineteenth-century effort to characterize gold deposition was James Dwight Dana, who was a student of the eminent geologist Benjamin Silliman at Yale College. As we saw earlier, Dana had previously been in California as part of the Wilkes Expedition, and he was interested in providing geologic knowledge of practical value to miners. In 1851, he published his *Manual of Mineralogy*, which he advertised as an attempt to be "as far as possible, practical and American in nature."[42] Of particular interest is the following passage:

The gold rock of the United States is to a great extent a micaceous or talc-ose schist, with veins or beds of quartz. The gold is mostly confined to these veins, though also found to some extent in the rock on either side. . . . Iron pyrites is frequently present, and by decomposition it stains the rock with iron rust. . . . The grains of gold may sometimes be seen in the cavities of the quartz, or it sparkles on a surface of fracture. But very commonly a mass of quartz that shows nothing to the eye, yields gold on trial.[43]

Given Dana's leading reputation, it is safe to interpret this passage as reflecting the scientific frontier of geologic understanding of gold deposits at the time, especially their association in nature with quartz and the frequent presence of iron pyrites, which would leave telltale signs of reddish rust-colored rocks upon decomposition. If such information was available to miners in California, it would have provided a certain amount of practical guidance to miners regarding where to look for gold.

As it turns out, much evidence suggests that this information was indeed available to many miners in California, and that many of them probably acted on it. One important source of information that we know of is a book by Felix Wierzbicki entitled *California as It Is and as It May Be*, which was published in San Francisco in September 1849. Wierzbicki was a Polish physician who was living in San Francisco at the time of the discovery. His book was essentially a newcomer's guide to California, but it was obviously targeted at the multitude of gold seekers arriving weekly in San Francisco by the thousands, as it was chock-full of useful information on mining, including provisioning; what tools to bring; how to mine; things to consider in forming a partnership with other miners; and detailed descriptions of the different mining localities. Among the many useful tidbits of information in the book was the following advice on prospecting:

On arriving at any spot containing gold deposits, the first step to be taken is to examine the general appearance of the country. The hills should be covered with brick-red soil . . . slate rock should be found . . . Likewise quartz should be found scattered about on the ground . . . The presence of these three signs jointly is sufficient to authorize one to look for gold by digging in some convenient spot, but any of them singly is of no validity in this respect.[44]

This advice is obviously highly derivative of Dana's statement contained in the *Manual*, suggesting that indeed, reliable science-based guidance on prospecting was available to the gold seekers. The clear markers provided by Wierzbicki on what to look for would have provided useful guidance to prospecting miners.

Because this book was highly informative and written in a credible, dispassionate tone, it was an instant sensation, quickly selling out and going to a second printing within three months.[45] Adding to its influence was the fact that extended excerpts from the book were published in the *Alta Californian* in early October, shortly after it was published.[46] All of this strongly suggests that significant numbers of miners would have used this information to guide them in their search for gold deposits. Certainly it was known by the miner Alonzo Delano, who wrote in the early 1850s:

> "I believe that the best diggings are generally found where the formation is talcous slate, or, where there is an abundance of auriferous quartz—where the soil is covered with peroxide of iron. Sometimes rich earth is found, where the earth is not highly colored with iron, but there is a superabundance either of slate or quartz in its vicinity."[47]

Some additional anecdotal information is available from none other than the event of the original discovery itself at Sutter's Mill. Writing years later, one of the workers at the Mill, James Brown, recalls Marshall's reaction to the discovery and why he thought it might be real gold. Said Marshall:

> "I believe it contains minerals of some kind, and I believe there is gold in these hills."
>
> At this statement I inquired, "What makes you think so?" He [Marshall] answered that he had seen blossom of gold, and upon my asking where, he said it was the white quartz scattered over the hills; in my inquiring further as to what quartz was, he told me it was the white, flint-like rock so plentiful on the hills. I said it was flint rock, but he said no, it was called quartz in some book he had read, and was an indication of gold.[48]

This passage suggests two important things about the printed information available to prospecting miners. First, geological formations could help identify where the gold was likely to be. Second, they could help determine whether or not what miners found was really gold. Both would have been of practical value to miners looking for gold.

What do we conclude about the predictability of prospecting? The overall body of evidence suggests something that falls far short of the caricature that prospecting was a great lottery. The miners in California had access to the best scientific information available at the time, and no doubt many of them used it. But even the best scientific information would not have ensured favorable outcomes in what remained a largely probabilistic venture. And given that there was no guarantee of success, miners would have been more than human if they did not react, and in some cases overreact, to less-than-fully substantiated rumors of strikes elsewhere, thus reducing the effectiveness of the principles of scientific prospecting that were available at the time. The overall conclusion must be that prospecting was far from random, but that there was a certain amount of irreducible uncertainty, which made it extremely difficult to predict where the next successful strikes would be. As we shall see later, this fact would have an upside: the mitigation of racing dissipation in competition for mining, and especially water, claims.

3.4. Water and the Technologies of Placer Mining

Once miners discovered gold deposits, of course, the next step was to mine the deposits. This would turn out to present numerous technical challenges that rapidly evolved over time as the gold was steadily depleted. In response, miners would devise new production methods in order to increase mining productivity, the overall effect of which was to steadily increase the importance of both water and capital in the gold production process.

As we have seen, in the earliest days of the Gold Rush miners tapped surface diggings in river beds and banks, gulches, and ravines. After the earliest flush days of 1848 when many miners could simply pick flakes and nuggets of gold from crevices and stream beds using crowbars, knives, and pickaxes, gold generally took the form of smaller flakes or fine particles embedded in dirt, mud, or gravel. It was at this point that miners turned to other processes to extract the gold, processes in which water figured prominently. The quintessential early method of mining was the well-known *panning* method, an ancient method which had been illustrated by Agricola and had been used by miners in the earlier Georgia and North Carolina rushes.[49] Panning involved taking a circular pan made of wood or metal, placing muddy gravel suspected of contain-

FIGURE 3.8. Early mining technologies, ca. 1850
Courtesy of the Bancroft Library, Zelda Mackay pictorial collection, University of California, Berkeley.

ing gold into the pan, agitating the pan with a circular motion that was strong enough to suspend the lighter debris while the gold would sink to the bottom of the pan, and then skimming off the debris, leaving the gold in the pan.[50] Panning was easy to learn and required very little in terms of factor inputs other than muscle and water, and was thus a popular method for the early miners. On the other hand, it was not possible to process much debris quickly, and it was physically taxing because of the constant repetitive motion, and because the pan could be quite heavy when filled with water and debris.[51]

Nevertheless, pans would continue to be used throughout the 1850s, both by solitary miners and as part of the prospecting process for larger-scale operations. In the latter capacity, panning would be used to assess the richness of new diggings as miners looked for "color." Once they found sufficient color—that is, evidence of gold in the local placers—they would then start to work the deposits using more advanced methods, to be described here shortly. Furthermore, pans underwent some modest improvement over time.[52] The pan of the late 1850s probably closely resembled the pan of the late 1840s, though it was probably lighter and less expensive than its earlier counterpart in part because of advances in methods of manufacturing. By 1856, for example, the following item on pans appeared in the *Alta Californian*:

> Mining Pan Manufacture.—This article is one of the most useful in California, and in order to facilitate and improve its manufacture, . . . Messrs. Dickens & Hillhouse have just finished a new and very simple machine for the manufacture of sheet iron mining pans, without seams and perfectly solid, which is a very great improvement on the old pan. The machine is made on the die and level principle, and has a stamping power of nearly a ton. With steam power two gross of these pans can be turned out in a day, while four men can make and perfect one gross with ease in the same time. A patent has been applied for.[53]

In addition to indicating that this was a new production method, this news item suggests that there was still significant demand for pans by late in the decade.

Another technology that was available to miners from the very beginning of the Gold Rush was the so-called *rocker-and-cradle* method. In its earliest form, a hollowed-out log was affixed to a rocking mechanism, debris was shoveled into a sieve attached to the top end of the log, water was fed into the log, the cradle was rocked, and debris and water discharged from the bottom of the log. Riffles or cleats made of wood or metal were attached to the floor of the log to catch the gold as the debris was fed through. Thus, the rocking motion served the same agitating function as had the circular panning, keeping the lighter debris suspended during processing while the heavier gold sank to the bottom of the mechanism. Successful use of the rocker-and-cradle method required at least three or four men: one or two men to shovel in the debris, another to feed in the water, and another to rock the cradle. It was not a terribly efficient process because much gold escaped over the riffles, but it increased productivity by permitting miners to exploit the advantages of specialization and division of labor. It also underwent modest technical improvement early on, moving beyond a hollowed-out log to boards fastened together. Like panning, the rocker-and-cradle technology had been used in the previous gold rushes in Georgia and North Carolina, after which the technology migrated to California. The existence of the technology in California is known to predate the great emigration of 1849. It was, for example, well-known in Oregon by summer of 1848, according to one miner, Peter Burnett, who relates that he made sure he had brought "new and suitable plank for a rocker" in his wagon before he set out for California.[54]

Compared with the basic pan, the rocker-and-cradle device probably underwent more extensive modification and refinement early on. Whereas Burnett's rocker-and-cradle in late 1848 was little more than three boards nailed together, by late 1849 rocker-and-cradles had become much more elaborate. The Jackson-Burke rocker, which had been used for some time in Virginia and which was introduced into the gold fields in 1849, consisted of a nine-foot-long trough whose bottom was made of perforated cast iron plates, into which water was pumped. In the bottom of the trough were holes that gradually increased in size toward the lower end, underneath which were placed mercury-filled drawers to catch and amalgamate the gold. By April of the following spring, however, the *Alta Californian* was able to report that this rocker was already being replaced by more advanced versions that were lighter and cheaper:

> In place of the ponderous Virginia rocker, costing last fall a small fortune to purchase and another to locate it, we now have an elegant substitute, fully equal to the original and accurately accommodated to all, its peculiar and well-established points of merit, united with the greatest attainable lightness and cheapness. The price for one of these is about $200, and it weighs little more than half as many pounds.

The *Alta Californian* went on to summarize the rapid changes that had already occurred in the rocker-and-cradle technology:

> Only a few months ago, and the great essential apparatus, the cradle or common washer, had not advanced in its construction from the rudely dug out log, or an ill-shaped combination of rough remnants of boxes and other incidental "stuff". Now the elegant specimens of handicraft in these articles would adorn the exhibitions of our mechanic fairs in the East.[55]

As we have seen, prosecution of mining using the panning and rocker-and-cradle methods could be done by either one or a handful of men. Neither method was, however, terribly efficient at separating gold from debris, as each required miners to process individual piles of debris, either pan-sized or somewhat larger cradle-sized. At some point in late 1849 or early 1850, however, miners first used a continuous feed system in a device that became known as a *long tom*.[56] The long tom was a long, open-ended box into which debris was shoveled, water was piped into the top of the box, the debris was stirred, and the heavier gold flakes fell through perforations in the bottom of the box into a second box with a riffled bottom to catch the flakes. The long tom increased productivity by applying water in a continuous flow, permitting more debris to be processed in a given period, and it quickly came to enjoy widespread adoption. By February 1851, a letter to the *Alta Californian* described a "great many" miners around Sonora in Tuolumne County using long toms, which was said to wash as much dirt as four cradles.[57] By June, long toms were described as being "in general use" around Sutter Creek in Amador County. By the time the miner John Borthwick arrived in Placerville in fall of 1851, he described long toms as the apparatus "generally used for washing." By mid-1852, long toms had come to enjoy such widespread adoption that waterways were being measured in terms of how many toms they could serve, with the *Sonora Herald* describing a big watercourse as a "500 to 1,000 tom stream."[58]

The miners soon discovered, however, that by lengthening the trough

FIGURE 3.9. Mining with a Long Tom, Murphy's
Courtesy of the Bancroft Library, Charles L. Camp Collection, University of California, Berkeley.

FIGURE 3.10. Sluicing, Murphy's
Courtesy of the Bancroft Library, Charles L. Camp Collection, University of California,
Berkeley.

through which the flow of water was piped, they could dispense with
the perforations in the bottom of the trough, using riffles attached to
the bottom of the trough to catch the gold flakes: thus was the *sluice*,
or *sluice box*, born. In this manner, the long tom technology was trans-
formed into what was in essence merely a long, shallow trough through

which water was piped, the gold being caught by riffles attached to the bottom of the trough. According to Rodman Paul, miners may have begun experimenting with the sluicing technology sometime in the winter of 1849–50, though actual adoption lagged by a full year.[59] Sluices began to be mentioned in news accounts by spring of 1851.[60] By December, the sluice technology was enjoying widespread adoption in Calaveras County, where "a number of" sluices "one hundred to a hundred and eighty feet in length" were being built. The greater amount of throughput possible made sluices considerably more productive than cradles, according to the *Calaveras Chronicle*:

> Miners should remember that it takes earth averaging from one to two bits per pan to pay a cradle, but that one cent per pan will pay a well constructed sluice when properly worked.[61]

Miners continued to tinker with the sluice box and over time, refinements were made that further increased its productivity. One homely little refinement involved nailing down old pieces of woolen blankets to the bottom of the sluice, which would capture the finer gold particles as they passed through.[62] Other refinements involved widening and lengthening the sluice boxes, thus providing a greater surface to catch the gold flakes, which further increased gold discovery. A further modification was to make the sluices slightly narrower at one end, allowing multiple sluices to be deployed sequentially.[63] Thus, over time sluicing operations came to require ever-greater upfront capital investments.

The timing of the adoption of sluice technology strongly suggests that water availability may have been an important constraining factor. Given the similarity of the long tom and sluice technologies, it is not surprising that the idea of sluicing came quickly on the heels of the long tom, as Paul suggests.[64] Yet as we shall see shortly, actual diffusion of the sluice technology lagged behind the adoption of long toms, despite much evidence that sluices were considerably more productive than long toms as long as sufficient water was available, as one miner explained in 1853:

> I could adduce the experience of hundreds of miners who have for a long time used the tom or cradle, and afterwards have substituted the sluice, and when they have supposed they saved all the gold by the first processes, they have found that with a long sluice, having the proper pitch and an abundance of clear water, they could get a much larger quantity of gold from the same

quantity of the same kind of dirt. The sluice is undoubtedly the best thing yet
employed for saving the fine gold.

At the same time, where water was less plentiful, adoption of sluices
lagged behind long toms; as, for example, in relatively water-scarce Mariposa County.[65] Miners may well have wanted to avail themselves of the
superior sluicing technology, but in many locations, this would have
to wait until water was developed in sufficient quantities to make this
possible.

The trend toward more heavily water-intensive mining technologies
did not, however, stop with the long tom and sluice box, both of which
required debris to be manually shoveled into the sorting mechanism.
The next step was to use water to continuously feed debris into the
sorter. This was initially accomplished by the process known as *ground
sluicing*, in which water was directed to run over a suspected lode-
bearing hillside, and the debris was eroded down and either dug out
of the ground or directed into sluice boxes, where again the gold was
separated out. Thus, it was at this point that sluice boxes became complementary components in a process that continuously fed both water
and debris into the sorting mechanism. Histories do not make clear
the precise timing of the introduction of ground sluicing, but they suggest it was no later than early 1852 and possibly earlier. In any event,
according to contemporary accounts, in the winter of 1852–53 ground
sluicing was being done "to a large extent" at Mormon Camp, near Sonora. By 1857, the *Sacramento Age* was describing ground sluicing as
"a common way of collecting gold."[66] Shortly I will present evidence
that clarifies the timing of the introduction and penetration of ground
sluicing.

The next important technological advance was the invention of the
process of hydraulic mining, or hydraulicking, in 1853 by Edward Matteson (see Figure 3.11).[67] In hydraulicking, a nozzle was attached to a
length of hose, through which a high-pressure jet of water was directed
at a suspected gold-bearing hillside, and the debris was again directed
into sluice boxes. Doing so vastly increased the amount of debris that
could be processed, while the remaining valueless debris was flushed
into creeks that bore it away downstream, eventually exiting the gold
mining regions, mostly into the Sacramento Valley. The first mention of
this process in the *Alta Californian* occurred in June 1853:

FIGURE 3.11. Edward E. Matteson, inventor of hydraulic mining
Source: *The Miners' Own Book*. Courtesy of the Book Club of California.

A new method of mining in hill diggings has lately been introduced in this place [Nevada County], as novel as it is efficient. The usual cut is made from the outer edge at the base into the centre of the hill. From a reservoir on its summit, (made with a barrel, to preserve a steady pressure) the water is conducted by a leading-hose of strong canvas, terminating with a pipe, similar to that of a fire engine. The column of water thus produced ranges from twenty to one hundred feet according to the height of the hill. The pipe is taken into the area of the cut and brought to bear upon its sides; and such is the immense power of the water as it escapes from the pipe, that no alluvial deposit can resist the force for an instant.[68]

Early versions of hydraulicking could be quite crude, using hose made of rawhide and nozzles made of wood. However, miners contin-

FIGURE 3.12. Hydraulic mining near French Corral
Source: Lawrence and Houseworth Albums, Society of California Pioneers.

ually tinkered with the technology in attempts to make it more efficient and productive. Rawhide hose quickly gave way to more durable
wire-reinforced canvas and wooden nozzles gave way to iron ones. In
1854, a mining company attached a perforated iron grate to the head of
the sluice, which was pitched at a steep angle. The grate would direct
larger rocks away from the sluice, while the smaller debris would enter
the sluice through the grate. By 1855, the "gooseneck" nozzle was introduced in Yuba County, which increased the volume of water that could
be directed against a hillside. In late 1858, the *North San Juan Press* reported that a mining company had achieved good success in blasting the
hillside with gunpowder in order to loosen up the debris prior to application of the water. Miners also experimented with using stamp mills
to break up large debris and "undercurrent" sluice boxes—secondary
sluice boxes positioned underneath the main one that processed finer

debris that fell through grates in the bottom of the main sluice box—that were designed to increase gold recovery.[69]

The rate at which hydraulic mining methods were adopted depended upon two key factors that varied locally. Most obviously, hydraulicking was an extremely water-intensive process, so that the presence of large quantities of water in a mining locality was a considerable advantage, at least until sufficient water could be brought in from outside. But successful hydraulicking also required localized sharp changes in elevation, in particular so that water could be imported to a terminus situated well above the diggings, which created a significant "head," thus generating sufficient water pressure for effective mining.[70] The presence of elevation changes also helped when it came time to dispose of the tailings left over from the production process, as tailings could be vented into streams that would carry them off, away from the diggings. As we shall see, this was not the end of the story, as venting could generate disputes with downstream mining operations, not to mention inflicting sizable damages on the local environment.

It will be useful to convey a quantitative sense of the pace of technological advance and the rate at which the new technologies penetrated the gold fields, in order to correctly interpret the later developments in provisions relating to mining and water rights. Figure 3.13 reports one measure of this: the cumulative number of times each of the different technologies was mentioned in a database of over 900 news accounts

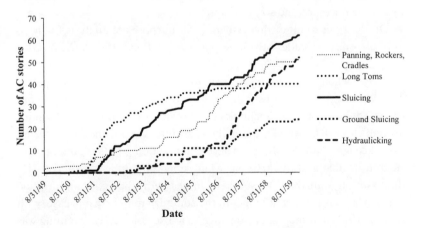

FIGURE 3.13. Penetration of mining technologies, 1849–1859. AC, *Alta Californian.*

pertaining to gold mining that appeared in the *Alta Californian* from 1849 to 1859.[71] Each of the observations in Figure 3.13 is an actual eye-witness account of the mining technology being deployed somewhere in the gold fields. Several important patterns may be discerned in the data. The first is that what I shall term *primitive* methods (panning, rockers-and-cradles) were clearly dominant in the early Gold Rush, being the only methods mentioned in 1849 and 1850. In 1851, we begin to observe the penetration of long toms and then sluice boxes the following year. These new methods quickly overtook the primitive methods and for a while dominated mining. However, whereas the use of long toms slowed dramatically after 1853, the use of sluice boxes continued unabated for the remainder of the decade. The other important trend is that ground sluicing started to make significant inroads in 1854, while hydraulicking witnessed gradual adoption from its onset in 1853, noticeably accelerating after 1856. These patterns largely confirm the anecdotal information presented earlier.

Further evidence on technology adoption is reported in Figure 3.14, which breaks down the observations between the northern mines and the southern mines. The reason this might be of interest is that the northern mines had considerably greater access to water, so Figure 3.14 might reflect the impact of water scarcity on technology adoption. Sure enough, miners in the drier southern mines relied much more heavily on primitive technologies and long toms. Northern miners, on the other hand, relied on sluice boxes and hydraulicking much more extensively. In the discussion to come, it will help to keep in mind this distinction between the northern and southern mines.

On the basis of all of this evidence, for purposes of analysis I will divide the entire decade into three periods I will call the *Early*, *Middle*, and *Later* periods. The Early period consists of the first two years, 1849 and 1850, when, as we have just seen, primitive technologies dominated. The Middle period begins in 1851 with the growing adoption of continuous flow separation technologies. Finally, the Later period begins around early 1854, when the heavily water-intensive technologies started to make significant headway.[72] These demarcation points should be considered flexible and to vary somewhat depending upon whether we are discussing the northern or southern mines, with the Early and Middle periods lasting somewhat longer in the southern mines. In any case, with these periods in mind, let us now turn to a discussion of how mining was organized.

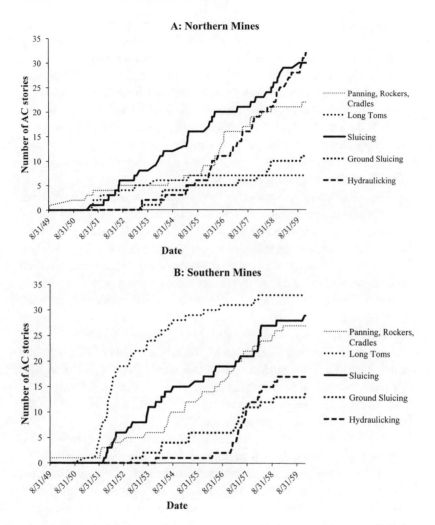

FIGURE 3.14. Penetration of mining technologies, 1849–1859. A, Northern mines vs. B, Southern mines

3.5. The Organization of Mining

The technological progression of mining that we have just seen, from digging nuggets out of crevices to using pans and rockers in the shallow streams to sluicing to hydraulicking, had implications for the organization of mining operations and how it evolved over time. By their very nature, digging nuggets out of crevices and panning were activities that could be, and often were, done individually. Furthermore, both were highly labor-intensive production methods, requiring very little capital or water for successful prosecution. This is not to argue that there were no advantages for panners to work together, such as sharing cooking duties or for mutual protection, but these were more ancillary to the primary task of gold extraction. Consequently, as long as the gold was sufficiently rich and plentiful, as it was in the halcyon days of early 1848, mining could be effectively done at a very small scale of production with little need for cooperation or organization.

The adoption of rockers-and-cradles was the first step toward company organization, albeit at a relatively small scale. As we have seen, compared with panning, mining with rockers-and-cradles required a somewhat greater investment in capital along with a modicum of division of labor, as miners divided up the tasks of digging, hauling dirt, and pouring water into and rocking the cradle. As a result, whereas panning could be successfully done by one miner working alone, mining with rockers-and-cradles required at least three and ideally more like five or six miners. Early coyoteing was also greatly aided by miners working in tandem, as it involved digging down, working around the bedrock, and hauling dirt up to the surface. All of this meant that modest incentives for team production were present from the very beginning of the period, even in the Early period. However, as of yet, there was very little in the way of meaningful economies of scale.

One exception to this statement is the river mining operations discussed earlier, which we saw had a significant presence in parts of the gold fields as early as late 1848 and required teams of men to construct the dam and diversion ditch, and to work the exposed stretch of river. River mining thus had a substantial initial investment component that was absent from all other placer mining operations during the Early period prior to 1851. The wish to protect these investments would have certain implications for the desired security of river mining claims and the protections afforded them by emerging institutions, to be discussed later. However, unlike later investments in ditching capacity, the wish to protect the security of water rights would be largely absent. For the river mining companies, water was mostly a nuisance to be gotten rid of, not a valuable input into gold production.

Another area where we did observe significant economies of scale during the Early period was in the early emergence of a quartz mining industry, which began with the discovery of gold quartz at Mariposa in 1849 and Nevada County in 1850, as we have seen. From the very beginning, the technology for quartz mining was considerably more capital-intensive than placer mining. Since the gold was encased in quartz rock, there was a preliminary step prior to gold separation in which the quartz rock was crushed up into fragments that were fine enough to permit separation through application of water. This crushing was accomplished by feeding the quartz rock into large stamping mechanisms in stamp mills, in a process not unlike grinding up substances using an enormous mortar and pestle.[73] To create a working stamp mill thus required a sizable upfront capital investment, as well as considerable throughput in order to make the investment worthwhile. As it would turn out, however, quartz mining experienced major technical challenges that took some time to be successfully addressed.[74] Consequently, after a brief flurry of investment activity in the early 1850s including considerable interest from eastern and British investors, quartz mining quickly flamed out and did not contribute significantly to mining output for the remainder of the decade.[75] By one informed estimate, quartz mining contributed less than one percent of total state gold production during the 1850s.[76] As a consequence, the remainder of our discussion will largely exclude consideration of quartz mining.

The movement to the Middle and Later periods, however, saw modest and later, sizable, economies of scale, which led to major expansions in the minimum efficient scale of operations and the tendency to team production. The movement to long toms and sluices moderately expanded the upfront capital requirements both in the separating mechanism itself and in the diversion of water through the mechanism, while the increased throughput kept more men busy hauling dirt for processing. Ground sluicing and hydraulicking required significantly greater investments in infrastructure for diverting water, especially as mining migrated to sites remote from water sources. And tunneling in the deep diggings required a major upfront investment in digging to gain access to the gold that increased dramatically through these later periods, as we have seen. To summarize, the technological changes that were occurring in the Middle and Later period all effectively increased the initial capital requirements and raised the minimum efficient scale of mining operations, thus providing the economic impetus for ever-larger companies to emerge.

The organizational form of mining companies also underwent an evolution over time that mirrored the technological changes that were taking place. During the early Gold Rush, most miners formed partnerships
or joint stock companies with other miners. Under these arrangements,
they would agree : to labor together to wash gold or to construct a dam
and diversion ditch for a river mining operation; to either buy shares in
the company or contribute whatever funds they could toward company
expenses; to share in the profits of the venture; and to subject many decisions to a vote of company members, including selection of a foreman,
admission of new members, and increases in company stock.[77] Some
miners formed lasting partnerships with others connected by kinship,
a common home-town or religion, or acquaintanceship formed on the
journey to California, but these tended to be the exception rather than
the rule. On the whole, early partnerships tended to be fluid, forming
whenever the need for one arose and disbanding when the need no longer existed.[78]

The early dominance of partnerships is striking given the existence
of evidence that suggests that very early on, the hiring of wage labor by
miners was a feasible alternative business model. Indeed, diaries and
other contemporary accounts contain numerous references to miners
hiring other miners to work for them.[79] Rodman Paul has explained the
early dominance of partnerships over wage labor as due to the fact that
miners could make so much money working independently.[80] However,
this does not really explain the dominance of partnerships because it
does not explain why wages would not adjust to compensate, and some
evidence actually suggests that they did compensate enough to attract at
least some workers.

Part of the answer may have been voiced by one miner when describing an acquaintance who did hire himself out:

> One of our boys has hired out to work at $100 a month and board. This
> is good pay, but when I mine I wish to work for myself, even though I may get
> less.[81]

The wage premium for working independently described here was likely
shared by other miners. However, another part of the answer is contained in some of the same accounts that describe wage labor contracts.
One miner, for example, describes one such contractual arrangement
around Placerville that did not last long:

Mr. Rucker hired out to a man by the name of Jobe at the rate of ½ ounce or $8.00 per day and boarded; they had a written article drawn up and signed. Rucker set into work for him on Monday 29th of April 1850 and was obligated by the contract to serve him six months. But during the first week of his service at mining (for his employer) who was out prospecting and trying to find diggings to set him in, he, Mr. Rucker, took the liberty to work when he pleased and gamble when he wanted to which he is very fond of and does a good deal at. And on Monday, 6th inst., he took the privelege [sic] to go out with some 50 men on a tramp after Indians which had been doing some stealing from the whites and thought that they would punish them severly [sic] if they could find them, but the company returned in a few days and did not get nearer than ½ mile to any of the Indians—so they effected no good. Since then Rucker has not done any work for his employer and, I spose [sic] by mutual consent on both parties, they dissolved as Rucker has since started out in the mountains with some other persons on a prospecting tour. And I also heard the man say that had him hired, that Rucker was not a going to work for him any more as they agreed to break up.[82]

This account strongly suggests extreme difficulty in enforcing the terms of this labor contract for two related but distinct reasons: costly supervision giving rise to shirking behavior, and the fact that alternative employment opportunities were readily available for the employee. Under these circumstances, partnerships or associations would tend to emerge instead of wage labor in order to economize on transaction costs.[83]

It was not long, however, before the partnership/joint stock company form began to give way to mining corporations as miners took advantage of a new statute enacted by the state legislature in 1850 that allowed companies to incorporate.[84] An important reason for this shift, of course, was the growing capital needs of mining operations as they grew in size and scale, outstripping the ability of many miners to self-finance. It should be added, however, that the cost of borrowing from alternative sources was likely quite high, with interest rates as high as four to eight percent per month in San Francisco as late as 1851, and likely considerably higher in the previous two years.[85] And after 1852, banks in San Francisco experienced hard times with the decline of gold production, resulting in several panics and bank closures in 1854 and 1855.[86]

The very first company to be incorporated under the new law was a mining company, the California State Mining and Smelting Company,

in May of 1850, and this was followed by hundreds of additional incorporations over the remainder of the decade (see Figure 3.15). In total,
from 1850 through 1859, 576 companies were incorporated in the state,
of which 214, or 37 percent, were mining companies, and another 218
were water companies or integrated mining and water companies. Virtually all of these water companies were in business to service miners' demands for water to prosecute mining. In all, Figure 3.15 reveals that the
first decade of incorporation in the state of California was unquestion-
ably dominated by the mining sector, with 75 percent of all new corporations consisting of companies either participating in, or operating in service to, the mining industry.

To provide more insight into this temporal pattern of incorporation, Figure 3.16 shows the number of incorporations of mining companies alone, without water companies. The overall pattern includes two
components. The dramatic jump in incorporations in 1851 and 1852 reflects the brief speculative interest in quartz mining on the heels of the
quartz discoveries at Mariposa and Nevada County, which quickly died
out. During those two years, quartz company incorporations comprised
over 85 percent of all mining incorporations. When we strip away the
quartz company data, the remaining pattern is of a trickle of mining incorporations through 1853, followed by a steady and accelerating increase to 1856 and 1857, after which new mining incorporations fall off

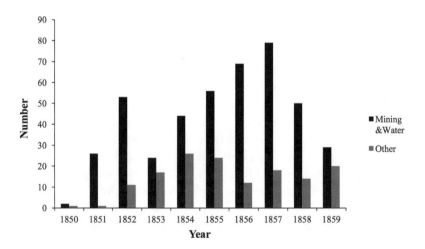

FIGURE 3.15. Total incorporations per year, 1850–1859

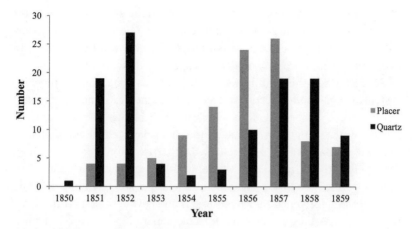

FIGURE 3.16. Number of incorporations per year, placer and quartz companies, 1850–1859

dramatically. In other words, mining incorporations are virtually non-existent during our Early and Middle periods, and then take on increasing importance during our Later period, which just happens to coincide with the adoption of heavily capital- and water-intensive mining methods. The overall pattern suggests that the new technologies dramatically upped the financial requirements for mining companies to operate successfully, as reflected in the need to incorporate in order to raise necessary funds. The decline toward the end of the decade likely reflects both growing depletion of the gold fields and a financial crisis and retrenchment in the mining industry that occurred after 1858.

3.6. Conclusions

Let us recap what we now know about the early mining industry. The initial rush to the gold fields in 1848, followed by the massive influx of forty-niners the following year, resulted in rapid depletion of the easily accessed gold in the shallow streams, and the banks and bars in those streams, throughout the gold regions. We saw that initially, this was concentrated in two main areas: the watersheds of the American and Yuba Rivers in the northern mines, and the watersheds of the Mokelumne and Stanislaus Rivers in the southern mines. This temporal pattern will help interpret the early emergence of property rights in mining claims that we will see later on, which will be concentrated in these areas that saw the earliest rates of depletion and therefore, the greatest early potential for disputes over available gold. A visible connection between growing scarcity and the emergence of informal property rights will be apparent, in line with our basic scarcity model of property rights formation.

Second, when this readily accessible gold was gone, some miners invested in dams and diversion ditches and flumes to mine the beds of deeper rivers. Others began to search for gold farther afield away from surface water sources, in a process that had major elements of chance but also, in many cases, science-based expertise. However, it remained extremely difficult to predict where gold was going to be found. The miners were also led by deduction and surface evidence to look for gold underground, for which they dug tunnels and coyote shafts. At the same time, they devised new methods for gold separation that used increasingly large amounts of capital and water, which generated economies of scale while giving impetus to team production. The ever-increasing capital requirements of successful placer mining were met by a generalized movement away from partnerships and joint stock companies toward new corporate enterprises capable of raising larger sums of money through stock issues.

Of interest here is the timing of when things happened. The central importance of gold separation technologies, and the clear implications for trends in capital- and water-intensity, provides an analytical basis for interpreting mining developments, especially with regard to company size, investment requirements, and the associated need for financing. Being able to pinpoint when technological changes occurred makes it sensible, for example, that the Early period, with its almost exclusive reliance on primitive labor-intensive technologies, witnessed very few incorporated mining companies. It similarly helps explain the dramatic acceleration of incorporation activity in the Later period, when water- and capital-intensive ground sluicing and hydraulicking methods were being adopted with increasing frequency. As we shall see shortly, identifying when technological changes occurred also informs interpretation of the evolution of rules governing mining and water rights. But before we see exactly how, let us first examine the other key industry of our study: the independent ditch industry.

CHAPTER FOUR

Watering the Diggings

The Development of the Ditch Industry

The great complaint from the mines is want of water. Only give us water, say the miners, and we will make business good all over the State. But if the rains won't come, what are they to do? If the mountain won't go to Mahomet, Mahomet must go to the mountain. If the water won't come to the miners, the miners must go to the water. —*Alta Californian*, 2/9/1855

4.1. Introduction

Coincidental with, and mirroring, the movement of placer mining to dry diggings and the increasing water-intensity of placer mining was the creation of an extended and elaborate water supply system throughout much of the mining regions. As we have seen, water was an essential factor input in gold separation and became increasingly important over time as miners adopted ever more water-intensive technologies. This in turn gave impetus to the development of water supplies in support of the burgeoning mining industry. This chapter describes this process of development, from the initial halting steps of mining companies to supply their own water, to the creation of massive integrated companies that constructed enormous reservoirs and miles of water delivery infrastructure. As we shall see, the development of water throughout the gold regions in turn gave rise to water disputes of various kinds over the origination of those rights and how they were exercised through the delivery and application of water for mining. The story of water law in 1850s California is ultimately the story of how these disputes over water were addressed and resolved. In order to understand how disputes over water arose in the operation of the industry, it will help to begin by describing the origins and development of the ditch industry itself.

4.2. The Origins of the Ditching Industry

You know we have preachers in the mines; well, they have been praying, and the miners have been cursing, for rain, but all has availed nothing. Saints and sinners can do nothing with the stubborn elements.—(Letter from Yankee Hill, *Alta Californian*, 2/15/1851)

Prior to the development of local water supplies, mining operations were arranged around the natural availability of water. As we have seen, most of the gold fields were located in a swath of the Sierra foothills from Butte County in the north down to Mariposa County in the south, an area roughly 200 miles long and 50 miles wide. As the weather fronts came through, they dumped rain and snow in the mountains, which was funneled back through the gold fields in a series of westward-flowing rivers and their tributaries, which eventually emptied into the great north-south flowing Sacramento and San Joaquin rivers. Then as now, precipitation was seasonal, concentrated in the months from November until February or March. In the springtime, the accumulated snow-packs high up in the mountains would melt and fill the mountain streams that fed the rivers. Through spring into summer, water levels in the rivers steadily declined as flows from the spring thaws subsided, and they would remain low until the November rains came. However, the seasonal ebb and flow of the rivers would occasionally be punctuated by storms that created freshets that could raise river levels quickly and sometimes violently.

Because miners were crucially dependent upon the availability of water, they had to be constantly mindful of when and where they could get it. This meant, first of all, that gold separation was easiest by far for miners located right at the naturally flowing water sources, the ones working the beds and banks of rivers and streams. Miners working at nearby bars could, and often did, lug their dirt to the nearby water. Daniel Woods describes, for example, conditions near Weber Creek in September of 1849:

> More than a hundred men are at work upon the bar. The auriferous dirt must be taken a quarter of a mile to the river to be washed. Some do this by packing the dirt in bags upon mules, and some pack this upon their own backs.[1]

Miners working farther away could still transport their dirt, which they did using every mode of transportation available, including not only mules and their own strong backs but also carts, horses, oxen, and later on, railcar. In some cases, the dirt was hauled several miles to water.[2] But there were obvious limits to this strategy, especially as the gold deposits became increasingly less rich and the new discoveries occurred either further away from water or at higher elevations. A miner, who wrote in February 1851 to the *Alta Californian* about the discovery of a very rich placer on the side of a local peak at an elevation of 300 feet above the river, must have been wondering how in the world miners were going to take advantage of that fact.[3]

Some miners apparently tried to sink wells to access groundwater for their mining operations and were reasonably successful at it. As early as summer of 1851, it was reported that miners near Shaw's Flat in Tuolumne County had sunk some twenty wells to supply their long toms. The following January, another company reportedly sank a well at Dragoon Gulch, also in Tuolumne County, and used horsepower to raise the water. Then in 1854, a French company reportedly sank a well above Carsontown in Mariposa County and was able to raise sufficient water to operate three long toms.[4] It is probably not coincidental that all three of these news accounts, the only ones I have been able to find, described developments in the southern mines, where water was relatively scarce. But the Mariposa correspondent probably spoke for many when he wondered aloud:

> Why would not the plan of sinking wells operate equally well in some of our other dry camps?[5]

The answer might well be partly economic, as one of the wells at Shaw's Flat reportedly cost one thousand dollars to drill, as it had to be sunk through solid rock. But more likely it was a question of capacity, each of these wells apparently producing enough water for long toms but perhaps not enough for more water-intensive methods. It is hard to imagine powering a hydraulic mining operation using groundwater.

The other strategies available to miners early on dealt with the seasonality of water. For miners unwilling to make the herculean effort of transporting their dirt to water, the disappearance of water by early summer often meant simply closing up shop and moving to wet diggings near the rivers and streams. By early August of 1851, for example, miners were abandoning the gulches around Sonora "on account of the scarcity of water" and "flocking in great numbers to the Tuolumne River."[6] Others, however, continued to work their claims by accumulating huge mounds of earth, in anticipation of either washing them when the waters returned, or selling them to other miners. Edward Buffum describes an early example of miners being at the mercy of the rains near Weber Creek in December of 1848:

> On descending the hill, we found the dry diggings in a pretty little valley surrounded by hills, and forming a town of about fifty log houses. Very little was doing there, however, at that time, as the gold was so intermixed with a clayey soil, that water was necessary to separate it, and the miners were patiently waiting for the rainy season to set in. Many had thrown up huge mountain-like piles of earth, and making thereby a large excavation intended, when the rain came, to catch the water in which the golden earth was to be washed.[7]

Accumulating a dirt pile in anticipation of the availability of water would be a recurring theme throughout the decade, even as late as 1859 in the southern mines. Notice that in this particular case, digging these piles of dirt served two functions, the first being the more obvious one of readying the dirt for washing. However, it also created an artificial catchment device to capture water for washing, perhaps one of the very first known methods in the gold fields of creating an artificial source of water to support gold separation.[8]

It should be apparent that the absence of water, and its gradual disappearance in what should have been prime mining seasons in the summer and fall, created real headaches for many miners. Sometimes miners got lucky with unexpectedly late or early rains, but this must have made them even more keenly aware of how important it was to procure reliable sources of water. Said one miner who wrote to the *Stockton Times* in spring of 1851:

> The effect of the late rains has been of the most favorable character. The gulches in the mountains have been well filled, and a gentleman just from Jamestown says that the miners who could not make three dollars a day by packing the dirt, are now earning from eight to twenty dollars. He says that each shower was worth a million of dollars.[9]

And so it is not surprising that miners began to take water from rivers and streams and direct it in artificial channels to where the water was needed for washing. Ditching began in early 1850 in the relatively water-rich northern mines, especially Nevada County. Perhaps the very first significant ditch in the gold fields was undertaken in Nevada County in March of 1850, to bring water to diggings at Coyote Hill (now part of Nevada City), a distance of one and a half miles.[10] This was the first of a series of at least eleven separate ditches projected in Nevada, Yuba, El Dorado, Amador, and Placer counties by spring of 1851, six of them in Nevada County alone. All of them were subsequently brought to completion.[11] By early 1851, then, small-scale ditching to dry diggings was beginning to take hold in the northern mines, tapping primarily the Yuba and American Rivers and their tributaries.

In general, ditching was slower to take off in the drier southern mines, though Tuolumne County saw the beginnings of its ditch industry as early as late 1850. Between then and the spring of 1851, several small companies organized to supply water to miners in dry diggings.[12] Ditching activity lagged in Calaveras County, where major gold deposits at Mokelumne Hill, one of the oldest and richest strikes in the southern mines, remained unmined in spring of 1852 for lack of water.[13] Ditching lagged even further behind in Mariposa County, the southernmost and hence driest, in the southern mining regions, where complaints about lack of water as an impediment to mining were heard in the newspapers well into the latter half of the decade.[14] But all of the southern mining counties suffered longer than their counterparts in the north for lack of water.

By modern standards, all of the ditches just mentioned were small affairs that generally did not convey large amounts of water and extended at most a few miles—the longest was fifteen miles, and almost half of them were shorter than four miles. However, by spring of 1851 we begin to observe the stirrings of plans for considerably larger ditching projects. The very first incorporated water company in the state, and among the first corporations, was the Bear River and Auburn Water and Mining Company, which incorporated in May of 1851 with an initial stock issue of $75,000 for the purpose of diverting water from the Bear River to diggings in Auburn.[15] It turns out that the Bear River company had grossly underestimated how much it would take to complete its project and made another supplemental stock issue for $200,000 the following January. However, by November of 1852, the *Alta Californian* announced that its forty-five mile canal was completed and that water had arrived in Auburn.[16]

The Bear River and Auburn Water and Mining Company was followed in close succession by four additional incorporations of water companies in 1851, and then an additional thirteen the following year. Two other early water companies of note are the Bradley, Berdan Company and the Tuolumne County Water Company. Bradley, Berdan was incorporated in December of 1851 for the purpose of taking water from the Cosumnes River and conveying it to diggings around Placerville, a distance of almost thirty miles. Like the Bear River company, it also grossly underestimated the resources needed to complete the project, and it followed up its initial $54,000 stock offering with three additional ones, eventually ending up with a total capital stock of $150,000. It eventually completed its project by December 1853, which consisted of a large dam on the Cosumnes, a twenty-seven mile long main canal, and additional supplemental feeder canal lines, for a grand total of almost one hundred miles of canal.[17] Bradley, Berdan was immediately successful, shares of its stock selling well above par when it was completed, and in 1856 it was combined with other ditch companies to become the Eureka Canal Company.[18]

The Tuolumne County Water Company was organized in June of 1851 for the purpose of taking water from the Stanislaus River and conveying it to various mining localities within northern Tuolumne County. It started out as a joint stock company, but subsequently incorporated in September 1852. By April 1853, the total length of its entire system was estimated at about eighty miles including collateral branch canals, servicing some 1,800 miners.[19] It would turn out to be the largest and most successful ditch company operating in Tuolumne County for the remainder of the decade and beyond, eventually servicing a number of mining localities in the vicinity of Columbia. Its size and prominence in an extremely rich section of the gold fields would involve it in many disputes over water throughout the decade. We will encounter a number of these disputes in our subsequent discussion.

To see the general temporal patterns in ditch length during the early 1850s, I have collected information on fifty-four ditches constructed from 1850 to 1856 in seven mining counties.[20] These were all new ditch projects, designed to tap a new water source to convey water to

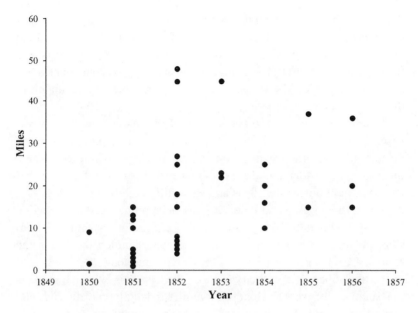

FIGURE 4.1. Ditch length by year of completion, 1850–1856.

dry diggings for mining. Figure 4.1 shows a scatterplot of ditch length (in miles) against the year that the ditch was completed, for the thirty-seven ditches for which I have both pieces of information. These data largely confirm the previous discussion: first, that the very earliest period of ditch construction from 1850 to 1851 was the era of small ditches. However, though small ditches continued to be constructed after that, there was also a noticeable jump in the average length of ditch endeavors shortly thereafter. Notice also that there was a generalized upward trend in the length of ditches, though the last few years witnessed nothing like the several massive projects of 1852 and 1853.

This pattern of data probably reflects several factors. First, recalling our earlier periodization of mining technologies, 1851 was the beginning of the Middle period, which saw the introduction and spread of long toms and sluices: new technologies based upon a continuous flow of water. This development likely generated a significant increase in the demand for water, with the ditch industry expanding to meet this demand. Second, as we have seen, there was a generalized movement of mining toward dry diggings with the steady depletion of the more accessible wet diggings. Ditches likely became longer in order to service diggings that were increasingly remote from surface sources of water. Third, as gold was discovered in a greater number of remote locations, individual ditches could be expanded and extended to service more diggings. Extending ditches to multiple diggings would enable ditch companies to realize the economies of scale associated with large upfront investments in ditch capacity.

As might be expected, one corollary of increasing ditch length was rising cost of construction. Figure 4.2 shows a scatterplot, for twenty-seven companies in Amador County, of the length of the company's ditch against the ditch's final construction cost. These are all ditches that had been built during the 1850s and were still in operation in 1861.[21] As expected, there was a definite positive association between construction cost and ditch length, along with a strong suggestion that this relationship was nonlinear. This nonlinearity perhaps signified the increasing technical challenges associated with constructing long ditches, as well as the likely increased capacity of those ditches. This evidence suggests that small ditches shorter than twenty miles in length typically had relatively modest capital requirements, but that the financial ante was upped dramatically for the new emerging longer ditch systems.

Another development that dramatically increased the financial stakes for many ditch companies was the consolidation of individual ditches into larger systems. We have already seen, for example, that the fate of the Bradley, Berdan ditch was to be combined with other ditches into a larger company, the Eureka Canal Company. Indeed, we observe a great

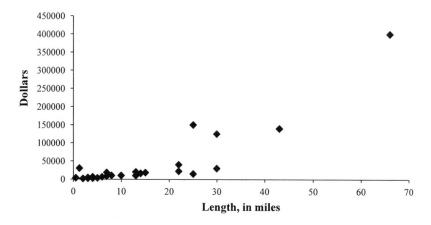

FIGURE 4.2. Construction cost as a function of ditch length, Amador County. 1850s

many instances, particularly later in the decade, of ditch companies being consolidated with other ditches or being absorbed into larger ditch companies, some of which were mind-bogglingly massive. By 1856, the Eureka Canal Company was the largest in the state, consisting of dams, reservoirs, and 247 miles of ditches, which altogether had cost $700,000 to build.[22] Consolidating ditches served the important economic function of rationalizing existing ditch systems, avoiding duplication of ditch lines, and enabling mining communities to be supplied with water more efficiently. It was also sometimes used to resolve disputes over water rights, competing companies often choosing to join forces rather than fight each other over water.

The introduction of water by ditch companies into previously dry areas commonly permitted dramatically increased gold production. Most obviously, it permitted the working of diggings that could not be worked at all before. The introduction of water into the southern mines surely opened up vast areas for mining that had previously remained largely untouched. But even in areas with some natural water supplies, the coming of artificial ditches allowed many miners to work well into the late summer and fall, whereas when they were at the mercy of the elements, they might have to call it quits weeks, or even months, earlier. Commenting on a newspaper account in Calaveras County in August of 1853, for example, the *Alta Californian* observed:

> The lateness of the season and lowness of some of the mountain streams do not appear to affect the general prosperity that has been exhibited in the Southern mines this summer. In former times the month of August was characterized by a depression in business among the miners, in consequence of the decline in the facilities of water; this year finds them with hands full of work, and holes full of water, from the flumes, canals and reservoirs that have been constructed in the various mining regions.[23]

By eliminating or reducing the seasonal availability of water and thus encouraging miners to stay put throughout the year, the development of local water supplies also imparted a measure of added permanence to local economies. As early as December of 1852, the *San Joaquin Republican* proclaimed that local development of water had not only resulted in a "great revolution" in mining, it had also given "a permanent character" to the local population.[24] Such permanence encouraged the found-

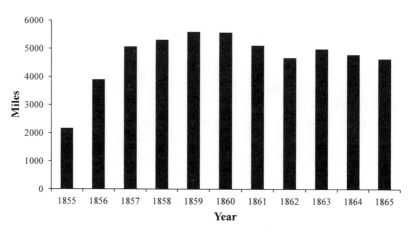

FIGURE 4.3. Total ditch miles, state of California. 1855–1865

ing of stores, churches, boarding houses, and restaurants, and sometimes even the sustained development of the local economy over time.

To convey a quantitative sense of the extent of ditching activity over time, Figure 4.3 reports total ditch mileage in the state beginning in 1855, the first year in which comparable statewide data are available.[25] This figure shows that by 1855, over two thousand miles of ditches had already been constructed throughout the state. Total mileage grew rapidly over the next two years, exceeding five thousand miles by 1857, and then leveled off and began to decline after 1859. Clearly, the period from the early 1850s up through 1857 was the golden era of ditch construction in early California.[26]

The aggregate data in Figure 4.3 do not reflect the fact that the vast majority of ditch construction occurred in the mining regions in order to support water-intensive placer mining. Almost all of the ditch construction up through 1855 occurred in a few select counties, with four mining counties—Amador, El Dorado, Nevada, and Trinity—accounting for nearly 94 percent of all ditch mileage in 1855. By 1857, however, significant ditch construction activity had spread to many more counties, with fourteen counties—mining counties all—containing at least one hundred ditch miles.[27] By this time, these fourteen counties accounted for over 97 percent of all ditch miles in the state. However, it is also clear that the southern counties lagged behind: located at the southernmost end of the Mother Lode, relatively water-scarce Mariposa County had only sixty-three miles of ditches by 1857.

4.3. The Technology of Ditching

The first miners to divert water from surface sources to dry diggings probably drew from the experiences of miners who mined the beds of rivers. We have seen that early river mining involved damming a river and diverting the water into a canal or flume, rudimentary versions of which were being undertaken in the gold regions as early as late 1848. We have also seen that early river mining projects tended to involve short earthen ditches and relatively crude dams made of timber, brush, boulders, canvas, and clay. However, by no later than 1849 teams of miners were beginning to drill and blast through solid rock or building wooden flumes to carry water around river mining operations, sometimes using auxiliary pumps to keep stream beds dry. Both the basic technology for river diversion and the practice of team production were well known to the miners by the time the first known diversion ditch was built in Nevada County in the spring of 1850.

The major new challenge facing miners, of course, was the need to divert water away from the rivers and streams to the dry diggings. As long as the water had to be diverted only a short distance, this did not present major problems. However, diverting and transporting water long distances presented major challenges for miners because ditch systems had to be gravity-fed. River miners who wanted to expose a stretch of river bed could build flumes parallel to the river and take advantage of gravity to carry the water away and back into the river at some point downstream. Miners who wanted to build diversion ditches to convey water any significant distance to dry diggings, on the other hand, had to consider the altitude of the target diggings and choose a diversion point from a suitable water source that was above the diggings and a path from that diversion point to the diggings that was entirely downhill. One reason that ditch systems became larger and longer over time was that a suitable diversion point might be many miles away from a diggings. Speaking in 1851, one miner described the problem in getting water to a hill diggings at Mokelumne Hill in Tuolumne County:

> The want of water was the great obstacle in the way of mining at Moquelumne Hill. As it stood so much higher than the surrounding country, there were no streams which could be introduced, and the only means of getting a constant supply was to bring the water from the Moquelumne River, which

flowed past, three or four thousand feet below the diggings. In order to get the requisite elevation to raise the waters so far above their natural channel, it was found necessary to commence the canal some fifty or sixty miles up the river.[28]

Once a diversion point had been selected, a dam would be constructed at that point, creating a reservoir from which diversion ditches or flumes would transport water. For this purpose, it was necessary for dams to be constructed to be sturdier and more durable than had sufficed for early river mining operations. Reports of plans for "permanent" dam structures in some of the major rivers began to be reported in the *Alta Californian* as early as August 1851. In 1853, the Tuolumne Hydraulic Association constructed a dam eighty-five feet wide and twenty-five feet high, at an altitude of 5,000 feet, to conduct water to Sullivan's Creek and thence to a number of mining localities in Tuolumne County. By spring of 1855, a dam had been completed above Mississippi Bar in Placer County creating a reservoir covering over forty acres.[29] By 1857, a much sturdier and more massive dam had been constructed at French Corral on the Yuba River. According to the *Alta Californian*:

> [This dam created] an immense reservoir, covering 200 acres, with an average depth of 22 feet. This is formed by a circular range of hills, which enclose it naturally, to within a few hundred yards, across which has been built an embankment, 55 feet high, 350 through at the base, and containing 88,000 cubic feet of earth. This forms a deep and permanent lake, . . . and supplies 26 companies with water.[30]

To transport water from the reservoir to a diggings, a route would be carefully surveyed to follow the contours of the land while achieving a continuous gentle downward pitch over the entire route.[31] Miners and ditch companies exhibited much ingenuity in surveying their ditch routes, using everything from simple levels with plumb lines to professional surveying equipment called *theodolites*. One miner describes a simple, albeit laborious, process he used to survey the route for a canal to Chambers Bar in Tuolumne County in 1855:

> I devised a simple instrument to mark the line of survey. This was nothing more than a straight-edge strip six feet long, to which was attached at right

angles another strip five feet long. A plumb bob in the center of the straight-edge fell along the upright leg, which had a hole for the bob to rest when the leg stood perpendicular, and when it did so, the straight-edge was of course perfectly level. A pole five feet one inch long was prepared and sights were taken every two rods. When this pole stood on the ground so that a sight along the level straight-edge struck its top, its bottom was just one inch lower than the bottom of the leg of the straight-edge; a stake was driven to mark the spot, and the level was moved up to the stake for another sight. This gave the ditch a fall of half an inch to the rod.[32]

Similarly, John Wallace, a trained engineer working for the Tuolumne County Water Company, describes how he went about surveying the route for a portion of the Company's ditch system in 1851:

We all commensed [sic] in high spirits the following Monday, which was the first of July, commencing at a pass in the mountains, which we named "Summit Pass", & working from thence toward the river. Our first object was to grade a road on the side of the mountain, 6 feet wide, following all the inequalities of the rugged mountain side, but keeping a perfectly level road as regards the height. I say a perfectly level road but that is not strictly true. As we progressed we kept the road on a gradual rise of about 10 feet to the mile, so as to allow the water to flow when we have completed the work. The setting out of the road or grade was of course my work, so I had to keep ahead, and put down pegs at every road for the men to work to. I had 3 or 4 men constantly with me cutting pegs & driving them in, measuring the distances, & holding the staff, etc., while I carried the Theodolite & levelled [sic] & directed the driving of the pegs, etc. It thus took us about two months before we graded the road to the river, a distance of fifteen miles from the place we started from.[33]

With the need to follow the contours of the terrain, the actual construction of a ditch segment could be extremely laborious and time-consuming. Given that it took two months to grade fifteen miles, grading of the ditch route described above by Wallace would have advanced at what must have felt like a snail-like pace of a quarter of a mile per day. But grading was only the first step in constructing a ditch system. If the surveyed route happened to be upon solid rock, digging earthen ditches was literally impossible and companies would be forced to erect wooden flumes or to drill or blast a channel through the rock.[34] In some cases,

FIGURE 4.4. Cliff flume over the Yuba River, Nevada County
Courtesy of Searls Historical Library, Nevada City.

following the contours of the land led ditch companies across sheer cliffs
or rock faces to which they would attach supports on which to build the
flume, dozens or even hundreds of feet in the air.[35]

Another early development during this period was the construction
of flumes built on wooden trestles or bridges. The purpose of these elevated flumes was to allow companies to traverse a valley or depression,
or to avoid having to follow land contours, in order to maintain the water
on its downward trajectory.[36] When the local topography was more rugged or uneven, the trestles supporting these flumes could be built quite
high, and had to be secured with a broad reinforced base for stability. As
trestles got higher over time, they would sometimes have to be supported
with suspension cables to keep them from toppling over. Consider, for
example, the following description of a suspension flume built in 1857
that spanned Murphy's Creek in Calaveras County:

> The flume is built on the Penstock or water-tight-box principle, and is held up
> with two wire suspension cables, one and a half inch in diameter, and 1000
> feet long, with two guy cables to support the towers, over which the cables

FIGURE 4.5. Elevated flumes, Georgetown Water Company
Courtesy of the California History Room, California State Library, Sacramento.

FIGURE 4.6. Elevated flume near Smartsville
Courtesy of the California History Room, California State Library, Sacramento.

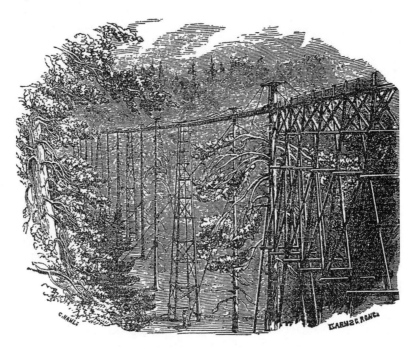

FIGURE 4.7. Suspension bridge across Brandy Gulch
Source: The Miners' Own Book. Courtesy of the Book Club of California.

are sprung. The northern tower is 94 feet high, the southern 124 feet; the cables are firmly anchored at the ends, in the bedrock, sufficiently secure to
hold twice as much necessary force. From the flume down (perpendicularly)
to the bed of the creek, it is 250 feet; the entire length of the flume 1,500 feet;
the box will carry 50 inches of water, forced by a fifteen foot heading; sag of
wire, 45 feet.[37]

The following description of the ditch system of the Tuolumne County
Water Company in August of 1852 is worth reproducing in its entirety, as
it provides an excellent sense for how far along the technology of ditch
system construction was early in the decade:

[The Tuolumne Canal] must have originated with men of gigantic energy and
enterprise, for few persons would have ever made the attempt to construct a
flume for miles on the side of a precipitous rock, where a single misstep would
send them a thousand feet into the ravine below. This portion is entirely com-

pleted, and the water running through to the ditch, three miles from the dam where the work commences. Here there are four lengths of two rods each, the trusses laid and planked, wanting the siding only to complete it, which we met on the way up the hill. On Saturday the water can be turned on a mile farther, where a quarter of a mile of siding and caulking remains to be done, which, with the assistance of the men above, who would finish their work on Saturday, can be fully completed by Wednesday, and the water let on the whole route. Five miles from the dam is a bridge, 30 feet high and 800 feet long, that conveys the water across a ravine; and a few rods farther on, a tunnel, 300 feet long, 4 by 6 feet, arched and well supported, conveys the water to a deep ditch, winding and turning on the side hills, to a distance of fifteen miles from the dam. Here a natural ravine, crossed at right angles at the bottom by Five Mile Creek, takes the water, and by a flume ten miles long, the creek is tapped and the water carried direct to Columbia. From here a ditch has been constructed, ten miles in length, that takes the waste water to the various diggings below.[38]

4.4. The Organization and Operation of Ditch Companies

The construction of a ditch system was not, of course, merely a technological feat but rather, an investment in a business concern that required financing and ongoing operations management. As we have seen, the earliest ditches were small affairs. When working on a modest scale, financing could be accomplished by a team of miners, each willing to donate his labor and modest resources. One miner, for example, attests to the ease with which miners could become involved in a fledgling ditch company during the early 1850s:

> This affords another instance of the successful employment of capital originally procured by gold digging; and if you wanted a few shares in one of those young companies, you could procure them without money, for by taking your coat off and helping to cut the ditch, you could in six months work yourself into a very respectable stockholder.[39]

If miners happened to have sufficient cash in addition to labor, they could form a joint stock company, each member buying a share and thus contributing to the resources of the company for buying materials and supplies. Early ditch companies would also go into debt for materials and labor and in some cases, they were even known to borrow money from miners who were in a position to front significant amounts of cash.[40]

However, as ditches became longer and ditch systems became more elaborate, they came to require a great deal of capital and were beyond the limited means of many miners. Furthermore, high interest rates, which could easily be three percent per *month*, discouraged many miners from borrowing money from lending institutions. These realities were undoubtedly a key reason that beginning in 1851, miners and entrepreneurs began to take advantage of the state's new incorporation laws to raise capital for ditch construction. The very first incorporation law for the state, enacted in April of 1850, permitted companies to incorporate simply by filing a written statement with the clerk of the county in which they intended to operate, thus greatly facilitating the raising of money by ditch companies through the selling of corporate stock.[41] Investors would invest in stock in ditch companies in anticipation of returns on their investments both from capital gains and the disbursement of dividends on revenues in excess of operating costs.[42] And while early companies tended to sell their stock locally, it was not at all long before ditch companies had access to a broader in-state pool of investors in Sacramento and San Francisco.[43] As a consequence, dozens of ditch companies took advantage of the state's incorporation laws to raise money for water production during the 1850s, as we have seen.

Initial financing was, of course, only the first step toward making a ditch company a successful ongoing business concern. Companies had to purchase materials and supplies, secure rights to water from the target source, survey ditch routes, and hire contractors (sometimes including construction laborers), all toward construction of the ditch system itself. Then once a system had been constructed, companies had to hire engineers, supervisors, ditch tenders, and bookkeepers in order to maintain the system and to manage ongoing operations. Along the way, countless actions had to be taken including contracting for additional materials, securing rights of way, negotiating the terms of agreements with miners receiving water including how much to charge, and addressing and resolving disputes that might arise over water rights and damages resulting from breaking ditches and dam failures.

To accomplish all of these myriad tasks, ditch companies began to set in place formalized operating procedures for addressing the countless concerns they were likely to face. In this, many were guided by the 1850 incorporation law, which required incorporated companies to have elected boards of trustees who were empowered to create operational bylaws, and who in general had fiduciary responsibility, for the company. Incorporated companies were required to have officers and to make their finances a matter of public record, and they were given procedural guidelines for, among other things, issuing new capital stock and changing their line of business. This law also made company trustees personally liable for any debt in excess of the company's capital stock while exempting stockholders from liability. State legislators, however, apparently decided this law provided insufficient safeguards to lenders, as they subsequently enacted another incorporation law in 1853 that established stricter guidelines regarding debt, including outright prohibitions on assuming any debt in excess of outstanding capital stock, and making stockholders personally liable for their proportion of any debts assumed by the company while they were stockholders.[44]

An examination of the minutes of meetings of the boards of trustees and stockholders of three ditch companies—the Tuolumne County Water Company, the Columbia and Stanislaus River Water Company, and the Tuolumne Redemption Company—that operated in Tuolumne County in the 1850s indicates they had all adopted highly formalized procedures for running all aspects of their respective businesses, in the spirit of the incorporation laws. These included the use of parliamentary procedure and committees for dealing with a whole host of issues relating to operating a ditch business, including resolving disputes over water rights, developing new sources of supply, contracting with miners for water supplies, setting pricing policies, and writing contingency language to guard against breach of contract resulting from damage to company ditches or flumes.[45] A few entries from the minutes of meetings of the board of trustees of the Columbia and Stanislaus River Water Company during an 1856 dispute with its rival the Tuolumne County Water Company provide a sense of the formality of the procedures they were following at the time:

April 25, 1856 (8 pm): Bill presented from T. C. Water Co for breakage of their Five Mile Flume—amts to $200.00—on motion Secretary was instructed to communicate with that Co. asking for explanation of the bill & disclaiming all knowledge of injuring their flume.

May 2, 1856 (9 pm): Communication with T. C. Water Co., in answer to our last requesting explanation of their bill, giving explanation, & enclosing amended bill, read, &, on motion, received, & Secretary instructed to reply, to the effect, that the Trustees of our Company consider the charge unjust— that we are credibly informed that their ditch would inevitably have broken in that place without the pressure of our schute [*sic*] and that we consider that they should have assisted in the repair, without thinking of making a charge for damage; but that if they insist upon the bill, we are willing to refer the matter to an arbitration of disinterested persons, to go onto the ground and decide between the two Companies.

May 6, 1856 (9 pm): On motion, Secretary instructed to communicate with the T. C. W. Co. regarding the breaking of their ditch and inform them that this Board is willing to settle the matter by arbitration.

May 12, 1856 (9 pm): Communication from T. C. Water Co. respecting breakages of ditch, & refusing to submit the matters to an arbitration, read, & on motion Secretary instructed to return communication & reply to same.

The bottom-line objective of ditch companies was, of course, to make money for owners and stockholders, and they accomplished this in two ways: either using the water themselves to prosecute mining, or vending water to miners for their own use. The experience of ditch companies varied widely, with a great many failing as a result of insecure water supplies, poor business practices, or insurmountable technical challenges. But many of the ones that did survive did well financially, by developing a secure water supply, constructing a durable ditch system, contracting with miners for water delivery, and collecting revenues to pay off debt, cover operating expenses, and provide a return to owners or stockholders.

The pricing policies of ditch companies deserve a closer look for what they reveal about the value of water during this period and about the challenges involved in vending water. When a ditch company extended service to a mining locality, actual sales or rentals were made challenging by the fact that at the time, measurement technologies were extremely crude—way too crude to even come close to accurately measuring a unit of water such as an acre-foot, or a cubic foot per second. One common way to measure water was to conduct it from a ditch or flume into a large wooden measuring box into which had been cut square or rectangular apertures, through which water would be delivered by flumes or later, pipes, to mining companies.[46] The quantity of water that actually flowed through an aperture depended both upon the size of the aperture and the pressure with which the water was forced through it. A so-called *miner's inch* was the amount that flowed through a square-inch aperture placed so many inches below the surface of the water (which produced a "head" of pressure) during a certain period. Apertures submerged farther below the surface had larger heads that generated greater pressure. The head varied in practice from four to twelve inches and the length of time also varied, with 10-hour and 24-hour inches being common, for example, in the area served by the Yuba and Bear Rivers in Nevada County.[47] Another complicating factor was the fact that ditch systems constructed in the mining regions varied widely with regard to the grades at which the ditches were pitched, with declines in elevation ("falls") per horizontal mile of ditch varying anywhere from six to 25 feet. Steeper grades meant that a greater volume of water would flow through a ditch in a given period. All of this meant that the actual amount of water delivered to a mining company and called a miners' inch could vary dramatically. Even years later, an engineering study conducted at North Bloomfield in Nevada County in 1891 found that a 24-hour miners' inch averaged about 2,230 cubic feet but varied anywhere from 2,000 to 2,600 cubic feet.[48] As large as this variation was, it was probably dwarfed by the variation in a miners' inch measured forty years earlier with immensely cruder measurement technologies.

So when miners purchased water from a ditch company, exactly how much water were they purchasing? The answer seems to be that ditch companies used crude proxies for quantity that sufficed because the value of accurate measurement was not terribly high. Miners who wanted water to feed through their sluices or hydraulicking equipment did not require specific amounts of water, only flow sufficient to accomplish their purpose of separating out the gold from the surrounding debris. Thus, when they purchased water they tended to pay for periods of service rather than contracting for specific amounts. Consider, for example, the following early rudimentary contract for water supply from Placer County:

We the undersigned miners on the Auburn Ravine having claims located on said ravine which claims we are unable to work owing to the want of water, we therefore petition the Bear River and Auburn Water and Mining Company to introduce and suffer to pass down said Ravine a sufficient amount of water to supply the demand or so much as the company may have space and *for the use of which we agree to pay the collector for said company each week the sums set opposite our respective names*; we recognize the right of the Bear River and Auburn Water and Mining Company to the use of Ravine for conveying their water and parties using the water of said company are justly bound to pay for the same at all times when there should not be sufficient natural water in said ravine for mining purposes.

Auburn September 22, 1853[49] (emphasis added)

Thus, in this contract, the miners are agreeing to pay a certain amount of money per week, with no guarantee of receiving any specific amount of water. All they are asking for is "sufficient" water to meet their mining needs. The vagueness of this contract makes sense given both the measurement difficulties and the fact that as long as miners were able to prosecute mining, it really did not much matter precisely how much water they received. We will see later that the issue of measurement would also plague the courts, which during this period would decide rights entitlements largely on the basis of diversion capacity—for example, the physical dimensions of wooden flumes, taking into account grade steepness—which was considerably less informationally demanding than actually monitoring flow. All of this appeared to support water sales and judicial rights allocation reasonably well under the circumstances.

Regarding the pricing of water, in principle ditch companies and miners negotiated a price at which water would be vended, and this price reflected both the value of water in mining production and the marginal cost of developing the water. At the same time, larger and more extensive ditch systems likely resulted in greater upfront capital costs along with lower marginal costs of supplying water. All of this implies that, during most of this period, both the demand and supply of water were increasing. Figure 4.8 shows what was happening to the price of water in the later 1850s, during which price observations periodically appeared in the *Alta Californian*. The "Price" graphed on the vertical axis is in dollars per miner's inch, and is graphed against "Date" which is the date on which the price quote appeared in the *Alta Californian*. The overall pattern appears to be trending downward, suggesting two possibilities: that demand increases were falling short of increases in supply, and/or that

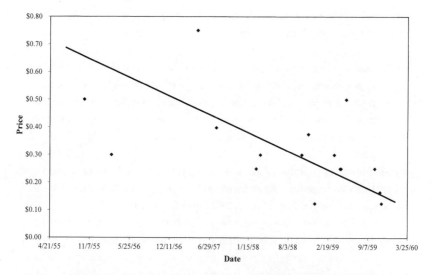

FIGURE 4.8. Water prices charged to miners by ditch companies, 1855–1859

increased competition among ditch companies was forcing ditch companies to lower their prices.[50]

In order to understand the overall pricing experience, it should be recognized that throughout this entire period, miners and ditch companies were locked in a vigorous struggle for distribution of the quasi-rents associated with ditch systems once constructed. On the one hand, miners recognized that sufficient water supplies were absolutely necessary for working their claims, and they persistently encouraged ditch companies to come in and develop their local supplies. These entreaties became more urgent over time, particularly after 1855 when hydraulic mining was making major inroads as a mining technology, and particularly in certain counties such as Mariposa where water supplies were scarcer. On the other hand, once water was developed in a locality, it was quite common for miners to chafe under the terms of water supply, which they often perceived as being unilaterally dictated to them by the ditch companies.

Probably the most common issue in the struggle between miners and ditch companies concerned the prices charged by the ditch companies. Complaints by miners that ditch companies charged too much for water began to be observed not long after the completion of the first ditch projects. As early as February 1853, miners near Columbia and Springfield in Tuolumne County were publicly complaining about water rates charged by the Tuolumne County Water Company:

> The amount of ground about Columbia and Springfield that will pay moderate wages is immense, but is not rich enough to justify working with the present rates for water. The Tuolumne County Water Company are so illiberal as to refuse water on anything like reasonable terms. The consequences are that the miners are almost all provoked and indignant.[51]

By 1856, such complaints were becoming much more frequent, and were thereafter observed in a number of other mining counties, including Nevada, Calaveras, Amador, Shasta, El Dorado, and Butte.[52]

It was not merely that prices were high that concerned the miners. Many believed that the ditch companies often took advantage of their local position to charge monopoly prices. In 1853, for example, miners in Tuolumne County were heard complaining that the prices charged by the Tuolumne County Water Company were higher in Columbia than at Shaw's Flat, where the Company happened to face competition from another ditch company. They further accused the Company of engaging in hardball tactics by cutting off service to miners who complained about high prices.[53] Their suspicions about the Company were probably correct. In a letter dated January 10, 1853, John Wallace, chief engineer and then president of the Company, provides a revealing look at the company strategy toward the miners that essentially corroborated the miners' charges:

> When we first introduced our water, and when we had only a small supply, we placed the price rather high, but still we had plenty of applications for it, but some of the miners thought the price was too high and there was a great deal of talk about it. A public meeting was called to discuss the matter, speeches were made and threats if we did not come to their terms and reduce the price. A deputation was appointed to call on the company. I being at the time President, had to receive them, after they had fully stated their case, I simply told them that as far as threats went, it was entirely the wrong way to go about it, as it would only make the company more determined, might cause bad feelings, that if any gentlemen could not afford to pay the price he was not compelled to use it, that there were plenty others who would, and that it was a new feature in mercantile transactions for the buyer to set the price. I finally told them that the company would reduce the price as soon as they had a suf-

ficiently copious supply to warrant them in so doing. They afterwards had
another meeting to hear the report of this committee, some speeches were
made but they were much calmer and without threats. A few of the more ra-
bid ones were marked, and for some time we refused to sell them water at any
price, that took the shine out of them and deterred other [sic] from acting in
a similar manner.[54]

Miners did not stop at merely voicing their grievances over the pricing practices of ditch companies. In November of 1853, it was reported
that miners in Tuolumne County were carting their dirt over a mile to
springs at Springfield "rather than paying an exorbitant price to the water companies for muddy water."[55] There were, however, obvious limits
to such a strategy of avoidance. Other miners, with limited success, pe-
titioned ditch companies in an attempt to induce them to reduce their
rates.[56] The larger response, beginning in 1855, was for miners in a locality to organize and go on strike to try to obtain lower rates. One of the
first instances of a miners' strike occurred in March of 1855, when miners around Columbia in Tuolumne County went on strike and refused to
take water from the Tuolumne County Water Company until it had reduced its rates. This was followed in November of that year by a miners'
strike at Red Dog in Nevada County, where the miners were demanding
a rate reduction of eight cents per inch. These miners were later joined in
their strike by miners from the nearby mining camps Waloupa, Brown's
Hill, and Pine Hill. In March 1856, nearly one thousand miners at Mokelumne Hill in Calaveras County were on strike demanding a rate reduction by the Mokelumne Hill Canal. Later that month, the *Nevada
Journal* reported that such strikes had taken place "in various parts of
[Nevada] county." A few days later, miners in Calaveras County were reportedly out on strike over water rates.[57]

The success of miners in achieving price reductions through strikes
depended upon their ability to overcome the transaction costs of orga-
nizing. One particularly unsuccessful strike in Amador County in late
1857 collapsed within a month when miners apparently began defecting
en masse.[58] However, miners also took steps to try to reduce the likelihood of defection. In their battle with the Tuolumne County Water
Company in 1853, for example, the miners around Columbia ordered
that all miners who adhered to the strike would have their claims protected against claim jumpers and appointed a Recorder to keep written
records of all claims where work had been suspended in support of the

strike.[59] Another strategy that helped miners to maintain a united front, when it was available, was to negotiate with a competing ditch company to extend service to their locality, or to organize into a ditch company of their own.[60] In some cases, the result was to avoid having to pay the offending ditch company at all, or to allow miners to exert pressure on the company for lower prices. At times, this was a successful strategy, as ditch companies would respond to competition by reducing their water rates, as the Tuolumne County Water Company did in early 1857 when faced with competition from another ditch company:

> On motion Resolved, That the price of a 9 inch tom stream of water be re-duced to $3 per day and larger streams to proportion in places *where the new ditch comes in contact with ours*, the time of said reduction to take effect at the discretion of the water agent.[61] (emphasis added)

4.5. Legal Disputes over Ditching Operations

The challenges of implementing pricing policies notwithstanding, it is probably fair to say that the main challenge confronting ditch compa-nies during this period was the resolution of disputes that they became involved in over water development and production. Probably the most common dispute occurred when the diversion of water from a river or stream by a ditch company threatened to deprive a downstream claim-ant of water. Since the construction of a dam and ditch system could take months, sometimes these disputes could be preempted by notification by the downstream party of a potential conflict if the company went ahead with its plans.[62] In some cases, companies who considered themselves to have a superior claim to a water supply would issue peremptory notices to other companies not to proceed with their plans to develop it.[63] In other cases, ditch companies would consolidate their systems in order to avoid duking it out over competing claims.[64] In a good many instances, miners working at or near a stream would organize among themselves and resolve to resist ditch companies with designs on the water in the stream.[65] However, none of these strategies would be sufficient to pre-clude a large number of suits being brought before the state courts to re-solve disputes over competing diversions of water, a topic we will return to in chapter 7.

An important variation on the theme of diversions depriving downstream claimants of water involved diversions that degraded the quality of water reaching those downstream claimants. This issue began to arise after the adoption by miners of water-intensive separation technologies, beginning with long toms and sluices, which involved a continuous flow of water that carried off sludge and debris in tail waters that were vented back into local waterways. When a ditch company diverted water from a stream and the water was used in this way, the result was inevitably reduced water quality downstream, rendering the water of considerably diminished value for downstream companies. Given the evidence presented earlier that continuous-flow separation technologies began to be adopted no later than 1851, it is not surprising that we observe the appearance of this type of dispute quite early on as well. An early instance of the problem is illustrated in the diary of one miner in summer of 1851:

> I have not mined any for a number of weeks, but have a claim in view to work shortly, providing arrangements can be made to keep the muddy water and dirt that washes down from the hills where others are mining, from washing in upon it, which settles and fills up so that the claim is not workable until it can be turned off.[66]

In 1852, a miner wrote to the *Alta Californian* from Sonora in Tuolumne County describing a lawsuit brought by miners against a ditch company, which allegedly both deprived them of water and rendered it muddy and filled with debris:

> The next difficulty to be encountered was in the shape of a lawsuit instituted by certain persons mining lower down the creek, just below the mouth of the company's race. They sued for damages on the following grounds: First, that the company had directed the water of Sullivan's Creek from its original channel; secondly, that the water was wasted by running through a new race, and as a consequence the plaintiffs had not sufficient for their mining operations; thirdly, that the water was returned to them not only diminished in quantity, but turgid [*sic* turbid] and muddy.[67]

By mid-decade, complaints over degradation of water quality by upstream companies were being regularly heard in Nevada and Placer Counties.[68] Degraded water quality would become an omnipresent fact of life in the gold regions throughout the 1850s, embroiling water claimants in protracted court cases as well as affecting the pricing policies of ditch companies, who would attempt to sell the water at reduced prices that reflected its diminished value in gold production. The influence of disputes over water quality on the development of the common law of water rights will be the subject of chapter 8.

A quite different genre of disputes involved damages inflicted on nearby or downstream companies from leaky or breaking ditches and collapsing dams. Leaky ditches would present difficulties, for example, for coyoteing or tunneling miners working nearby whose excavations would become filled with water.[69] Collapsing ditches and dams would abruptly release water that would inundate nearby or downstream mining operations, inflicting damages by burying claims, destroying tools and supplies, and in some cases, even resulting in loss of lives.[70] As dams became stronger and more durable over time, damages to downstream operations from dam failures appear to have occurred with lower frequency but when they did occur, the consequences were often considerably more devastating. Dam failures, the strategies of companies to deal with them and their aftermath, and the development of common-law rules to deal with them are all the subject of chapter 9.

4.6. Conclusions

Given the importance of water in the placer mining process, it was perhaps inevitable that an extensive ditch industry, consisting of hundreds of ditch companies, would develop to service the miners' demands for water. What is striking is how quickly the industry emerged and spread throughout the mining regions, as companies tapped every significant source of water available that could be economically brought to paying claims. Ditch companies showed remarkable ingenuity and resourcefulness in projecting and engineering ditch systems that transported large amounts of water dozens, or even hundreds, of miles over rugged and sometimes treacherous terrain. Though there were undoubtedly many companies that were ill-conceived or poorly managed, some companies thrived by following thoughtful and prudent business practices. But even the more successful ones experienced numerous difficulties in the form of challenges to their legal rights to water, and disputes over damages inflicted on other parties through water diversions, venting of tail waters, leaky ditches, and collapsed dams.

In these disputes, much was at stake. As we have seen, ditch systems very quickly came to require enormous upfront investments in dams, ditches, and flumes. In the operation of these ditch systems, the returns from these investments were under constant attack from threats of various kinds, not the least of which were legal challenges to the water supplies of the ditch companies. The development of water law during this period, to be discussed at length in chapters 7 through 9, largely reflects rulings made by the courts, which were attempting to lay down a coherent set of principles for resolving disputes over water rights. However, water law would ultimately be shaped as well by the actions of miners who self-organized in the gold fields into mining camps and created their own sets of rules for governing mining and water use. The way these rules were generated is of interest both for the influence they exerted on official court rulings and for what they reveal more generally about the economic currents shaping the creation of rules governing water rights. Let us now turn to a closer examination of the rule-making process within the mining camps.

CHAPTER FIVE

The Informal Law of the Mining Camps

The mining population have been allowed to constitute their own laws relative to the appointment of "claims," and it is astonishing how well this system works. Had the Legislature, in ignorance of the miners' wants, interfered and decided that a man should have so much, and no more, of the soil to work on, all would have been anarchy and confusion.
—Marryat, p. 124

5.1. Introduction

The first miners who scoured the gold fields in 1848 in the immediate aftermath of the initial discovery had little in common except their quest for golden riches. They probably thought little of rights or government or institutions of any kind. Their concerns were simple: get the gold before someone else did. And indeed, with only some five thousand of them combing a vast area, there was little need to worry about disputes, let alone mechanisms for resolving them, for deciding who got what. In a very real sense, there was plenty for all. However, this could not last, not with the biggest gold chunks getting scooped up quickly, not with the forty-niners on their way from every corner of the globe. At some point, the miners were going to have to confront the awful truth: there was going to be scarcity, there were going to be disputes. And if they did not want things to deteriorate into a free-for-all, there would have to be rules. And with no government around, not really, they were going to have to make the rules themselves.

They did not, of course, sit down in some mega-assembly hall and work out the rules in an orderly, parliamentary fashion. This would have been impossible anyway, as they were scattered all up and down the southern and northern mines, and getting more scattered by the day. No, the process was a truly organic one, with every locality working things out for itself, not really caring what the next locality down the road was doing. And there was no time table for figuring out what needed to be done: things happened when they needed to happen. What they ended up working out was deliciously varied and scatter-shot, with every set of local rules different from the others. How much land should we let people mine? How do we go about settling disputes? More generally, how do we maintain order? All of these questions were answered through a political process, as local politics was a huge determining factor. Yet, as we shall see, there would be an economic logic to the rules they came up with, because there were certain economic realities that simply could not be ignored.

5.2. The Creation of the Mining Camp System

What we do seem to know, and we shall return to this issue shortly, is that the formation of semi-organized gold camps complete with rules for working claims probably began sometime in 1849, after enough forty-niners had arrived to make localized scarcity a reality. It is important to keep in mind the institutional setting in which the formation of the camps occurred. Under the Treaty of Guadalupe Hidalgo that ended the Mexican War in February of 1848, Mexico ceded a large expanse of territory of over one-half million square miles to the United States including all of the present-day state of California.[1] The vast majority of this land was then designated part of the public domain, including virtually all of the gold fields into which the miners swarmed. Legally then, the gold seekers were trespassers on public lands belonging to the federal government who went about busily expropriating gold that technically speaking was not theirs to take. The federal government, however, did nothing to uphold its claims to the gold resources nor did it establish any regulations to manage the development of the gold fields.[2] Consequently, the growth of mining camps in the early 1850s occurred in the almost complete absence of effective institutional governance by the federal government.

It may seem strange that the federal government would not enforce its rights to gold resources that would turn out to be of immense value.

Certainly the local representatives of the federal government were aware that the gold fields were on federal lands and they believed very early on that the gold deposits were extremely rich. When Governor Mason toured the gold fields in the summer of 1848, he quickly became convinced that gold was present in massive quantities. In reporting on his trip later, he remarked on "houses vacant and farms going to waste" en route, and "hill sides . . . thickly strewn with canvass tents and bush arbors" at Mormon Diggings, his first destination.[3] Upon reaching Weber Creek, he discovered:

> "The country on either side of [the] creek is much broken up by hills, and is intersected in every direction by small streams or ravines, which contain more or less gold. Those that have been worked are barely scratched; and although thousands of ounces have been carried away, I do not consider that a serious impression has been made upon the whole. Every day was developing new and richer deposits; and the only impressions seemed to be, that the metal would be found in such abundance as seriously to depreciate its value."[4]

Despite the apparently enormous amount of gold to be found, however, the lack of enforcement makes sense when one considers the enormous challenges any attempt to enforce federal rights would have entailed. The gold fields spanned a large geographic extent and the resources available to the government in the area to maintain order were quite limited. Even in 1848, when the nonnative population of California numbered only in the few thousands, there was little that could be done by the government to effectively exclude gold seekers from the goldfields. As early as May of that year, for example, the *Alta Californian* could be heard editorializing that the government was helpless to stop the digging:

> As to Gov. Mason's interference we do not anticipate any trouble in that respect, and even if the U.S. authorities were to endeavor to put a stop to individual digging, it would take quite a large army to effactually occupy "thirty miles square."[5]

Mason himself was not sanguine about his ability to uphold federal rights in the gold fields:

> The entire gold district, with very few exceptions of grants made some years ago by the Mexican authorities, is on land belonging to the United States. It

was a matter of serious reflection with me, how I could secure to the Government certain rents or fees for the privilege of procuring this gold; but upon considering the large extent of country, the character of the people engaged, and the small scattered force at my command, I resolved not to interfere but to permit all to work freely.[6]

Indeed, many of the very soldiers that Mason relied on locally to maintain order were themselves deserting their posts to look for gold. Writing from the gold fields in late 1848, William Tecumseh Sherman, then a young officer and adjutant to Mason, plaintively described the difficulties of preventing desertion among his own troops:

> I see that nearly all the recruits have deserted and I fear all the Company will be gone, for as to apprehending deserters, it is now out of the question. We have not the power, and the mines are so wide spread that the devil himself could not find one . . . I really hope I will not stumble on any as we cannot guard them.[7]

Rather than try to stop desertions, sometime in 1848 army units began to grant two-month furloughs for soldiers who wanted to look for gold.[8] Needless to say, the challenges to the federal government to enforce its rights to the gold fields would only become greater when the forty-niners started flooding into California the following year, at the end of which the nonnative population had grown to nearly 100,000.[9]

Nor could the few private landholders then in existence hope to keep the flood of gold seekers off their lands, even if they enjoyed official sanction of their ownership claims. On the basis of a grant from Governor Mason, Sutter himself officially owned some 50,000 acres of land that included his mill, Sutter's Fort and, it would turn out, large tracts of land in the foothills containing gold.[10] Once the Gold Rush was on in earnest, however, it became impossible for him to maintain any semblance of control over access to these lands. One miner described numerous "squatters" on Sutter's land who considered Sutter's claim to be an "usurpation" and who were "determined to maintain their possession at all hazards."[11] He goes on to describe the situation right outside Sutter's Fort, where

> the squatters have recently staked off lots, in accordance with an arrangement made among themselves, at one of their meetings. They voted that each

man should be entitled to a lot, forty by one hundred and sixty feet, wherever
he could find one unoccupied. They have accordingly laid out their lots, and
expect to hold possession against Sutter and all other claimants.[12]

Similarly, after statehood occurred in early 1850, the State did not interfere with the internal workings of the mining camps, largely leaving
the allocation of mining claims and water rights and the resolution of
disputes to the miners themselves. In 1851, the state legislature gave official sanction to this hands-off policy when it enacted a law that declared
that local miners' customs and traditions were to govern resolution of all
disputes over mining claims. As we shall see, even after the courts came
to be increasingly relied upon after the mid-1850s, they would still defer
to the mining codes that are the subject of this chapter. Many in the legislature were interested in tax revenues that could be raised through taxation of mining claims and other mining property, but mining supporters
managed to push through legislation that for a while exempted mining
claims from property taxation.[13] During the early 1850s, then, there was
little the state legislature would do to regulate mining in any way.

In short, the absence of enforceable official institutions in the gold
fields well into the early 1850s created the circumstances for a natural
experiment in property rights formation to take place, largely free from
institutional governance structures. It was into this situation that tens of
thousands of miners walked within an extremely short period, to extract
an extremely valuable resource in ways that were certain to result in congestion and the potential for disputes. What would happen?

5.3. The Beginning of Formal Mining Rights

In 1848, prior to the onset of the full-blown Gold Rush, many accounts
suggest that individual property rights in mining were virtually nonexis-
tent. According to the miner James Carson, for example, miners in 1848
had "no division of the ground into claims—they dug where it was richest."[14] When Carson arrived at Mormon Island on the south fork of the
American River in mid-1848, he found there "some forty or fifty men"
working the diggings with rockers-and-cradles. He goes on:

> But a few moments passed before I was knee deep in water with my wash ba-
> sin full of dirt, plunging it about, trying to separate the dirt from the gold.[15]

Nowhere was there a sense that he had to ask permission from the miners already there, or be assigned a location to work, or purchase a claim. This impression is corroborated by the observations of many observers of conditions in the gold fields during that year. Walter Colton, alcalde of Monterey, similarly described diggings along the Stanislaus River in 1848:

> A new deposit was discovered this morning near the falls of the Stanislaus, and in the crevices of the rocks over which the river pours its foaming sheet. An Irishman had gone there to bathe, and in throwing off his clothes, had dropped his jack-knife, which slipped into a crevice, where he first discovered the gold. He was soon tracked, and in less than an hour a storm of picks and crowbars were shivering the rocks.[16]

Similar descriptions of extreme informality in claiming rights to dig for gold may be found in the accounts of the miners Heinrich Lienhard and William Ryan.[17] In 1848, if you came across a promising location, it was generally possible for you to simply dig in, even if plenty of miners were already there.

Yet in 1848 we also see the very beginnings of movement toward more formal mining rights. In late 1848, for example, a miner Edward Buffum writes of conditions on the Yuba River:

> All the bars upon which men were then engaged in labour were "claimed," a claim at that time being considered good when the claimant had cleared off the top soil from any portion of the bar.[18]

The legal scholar Andrea McDowell has noted the existence of scattered references to "claims" contained in a variety of sources, beginning in July 1848. These sources refer to the beginnings of rules for staking a claim and some degree of exclusiveness in the right to dig.[19] These features are, of course, elements of property that economists predict would emerge under conditions of growing scarcity. Indeed, some evidence suggests that localized scarcity was associated with, and may have been at least partly responsible for, these particular instances of more formal mining rights. All of the references cited by McDowell, as well as Buffum's, involved diggings on either the American or Yuba Rivers, which were among the very earliest sites of gold discovery to which miners first swarmed. In a couple of the references, it seems clear that gold was beginning to be noticeably depleted. One case involved subsurface dig-

gings where miners had to dig down twelve feet before they reached the
gold. One would think that such a significant expenditure of time and
effort would generate pressure to support an exclusive right to dig. The
distinct impression is that growing congestion was giving rise to localized movements toward a rudimentary form of property rights in mining. However, in 1848, these were largely the exception, not the rule.

Other evidence supporting this impression of extreme informality
in the mines in 1848 is provided by numerous accounts of how early
miners felt about crime and personal safety. When Governor Mason
toured the goldfields in summer of 1848, he remarked on the orderli-
ness of mining:

> All live in tents, in bush arbors, or in the open air; and men have frequently
> about their persons thousands of dollars worth of this gold, and it was to me
> a matter of surprise that so peaceful and quiet state of things should continue
> to exist.[20]

This impression is corroborated by one miner, who described conditions
in the southern mines near Sonora in 1848:

> On inquiring whether, as there existed such strong temptation, robberies
> were not very frequent, I was informed, that, although thefts had occurred,
> yet, generally speaking, the miners dwelt in no distrust of one another, and
> left thousands of dollars' worth in gold-dust in their tents whilst they were ab-
> sent digging.[21]

And though one can find instances of crime in the 1848 gold fields, these
were by far the exception rather than the rule, just as was the case with
mining claims. The consensus of historians regarding the situation in
1848 is summarized by John Hussey:

> Everyone who has written about the days of '48 has noted the relative absence
> of crime in the diggings during that first year of the rush.[22]

The movement toward formal claims became more pronounced in 1849
as gold seekers continued to swarm into the mining regions. At first,
the rules governing claims were loose and informal. Claims were maintained by the custom of leaving tools at the claim site, which was gen-

erally respected by other miners.[23] Disputes were resolved in relatively informal ways as, for example, described by one forty-niner who was working along the American River in the summer of 1849:

> Two foreigners, who had been some time in the mines, began to work their respective claims, leaving a small space between them. The question arose to which of them this space belonged. As they could not amicably settle the dispute, they agreed to leave it to the decision of an American who happened by, and who had not yet done an hour's work in the mines. He measured off ten feet—which is allowed by custom—to each of the claimants, taking for his trouble the narrow strip of land lying between them.[24]

In another early instance, another miner describes, upon having his claim jumped, "appeal(ing) to the crowd" of other miners in the vicinity, who arbitrated the dispute and upheld his claim.[25]

Marking claims with pickaxes, tapping random passersby, and "appealing to the crowd" may all be understood as low-cost ways of maintaining property rights where the stakes in creating a more formal property rights system were still relatively low. Low stakes (given the presence nearby of plenty of other comparable claims) would have reduced the incentive to "horn in" on another miner's claim and would have enhanced the stability of even such an informal system. The arrangement was not foolproof and led to tensions, and in some cases disputes, among competing miners.[26] However, the universality of informal arrangements early on in the Gold Rush strongly suggests that they worked reasonably well, at least until continued growth and congestion in the gold fields spurred the emergence of more formal property rights and methods of enforcement.

The emergence of claims was associated with another important early development, the apparent existence of a thriving market in which claims were freely bought and sold. Even as early as late 1848, the miner Peter Burnett recounts being able to purchase a claim fronting on the Yuba River, suggesting that transferability was part and parcel of the notion of a claim from very early on, perhaps as soon as the notion emerged in the gold fields that a piece of land containing gold could belong to someone.[27] As might be expected, the agreed-upon price generally reflected the perceived richness of the claim. And though abuses did undoubtedly occur through such deceptive practices as "salting" a claim in order to attract buyers or elicit higher offers, these were apparently not widespread enough to cripple the operation of these markets.[28] One reason was that miners could sometimes collect reasonably reliable information on the richness of claims through observing the richness of neighboring claims as, for example, described by one miner:

> After working our claim for a few weeks, my partner left me to go to another part of the mines, and I joined two Americans in buying a claim five or six miles up the creek. It was supposed to be very rich, and we had to pay a long price for it accordingly, although the men who had taken it up, and from whom we bought it, had not yet even prospected the ground. But the adjoining claims were being worked, and yielding largely, and from the position of ours, it was looked on as an equally good one.[29]

Also supporting the operation of markets in claims was the fact that miners apparently devised various arrangements to share risk or overcome short-term liquidity problems. For example, Peter Burnett bought his claims on the Yuba River on credit for $300, to be paid back from proceeds of the diggings. And in 1851, another miner Lorenzo Stephens sold his claims for $30 on condition that he was to share in any additional proceeds.[30]

On the broadest level, the experience of 1848 and 1849 is consistent with the standard economic interpretation that increasing resource value will generate pressures to define property rights in ways that enable claimants to appropriate that value. In the period of extreme abundance that was 1848, it was almost entirely unnecessary to create property rights that defined use privileges and what they consisted of, because in a real sense there was plenty for all. This changed, however, in 1849 as miners poured into the gold fields. As the gold began to get scarce, we saw the appearance of exclusion rights that addressed the danger of disputes, mitigated rent dissipation, and permitted more complete appropriation of the value of the gold. This apparently included free and unimpeded exchange of rights, permitting rights to flow to those who valued them the most. It is, however, extremely hard to imagine that the rudimentary informal mechanisms to enforce rights and resolve disputes that we have just seen would long suffice, as the gold fields filled up with miners. With no controlling institutions present in the gold fields, miners had every incentive to devise for themselves more robust mechanisms that would serve these functions in a reasonably expeditious and consistent manner. Here is where mining camps entered the picture.

5.4. The Emergence of Mining Camps

Some evidence suggests that miners may have initially organized not to settle disputes over claims, but to maintain order in the diggings. Even though the gold fields were largely orderly and peaceful in 1848, there was still the need to deal with transgressions such as burglary, shootings, horse theft, and the occasional murder. This was accomplished with what the miners referred to as *lynch law*, summary justice quickly executed, so that the problem could be dealt with expeditiously and everyone could get back to work. However, it is clear from many accounts that the process often involved some semblance of due process. Judges would be chosen, juries would be empaneled, testimony would be taken, not everyone was convicted, and the severity of the punishment corresponded to the severity of the alleged transgression.[31] None of this is to argue that there were not miscarriages of justice: there undoubtedly were, perhaps many. The only point here is that administering lynch law required coordination and a modicum of organization among miners. However, in form if not in substance, its apparent impromptu manner made lynch law more closely resemble the informal techniques for maintaining claims and resolving disputes that we discussed earlier, rather than any sort of formalized governance structure.

In any case, the same procedures and predilections for due process soon made their way into disputes over claims. In these instances, one party would bring a complaint before a miners' court, which would hear the case, empanel a jury, summon witnesses, hand down a verdict, and assess appropriate penalties. One miner describes participating in one of these in early summer of 1850:

> Even as late as June, 1850, I was one of a jury in the mines, to decide on a case of litigation, where one party sued another before a self-constituted miners' court, in the absence of higher law, for flooding the water on a river claim, and thus preventing its being worked. The court was duly opened, the proofs and allegations adduced, and the costs of the trial *advanced*. Judgment was rendered against the plaintiff, in favor of the oldest occupant of the adverse

claims, when the plaintiff submitted without hesitation, and paid $102, costs, with as much cheerfulness as if it had been done by a legally constituted court of the United States.[32] (emphasis in original)

When this occurred—June 1850—is of significance here, as by this time California was officially a state of the union and its first legislature had already enacted a statute creating the official state court system. However, because it took time to establish court districts and select judges and sheriffs, the courts were not yet operational in most areas of the State. The miners stepped into this early void and constituted courts of their own to meet the growing demand for mechanisms to resolve disputes over mining claims. And this passage indicates that these early miners' courts enjoyed legitimacy in the eyes of many miners.

But the miners went much further than merely creating unofficial, rudimentary courts complete with many of the trappings of official courts. They self-organized into entire local communities—mining camps—whose economic life centered on mining the local deposits, where each camp designed and collectively agreed upon a set of principles to govern mining within the camp. All who wanted to mine in the camp had to abide by these principles, which were designed with three primary purposes in mind: to establish orderly ways of assigning claims, to ensure local diggings were fully utilized, and to resolve disputes over claims to both gold and water.

It is not known with certainty when the first formal mining camp came into existence in California, complete with specific principles governing local mining. But it must have occurred sometime soon after the forty-niners started arriving in droves in late summer of 1849. As one miner put it: "owing to the mass of beings in the mines in '49", the miners in "different mining districts" formed courts that "settled disputes arising out of disputed claims."[33] One of the earliest known examples of specific arrangements and procedures for governing mining is provided by the miner Amos Batchelder, who described conditions on the south fork of the Feather River in December of 1849:

They divided the river into three districts, chose a president for each and decided that to hold a claim a company should post up a notice stating its bounds in writing, which should be good for ten days, after which the ground must be occupied by one or more of the company. All difficulties arising about claims made previously are to be settled by arbitration. Everyone is to have the privilege to work the banks of the river above a medium height of water—a provision to accommodate those who do not belong to any company. The river is mostly taken up in claims from twenty to seventy-five rods long.[34]

As can be seen from Batchelder's description, these miners had answered several key questions regarding the nature of a claim: who was entitled to stake a claim (everyone), how claims were to be asserted (by posting a written notice, followed by actual occupation), and how disputes over claims were to be resolved (by arbitration). Another miner recounts in early March 1850 that these miners also provided for a system of recordkeeping, in which each claimant on the south fork was required to register his claim on the books of an "Association" of the miners on the river.[35] What many would consider to be key substantive and procedural elements of a formal rudimentary system of property rights had been created.

These miners were describing one of the first formal mining camps in the State and the essence of its mining code: the rules and procedures that it created to govern mining within its own locality. Similar rules and procedures would be replicated over and over within the coming decade by miners in a great many localities throughout the gold fields of California. Ultimately, there would be hundreds of mining camps, many of which created written bylaws that survive to this day. These rules and procedures would form the basis for a system of mining law that existed outside the official legal system of the State. For a time, this extralegal system of law created a reasonably effective governance structure for mining activity in the gold fields. And as we shall see, it would turn out to exert an important influence on the official system of law created by the courts and legislature.

5.5. Understanding the Mining Camp System

In this and the next chapter, I will be developing a positive explanation of, and normative interpretation of, the workings of the mining camp system. The challenge here is that the picture is complicated, especially since I will be trying to explain and interpret two seemingly distinct phenomena: the operation of the mining camp system itself, and the transition from the mining camp system to the official laws of the state as promulgated in the courts and legislature. But the two are related both in fact and conceptually.

In the gold fields, gold and water had the character of *common-property resources*, a notion we encountered in chapter 2. With common-property resources, resource use imposes external costs on other users, and it is difficult to exclude outsiders from entering to use the resource themselves.[36] Under these conditions, there is a tendency for the resource to be depleted too quickly, to the extent that users with access are homogeneous and do not consider the impacts of their activities on others. The result can be significant dissipation of rents, especially for complex resources such as gold and water where there may be many difficult-to-measure margins that can be exploited by users. In extreme cases, all of the rents associated with the resource may be dissipated, an eventuality often termed a *tragedy of the commons*.

As we have seen, entry into the gold fields was easy and fortune-seeking miners arrived at the gold fields with little difference in abilities or experience, at least in terms of looking for gold. Since gold was obtained under a rule of capture, all of this suggests the possibility of significant rent dissipation. The extent of rent dissipation, however, would have also depended upon the ability of miners to self-organize to enact rules that would permit them to forestall rent-dissipating activities.[37] If miners in a locality could contract with each other at low cost to limit or manage entry and to set up an orderly process to allocate mining claims and water rights, then it is possible that much rent dissipation could be avoided. The magnitude of these transaction costs would have determined not only whether they could sit down and write a governing code at all, but also the particular content of the provisions in that code. Lower transaction costs meant, of course, a greater likelihood that a code would be written. However, with lower transaction costs, we would also expect the content of code provisions to be more effective in deterring rent dissipation. In particular, as we shall see shortly, when transaction costs were low, code provisions designed to reduce rent dissipation would have been more likely to reflect economic considerations, such as economies of scale and externalities, both negative and positive, resulting from mining operations.

There is reason to believe that transaction costs were sufficiently low that such considerations might well be discerned in the codes. For one thing, hundreds of camps were formed and many codes were in fact written, implying that the transaction costs of self-organization could not have been extraordinarily high. Several factors would have kept transaction costs down and made it possible for camps to write effective codes. In the miners' meetings in which codes were written, everyone was permitted to participate, miners were in face-to-face communication with each other, and general interest in fairness would have enhanced the legitimacy of the codes in the eyes of the miners.[38] But a crucial factor was the fact that in a given locality, exclusion of newcomers was possible, in an extremely important sense. Though miners came and went, it was possible for camps to craft enforceable rules regarding who enjoyed access to the placer deposits and available water supplies within the camp. Limits on claim size effectively allocated available deposits to a fixed number of miners, and then a thriving market in claims effectively excluded all who were not willing to pay the prices asked. Exclusion from water supplies was achieved in two ways, either by allocating on a first-come, first-served basis, or by permitting only miners located on waterways to use the water.[39] This is not to argue that exclusion from available gold and water was costless, but there are good reasons to believe exclusion costs were manageable.

So we have a framework with which to understand the creation of the camps and the content of the rules they crafted for governing mining locally. At this point, the discussion in this chapter will turn to examining the content of the mining codes to explore the ways in which they may have mitigated rent dissipation within the camps. The other issue—how we understand the subsequent move away from the mining camp governance structure into the official court system—will be explored in chapter 6.

Ever-growing congestion was chiefly responsible for the spontaneous creation of the network of mining camps that penetrated virtually every part of the gold fields, as miners continued to arrive. Through the process of staking claims and working the diggings, it was inevitable that disputes over mining and water claims would occur. These included disputes over claim boundaries, whether a miner was in right possession of a claim, whether he was attempting to work too much land, and whether he was prosecuting mining consistent with the local understanding of due diligence. Mining camp rules and regulations were designed to address these issues, by clarifying expectations regarding what activities could and could not be done, and by providing mechanisms for resolving disputes among mining companies. They thus addressed a central cause of rent dissipation: resources wasted on disputes over mining claims. All miners in a locality would have had an interest in establishing fair rules applied consistently that resolved costly disputes and perhaps, pre-empted them before they even occurred.

It is telling, first of all, that an almost universal feature of the mining codes was the imposition of limits on the permissible size of an individual claim that applied to everyone in the camp. This provision had several advantages, not the least of which would have been to mitigate disputes over where miners could dig; namely, only within the boundaries of a claim. Furthermore, such a rule would have been considered fair, and would certainly have been supported by a majority of miners in a camp, which helps explain its virtually universal adoption. And the particular permissible size chosen by a camp would have reflected both the richness of the local placers and the number of miners locally wanting to work a claim.[40] The extent to which the policy of establishing a maximum claim size was driven by economic considerations is a question we will return to shortly. The point here is merely that it was quite possible to achieve agreement among miners on this provision.

A related provision was the requirement that a claim needed to be worked in order for the miner to maintain possession. The work requirement provision was nearly as universal as the claim size limitation though as we shall see, it underwent a subtle, explicable evolution over time. The work requirement would have served the function of ensuring the deposits would be worked, possibly preventing waste and rent dissipation.[41] The notion that one needed to work to keep one's claim would also have comported with miners' notions of fairness, albeit in a different sense than the claim size limitation. Some evidence suggests that miners were concerned with fairness in the sense of John Locke: that "mixing one's labor" in with a natural resource entitles one to a property right in the resource.[42] In this sense, a work requirement would be a mechanism to ensure that miners got their Lockean "just deserts." It would have also seemed fair to miners for the work requirement to contain exceptions for extenuating circumstances such as accident, illness, or lack of water to prosecute mining. It is not surprising that many codes contained precisely such exceptions.

Another feature of the mining codes was to encourage and support the buying and selling of claims. In general, freely buying and selling property was a very powerful impulse in mid-nineteenth-century America. However, in the camps, it ran up against a conflicting current which was perhaps every bit as powerful: fear of monopoly. Early codes almost universally allowed the purchase and holding of an unlimited number of claims, reflecting the gut instinct prevalent at the time that people should be allowed to do what they want with their property. In the absence of negative externalities, of course, such a provision supports the efficient working of claims. Given that this would have mitigated rent dissipation and seemed fair to miners in this libertarian sense, it is not surprising that they were able to agree on inclusion of these provisions in the codes—at least until the bitter experience that this could, and often did, lead to monopolization of claims made miners increasingly reluctant to include this provision in their codes over time.

Given that miners could agree on a number of principles to govern mining, the question we turn to now is whether there was a compelling economic logic to the specific provisions they crafted. Let us begin by exploring this possibility within the context of river mining, by examining codes through the lens of transaction cost determinants of property rules, as developed in chapter 2. In river mining, perhaps the most common dispute occurred when a company built a dam that backed water over the dry river bed claims of a company situated immediately upstream. When there were only a handful of companies situated on a stretch of river and they were not physically adjacent to each other, they would have been unlikely to interfere with each other's operations and peace and harmony would have reigned. However, when companies organized "along the whole extent of the river, and at every available point it will be dammed and turned," as they apparently did on the Tuolumne River in summer of 1850, one can imagine that disputes might well occur.[43]

Some might reasonably anticipate that river miners placed in this position might resort to taking matters into their own hands by tearing down offending structures, or worse, if they believed they had a superior claim to mine the river. During this period, however, there is little evidence that they pursued such confrontational strategies. On the contrary, there is much more evidence to suggest that river miners tried to resolve matters cooperatively and amicably by establishing guidelines that governed the taking of river claims and disputes that might arise between companies.

For example, in the summer of 1851, two separate assemblages of

river miners on the American and Mokelumne Rivers convened to create guidelines for resolving disputes over river claims. In the first meeting, which took place on July 12th, damming companies on the Mokelumne River called for the election of two arbitrators to resolve disputes
among companies and if needed, a system of jury trial to hear cases. It
also attempted to clarify what companies were entitled to; namely, all
ground drained or dried by damming or wing-damming. Later that
month on July 29th, a second set of miners convened at Mormon Island
on the American River and passed a more extensive set of resolutions
specifically enjoining damming companies from backing water over
claims "which do not belong to them," which constituted an injury to the
upstream party "and as such abated." Furthermore, the injured party
was explicitly entitled to damages. The resolutions also required damming companies to clearly establish the limits of their claims by staking
them off, and that others were explicitly empowered to work up to those
stakes "without any hindrance from the said company."[44]

The difference in the approaches taken by the two sets of miners is
striking to someone familiar with the modern law-and-economics tradition. Whereas the Mormon Island resolutions may be interpreted as
attempts to create bright-line property rights to individual stretches of
the river, the Mokelumne River resolutions were considerably more ambiguous, basically leaving the rights in the hands of arbitrators or a jury,
and providing no guidance regarding the basis on which to settle disputes. What makes this interesting is that the typical dispute that both
of these sets of resolutions were intended to address probably involved
low transaction costs. There would have been only two parties involved,
and the injury—a dam that backs water over the claims of the adjacent
party upstream—would have been easily observable and the identity of
the offending company extremely easy to determine.[45] Under these conditions, efficiency might dictate the creation of clearly defined property rights protected by a rule of trespass, which would facilitate Pareto-
improving trades such as a buyout by one company, or consolidation of
the two companies accomplished in some other manner. Such property
rights were clearly provided by the Mormon Island resolutions and decidedly not by the ones from the Mokelumne River.

It is difficult, of course, to draw definitive conclusions regarding efficiency based merely on these two sets of resolutions. We do not know,
for example, how long these resolutions were in effect or how stringently
they were enforced. Some evidence, however, suggests that the Mormon

Island provisions may have been more broadly reflective of miner preferences in general regarding how to address river mining disputes. Another surviving set of bylaws that governed river mining in the 1850s are those of Lower Humbug Creek, a mining district in Siskiyou County. These bylaws, which were written in 1855, were explicit about the treatment of backwaters in disputes involving adjacent claimants, mandating that the backwaters created by a lower claimant "shall in no case be allowed to interfere with the other" when claims were made "at one and the same time." However, when a claimant arrived first, his backwaters were not "considered an incumbrance [*sic*] to the one above."[46] As in the Mormon Island resolutions, this wording is suggestive of a trespass rule in disputes involving backwaters. And as we shall see, the use of temporal priority in governing such disputes in this manner is broadly consistent with other provisions crafted by miners to resolve disputes over mining claims.

It should be added that other provisions in the Mormon Island resolutions also mirrored similar ones widely seen in other mining codes. Among these was a work requirement: that claims were subject to forfeiture if work was not done on them regularly. However, the Mormon Island resolutions also stipulated that claims were not forfeited if work was prevented by illness or back waters. A separate resolution entitled the first discoverer of gold in a ravine to an extra claim. As we shall see, all of these principles—work requirements, specific exceptions to work requirements, and additional claims for first discovery—would appear regularly in mining codes. And though these principles have efficiency interpretations of their own, the only point here is that the seemingly more efficient definition of property rights in the Mormon Island resolutions appears to more closely echo the sentiments of the larger community of Gold Rush miners than did the Mokelumne River resolutions.

The vast majority of miners' codes available to modern researchers governed diggings not in the beds of rivers but rather, in their bars and banks, or in locations remote from water such as ravines, gulches, flats, and hills. In these settings, the nature of the disputes that could occur over mining claims was not about flooding each others' claims by building dams but rather, was about other forms of interference with mining such as claim jumping, claiming too much land, and diverting water supplies. In order to investigate the way miners' codes treated these sorts of disputes, I have assembled sixty-one non-river mining codes spanning

the years from 1850 to 1857. The following discussion will focus on several types of provisions that appeared regularly in the codes: limits on
claim size, limitations on the number of claims individual miners could
hold, work requirements, the ability to associate together to prosecute
mining jointly, extra claims for discoveries of new deposits, and formal
procedures for resolving disputes over claims.

Without exception, the mining codes governing non-river placer diggings sustained the notion of a claim largely as a right that enjoyed first
possession protection against newcomer encroachment. Along rivers,
streams, and creeks, claims comprised so many feet of frontage land extending so many feet back from the waterway. In gulches, ravines, flats
and hills, surface claims were mostly rectangular, so many feet by so
many feet. All provided a perimeter that in principle excluded other miners from interfering with prosecution of mining within the area of the
claim. On the surface, defining claims in this way would appear to promote efficiency to the extent that mining within one's designated claim
area inflicted no externalities on other miners.[47] On the other hand, the
limitation on the permissible size of a claim has been interpreted by
some as reflecting miners' interest in maximizing the number of miners
who were able to work the gold, and thus in ensuring allocative fairness.[48]
The following discussion, therefore, will speak to this debate in the scholarly literature, which I will refer to as the *efficiency vs. fairness* debate.

It turns out that the claim size limitation cannot be correctly interpreted without considering certain other relevant factors. First, the mere
fact of a claim size limitation is not in itself sufficient to allow us to conclude that either efficiency or fairness was the decisive operant factor.
The question is how the claim size limitation compared with the minimum efficient scale of a placer mining operation during this period. If
the minimum efficient scale was considerably larger than the claim size
permitted by a code, then imposing the size limit could have resulted in
significant losses in productivity, making it harder to argue that this provision promoted efficiency. If it was not, however, then it is impossible to
tell, on the basis of this factor alone, whether efficiency or fairness was
the driving factor.

However, even a minimum efficient scale of mining significantly in
excess of the claim size limit *in itself* tells us nothing about efficiency vs.
fairness unless there were additional proscriptions contained in the code
against aggregating individual claims, either by locating or purchasing
claims, or working together with other miners. If there were no such pro-

scriptions, then miners could have been free to expand the scale of operations to take advantage of economies of scale by combining claims and resources, laboring together, and prosecuting mining on a larger scale. At the same time, these codes may not have promoted fairness in the egalitarian sense because they would have facilitated, or at the very least done nothing to block, concentrations of resources and wealth in the hands of a few. Enhanced concentration of wealth could have occurred in a variety of ways, the most obvious perhaps being the concentration of Ricardian rents in companies of miners favored by circumstances to mine the most productive placer deposits. Wealth concentration could also occur, however, if technological change was rendering mining more capital-intensive, thus increasing the return on labor. Finally, in the instances where miners were hiring others to work for them, they may have been able to gain significant rents as the residual claimant on the revenues of the company, to the extent laborers could not easily exploit hard-to-measure margins of effort or were risk-averse, or Indian labor was available.[49]

More generally, the appropriate comparison to make is between the minimum efficient scale and the total claim size—what I shall call the *potential* claim size—that reflects the individual claim size limitation but is also adjusted to take into account the possibility of locations or purchases of multiple claims and the possibility of individual miners being permitted to work in association with each other. When one examines the codes in my sample, the potential claim size turns out to be commonly much larger than the individual claim size limitation. For example, of the forty-six codes for which I have specific information on individual claim size limits, twenty-two permitted unlimited purchase of claims, and thirteen explicitly allowed individual miners to work in association with each other. Only five of the forty-six codes limited miners to one claim without the explicit possibility of working in association with other miners. All of this means that studies that focus on the individual claim size limitation without considering the possibilities of holding multiple (often unlimited) claims or working in association with other miners may provide a highly misleading picture of the restrictiveness of the individual limit. Since holding multiple claims and working in association with other miners would have promoted the concentration of wealth in companies of miners for the reasons given earlier, the case for fair outcomes, as embodied in egalitarian policies on claim sizes, becomes considerably weakened.

More insight into the economic determinants of the mining camp system is gained by examining how relevant provisions of the codes evolved over time. The interpretive exercise here is to examine code provisions in connection with what we know of the use of placer technologies and the implications for the likely minimum efficient scale of gold production. Figure 5.1 reproduces Figure 3.13 from chapter 3, showing the temporal pattern of technology adoption. This evidence will be exploited to shed light on the mining code provisions, where in addition to the provisions relating to claim size, the holding of multiple claims, and miners working in association, we will also consider work requirements and rules that awarded extra claims for new discoveries.

In the following discussion, I will divide the analysis into what I earlier called the Early, Middle, and Later periods, which provides the basis for characterizing the temporal progression of the provisions in a systematic way based upon the adoption of technology. To summarize much of the information quickly in advance, Figure 5.2 shows the cumulative number of codes over time that contained each of three key provisions: (a) no limits on purchases of claims (*Unlimited Claims*), (b) explicit permission for miners to associate together to work their claims (*Association*), and (c) an extra claim for discovery of a new deposit (*Discovery*).

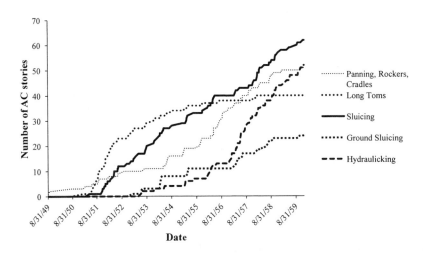

FIGURE 5.1. Penetration of mining technologies, 1849–1859. AC, *Alta Californian*.

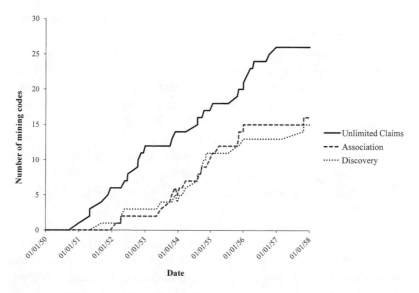

FIGURE 5.2. Various provisions of mining codes, 1850–1857

Early Period (1849–mid-1851)

Only four codes in total were written prior to summer of 1851, during which period placer mining was dominated by the primitive technologies: panning and rockers-and-cradles. Two of them were written in late 1850: Chinese Camp in Tuolumne County, and Gold Mountain in Nevada County. Both codes specified small claim sizes (20 by 20 feet and 30 by 40 feet) consistent with the prosecution of small-scale mining. Neither proscribed the acquisition of multiple claims, however, and Gold Mountain explicitly permitted miners to purchase as many claims as they wished, though all exchanges needed to be entered in the books of an elected recorder.[50] The other two codes that were written in this early period were for Kentucky Hill and Prospect Hill, both in Nevada County. These codes, which were written in spring of 1851, were virtually identical and did little more than establish individual claim sizes and a recording requirement and as might be expected, the claim sizes remained relatively small—60 feet by 60 feet. As with Gold Mountain, both permitted any miner to purchase as many claims as he wanted.

Despite the fact that these early codes mandated relatively small individual claim sizes, the fact that accumulation of claims was possible (and even facilitated by these codes) makes it unlikely that there was much loss of rents through miners being forced to operate at inefficiently small scales. Furthermore, the danger of monopolization of claims was probably mitigated by the fact that only primitive technologies were available to actually work the claims. It is also telling that the work requirements of these early codes were extremely informal and much less directive than many of the work requirements contained in later codes. The work requirement of Kentucky Hill, for example, read in its entirety:

> A claim properly staked and registered need not be worked, nor tools left upon it until the first day of August next.[51]

This provision, phrased more as a grace period rather than a requirement to work, does not seem designed to facilitate turnover of claims or maximize gold production, as some have suggested. It should be added that the work requirement provisions of the Prospect Hill and Gold Mountain codes contained extremely similar wording.

The work requirement of Chinese Camp tells, however, a slightly different story. It simply reads:

> That all claims now made and worked by the present settlers, shall be held by them.[52]

This passage reads more as a requirement to work than a grace period before work needed to be commenced, though it is not at all specific about what constituted work, nor how much work needed to be done, as later work requirements found in other codes would be. The difference between Chinese Camp and the other codes may lie in the fact that Chinese Camp was probably settled and mined earlier than the others. If depletion occurred earlier, this might have given rise to earlier pressures to promote use through actual requirements to work. This interpretation is consistent with some other evidence that depletion generated work requirements. The miner Alonzo Delano, for example, recounts that when he visited diggings at Dawlytown in late 1850 (a camp not contained in my sample), miners were required to commence work on a claim "within ten days after it was located."[53] Dawlytown was located on the middle fork of the Feather River near Bidwell Bar, which was one of the earliest areas to be mined, as we have seen.

The foregoing evidence provides a more refined picture of the Gold Rush period than is found in some recent scholarly studies, which stress limits on claim sizes, restrictions on holding multiple claims, and work requirements to conclude that miners' codes were crafted to prevent monopolization of claims, to spread the wealth among miners, and to facilitate the turnover of claims.[54] The evidence contained in the earliest codes considered here is more consistent with an interest in permitting miners to work claims at their discretion, to operate at whatever scale they saw fit, to buy and sell claims as they pleased, and to support production through creation of rights that effectively excluded other miners. Work requirements were generally vague and not at all directive in terms of requiring work, though they seemed to be more directive in the parts of the gold fields that had been mined earlier. Finally, the virtual absence of provisions that rewarded miners for gold discoveries also makes sense for this early period: the incentive effects of such provisions were probably largely unnecessary given the relative availability of gold during the Gold Rush period.

Middle Period (mid-1851–1853)

Beginning in mid-1851, we begin to observe some subtle changes in the content of the codes relating to claim size, mining associations, and incentives for new discoveries. As we shall see shortly, through the Middle period we do not observe a noticeable trend in the permitted individual claim size limit contained in new codes. However, during this period we do begin to observe mining camps imposing significant restrictions on the acquisition of claims and on mining practices on those claims. Some codes written in 1852, such as those of Constitution Hill and Washington Hill, continued to permit miners to purchase as many claims as they wished. Similarly, the mining code of Jackass Gulch also seemed to permit the purchase of multiple claims, but that purchases needed to be made "in good faith and under a bona fide bill of sale" and certified by two disinterested parties, suggesting that sufficient fraud or confusion had surrounded the selling of claims that the miners considered some procedural guidance to be desirable. Weaver Creek, on the other hand, was explicit in limiting "each and every miner" to one claim. Rockwell Hill also appeared to limit miners to only one claim when it specified that "No person shall hold more than one claim by location," though this could be interpreted as leaving open the possibility of holding other

claims by purchase, a contingency the code was silent on. Similarly, Volcano Hill permitted miners to hold two claims by location, while also not
being explicit on purchases. Upper Yuba and East Fork of North Trinity
both struck a middle ground by permitting miners to hold one claim by
purchase and one claim by location.[55]

Another way to see the new trend in restrictions on claims is to consider the new codes that permitted an unlimited number of claims. Figure 5.2 shows that over time, miners continued to write into new codes
provisions permitting an unlimited number of claims, mostly through
purchase. However, whereas the presence of unlimited claim provisions
was virtually universal through 1851, a growing number of new codes
written thereafter did not contain such provisions. This is seen in Figure 5.3, which shows the cumulative percentage of codes over time that
permitted an unlimited number of claims. The peak was in December
1851, when six out of seven existing codes did so, but we see a steady
decline after that through the remainder of the period. Nevertheless,
through the Middle period, nearly half of all codes permitted unlimited
claims. When you combine this with the fact that many other codes, if
they didn't permit an unlimited number, permitted at least two, it is apparent that again, the potential claim size well exceeded the official individual claim size in a great many cases. [56]

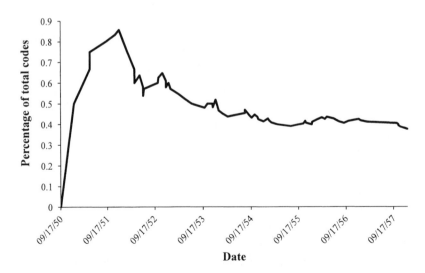

FIGURE 5.3. Cumulative percentage of mining codes that included unlimited purchase provision, 1850–1857

At the same time, however, provisions began to appear in some codes that explicitly permitted miners to associate to work together and pool claims. The code of Volcano Hill, written in 1852, explicitly permitted miners to form joint stock companies that could work "any part of their joint claims as best suits their convenience." The 1853 code of Columbia, after specifying that each miner within the district was permitted to hold only one claim, went on to say that

> Nothing in this article shall be so construed as to prevent miners from associating in companies to carry on mining operations; such companies holding no more than one full claim to each member.

Since a "full claim" in Columbia was one hundred feet square, or 10,000 square feet, four miners could in principle pool their claims to amass a total working area of nearly an acre. Similarly, Vallecito, written in 1853, allowed sixty feet square to "each individual, or to each member of any company." East Fork of North Trinity also explicitly permitted miners to associate together to work their claims.[57]

Another significant change that occurred during the Middle period was that the work requirements became more explicit and binding as the period progressed. The work requirements of the 1852 codes of Constitution Hill and Washington Hill took the earlier form of permitting a grace period, with Constitution Hill explicitly permitting claims to be held "without labor done" for an entire year. The 1852 code of Rockwell Hill was directive about how much work needed to be done, but did not require much: only one day in sixty. The most stringent work requirements found in the 1852 codes were those of Jackass Gulch and Weaver Creek, which required miners to work one day in five and one day in ten in order to hold claims. However, the 1853 codes virtually all imposed relatively strict work requirements. Representative of the 1853 codes were Warren Hill, Empire, and Jamestown, which required miners to work one day in six, and New York Diggings, which required one day in seven.[58]

This evolution in the work requirement is suggestive of generalized growing gold scarcity after 1852, since it is hard to imagine miners forcing each other to work when there is plenty of gold for everyone. To this extent, the evidence is consistent with the claim that the work requirements helped maximize production by facilitating turnover of claims.[59] Aside from signaling growing gold scarcity, however, the trend toward universal work requirements also reflected some of the technological advances described earlier that promoted team production. This is seen in the fact that work requirements sometimes complemented the association provisions, as for example, in Brushey Canyon (1853), which stipulated that miners holding contiguous claims could work "one or more of such claims leaving the others unworked."[60] This provision made it possible for miners associating together to concentrate their efforts on one part of the combined claims without fear of losing the rest. During this period, we also begin to observe work requirement provisions that reflect the rise of a separate and distinct ditch industry that was in the business of selling water to miners. The work requirements of Columbia (1853), for example, had to be satisfied within three days after water could "be procured at the usual rates." This tendency would become more pronounced in the next few years.[61]

Later Period (1854–1857)

The patterns that emerged in 1852 and 1853 would become more clearly defined over the ensuing years to 1857, and new patterns would become noticeable as well. First, it was only in this period that we observe a significant increase in the permissible claim size (see Figure 5.4). After the

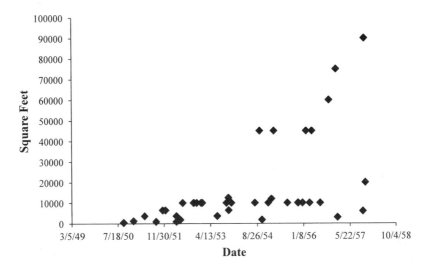

FIGURE 5.4. Claim size limits over time, 1850–1857

summer of 1854, we observe virtually no codes mandating claim sizes less than 10,000 square feet and a significant number 20,000 square feet and larger, up to a maximum of 90,000 square feet in one case. At the same time, with greater regularity miners' codes would restrict the number of claims individual miners could hold. The provisions varied across codes and over time, but the modal provision imposed a maximum of anywhere from one to two claims. Similarly, over time we observe fewer codes that permit unlimited purchases of claims, though it needs to be emphasized that such provisions did not disappear from the codes. From 1854 through 1857, ten out of twenty-six codes permitted unlimited purchases. However, as with the previous period, this restrictiveness was partially offset by the inclusion of association provisions, which continued to be written during this period: eight such provisions appeared in new codes written during this period. The result was that fifteen of the twenty-six codes—nearly 58 percent—written during the Later period allowed miners either unlimited claims or explicit freedom to associate in mining. Even by mid-decade, the potential claim size well exceeded the individual claim size limit in a majority of mining camps.

As we have seen, directive work requirement provisions began to be universal in the codes in early 1853. The Late period witnessed a continuation of the trend that they reflected technological advances in mining that promoted team production of gold. Some codes, such as Smith's Flat (1855), permitted water development in digging ditches and constructing reservoirs—team activities—to count towards satisfying the work requirement. Some codes that made work requirements conditional on sufficiency of water, for example, based them on the new evolving technologies for water application. The code of Garote (185?), for example, stated that sufficiency meant enough water to "work a (long) tom," while Smith's Flat (1855) stipulated that a "sluice-head" was sufficient to work a claim. Still other work requirements clearly reflected a new orientation toward a separate ditch industry that supplied water to miners. Saw Mill Flat (1854), for example, stipulated that miners not working their claims would not forfeit them if water was either not available to work them, or if it was too expensive. French Creek (1854) went even further when it did not require claims to be worked unless water could "be had free of charge." Ohio Flat (1856) specified that claims would be forfeited if not worked within ten days after water was available at a "reasonable" price. The thrust of the work requirement provisions involving water was, of course, to acknowledge not only the technological reality that placer mining was difficult to prosecute without water, but also the economic reality that cheaper water in greater quantities was also important to miners. Miners saw fit to superimpose increasingly sophisticated work requirement restrictions on the basic exclusion right that reflected the importance of water and the new industrial organization that involved separate suppliers of water furnishing water to miners in transactions resembling a market.[62]

As Figure 5.2 also indicates, one other important development during this period was the emergence in the codes of a provision that gave the discoverer of new deposits the right to an extra claim. Such a provision had appeared sporadically prior to late 1853, appearing in a primitive form in 1851 in the code of Poverty Hill, Yorktown and Chili Camp, which allowed the discoverer of a new lead sixty feet upon the lead. Two other codes that gave discoverers an extra claim were Vallecito and Volcano District in 1852, which stated that the provision was included in the code "in order to encourage industry and diligence within this district." Beginning with the code of Brushey Canyon in late November 1853, however, the vast majority of codes written up to early 1856 contain such a provision. Granting extra claims to the discoverers of new lodes would appear to have been designed to reward prospecting, which if successful would have led to the enrichment of all. And some evidence suggests that miners would sometimes attempt to free-ride on the prospecting of others, as Frank Marryat described in 1851:

> There are plenty of "prospectors" in the mines, but the profession scarcely pays, for the "prospector" is the jackal who must search for many days, and, when he has found, the lion, in the shape of the old miner, steps in and reaps the benefit. So that there is something to be learnt in the diggings, for undoubtedly one of the first principles in life is to look on while others work, and then step in and cry "halves."[63]

Additional miners' accounts confirm that free-riding on the prospecting activity of others was an issue in the 1851 mining season.[64]

To the extent that free-riding was a serious issue, the extra claim provision can be viewed as an attempt to address the problem by providing greater rewards to prospecting activity. However, this explanation by itself is not entirely adequate as it does not explain why the provision did not begin to appear regularly in new miners' codes until nearly 1854, more than two mining seasons after free riding began to be documented to be an issue in the camps, nor why it largely vanished after 1855. A clue is perhaps provided by Figure 5.2, which reveals a striking similarity in the time patterns for the association and discovery provisions. My suspicion is that economies of scale, team production, and the search for new placer deposits all intensified in the 1853 season, which, perhaps not coincidentally, is when placer mining took a leap upwards in terms of capital- and water-intensity with the invention of hydraulic mining. By 1855, however, larger scale operations had perhaps become regularized and part of industry norms and few new discoveries were being made by small-scale mining operations.

Overall, the evidence presented in this section provides very little support for anything like a generalized egalitarian notion of fairness emerging from the miners' codes relating to mining claims. On the contrary, early codes virtually unanimously permitted individual miners to collect as many claims as they had resources to purchase and imposed very little in governance constraints on their behavior in mining their claims. Over time, we observe limits being imposed on unlimited purchase of claims but at the same time, a number of codes compensated by permitting free association of miners and the pooling of claims. The latter association provisions track the likely expansion of the minimum efficient scale of mining through the invention and application of more heavily water- and capital-intensive mining technologies, permitting miners to team up to take advantage of these new technologies. Fairness may well have been an important concern for the minority of miners' codes that explicitly limited miners to one claim apiece, as well as the ones that made their work requirements contingent on the availability of water or being free from illness.[65] The fact that work requirements were largely absent during the Early period and then became universal after late 1853 seems, however, more consistent with growing scarcities in placer deposits over time than with promoting fairness. The dominant pattern suggests a tracking of the imperatives of gold production: supporting investment security, providing exclusion rights, and permitting miners to take advantage of technological advance and growing economies of scale over time.

5.6. Water Rights in the Mining Codes

Economists have not been unaware of the mining district codes and the wealth of information contained within them.[66] Little scholarly attention has been paid, however, to the provisions relating specifically to water use, despite the fact that water was a crucial factor input in the gold production process, as we have seen. The importance of water as a factor input into gold production was reflected in many provisions in the miners' codes that governed water use, including ones governing work requirements and claim size. As we have seen, virtually all codes mandated some sort of requirement to work a claim or risk forfeiture. However, many work requirement provisions did not mandate forfeiture of claims if no water, or insufficient water, or no inexpensive water, was available to work them.[67] Regarding claim size, the codes tended to permit miners to claim larger areas when water was either not available or needed to be purchased.[68] All of these provisions reflect an implicit recognition that water significantly increased the productivity of the mining process.

If water was so valuable to miners, the model developed in chapter 2 suggests that we should observe selective movement towards quantification, the ability to transfer water (to increase total available rents), and greater security of water rights (as reflected in first possession rules), depending upon the degree of "publicness" of water use. And indeed, the codes contain considerable information that suggests these issues were considered important by miners.

A. Quantification

Of the three issues, quantification is the one to which the codes make the least explicit reference, showing up occasionally in work requirement rules as attempts to define what is meant by a "sufficient" amount of water to work a claim.[69] However, code provisions that quantify water rights are uncommon and when they do occur, they are typically highly imprecise. Among the few codes that make any attempt at quantification is Garote (185?), where sufficiency meant enough water to "work a (long) tom." In addition, Bodie District (1860) required "sufficient water to work with a long tom or rocker," Smith's Flat (1855) stipulated that a "sluice-head" was sufficient to work a claim, and Oregon Gulch (1855) considered a claim workable when a "tom-head" of water was available without purchase.[70]

The dearth of evidence of quantification in the codes needs to be interpreted in the context of our earlier discussion of the state of water measurement technology in the 1850s. As we have seen, during this period it was extremely difficult to measure water flows with any precision in the California gold regions, which explains why water markets specified times of service rather than actual quantities of water. It is thus not surprising that miners' codes would be largely silent on quantifying water rights. Nevertheless, it is telling that the few codes that did make the attempt phrased it in terms of the amount of water required to successfully work a claim. This seems completely consistent with miners contracting with water companies for times of service, as we saw earlier in the contract between the Bear River and Auburn Water and Mining Company and miners in Auburn Ravine. What was important was the amount of water needed for successful mining, not a specific quantity.

B. Transfer Restrictions

Restrictions on transfer, when they occurred, were commonly manifested in provisions that conferred special status upon miners within the locality when it came to water use, typically at the expense of ditch companies. Some codes, for example, singled out mining as the preferred use to which water could be put. Weaverville (1853) protected water claimants who constructed races to convey water and kept those races in good repair, "provided such water be used for mining purposes." Others protected miners within the district from harmful diversions, possibly for other purposes. Little Humbug Creek (1856), for example, prohibited diversions of water from the creek "to the prejudice of the miners" working thereon. Brown's Flat (185?) stipulated that all the water available in the local creek "shall be reserved for the use of miners in this precinct." Others such as Brushey Canyon (1853) simply stipulated that water had to stay where it was, save possibly for any water surplus to the needs of the local community, and could not be taken out of the local watershed by ditch companies, who were derided as "nothing more than water carriers." Finally, Columbia (1853) permitted diversions of surface water from "gold-bearing ravines," but only with the consent of parties working the ravines, and even then the water could be recalled by "any party interested."[71]

C. First Possession

The notion that water rights were subject to first possession also appeared in the miners' codes, though with considerable variation across different camps. One way in which first possession appeared was in governing companies whose dams backed water up on an upstream company. Here we observe variation in the extent to which relative rights were based upon first possession. In some cases first possession is explicitly invoked, as in the case of Lower Humbug Creek (1855) which clearly awards property rights to the downstream company if it is there first:

> When a claimant occupies a claim previously to the taking of the adjacent one next above, he shall be allowed the privilege of putting in a dam at the upper end of his Claim(,) the subsequent claimant above if any being compelled to terminate his race at the head of the race below nor shall the backwater of the lower claim in such case be considered an incumbrance [*sic*] to the one above.[72]

However, the same is decidedly not the case when claimants arrive at the same time:

> Where two or more adjacent claims are taken by different individuals at one and the same time the backwater of the lower claimant shall in no case be allowed to interfere with the other.[73]

Though not explicitly stated, the a fortiori suggestion is that downstream claimants who arrive after upstream claimants will also not enjoy a superior right. On the other hand, the bylaws of Little Humbug Creek (1856) are more ambiguous on the issue of temporal priority:

> Resolved, that no miners or company of miners shall back water by a dam or otherwise upon the claim above them to the injury of the party holding the upper claim without their, the upper parties, consent.[74]

This provision seems to simply award the right to the upstream company, though it could also be interpreted as basing this award on its being present first, in which case the ultimate basis for the right would be first possession. In any case, this provision is nowhere near as explicit as the previous one in defining the relative rights of newer versus older claimants.

More commonly, first possession entered into the codes either as a basis for acquiring water rights or for resolving disputes. Some codes were quite explicit that acquisition of water rights was to be based upon first possession, though explicitly reserving this privilege only for miners. Jamestown (1853), for example, stipulated that:

> Miners shall be entitled to the priority of water, according to the date and situation of the location of their claims.[75]

The code of Lovelock (1864) contained a similar relatively unconditional statement of first possession, however again making it clear that it was miners who enjoyed this right:

> That the first location shall be entitled to the natural water which may accumulate in his claim, ravine or what not for mining purposes.[76]

Weaverville (1853) permitted race companies to obtain first possession rights to divert water to the capacity of their races, which were, however, conditional on their leaving at least "four tom-heads" of water in the local creeks "for the benefit of miners at present working or who may hereafter work" said creeks.[77]

Some districts, however, did not obviously base the acquisition of water rights on first possession. Hungry Creek Diggings (1857) simply stipulated that no one could construct a dam or other obstruction in the local creek "to the detriment or hinderence [sic] of any other individual or company." Ohio Flat (1856, 1858) stated that water in the district "shall be governed by the usages in" the district, with no explicit reference to temporal priority. According to the code of Upper Yuba (1852):

> Resolved, That no Company shall monopolize a Stream of Water for Speculation or unnecessarily use it to the injury of others.[78]

These latter statements are obviously a far cry from any sort of unconditional first possession right.

Regarding the resolution of disputes over water, I could find only one district—Brown's Flat—that explicitly mandated that first possession would be the controlling principle. Brown's Flat (185?) simply stated: "In all disputes concerning water, priority of use shall have precedence." The statement in the code of Ohio Flat (1856, 1858) to the effect that water "shall be governed by the usages in" the district, presumably included disputes over water and nowhere else in the Ohio Flat code was mentioned any notion of first possession rights. Most codes that explicitly treated water disputes, however, created a system of arbitration in which water disputes would be resolved by a set of disinterested persons. This was true, for example, of Springfield (1852), Saw Mill Flat (1854), Little Humbug Creek (1856), and Maine Little Humbug Creek (1856).[79]

In chapter 2, I derived the general hypothesis that the adoption of individualized water rights should be negatively correlated with the "publicness" of water use, as well as the specific hypotheses relating to quantification, transfer restrictions, and first possession. The question becomes how to test these hypotheses. Inspecting the miners' codes, one piece of information available to us is whether a particular district happens to comprise dry or wet diggings, or some combination of the two. Water used in wet diggings was typically not used in a way that physically consumed it. Panners, and miners using rockers-and-cradles, had little effect on the river. When water was diverted for the purpose of river bed mining, it was not taken far: the wooden flumes typically turned the water back into the river just downstream of the diggings. Water taken to dry diggings, however, was transported from rivers and streams that were physically removed from, and sometimes some distance from, the diggings. This water was often not turned back into the river from which it was taken and when it was, it could be laden with silt, dirt, and debris, all by-products of the gold separation process. In short, dry diggings were generally much more consumptive of surface waters, both in terms of reduced quantity and quality. In terms of our model, miners in wet diggings tended to have larger recharge coefficients than their counterparts in dry diggings. Consequently, use of the water took on more of the character of a private good in dry diggings.

Given the data available in many mining codes, there are several testable hypotheses here. The first is that water rights would be more likely to be quantified in dry diggings. In our earlier discussion of quantification, we identified five mining camps whose codes had quantified water rights in some form: Garote, Bodie, Smith's Flat, Oregon Gulch, and Weaverville. Available evidence strongly suggests that each one of these camps were largely, if not entirely, dry diggings. None of these camps were located on significant waterways. A contemporary description of

Garote mentions its "extensive" placer mines including some underlying a mountain where tunnel mining was being prosecuted, and the need to divert and bring water from the nearby Tuolumne River to the mines.[80] Bodie comprised a ten-mile square area containing various types of claims including flat, hill, ravine, and gulch claims.[81] Smith's Flat contained surface, ravine, and hill claims, including an entire set of laws devoted to hill claims exclusively. It also explicitly considered water development, including digging a ditch or constructing a sluice, to fulfill its labor requirement for maintaining a claim.[82] Oregon Gulch exclusively contained surface and hill claims, and considered claims to be workable only when water could be "conveniently obtained."[83] Many of the miners of Weaverville relied heavily on certain ditches for water supply, in the building of which ditch companies had incurred "considerable expense."[84] Given the predominantly dry diggings of these five camps, it makes sense that they would have attempted to quantify water entitlements, even if they were limited by the primitive measurement technologies of the time.

As for our other hypotheses, Table 5.1 summarizes the water provisions in the miners' codes regarding right acquisition/dispute resolution and the exporting of water for those thirty miners' codes that explicitly treat water in a substantive way. In addition to these particular issues this includes, for example, work requirements and claim sizes that were conditional on water availability. Column (2) reports the county in which the camp was located. Columns (3) and (4) report the year the code was written and a rough characterization of the type of mining that occurred within the camp. These characterizations were arrived at as we did previously, through careful examination of the code provisions and corroborative material such as county histories and other historical accounts.[85] In Table 5.1, the difference between "wet/dry" and "dry/wet" is that the apparent predominant form of diggings is listed first. In column (5), "FP" means that acquisition of water rights was explicitly based upon the principle of first possession in some form while "NFP" means that the code either was silent on the issue or specified some other mechanism, such as arbitration or jury trial. Column (6) lists whether a code explicitly imposed restrictions on exportations of water from the mining camp.

The evidence in Table 5.1 suggests that dry diggings tended to adopt the principle of first possession and that wet diggings tended to restrict

TABLE 5.1. **Water provisions in mining codes**

District	County	Year	Diggings	Right Acquisition	Exportations Permitted?
Bodie	Mono	1860	Dry/Wet	NFP	No provision
Brown's Flat	Tuolumne	1853?	Dry/Wet	FP	Not allowed
Centreville and Helltown	Butte	1857	Dry/Wet	FP	No provision
Columbia	Tuolumne	1856	Dry/Wet	NFP	No provision
Con Cow	Butte	1851	Dry	FP	No provision
French Creek	El Dorado	1854	Wet/Dry	NFP	No provision
Garote	Tuolumne	1851?	Wet	NFP	No provision
Hungry Creek	Siskiyou	1857	Wet	NFP	Not allowed
Jacksonville	Tuolumne	1851?	Wet	NFP	No provision
Jamestown	Tuolumne	1853	Dry	FP	No provision
Lagrange	Tuolumne	1855	Dry/Wet	NFP	No provision
Little Humbug Creek	Siskiyou	1856	Wet	NFP	Not allowed
Lovelock	Butte	1864	Dry/Wet	FP	No provision
Lower Calaveritas	Calaveras	1857	Dry/Wet	NFP	No provision
Lower Humbug Creek	Siskiyou	1855	Wet	NFP	No provision
Maine Little Humbug Creek	Siskiyou	1856	Wet	NFP	Now allowed
Murphy's	Calaveras	1857	Dry/Wet	NFP	No provision
Ohio Flat	Yuba	1858	Wet/Dry	NFP	No provision
Oregon Gulch	Butte	1855	Dry/Wet	NFP	Restricted
Oro Fino	Siskiyou	1856	Dry/Wet	NFP	No provision
Rich Gulch	Butte	1852	Dry	FP	No provision
Saw Mill Flat	Tuolumne	1854	Wet/Dry	NFP	No provision
Shaw's Flat	Tuolumne	1854	Dry/Wet	NFP	No provision
Smith's Flat	El Dorado	1855	Dry	NFP	No provision
Springfield	Tuolumne	1852	Dry	NFP	No provision
Sucker Flat	Yuba	1855	Dry/Wet	NFP	No provision
Upper Yuba	Yuba	1852	Wet	NFP	No monopoly
Warren Hill	Plumas	1853	Dry	FP	No provision
Weaverville	Trinity	1853	Dry	FP	No provision
Weaverville	Trinity	1853	Wet	NFP	Not allowed

FP: First possession; NFP: Not first possession

exports from the camp. No wet diggings mandated first possession, whereas five out of seven entirely dry diggings did. To further investigate this impression, Table 5.2 reports the results of a series of logit regressions of both (a) adoption of first possession, and (b) restrictions on exports, on the type of diggings, sometimes controlling for a possible time trend. In these regressions, DIGGINGS is a count variable that takes integer values from 0 to 3 depending on the type of diggings where 0 indicates entirely wet, 1 indicates wet/dry, 2 indicates dry/wet, and 3 indi-

TABLE 5.2. **Did the type of diggings influence the adoption of first possession? Evidence from 30 codes**

	First Possession			Exportation		
	(1)	(2)	(3)	(4)	(5)	(6)
Diggings	2.72**	2.24**	1.71*	−1.22**	−1.25**	−1.20**
	(1.28)	(0.94)	(0.92)	(0.50)	(0.51)	(0.51)
Year	0.14		−1.46	−0.10		0.33
	(0.20)		(0.93)	(0.24)		(1.25)
Year X Year			0.11			−0.04
			(0.07)			(0.12)
Constant	−7.58**	−5.70**	−0.74	0.79	0.34	−0.23
	(3.84)	(2.25)	(3.84)	(1.32)	(0.68)	(3.04)
Percentage correct	83.3	83.3	90.0	83.3	83.3	83.3

N = 30.
Figures in parentheses are estimated standard errors.
* Significant at 10%.
** Significant at 5%.

cates entirely dry. The signs and significance level of the coefficients on DIGGINGS indicate that dry diggings were indeed more likely to adopt first possession and less likely to restrict exports.[86] It is also of interest that there is weak evidence that the adoption of first possession was a quadratic function of time, with the predicted probability of adoption starting to rise after 1857. This is only suggestive, however, as the estimated coefficients on the time variables are not significant at standard levels.

This overall pattern of results is consistent with the theoretical prediction that individual rights would tend to emerge when water use was consumptive and therefore, took on the nature of a private good, while group rights would tend to emerge when water use was nonconsumptive and therefore, took on the nature of a public good.[87] These findings are consistent with the conclusions of numerous scholars who note that restrictions on out-of-basin transfers from surface water sources may support more efficient use of water in the presence of significant return flows.[88] It is also consistent with my earlier 2003 study, which concluded that nineteenth-century water institutions were crafted at least in part to maximize rents from water use within the watershed.[89]

5.7. Conclusions

Considering that they were operating largely in the absence of official institutions with enforcement authority, it is striking how well the system of extralegal mining camps worked. They largely kept order, and they created mining and water rights that supported the successful prosecution of mining, including encouraging the investment in mining infrastructure that was becoming increasingly important to placer mining. Furthermore, in most cases the code provisions largely permitted miners and mining companies to operate at efficient scales of operation, and they responded to the steady depletion of local gold deposits over time with more rigorous work requirements and by providing extra incentives for new discoveries. With regard to water, the pattern of code provisions concerning quantification, first possession, and water exports reflected the setting in which water was used. In wet diggings, water rights were less likely to be quantified, less likely to be subject to first possession, and more likely to be subject to restrictions on export. These findings with regard to water are consistent with the prediction that individualized water rights would be more likely to emerge when water assumes greater private good properties, consistent with the rent-maximization model in chapter 2.

None of this is to argue that the mining camps were completely successful in keeping crime down and promoting efficient mining and water use, but they could have done a lot worse. The system, however, could not last. Over time, the official legal institutions of the state were coming on line and the costs of enforcing the official institutions were gradually decreasing for a variety of reasons. The system of mining camp law would slowly give way to a system of common-law principles created by the courts. The pressures that motivated the transition to the official institutions is the subject of the next chapter.

CHAPTER SIX

Origins of the Common Law of Mining and Water Rights

6.1. Introduction

The development of institutional rules governing water rights in the mining camps was, of course, merely the beginning of post-statehood water law in California. The "official" common law governing water rights would be left to the courts, who would determine within a far less democratic setting what a water right would consist of and how disputes would be resolved. They accomplished this in a series of rulings during the 1850s so that by the eve of the Civil War, the judicial treatment of many dimensions of water rights had been set in place. However, the transition from the mining camp system to the courts—the subject of this chapter—is itself worth considering for a couple of reasons. First, the mining camp system and the courts may be considered institutional alternatives designed to govern the same process: establishing rights to, and resolving disputes over, mining and water rights. Considering the move from one institutional regime to another will shed light on the relative costs of the two regimes, in terms of how well they serviced these objectives, and how they were changing over time.

In addition, examining the transition from extralegal to legal institutions raises certain questions that demand further reflection and explanation. Many of these questions are raised by the fact that mining camp bylaws were contemporaneous with the operation of the court system and indeed, continued to be written and revised for many years after the courts began to hand down rulings. Why did mining codes continue to be written even years after the court system was set in place? Why would miners bring their disputes to court if they had a local mechanism in place to deal with them? And more generally, how do we understand the observed slow but steady movement during this early period from the mining camp rules to the official common-law doctrine promulgated by the court system? It is hoped that this chapter will answer more questions than it raises.

6.2. The Creation of Legal Institutions and the Court System

The useful fiction we are adopting that the gold fields were devoid of official institutions when the gold seekers arrived was not, of course, literally true. Under Mexican rule, there had been a well-established system of organized civil government and a long tradition of Spanish civil law. The particulars of the Mexican system will not be described at any length here, but it is worth noting a few facts. First, when a change of government regime occurs, it is not the case that all of the previous governmental institutions and procedures vanish instantly without a trace. When the Treaty of Guadalupe Hidalgo was signed in early 1848, California had been under de facto military rule for about a year and a half, since Commodore Sloat had captured Monterey in an early campaign of the War in July of 1846. Since then, a succession of military governors had administered the region in anticipation of the end of the War and the establishment of a territorial government.

In line with prevailing customary law, the military governors had established a policy of honoring existing Mexican law in the conquered region. Scarcely one month after Sloat had captured Monterey, Commodore Stockton, the second military governor, proclaimed that the conquered region would be subject to military law until it became a Territory.[1] However, he went on:

> In the meantime the people will be permitted, and are now requested to meet in their several towns and departments, at such time and place as they may see fit to elect civil officers and fill the places of those who decline to continue in office; and to administer the laws according to the former usages of the territory.[2]

In principle, "former usages" meant the principles and operational structure of the previous system of civil law under Mexican rule. Mexican civil law largely persisted through the time of transition to statehood, and vestiges of Mexican rule continued after California became a state, but mostly in the form of rights to land granted to private citizens under Mexican rule.[3] As for operational structure, the Mexican system of civil government was based upon nonmilitary secular towns called *pueblos*. Depending upon its size, each pueblo was headed by one or more popularly elected magistrates known as *alcaldes*. Under the Mexican system, the alcalde combined judicial, legislative, and executive powers in administering a pueblo and resolving disputes among citizens, and he was a key component of the operation of the system.[4]

The alcalde system would continue throughout the era of military occupation and into early statehood, and it served two important functions in the transition from the Mexican civil law system to the California system, which would be based upon English common law. First, the alcalde system provided an operational bridge to the official court system until it got on its feet. For example, Stephen J. Field, forty-niner and future chief justice of the State Supreme Court, was elected as the first alcalde of Yubaville in January of 1850 when there was still uncertainty regarding whether the new state constitution was going to be recognized by Congress. He served until June 1850, when the first official judge of the Eighth Judicial District, William Turner, took over.[5] During his time as alcalde, Field was given very broad purview to address all sorts of disputes, both civil and criminal. Without the existing structure of the alcalde system, it is unclear whether any official legal structure and procedures would have been available to address the various legal issues that could and did arise, at least until the new state judiciary became operational.

Second, the alcalde system almost serendipitously served to smooth the doctrinal transition between the Mexican and California legal systems. At the outset of American occupation, existing alcaldes were invited to retain their positions and continue in their current magisterial capacity. Some, however, resigned and were replaced by American alcaldes appointed by Sloat and then his successor Stockton. In September 1846, Stockton called for a general election of alcaldes, which further accelerated the installation of Americans in alcalde positions. By 1848, most of the alcaldes in California were Americans.[6]

The turnover in the identity of the alcaldes gradually led to some fundamental changes in the application of the law. Many of the new alcaldes had little or no knowledge of Spanish law nor the ability to read what texts were available, most of which were written in Spanish. Consequently, there was a natural tendency for them to fall back on what they knew of common-law principles, many of them having come from common-law jurisdictions. Gradually, common-law influence began to seep into the practice of law. For example, Walter Colton, the alcalde at Monterey and one of the more successful early alcaldes, introduced the practice of a trial by jury in early 1847. This practice became common in the courts of other alcaldes prior to statehood even though the practice was unknown in Spanish and Mexican law.[7]

Not that the transition period provided by the alcalde system was always smooth and seamless. Field and Colton were probably unusual in the level of competence, background, and experience they brought to the job. Others may have had much less knowledge of the common law, and those who were unfamiliar with common law were likely at a severe disadvantage since law texts were extremely scarce in California during this period. Some may have simply borrowed wholesale and applied what little knowledge of the common law that they had, including James Zabriskie, an alcalde for Sacramento whose entire law library consisted of one volume of New Jersey law.[8] And in January of 1847, the *California Star* was heard to complain about another alcalde's decision on how to define the common law in his jurisdiction:

> We have heard a few days since that the alcalde of Sonoma had adopted the whole volume of Missouri statutes as the law for the government of people in his jurisdiction. If this is allowed, we will have as many legislatures in California as we have alcaldes or justices of the peace, and the country will be thrown into more confusion in a short time than ever existed in any part of the world inhabited by civilized men.[9]

It is worth adding that a single decision by this alcalde may have had quite a large impact, as Sonoma encompassed an area from the San Francisco Bay all the way up to the Oregon border.

Perhaps because of a somewhat checkered record of alcalde rulings, successive military governors of California attempted to impose quality control over alcaldes. When he became governor in 1847, General Kearny replaced naval officers who had been appointed by Stockton with civilians. He also closely monitored the decisions of some alcaldes in coastal areas, and sometimes circumscribed, or even reversed, their rulings. Kearny's successor Colonel Mason exercised care in his appointments of alcaldes, attempting to place the offices in the hands of "trust-worthy and capable people."[10]

The move to the state court system began in 1849, when the new state constitution established many of the particulars of the state court system-to-be while leaving others for the legislature to hash out. According to the constitution, the state Supreme Court was to consist of three justices elected to overlapping six-year terms. The state was divided into judicial districts, the precise number to be determined by the legislature, each presided over by an elected judge. District courts were given original jurisdiction in large-claims civil cases (where the amount in dispute exceeded $200), and thus handled the most important disputes involving mining and water. The state Supreme Court was the immediate court of appeal for rulings of the district courts. Justice courts were to handle small-claims civil cases and were to be presided over by elected justices of the peace whose jurisdiction encompassed the township in which they were elected. Appeals from Justice courts were to be handled in county courts.[11]

In the very first legislative session convened in late 1849, the legislature created a court system along these lines, headed by three elected Supreme Court justices and consisting of nine judicial districts, and it more fully spelled out the powers and duties of the district judges. District judges could administer oaths, issue subpoenas and writs of mandamus and habeas corpus, could punish for contempt with fines and imprisonment, and were required to recuse themselves in case of conflict of interest. In a separate act, the legislature set out detailed procedures for bringing civil actions in the district courts. Actions involving issues of fact were to be tried by a jury, unless waived by the parties involved. Since many water disputes centered on issues of fact, district cases involving water disputes commonly involved jury trials.[12]

The first legislature anticipated that it would take a while for the new court system to be fully functional and thus also provided for a managed transition from the court system existing under Mexican rule. Pending cases were assigned to the new Supreme Court for review. Once judicial elections had taken place and the new district courts were formed, the existing Courts of First Instance were abolished. Appeals from the Courts of First Instance were then remitted to the new district courts.[13]

Once the court system was in place, disputes involving mining and water quickly made their way into the system. The experience of the Placer

County district court is suggestive of the types and frequency of disputes involving water that were brought before district courts in mining country during the 1850s. The very first case brought before that court occurred in June 1851, when a contractor brought a complaint against a ditch company for nonpayment for digging a ditch, an indication of early vertical disintegration in the fledgling ditch industry.[14] This was followed by a similar dispute in July of the following year, and similar nonpayment cases occurred periodically for the remainder of the decade.[15] In October 1853, the first in a long series of cases occurred that involved an upstream diversion depriving a downstream company of water.[16] Additional cases for the remainder of the decade covered other issues, the most common of which were destruction of ditch facilities, mining operations degrading water quality, leaking ditches flooding mining operations, and destruction of mining or ditch operations from collapsing dams (see Table 6.1).

Mining and water cases quickly made their way into the decisions of the state Supreme Court as well. In its first judicial session in 1850, the Court handed down two mining-related decisions, one involving a shareholder dispute for a mining company organized in New York and the other ruling on the constitutionality of a statute levying a special tax on foreign miners.[17] In 1853 the Supreme Court handed down its first ruling involving a water dispute, in *Eddy v. Simpson*, reversing a district court decision that had permitted a diversion of water from a stream to the detriment of a prior plaintiff. For the remainder of the decade, disputes involving both mining and the development and use of water for mining purposes were regularly heard by the Supreme Court.

TABLE 6.1. **A taxonomy of water disputes, Placer County: 1851 to mid-1859**

Issue	No. of cases
(1) Nuisance/Tort	
Downstream damages	
Diversion/Water quality degradation	30
Bursting dam/Water releases	4
Destruction/Expropriation of ditch property	11
Upstream damages: Downstream obstruction/backwaters flood upstream	1
(2) Contractual	
Water supply: Nonpayment/Nondelivery	4
Ditch construction: Nonpayment/Nonconstruction	5
Shareholder dispute	1

6.3. The Instability of the Miners' Camp System

The creation of an official state court system, however, did not spell the end of the miners' codes and tribunals. Indeed, miners' codes continued to be written for years (see Figure 6.1) and miners' tribunals continued to play an important role in resolving mining and water disputes for some time. The simultaneous existence of both avenues for crafting mining and water rights and resolving disputes over a number of years speaks to the practical utility of such a dual system. It also raises questions regarding the respective roles of the courts and the miners' institutions. One might ask, for example, why the miners' codes and tribunals didn't simply disappear after the courts came on the scene. And given that they were presented with a choice, why would miners opt to take their grievances through potentially costly court proceedings rather than trying to solve them locally within the jurisdiction of a camp?

In the last chapter, we explored the notion of mining codes as the product of collective action at the local level, as a means of mitigating rent dissipation resulting from disputes over complex common-property resources; namely, gold and water. There we saw the economic logic of the codes as reflecting economies of scale in mining, depletion of mining deposits, and the external effects of water use on other miners. While

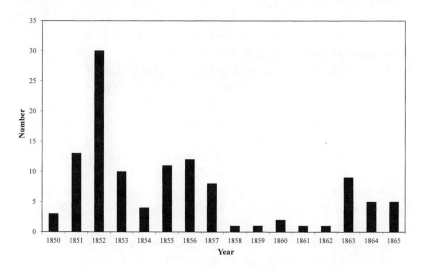

FIGURE 6.1. Number of miners' codes written per year, 1850–1865

we were able to document the importance of these economic factors, the analysis was incomplete in that it failed to consider the internal political dynamics of individual camps and how these might affect governance outcomes. In fact, the available evidence is suggestive of much tension internal to the camps among miners over various governance issues. These included camp rules on claim sizes, the buying and selling of claims, arbitrary enforcement of camp rules, and corruption of camp officials. The previous chapter did not examine these issues, in order to focus on the economic logic of the camps. But a complete understanding of the mining camp system requires an appreciation of the impact of these internal tensions on the operation of the system.

Traditional interpretations of the movement from miners' codes to the state courts in the 1850s have been largely apolitical, emphasizing structural changes that were occurring over time rather than examining the internal dynamics of the mining camp. Rodman Paul, for example, argues that local mining laws tended to be vague and were slow to change as mining conditions changed, which made them difficult to enforce, encouraging miners to either circumvent or ignore them. Furthermore, over time the pressures on the mining camp system only increased as stakes grew and the legal issues involved in dispute resolution became increasingly complex.[18] Charles McCurdy has emphasized the growing "multiplicity of interests" that threatened to cripple the rational development of the mining regions, which led to heavier reliance on the official court system.[19] However, the interests he refers to are not political but rather, the wide variety of economic uses to which the mining regions could be put.

Much evidence suggests that in fact, internal politics played an important role in influencing mining camp outcomes. As early as the summer of 1851, the *Alta Californian* was observed editorializing that mining codes notoriously supported special interests within the camps:

> The resolutions and expressions of opinion of the various conventions of miners are so dissimilar, so irreconcilable, and so partial in their character, that the matter appears to us to be getting more and more into the fog as the subject is more and more discussed. In the proceedings of none of the miners meetings do we see any approach to an attempt to bring forward a systematic and general plan for the regulation and government of the mines, and for the preservation and protection of the rights of all. *All the schemes proposed are merely local in their character, and appear more intended to protect the sepa-*

rate interests of some particular and individual company, than to evince a de-
sire to advance the interests of all by establishing the mining system upon a
good and just basis.[20] (emphasis added)

An intriguing example of the internal politics of mining camps occurred
in the winter of 1853 in Sonora, a mining camp in Tuolumne County,
when an elected council was accused of improperly awarding a valuable grant of land to a single mining company consisting of six individuals. The charge was that the council had been bribed by the company to
grant to it an exclusive right to mine an entire mile of Sonora Creek for
ten years.[21] This charge was strenuously denied by others who argued
that miners on the creek had failed to make living wages and that the
grant in question afforded "the only means of working (the) claims successfully."[22] The truth of these allegations aside, both of these items suggest a vigorous internal struggle over the distribution of available rents.

Perhaps because of suggestive evidence such as this, more recent
scholarship has begun to explore the internal politics of the mining
camp in order to understand the move toward increasing reliance on the
courts. Donald Pisani has, for example, emphasized the competing interests of groups of miners in the creation of water law in the mining
camps. In his view, one important source of conflict in mining camps
in the early 1850s was diversions of water away from surface sources by
large companies, to the detriment of smaller operations situated on wet
diggings along the waterway. One example of this occurred in Weaverville in 1853 when tensions over such a diversion led to a complaint being
filed in the district court of Trinity County in 1854.[23] But it seems fair to
say that existing scholarship has not fully developed the internal political
dynamics of mining camps, which may be a relevant piece of the puzzle
in understanding the movement to the courts.

The strategy pursued here will be to consider mining camps and the
official courts as alternative governance pathways for defining rights
and settling disputes. The very first camps were created at a time when
the official State courts did not yet exist and Mexican law could not be
readily enforced, nor did it command the deference of miners, in the
gold fields. This left the mining codes with what was, for all intents and
purposes, a legal monopoly in any particular locality. If miners chafed
under the local rules in a camp, they had four choices, not necessarily mutually exclusive: do their best working within the rules, work pri-

vately to circumvent the rules, work collectively to try to change them, or move on.

As the court system became operational, it provided a fifth choice for miners: instead of having to operate within, and settle for the options provided by, the camp codes, miners could choose to avail themselves of the court system. If, for example, a miner took a dispute to a miners' court and received an unfavorable outcome, he could take his chances in a county or district court. Or he could choose to go directly to the official courts, circumventing the miners' court entirely. The incentive to pursue a court solution would have been especially strong if mining camp procedures were viewed as biased, arbitrary, or favoring certain interests. Running to the courts for relief was counteracted to some extent by mining camp norms and customs, particularly when these resulted in social pressure, ostracism, or worse. However, it seems unlikely that it was eliminated entirely.

The optimal choice for a miner depended upon a variety of factors, including the magnitude of local enforcement costs; the negotiation costs associated with achieving effective collective action; and the relative costs of using the camp system instead of the court system. The more costly it was for a camp to enforce its regulations, the more likely it was that miners would try to exploit loopholes in order to capture more rents.[24] This would be especially true if there were not good opportunities elsewhere, making the opportunity cost of working within the camp system relatively low. It would also be true if the transaction costs of working to change those rules were high as well. These transaction costs would have depended upon a number of factors that affected the likelihood that effective coalitions for change could form. Keeping in mind the democratic nature of the process within the camps that produced the codes, these effective coalitions would have been more likely to form if large numbers of miners with large stakes in the outcome favored change, and these miners had interests that were similar enough for them to present a unified front.[25]

Much evidence suggests that the early camps were plagued with significant enforcement costs. First, as we have seen, the codes made an effort to be reasonably clear about how much claim land a miner was entitled to. Nevertheless, miners were afforded ample opportunity to capture extra rents by fiddling with the initial boundaries of their claims. According to Charles Shinn, for example, miners in Shaw's Flat ran the lines of their claims "irregularly as to include more of the good mining ground than they were entitled to," a problem which Shinn goes on to say was endemic to "hundreds" of early camps.[26] Part of the issue was topography. Establishing unambiguous claim boundaries in flats was relatively straightforward, where claims could be regular shapes, typically so many feet square. It was much more challenging in ravines, gulches, and hills, where claims followed the contours of the land and could extend an indefinite number of feet laterally underground. This meant that miners could exploit the opportunities generated by varying topography and the fact that it was costly for camp officials to monitor the drawing of claim boundaries. It should be added that this issue probably became increasingly problematic over time as claim sizes became larger in new codes, likely increasing monitoring costs.

Second, despite the attempts by the codes to promote orderly digging within the camp, disputes commonly arose over which mining company enjoyed the right to work a particular claim. The codes generally specified how claim limits were to be marked, typically by erecting "substantial" stakes at the corners of the claim, digging a shallow trench around the perimeter, posting a written notice somewhere on the claim or nearby, and/or notifying the camp recorder to make a record of the claim. The problem was that these were by no means foolproof ways of communicating one's claim to the rest of the world. As one miner put it:

> Of what avail is it to put up notices, which a breath of wind may blow away, which the weather may deface, and which any vagabond may tear down?[27]

Similarly, stakes and stones could be moved, trees to which claim notices were affixed could fall down, trenches could be filled in, recorders could be bribed. One can easily see how disputes over claims could arise, as well as the enforcement challenges presented to a camp.[28]

Work requirements also created enforcement challenges. This was partly attributable to the fact that miners were not literally working all the time. Indeed, most of the work requirements in the mining codes cannot be described as terribly onerous in terms of how much work they required miners to do to maintain their claims. Figure 6.2 reports the required number of days of work per six-month period for a sample of sixty-one mining camps.[29] Only one camp—Pilot Hill, in El Dorado County—required as much as one day's work in three, and this camp was a significant outlier. On the other hand, six camps required fewer

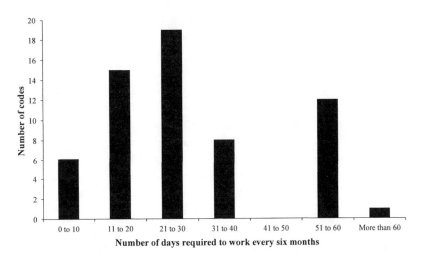

FIGURE 6.2. How onerous was the work requirement? Evidence from 61 camps.

than ten days' work over the entire six-month span. The median number of days of work was twenty-six, meaning miners were required to work their claims about once per week. This is not to argue that many miners did not work considerably more than this, and most undoubtedly did. But camp rules permitted miners to be away from their claims a lot.

It was when they were absent or not working their claims, however, that others were more likely to try to expropriate them. During the early Gold Rush, when technologies were simple, claiming methods were informal, and mining was largely itinerant, this could occur out of ignorance that someone was already there.[30] However, if one miner coveted another's claim, the fact that it was not being worked provided a convenient pretext for entering onto that claim. In this regard, the exceptions for accident or illness that most codes contained, though considered fair and humane, could actually make it more difficult for miners to hang onto their claims. Drummond and Martinez relate the story of a man who fell ill and thus, was not required by the local code to work his claim. But after repeatedly warning others off his claim, he lost it to claim jumpers when a ditch from Columbia was completed, thus dramatically increasing its value. It would have been considerably less likely that this miner would have lost his claim had he been actively working it. According to Drummond and Martinez, this was "a case picked out of many hundreds."[31]

The second factor that would determine the miner's choice of action involves the transaction costs associated with engaging in collective action to revise the codes. This is, of course, the arena in the camps where the politics would have played out. I will presume that engaging in private actions to capture rents at the operational level did not preclude efforts to alter the rules at the level of collective action, and conversely. But obviously the two are related: effective changes in the rules of the camp in one's favor may well have reduced one's propensity to try to circumvent the new, now-more-favorable rules. In this section, I will explore what was probably the most important way in which collective action politics would have played out: in the struggle between existing miners and newcomers over available rents in the local deposits.

Throughout much of this period, perhaps the most important persistent source of contention among miners derived from the fact that the population of a mining camp was extremely dynamic. The first miners to arrive in an area would sit down and devise a code that reflected the interests of every miner then present.[32] As we have seen, this would include regulations on the size of a claim, the buying and selling of claims, and the number of claims a miner could hold, all of which were designed to facilitate the maximal working of the deposits. This implied that regulations would be written that permitted the entire area to be "claimed up." When new miners arrived, they would naturally agitate for regulations that would permit them to work. The alternatives were to either purchase claims from existing miners, or to hire out to work for someone else, both vastly inferior alternatives to many miners.[33] All of this would have generated pressure for codes to be revised to accommodate more miners. Whether code revisions would actually take place depended upon the effectiveness of the new miners as a political coalition. As we have argued, if they were numerous and unified, and had large stakes in the outcome, they would likely have been politically effective and able to obtain change.

That the newcomers were all of these things is suggested by much anecdotal evidence, along with the fact that practically speaking, they were often indeed able to obtain revisions to the mining codes in ways that benefited them. When newcomers came into a camp and found the land taken up in large plots, they issued calls for public meetings for reductions in plot sizes to accommodate them, and they were often successful.[34] Early on, one miner commented on the challenges to miners who attempted to organize with the objective of keeping newcomers out:

However, it was possible for the first two or three men in an area to constitute themselves "a body politic" and organize a district before the stampede inundated them. Such tactics availed them little if they went in for trick legislation, for subsequent additions to the camp might refuse to sign any document that did not conform more or less to the general practice elsewhere.[35]

This statement speaks not only to the power of newcomers, but also to the importance of general norms that obtained throughout the gold fields, both of which imposed limitations on the ability of first-comers to have their way. He went on to say that in his experience, discontented miners were free to call for a reassessment of camp rules at any time merely by "posting a conspicuous notice, stating the time and place of a meeting and the subject that was to be the topic of discussion."[36] Thus, it seems that generally speaking, camps were set up to accommodate the interests and demands of newcomers. Since newcomers who desperately wanted to get at the gold were often likely to be numerous and highly united in their demands for generally smaller claim sizes, it is not surprising that they were often successful in achieving their political goals.

It is probably useful to square this argument with the observation made in the previous chapter that for mining codes in my database, claim sizes in new codes were steadily *increasing* over time, particularly during the Later period after 1854. It should also be noted that when existing camp codes underwent revision, it was commonly the case that the revised codes contained larger claim size limits.[37] The most plausible interpretation of these trends probably relates not to internal camp dynamics but rather, the growing use of new more capital- and water-intensive technologies along with ongoing depletion of the gold deposits over time. The new technologies increased the amount of deposits that could be processed, while the richness of the local deposits determined not the maximum claim size but rather, the *minimum* claim size. That is, claim sizes needed to be sufficiently large to make it worthwhile for individual mining companies to operate.[38] As depletion of existing deposits occurred and/or new, less-rich deposits were opened up, observed claim size limits would have reflected this reality. The fact that my database contains no downward revisions of claim size limits probably reflects considerable missing data on early codes, as well as the likely fact that political agitation for smaller claim sizes likely occurred most during the Early period corresponding largely to rush conditions.

The third factor that would influence a miner's actions in case of dispute in a camp was the existence of an alternative to the camp system, as well as the perceived attractiveness of that alternative. This alternative avenue was the state court system, which had official jurisdiction over all civil matters relating to property disputes. For disputes involving more than $200 in property value, parties had to file a complaint with the local district court, incur lawyer fees, and expend a perhaps considerable amount of time and energy in court proceedings. The advantage of going through this process was the prospect of procuring an injunction against a damaging practice, receiving an award of damages, or compelling the payment of an outstanding debt, all backed by the administrative apparatus of the state.

Existing scholarship paints a diverse picture of the movement to the courts. Rodman Paul emphasizes structural changes that were occurring, such as increasing stakes, growing legal complexities, and lack of standardization of the various mining codes, which made the mining camps increasingly inadequate for dealing with mining disputes.[39] Others have stressed miners' suspicion of the courts, which gradually diminished over time, a process that made miners less apt to want to settle matters on their own and more willing to bring their disputes to the courts.[40] Still others have argued that in fact, miners retained a general reluctance to cede their autonomy to any external authority, courts or legislature, throughout the period considered here.[41] Each of these positions has some validity and can be supported by evidence, but none touches sufficiently on the internal workings of the camps themselves and how they also contributed to the movement to the courts.

In fact, though the miners were indeed suspicious of external authorities, the institutions they designed themselves had problems of their own. We have already gotten a sense for this from our earlier discussion of the costs of enforcing and writing camp rules. Significant costs experienced by camps in enforcing their own provisions created the potential for disputes over staking claim boundaries and working claims. The ability of newcomers to take effective collective action resulted in miners' codes being rewritten to reduce claim sizes. Both of these developments promoted uncertainty regarding the security of miners' claims, which discouraged investment in mining and water development. As early as summer of 1851, calls were being made for the state to take legislative action to regulate the gold fields in order to render property more secure, such as the following statement that appeared in the *Alta Californian.*

Laws should be passed to secure property in mines, and to establish order
and preserve the peace among the miners. . . . [The] mines should be . . . under the direction of the State Legislature, . . . hav[ing] no power to alienate
or dispose of the soil, but . . . confined to the simple purpose of providing the
regulations which are demonstrated from day to day to be necessary.[42]

What is interesting about this statement for our purposes here is the
apparent willingness to be regulated by the state government, if it meant
more secure property rights and law and order in the gold fields. The
strong suggestion is that the mining codes and local tribunals were not
sufficient to accomplish these things. What the statement does not make
clear is why property rights were insecure, nor why it was important, as
if this would be stating the obvious. These issues were explicated by one
observer in early 1854, when the *Alta Californian* published correspondence from the southern mines, near Sonora:

> Every miner has felt that his claim was precarious in its extent, and the condi-
> tions under which it was held, as a convention of miners claiming equal rights
> to determine the amount or extent of a claim might resolve new laws, and
> *work a great injury to the plans which had been based upon the first laws.*
>
> Any legislative enactments having for their object the security of the
> holder of a mining claim must be benificial [*sic*] to the miners' interest, and
> serve most effectually, . . . to "develop the mineral resources of the State," by
> securing the outlay of labor and capital, *which in many cases are now with-
> held, because there is no security in the possession of the mines claimed.*[43]
> (emphasis added)

Apparently, this correspondent believed that the rewriting of mining
codes occasioned by the arrival of newcomers discouraged investment in
mining resources by rendering property rights less secure. Again, legislation was called for to rectify the situation.

In reflecting on these two news items, it is probably no accident that
the 1854 letter spoke specifically to the problem of discouragement of investment, while the 1851 news item was completely silent on the matter.
That investment might be discouraged by insecure property rights would
not have been much of an issue during the Early period, when technologies consisted of mostly pans, rockers-and-cradles, and the occasional
long toms, none of which required significant investment in either capital or water supplies. The issues being addressed in the 1851 news item

were likely personal security and freedom from theft. However, by 1854, sizable investments were being made in mining and water development, lending an added dimension to property rights security. It is probably not coincidental that in late 1853, the Board of Mining Water Companies, an association representing ditch companies, was urging "general concert of action" among miners "for the purpose of securing the passage of some general laws which will render property in water companies more secure."[44] Given the other two news items, it is no longer surprising that again, the legislature was being asked to take action.

While mining camps were having difficulties enforcing property rights, their credibility was also being undermined by signs that the mining camp system was subject to corruption in various forms. Some local magistrates were believed to engage in bribery, extortion, favoritism, personal enrichment, and making arbitrary decisions.[45] The episode related earlier regarding the grant by an elected council in Sonora to exclusive rights to mine Sonora Creek for ten years was characterized by some as "an outrageous assumption of power" by men interested in "lin[ing] their pockets."[46] To the extent that these events occurred with any regularity, they would have delegitimized the camp system, encouraging miners to seek relief in the courts.

The Sonora Creek episode is suggestive of another issue of general concern to many miners: the danger of monopolization of available placer deposits and water supplies. Opponents of the grant characterized it as an "obnoxious monopolizing ordinance" for placing a valuable right "worth millions" in the hands of a few.[47] In a nutshell, this statement expressed the concerns of many regarding any mechanism that would permit this to occur. But perhaps of even greater concern to many miners than the actions of a corrupt council were the provisions of mining codes that permitted the amassing of claims in a completely aboveboard fashion, especially provisions that explicitly permitted the purchase of multiple, sometimes unlimited, claims.[48] Newcomers commonly asserted that mining camp laws were allowing old-timers to monopolize the most valuable claims. In April 1852, for example, the *Alta Californian* editorialized:

> Newly arrived gold seekers have long complained of the injustice of the present system of holding claims in the placers; and there is no doubt but that as soon as they have the majority they will deprive the old miners of some of the

mineral land which they claim to hold "by right of purchase." Some of the richest and best claims in many of the placers have been purchased for a trifle, from men who had no title to them, and are monopolized under the present mining laws. Newly arrived miners begin to clamor for reform, and we may expect to hear of meetings for the adoption of new regulations.[49]

Notice that what seems to be centrally at issue here is the code provision that permitted miners to purchase claims, which was mostly a right to purchase an unlimited number during the Early period and well into 1852, as we have seen.[50] The following January, the *Alta Californian* published a letter by a miner complaining about the evils of monopoly at Montezuma, a mining camp in Tuolumne County:

> There is a great deal of rich mining ground to which water can now be got, but which is not worked at present, and will not be for a long time, unless the shameful monopolies that now are allowed are broken up. The laws that obtain here were apparently borrowed from the Chinese Camp. At the latter place it has been the custom to allow a man a claim of given dimensions for himself, and then he may hold by purchase as many as he is able to pay for. So I understand it to be here, and the practice admits of the greatest abuse. A man with a small capital may under it monopolize whole acres of ground to the exclusion of others, who ought to have equal privileges with himself.[51]

Eleven days later, he wrote about the same problem being prevalent at nearby Chinese Camp:

> In a letter from Montezuma few days since, I alluded to the monopoly of ground that was allowed there. In this place [Chinese Camp] it is the same, only the evil has been continued long, and is felt to be a more grievous misfortune. In the first place, the claims here are very small, but a person may hold as many as he can purchase. This gives the man with money every advantage to the exclusion of the miner without any.[52]

For a better quantitative sense for how widespread the practice of holding multiple claims was, let us consider the actual experience of one mining camp—Junction Bluff, in Nevada County. Junction Bluff was originally contained within the Mississippi Valley mining district, but split off from it in 1854. The mining code of Mississippi Valley had specified that an individual claim could be no larger than eighty feet by one-hundred

eighty feet (about one-third of an acre), and this claim size limit was retained by Junction Bluff when it split off. At the same time, Mississippi
Valley, while restricting each miner to one claim by location, permitted
unlimited purchases of claims, and this provision was also retained by
Junction Bluff.[53]

In Junction Bluff, mining claims were initially taken up by location
and then changed hands mostly through purchase, though occasionally
by forfeiture for noncompliance with camp rules. From 1853 through
1858, district records list fifty-two locations of claims totaling over two
hundred individual claims, as mining companies averaged about four
miners per company.[54] This suggests that local deposits potentially supported at least two hundred miners in total, assuming that the district
rule of one location per miner was adhered to, which seems to have been
the case. At the same time, throughout the 1850s there was an active
market for claims within the district, permitting individual miners and
mining companies to purchase and hold multiple claims. The question is:
under these conditions, how common was it for this to occur? And how
concentrated were these claims in the hands of individual miners?

To answer these questions, it will help to consider the relation between the physical size of the district and the dimensions of individual
claims. After splitting off from Mississippi Valley, Junction Bluff contained approximately 0.4 square miles, or about 260 acres, of land.[55] According to camp records, the entire district was divided up into fifteen
subsections. On average, therefore, each subsection contained about seventeen acres of land, though the subsections appear to have varied somewhat in size. Assuming that each claim was about one-third of an acre,
each subsection in Junction Bluff on average could therefore have potentially supported fifty or so individual claims, if every single acre within
the district was workable. In fact, actual workable acreage was likely less
than this, since it is unlikely that every square inch in the district was capable of being worked. Therefore, the following calculations on the concentration of claims within each subsection should be considered to be
lower-bound estimates of how much workable land was concentrated in
the hands of individual mining companies.

In terms of both the number and concentration of claims, district records suggest that there was much variation within the district. Table 6.2
reports, for each of the subsections, the maximum number of claims held
by the largest company at any point during this period, and the year this
occurred. This information is reported in columns (1) and (2). For refer-

TABLE 6.2. **Concentration of claims, Junction Bluff mining district**

Subsection	(1) No. of Claims, Largest company	(2) Year	(3) % Total district land, Largest company[a]	(4) No. of Claims, 2nd largest company	(5) Year
Hayton	24	1855	0.47	16	1854
Unnamed	18	1855	0.35	13.17	1858
Keene	19	1857	0.37	9.25	1858
Strowbridge	23	1859	0.45	17	1854
Chipman	11.25	1855	0.22	11.25	1856
Bowles and Pease	6	1854	0.12	3	1855
Singleton and Weston	15	1855	0.29	14	1855
Buckskin	40	1859	0.78	20	1858
Sinking Fund #1	8	1855	0.16	?	
Sinking Fund #2	10	1856	0.20	8	1855
Powell	4	1855	0.08	4	1855
Negro	8	1855	0.16	8	1857
Scott	4	1856	0.08	4	1858
Abbey and Fraser	9	1857	0.18	1	1857
Cook	10	1858	0.20	10	1858

[a]Assuming each subsection contains seventeen acres of land.

ence purposes, column (3) contains the implied percentage of total area within a subsection held by the largest company, assuming that each subsection contained seventeen acres of land, and each claim was one-third of an acre. Some subsections did not experience much concentration of claims in the hands of individual companies. For example, in Powell and Scott, the largest companies had only four claims, which comprised roughly eight percent of the total potential mining area of the subsection. And in each of these cases, the claims were divided up among at least three individual miners. Among the fifteen subsections, Powell and Scott came the closest to a completely egalitarian allocation of claims among miners.

On the other hand, a number of subsections experienced a great deal of concentration in the hands of one or a handful of companies. In nine out of the fifteen subsections, or 60 percent, the largest company had at least ten claims, an amount which comprised nearly 20 percent of all of the potential mining land in the subsection, at some point in the decade.

The heaviest concentration of claims was seen in Buckskin, where one company—the Buckskin Company—at one point had managed to amass forty claims, or nearly 80 percent of all potential mining land. Though Buckskin represents the extreme instance, we can see from Table 6.2 that it was not uncommon for one company to have a large fraction of all available mining land within a subsection of the district. Column (4) reports the number of claims owned by the second largest company within the district during this period, which indicates that the largest company was not alone in aggregating claims.[56] Apparently, many miners in Junction Bluff were taking advantage of district rules to amass claims and concentrate mining lands in the hands of a few.

To help interpret this pattern of data, Figure 6.3 shows a scatter plot of the number of claims owned by the largest company against the year in which this occurred. These data suggest an upward trend in the maximum number of claims as the decade progressed. As we have seen, the adoption of hydraulic mining accelerated in Nevada County after 1856. This development would have provided impetus for consolidation of larger and larger numbers of claims over time in the hands of individual companies. Thus, these data are consistent with an increase in the minimum efficient scale of mining operations, with companies working larger and larger aggregated plots of land over time. Not only did the rules of Junction Bluff permit aggregation of claims, but also many min-

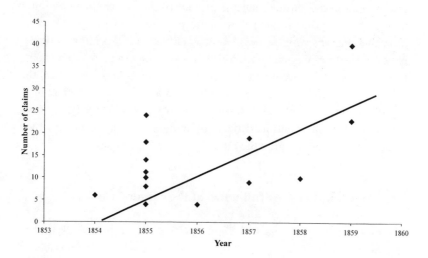

FIGURE 6.3. Number of claims, largest company, Junction Bluff. 1854–1859

ers within the district were apparently taking advantage of those rules, likely driven by growing economies of scale over time.

One might well wonder how miners were able to hold on to multiple claims when mining codes generally contained work requirements. Louisa Clappe relates how this was done at Indian Bar, on the north fork of the Feather River, in 1852. After describing the local rules regarding work requirements, she went on:

> There are many ways of evading the above law. For instance, an individual can "hold" as many "claims" as he pleases, if he keeps a man at work in each, for this workman represents the original owner . . . The person who is willing to be hired, generally prefers to receive the six dollars per diem [apparently the going wage], of which he is sure in any case, to running the risk of a claim not proving valuable. After all, the holding of claims by proxy is considered rather as a carrying out of the spirit of the law, than as an evasion of it.[57]

What is most striking about this description is not the method of using proxies to maintain possession, but rather, that using proxies was considered a perfectly acceptable way to hold multiple claims. It seems that early mining camp laws not only tried to accommodate attempts to amass claims but also actively facilitated them.

As we have seen, over time the unlimited purchase provision would become less common in new mining codes, though it continued to appear in new codes throughout this period. In the last chapter, we interpreted the temporal reduction in these provisions as partly reflecting growing concerns with fairness as the gold fields were coming to be depleted over time. We may now add that it may have also reflected some mixed success of newcomers in reining in early miners. However, the continued promotion of miners' ability to amass claims, and many miners' dissatisfaction with the resulting concentration of claims, may have contributed to the continued delegitimizing of the camp system over time, and thus encouraging the ongoing switch to the courts.

6.5. The Common-Law Influence of the Miners' Codes

The movement to the courts did not, however, mean that local miners' rules and customs gradually became irrelevant. Indeed, for a number of years local rules and customs exerted an influence over the content of court rulings and in doing so, directly affected the evolution of the common law of mining and water rights. Legal scholars and historians disagree over precisely how influential the miners' institutions turned out to be, but no one questions that they had some significant influence. The remainder of this chapter is devoted to exploring the issues of how influential the miners' institutions in fact were and the extent to which they influenced the content of the common law regarding mining and water rights.

To begin with, it is important to know that in 1851 the state legislature directed the state courts to consider and respect local "customs, usages, and regulations" in handing down rulings. The particular provision that mandated this was Section 621 of a lengthy statute that set forth rules governing proceedings in civil cases. The section read as follows:

> In actions respecting "Mining Claims", proof shall be admitted of the customs, usages, or regulations established or in force at the bar, or diggings, embracing such claim; and such customs, usages, or regulations, when not in conflict with the Constitution and Laws of this State, shall govern the decision of the action.[58]

This provision gave the miners' codes an important added dimension: they became evidentiary in official court proceedings.[59] Consequently, throughout the 1850s miners' code provisions and other evidence of local custom were commonly entered as evidence in court trials, where judges and juries would consider whether or not the rights asserted were consistent with local custom.

The most common way in which mining codes were invoked in mining disputes was as a source of legitimacy for claims made to land and water in order to protect them from expropriation by other claimants. In *Moran v. Driskill*, a mining dispute brought before the Nevada County district court in 1859, the plaintiff asked the court to instruct the jury to find for the plaintiff if they concluded from the evidence that mining claims "were located and appropriated in accordance with the customs and regulations of miners in that locality" and not abandoned. A similar stratagem had been tried in the same court in *Turner v. Morrison and Gray v. Johnson* the previous year. This stratagem was applied specifically to water rights in the 1855 Placer County case of *Bear River and Auburn Water and Mining Company v. New York Mining Company*, in which the plaintiff submitted a brief to the district court that argued that given that the claim was on public lands, water rights could be acquired only under the customs of the local mining district.[60]

The influence of the mining codes on court strategies is also observed in other cases that explored the limitations of mining code provisions in conferring legitimacy of land and water claims. In *Truxal v. Grant*, an 1857 Nevada County case, the defendant asked the court to instruct the jury that mining code revisions that expand the permissible size of claims do not apply retroactively to claims made under the old rules. In *Gray v. Johnson*, a Nevada County case handed down the following year, the plaintiff asked the court to permit it to retain a claim entered into in good faith under mining camp rules but accidentally to too much land. Finally, in *Lampman v. Gray*, a Nevada County case handed down in 1859, the plaintiff asked the court to instruct the jury that claims incorrectly recorded in a mining camp were not binding on subsequent claimants. In all of these cases, it is clear that disputants were clearly aware of the legal importance of the mining codes and invoked them when it was to their advantage to do so.[61]

The general response of the courts was largely to defer to the mining codes when they were explicit and their rules had been followed. The state Supreme Court set the tone early on in 1853 in *Hicks v. Bell* when it upheld a lower court ruling for a plaintiff in possession of claims made under local miners' customs. In *Hicks*, the fact that possession of the claim was "according to the customs of miners [in the locality]" was crucial in conferring legitimacy on the claim. Two years later, in *McClintock v. Bryden*, the Court explicitly invoked Section 621 of the 1851 Act when it took an expansive view of the rights of the miners to search for gold. In *McClintock* the Court argued that Section 621 implied that miners were empowered to seek gold "wherever (they) chose in the gold-bearing districts," including in lands already claimed and being used for agricultural purposes. The Court was clearly engaging in doctrinal overreaching at a time when gold fever was still prevalent and subsequently reversed itself in 1860 in *Smith v. Doe* and *Gillan v. Hutchinson*.[62] We will return to this issue in the next chapter.

Throughout the 1850s, the general deference to the mining codes is obvious at the lower court level as well. In an early Placer County court case, *Herrick v. Davis*, the jury found for the plaintiff in large part on the basis that he had complied with the local miner's code, which specified that claims were not considered forfeit if sufficient water was unavailable to work them. In *Gray v. Johnson*, the Nevada County district court judge explicitly instructed the jury that "complying with the requirements of the mining customs established and in force in the district" was sufficient to perfect a right. In *Turner v. Morrison*, the Nevada County judge accepted the plaintiff's instructions to the jury that complying with local rules and regulations was sufficient to constitute possession of a claim. Perhaps the clearest statement of the primacy of local mining camp rules is seen in the judge's charge to the jury in the 1859 case of *McDonald v. Vandeling*:

> Where rules, usages, and regulations have been established, and are in force in a mining district, no person can acquire the right to possession of a mining claim in that district, in any manner inconsistent with such rules, regulations, and usages.[63]

6.6. Conclusions

In this chapter, we have seen the numerous challenges experienced by the mining camp system as it struggled to provide for orderly mining of the placer deposits. The potential sources of rent dissipation were many, but they were not insuperable. In many ways, the camps were reasonably successful in promoting mining at the appropriate scale and addressing issues of externalities inflicted by mining operations, as we saw in the previous chapter. In this chapter, on the other hand, we have seen evidence of a number of issues that can, and did, arise in a largely decentralized effort to manage a common-property resource. These issues arose on both the operational level and the collective choice level. The result was a slow, halting, but clear move toward reliance on the official court system. At the broadest level, this move can be interpreted as the confluence of growing costs of the camp system and simultaneously declining costs of the court system. The argument being made here is related to Rodman Paul's position that structural change was occurring during this period, which gradually resolved the cost-benefit calculus for the two governance pathways—camps and courts—in favor of the courts. However, it goes further by understanding the ongoing changes as based in fundamental, inexorable economic realities and modulated by political rent-seeking.

But as it would turn out, far from dying out, the camps would maintain their influence through an important decision made by the state legislature: that the rules created in the camps would be controlling when brought as evidence to official court proceedings over mining and water disputes. Thus, in a sense, miners would have the best of both worlds: they would end up with the substance of many of their own rules, backed by the enforcement machinery and resources of the state. In any case, it would take some time for the courts to fully lay down a set of operational principles for governing mining and water rights, as the mining camps had provided only the most meager of guidance on a number of emerging issues. As we shall see, this judicial process occurred as disputes arose and the courts were confronted with a host of complex issues that required the crafting of a consistent set of legal principles for dealing with them. This process, and the legal principles that emerged, are the subject of the next section of this book.

The Origins of Prior Appropriation

7.1. Introduction

Toward the middle of the 1850s, the period of unofficial mining camp law ascendance gave way to emphasis on official judge-made law in the newly operational court system. It was here that the courts stepped in to craft legal principles to create mining and water rights and to resolve disputes over these rights. The Gold Rush itself was over by this point, but gold production remained strong for the rest of the decade (see Figure 7.1).[1] And the new gold mining industry bore little resemblance to the original placer mining of the Gold Rush. Instead of the small-scale, labor-intensive operations characteristic of the Early period, many mining companies were large and capital-intensive and made major demands on available water supplies. Ditch systems had become large enterprises as well, requiring sizable investments of their own. The new large-scale nature of mining and ditching, plus the fact that water development and use typically inflicted external damages on other users, created the potential for numerous conflicts to arise. Water became the subject of much litigation for the remainder of the decade, and the result was the creation of the basic doctrine of prior appropriation, which became the fundamental basis for water law not only in California but also in much of the rest of the western United States.

Three key legal concerns regarding water dominated the courts during this time. The first was a whole plethora of issues relating to defining the basic water right: precisely what it consisted of, how it was to be acquired, how it could be exercised, and how possession was to be maintained. The second and related issue was water quality: on what legal basis disputes over degraded water quality were to be resolved. The third

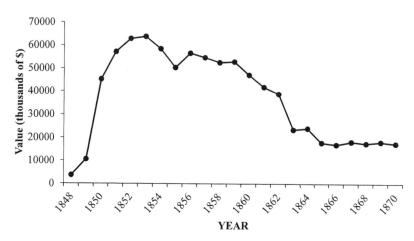

FIGURE 7.1. Gold production in California, 1848–1870

was dam failures: how disputes were to be resolved and again, on what basis. As we shall see, for each of the issues, the question of temporal priority would play an important role: who was first on the scene mattered greatly to the courts, and entered into their doctrinal positions in various ways. However, the courts struggled mightily with various issues regarding how to apply temporal priority to resolve these three types of disputes. Gradually, the courts iterated to a set of consistent principles and as we shall see, these principles all reflected a certain economic logic. Each of the next three chapters (7–9) is devoted to describing the common-law developments in the areas of basic water right definition, water quality, and dam failures. The present chapter is about the first of these issues: how the courts would go about defining the basic right to water, the primary objective being to support placer mining.

Many of the same economic currents and pressures, of course, would have been just as operant in influencing court rulings as in writing mining codes. However, the fact that the procedures for rule-making in the two settings were so different requires that we change our analytical approach now that we are switching our focus to the courts. To understand what happened in the camps, the approach was to model the camps as localized entities who self-organized to create governance structures for managing common-property resources. This was in essence the nature of the exercise for the many miners who clustered around gold deposits in various locations in the gold fields. The challenge was then to provide a sensible interpretation of their behavior as components of each of these localized exercises in collective action, in order to understand the economic properties of the overall picture. In focusing now on the courts, the spotlight will be on the courtroom, which created the official law, as situated within a broader constitutional and legislative environment. The evidence we will examine now all pertains to what happened there: not just the rulings themselves, but also plaintiff and defendant strategies, witness testimony, judges' instructions to juries, and last but not least, the content of the disputes themselves over water: what issues arose, and the circumstances. Here, the objective is to come up with a reasonable economic interpretation of the legal principles that emerged.

7.2. The Origins of First Possession in Water Rights

The available evidence suggests that the early official treatment of first possession in water paralleled, and was likely influenced by, the mining codes. It was not just a matter of the courts deferring to the codes. In fact, the same economic currents that governed the writing of the codes also affected the operation of the official court system. One way this can be seen is in the water claims that were staked by ditch companies and then subsequently submitted to county recorder offices. Consider, for example, the following water claim made by the Camp Seco Company in Tuolumne County in April of 1851:

> Said company claim that portion of said Wood's Creek which constitutes the head of said watercourse, and also so much of the water in said creek *as is not required for mining operations on said creek below our claim*. . . . They also claim the water as aforesaid in said creek, and also from the time it leaves said creek by or through said watercourse, until it returns again into said creek, including the water as distributed by said watercourse into gulches ravines and flats, and all water derived directly or indirectly from said watercourse.[2] (emphasis added)

There are several important things to note about the wording of this claim. First, given the primitive state of measurement technologies at the time, it is not surprising that the claim is not very specific about how much water is being claimed. Second, the influence of the miners' codes is observed in the deference to other miners who needed the water for their own mining operations, which was a common feature of the codes, as we have seen. This ditch company understood that its claim would have to recognize those miners' needs. But perhaps the most interesting thing about this claim is that it is *not a first possession claim*. It does not claim priority over those who may come later, if those happen to be miners. If miners required more water for mining operations below their claim, they would apparently have a right to it.

The Camp Seco Company subsequently went into operation happily developing and vending water, so it apparently got what it wanted. But given what we know of the story to come in which first possession will figure prominently, how do we understand the absence of a first possession principle in this particular claim? Part of the answer is that it reflected the early conditions of spring of 1851, when mining relied almost exclusively on panning and rockers-and-cradles; ditches were short, simple, and technologically primitive; and water measurement was extremely difficult. Under these conditions, one would not expect to observe detailed definition of water rights that provided ironclad assurance that the water could be diverted in the future. However, another important part of the answer is probably the same way we understand the variation in the miners' codes that we just saw in the last chapter. Note that the claim is for the right to take water from the creek, (virtually) all of which was to return to the creek. As we have seen, large amounts of recharge implies a large public good component to water, making an individualized right less likely to emerge. Indeed, as we saw in the last chapter, miners were less likely to mandate first possession in their mining codes under these conditions, nor did it make sense to.

For comparison purposes, consider a representative claim made six years later, in March 1857, by the Yorktown Ditch Company, which proposed to take water from Sullivan's Creek, also in Tuolumne County. After a detailed description of the location of the ditch, the claim went on:

> Said ditch is intended to carry forty nine inch streams of water; of which however the undersigned claim from Sullivan's Creek only what they are now entitled to, by right of claims purchased, and by them established as follows, to wit: for the Bennet Ditch commenced in January 1851, three streams of water of six inches each: for the Solesberry Ditch, commenced January 1851, four streams of six inches each: for the Bruce or Tucker Flat Ditch, dug January

1851, four six inch streams. Said ditches all intersected and ran water from Sullivan's *Creek and by priority of origin were and are entitled to the first water out of the said Creek, before any other Ditch or Ditches thereon.* The undersigned then claim for the Yorktown Ditch which is an extension and enlargement of the Solesberry Ditch twenty eight streams of six inches each over and above the original capacity of Solesberry Ditch. Said 28 streams are claimed over and before any other ditch except the one known as the Sonora Ditch commenced April 7th 1851, and entitled by original capacity to twelve streams from Sullivan's Creek of six inches each. The extension and enlargement of the Solesberry Ditch was commenced June 22nd 1851.[3] (emphasis added)

The difference between the two claims is striking. The Yorktown Ditch Company was extremely, some would say laboriously, careful to state exactly how much water it was claiming—twenty eight streams of six inches each—and precisely which other companies it considered to have superior claims based on temporal priority, and to how much water. Again, part of the explanation is temporal: by 1857, ditches were much longer and much more elaborate than they had been early in the decade. Much greater assurance would have been required for a company to be willing to undertake construction of a major ditch system. Certainly by all indications, the Yorktown Ditch Company was a good deal larger than the Camp Seco Company. However, in addition, the purpose of the Yorktown Company was to take water from Sullivan's Creek and conduct it several miles to Sonora and environs, which would have been highly consumptive of the water in Sullivan's Creek. As we have seen, this would have given added impetus to define this claim in a highly specific, individualized way, including the first possession feature.

If water claims are any indication, then, during the early 1850s there were growing economic pressures to define individualized rights that would support the mining that was occurring at greater distances from water with increasing frequency. A similar pattern is in evidence in early court rulings as well. Consider, for example, the 1853 Placer County case *Yankee Jim's Union Water Co. v. Moss.*[4] This well-documented case illustrates these economic pressures, as well as the challenges to the early courts in moving from the mining codes to official legal doctrine. In *Yankee Jim's,* a ditch company brought suit for damages and an injunction on upstream diversions on the basis that it had constructed its ditches prior to those diversions. The defendant upstream company maintained that its diversions of water, and the discharge of tail waters, occurred entirely within its own property. Significantly, the presiding judge refused to apply a rule of first possession. The plaintiff Yankee Jim's twice requested that the judge instruct the jury that its first possession status was to be controlling, and the judge twice refused to do so.[5] At the same time, the judge permitted a jury instruction requested by the defendant Moss that it had a right to use the water even though the plaintiff had been present and diverted the water first.[6] Not surprisingly, the jury found for the defendant, who was permitted to continue diverting the water and received a small damage award.

As it turned out, the *Yankee Jim's* case turned on two other separate, but related, points. Upfront, the plaintiff had conceded that his right extended only to water within the canon "not needed for mining and other purposes," echoing the Camp Seco claim we saw earlier. The fact that the upstream company was using the water for mining purposes would have to have been persuasive to the jury. The company fully took advantage of this fact, requesting, and receiving from the judge, a jury instruction that they were entitled to water to work their mining claims that were "located on the bank of the stream," even though they were not there first. This strategy alone may well have been sufficient to turn the tide in their favor. Taking no chances, however, they also requested the following jury instruction, keeping in mind their physical location relative to the stream:

> The right to use the water of a running stream belongs to the owner of the land over which it flows. A natural stream of water exists for the benefit of the land through which it flows, and is an incident annexed by operation of law to the land itself.[7]

This classic statement is one of the central principles of riparian law and in invoking it, the defendants undoubtedly were mindful of the fact that three years before, the state legislature had enacted a statute that directed judges to abide by principles of English common law.[8] The presiding judge certainly thought he was constrained to do so, as he allowed the instruction to the jury, thus locking in the verdict for the defendant. We will return to the issue of riparian law shortly.

The *Yankee Jim's* case is instructive on a couple of grounds. First, the influence of the mining codes is clearly in evidence. The plaintiff felt obligated to acknowledge the local rules that water was to be reserved for the use of miners, and this fact turned out to be determinative of the outcome. This was likely an important reason the judge did not instruct the jury that first possession was the governing principle: doing so would have flown in the face of the local rules favoring miners. This could not, and would not, last, but in the early 1850s, it was a logical outcome of early deference to the mining codes under the circumstances. Second, the institutional constraints on the courts are apparent, in the form of the legislative requirement that judges abide by English common law. It would turn out that the courts would struggle mightily with its charge to abide by this mandate. In this case, abiding by English common law happened to go hand-in-hand with the mining codes. But this could not last either, nor could the courts long ignore the benefits of a first possession principle, with the investment requirements of the ditch industry growing every year.

How did the courts begin to move down the path toward recognition of first possession as the governing principle in diversion disputes? The first step occurred that same year, in the very first water dispute case to come before the state Supreme Court, *Eddy v. Simpson*.[9] *Eddy* presented some factual similarities to *Yankee Jim's*. In *Eddy*, a ditch company who was first was located downstream from another mining company whose diversions were fully recharging the stream. There was thus no occasion for a dispute, until the upstream company undertook a second diversion that did deprive the downstream company of water. The upstream company defended its second diversion on the basis that its first diversion, by recharging the stream, was making up for the water lost in the second diversion. This reasoning was apparently persuasive to the district court, which instructed the jury that under these conditions, the "plaintiffs cannot be damaged."[10] Not surprisingly, the jury found for the defendants, despite coming after. The Court reversed this ruling, on the English common-law principle that water rights are only use (usufructuary) rights, so that the defendant could not claim rights to the recharge waters. This holding reduced the dispute to the competing claims of two diverters, and on this basis the prior claim prevailed.

Charles McCurdy has argued that in *Eddy v. Simpson*, the Court "summarily rejected appropriative principles," which leads him to conclude that the Court early on was pursuing an "erratic and often confusing doctrinal trail." [11] This does not seem to be the correct interpretation of *Eddy*, which ended up siding with the prior claimant. Rather, it seems that the Court rejected the district court's position that the tail waters could compensate for the waters lost in the second diversion. This was the departure from English common law that the Court was objecting to. This is an important interpretive point, as it spells the difference between an "erratic" Court and one that was responding to the beginnings of needs for investment security in diversion facilities. Douglas Little-field has since noted that *Eddy* was the "beginning of prior appropria-tion," even if it used a riparian principle to decide the dispute.[12] I would merely add that the two facts were not mutually exclusive. Ultimately, as we shall see, the courts were able to craft an appropriative doctrine that was not in conflict with riparian law given the conditions in California at the time.

It may well be that the ruling in *Eddy* reinforced the tendencies of the miners' codes to support first possession claims for diversions to dry diggings. Some evidence to this effect is provided by a series of cases brought before the Placer County district court from 1853 to 1855.[13] In each of these cases, the plaintiff brought a complaint in which it clearly claimed a right based upon having been present and diverting first. In one case, *Bennet v. Dingman*, the plaintiff charged the defendant with "tak[ing] the water entirely out of the canon and cause it to not return to its original channel but to fall into other ravines."[14] In another case, *Duell v. Bear River and Auburn Water and Mining Co.*, the defendants admitted constructing a large ditch from Bear River to conduct water "over the dividing ridges between Bear River and Auburn Ravine, be-ing about thirty miles in length."[15] As opposed to *Yankee Jim's*, where the water taken by the defendant was clearly remaining largely where it was, these latter cases involved definite diversions away from the source of water. These cases strongly suggest that where water was being physi-cally removed from the local watershed, being first was generally viewed by plaintiffs as controlling in disputes over diversions. This may well have also reflected the influence of mining codes, which tended to man-date first possession for diversions to dry diggings, as we have seen.

Equally telling are the arguments advanced by defendants in re-sponse to allegations of illegal diversions. Generally speaking, these de-fenses completely accepted the argument that temporal priority entitled the plaintiff to a superior right if clearly established by the facts. Rather than contesting that being first conferred a superior position, defendants defended their diversions by attempting to cast into doubt that the plain-

tiff really had been there first. The most common defense strategy centered on an expansion of capacity that occurred after the original diversion had been made. In *Duell v. Bear River*, the defendant based his
defense in part on the argument that the plaintiff enjoyed priority only
to the water diverted prior to an enlargement of the capacity of his ditch,
which enlargement occurred after the defendant began diverting. A very
similar defense was advanced by the defendant in *North Shirt Tail Ditch
Co. v. Union Canal Co.*[16] In an interesting variation, in *Taylor v. Gorman* the defendant argued he was entitled to the water in an expansion
of his own system, which occurred after the plaintiff had established his
own claim but where the original priorities were in question.[17] In all of
these cases, the court's ruling was based upon precisely how much water had actually been developed, either in an original diversion or subsequent expansion, prior to the diversion or expansion by the other claimant. In other words, establishing the relative priority dates was crucial,
and everything else followed from that determination.

The very fact that temporal priority was not questioned by either side
in any of these cases speaks volumes about its status at the time as a legal standard for deciding disputes. When a legal standard is clear and accepted by all, and it is easy to make a factual determination as to whether
or not it has been met, parties to a dispute tend not to litigate over it.[18]
Litigation is expensive, after all, and parties will prefer to settle in order
to avoid these costs. However, when a resource is complex in the sense
that it contains multiple attributes, there may be various other margins
along which users might try to expropriate rents. In the context of court
rulings over water diversions, it would not be surprising to observe disputes centered on less obvious factual and interpretive issues such as the
extra capacity associated with expansions of a ditch system, especially in
light of the measurement issues described earlier.

To summarize, this early evidence reflects several factors that influenced the development of early water law. The influence of the mining
codes is in evidence in both claims and arguments made in court to protect water rights. Reflecting our findings from chapter 5, the evidence
also suggests the importance of the distinction between water use in wet
diggings and water diverted for use in dry diggings. Ditch companies
had to acknowledge the demands of miners who were working wet diggings, and first possession likely did not emerge until the wet diggings
were largely worked out and mining started to migrate out to dry diggings away from surface water sources. When this happened, it was prac-

tically taken for granted by all parties that water rights needed to be decided on the basis of first possession. Finally, there is a strong suggestion that secure water rights were considered important to provide assurance to ditch companies before they would dare to undertake diversion projects that required large upfront investments.

7.3. A Complication: Riparian Rights

Let us now return to an issue that came up in the *Yankee Jim's* case: the claim of a riparian right by the defendants, based on the fact that the water flowed through their lands. Over time, remote diversions of water would come to dominate the gold fields as mining moved to dry diggings. However, there would remain plenty of instances where downstream companies might be working claims along a river or stream. Or water might be used on the waterway for other reasons, including power for a saw mill, or for municipal water supply.[19] But aside from the practical fact that claims for such uses were likely to continue to be made, there was a larger issue that the courts had to address: the fact that they had been directed by the legislature in essence to apply riparian law to govern disputes over water. The discussion so far has focused on the economic currents driving the creation of legal principles, especially first possession. The question is this: what role, if any, did this legislative mandate play?

To appreciate the potential difficulties facing the courts, it needs to be stressed that in many ways, riparian law was a highly inappropriate doctrine on which to base water rights in the gold fields, particularly as mining migrated away from the rivers and streams. As we saw earlier, under riparian law water is "an incident annexed by operation of law to the land itself," for the benefit of the land by which it flows. All riparian users, regardless of when they arrive on the scene, enjoy co-equal rights to use the water that flows by their lands. And in the early nineteenth century, jurists were in the process of transitioning from an earlier riparian doctrine that held that rivers must be preserved in their natural flow state to one that held merely that no one may "unreasonably" deprive other users of water.[20] To divert water from a river and convey it perhaps miles away to dry diggings is a direct violation of these fundamental riparian principles. All of this suggests that the previous discussion of water diversion based on temporal priority raised an enormous question: On what legal basis could these diversions be supported?

Legal scholars have long debated the extent to which it matters to judges that they respect and adhere to a received body of legal doctrine, such as English common law. Some scholars argue that judges are resistant to economic and social currents, stressing instead their tendency to hew to established doctrine.[21] Others argue that judges are very much interested in promoting economic and social objectives and minimize the importance of being consistent with established doctrine.[22] An extreme version of this view is that judges do whatever they jolly well please, a view that is captured nicely by Ambrose Bierce:

> Precedent, n. In Law, a previous decision, rule or practice which, in the absence of a definite statute, has whatever force and authority a Judge may choose to give it, thereby greatly simplifying his task of doing as he pleases. As there are precedents for everything, he has only to ignore those that make against his interest and accentuate those in the line of his desire.
>
> (Ambrose Bierce, *The Devil's Dictionary*)

Others have argued that over time judges may cycle between these two positions, depending upon circumstances. In the 1970s, for example, Morton Horwitz advanced his famous thesis that in the mid-nineteenth century, American judges moved from an emphasis on defining rights to promote industrialization to freezing rights to protect vested interests.[23] Though Horwitz's thesis has been vigorously critiqued on various grounds, the only point here is that legal scholars have disagreed, and continue to disagree, about the constraining influence of existing doctrine.[24]

This research will tread a middle path between these two positions. While I maintain that economic conditions matter greatly to judges in laying down doctrine, I also assume that being consistent with received doctrine also matters to them and that it influences them in English common-law jurisdictions through the mechanism of precedent. In economic terms, precedent provides a useful way for judges to economize on the cost of making a ruling in situations where disputes with similar fact patterns have occurred in the past.[25] In these cases, previous rulings provide guidance regarding the correct principles to apply, giving judges a reason to apply the same principles in the current case.[26] However, as conditions change over time, existing precedents become less relevant, and judges may need to devise new principles for resolving disputes. However, existing doctrine may still provide useful guidance, as long as conditions have not changed too dramatically.[27] The resulting emerging law thus strikes a balance between the economic demands of the new situation, and how previous judges have ruled under similar circumstances.

The legislative mandate to apply riparian law, then, should have forced judges to consider the principles in that law as not to be easily discarded, as they sought ways to define water rights that accommodated the demands of mining. This was no easy task, and there was a period when the courts struggled to lay down principles that were both consistent with riparian law and applicable to conditions in the gold fields. In *Yankee Jim's*, for example, the judge erred in permitting the defendants to claim a riparian right to their lands. Even though the stream ran directly through their lands, they did not own the lands and as we have seen, riparian rights are based on ownership of land adjacent to surface water. Therefore, they should not have been permitted to invoke riparian law to support their right to the water. This fact may have been a reason why the plaintiffs in *Yankee Jim's* ended up being awarded a new trial in spring of 1854 after they challenged the original ruling on the basis of errors in court instructions to the jury. By mid-1854, then, the courts were still struggling with the issue of riparian rights in trying to come up with consistent principles to govern water rights in the gold fields. The question was: How could the courts promote the widespread use of water in the gold fields while still honoring their legislative directive to adhere to riparian law?

7.4. Irwin v. Phillips and Its Impacts

The answer was to come the following year, in the landmark case of *Irwin v. Phillips*.[28] In this case, a mining company brought suit against an upstream company for diverting water from the local river, claiming riparian status entitled it to the water despite the fact that the upstream company was there first. So similarly to *Yankee Jim's*, this case pitted a company claiming a prior right against another claiming riparian status, the only difference being that the riparian claimant was downstream and therefore was the one to file suit. However, the outcome was entirely different: the Court affirmed a district court ruling that favored the upstream company, explicitly on the grounds that it was there first, arguing as follows:

The miner who selects a piece of ground to work, must take it as he finds it, subject to prior rights, which have an equal equity, on account of an equal recognition from the sovereign power. If it is upon a stream, the waters of which have not been taken from their bed, they cannot be taken to his prejudice; but if they have been already diverted, and for as high and legitimate a purpose as the one he seeks to accomplish, he has no right to complain, no right to interfere with the prior occupation of his neighbor, and must abide the disadvantage of his own selection.[29]

In other words, the plaintiff was safe from future diversions "to his prejudice," but he could not exploit his riparian status to deny the right of someone who was already present and diverting water.

It must be stressed how radical this statement would be in a riparian jurisdiction. As we have seen, under riparian law, rights to water are obtained by buying lands physically adjacent to surface waters, which entitles one to the use of the water, consistent with the reasonable rights of others. All users share equally in the water, regardless of when they acquire their riparian right, which is, however, "annexed by operation of law to the land itself" and for the benefit of that land. By contrast, in this statement there is no notion of co-equal rights, no notion that the upstream company is limited to any measure of reasonableness, no notion that the water is annexed to the land itself for the benefit of that land, and when one appears on the scene is completely controlling. All of these facts seem in direct contravention to the principles of riparian law. Given the legislative mandate to apply riparian law to water disputes, how did the Court justify ruling in this way?

The answer is illustrated by the error of the judge in *Yankee Jim's* to permit the defendant to stake a riparian claim to the water flowing through his land. The error lay in the fact that the defendant did not own his land. But the fact that he did not own his land provided the judge with a way out, if he had chosen to take it. Without land ownership, there was no basis for a riparian right, and the judge in *Yankee Jim's* could have nullified the riparian claim on that basis. In *Irwin*, however, the Court picked up on the fact that the dispute occurred on public lands where neither side could claim ownership, and it chose to declare that riparian principles did not apply for that reason:

It is insisted by the appellants that in this case the common law doctrine must be invoked, which prescribes that a water course must be allowed to flow in its natural channel. *But upon an examination of the authorities which support that doctrine, it will be found to rest upon the fact of the individual rights of landed proprietors upon the stream*, the principle being both at the civil and common law that the owner of lands on the banks of a water course owns to the middle of the stream, and has the right in virtue of his proprietorship to the use of the water in its pure and natural condition. In this case the lands are the property either of the State or of the United States.[30] (emphasis added)

Thus we see that the *Irwin* Court took existing riparian law seriously, and it still managed under the circumstances to make a ruling that respected riparian principles while creating a workable doctrine that would permit water development throughout the gold fields. It should be added that the *Irwin* Court seemed to be keenly aware of the economic importance of water in gold mining, a factor that disposed them to protect investments in water development:

[Certain principles have become] so firmly fixed as that they have come to be looked upon as having the force and effect of res judicata. Among these the most important are . . . the rights of those, who by prior appropriation, have taken the waters from their natural beds, and by costly artificial works have conducted them for miles over mountains and ravines, to supply the necessities of gold diggers, and without which the most important interests of the mineral region would remain without development.[31]

The implicit message is that without the protection afforded by being first, such "costly artificial works" might not be undertaken. The state Supreme Court would strongly defer to the first possession principle set out in *Irwin*, and its instrumentalist rationale of protecting investments in water development could often be heard during this early period, as for example in the 1857 case of *Hoffman v. Stone*:

The fact early manifested itself, that the mines could not be successfully worked without a proprietorship in waters, and it was recognized and maintained. To protect those who, by their energy, industry, and capital, had constructed canals and races, carrying water for miles into parts of the country which must have otherwise remained unfruitful and undeveloped, it was held that the first appropriator acquired a special property in the waters thus appropriated, and as a necessary consequence of such property, might invoke all legal remedies for its enjoyment and defence.[32]

It needs to be stressed that *Irwin v. Phillips* was not universally embraced by miners, some of whom worried that it would exclude them from access to water. In 1857, for example, a meeting of miners in Evansville, Butte County, stated in strong terms their opposition to *Irwin*:

> Resolved, That the decision of the Supreme Court in the case of *Irwin v. Phillips*, in which the Court held that . . . the single individual, or company, who diverted the water first from its natural channel, had exclusive right thereto, to the exclusion of any person or community who might afterwards require the whole or a portion of said water in its natural channel below, is a violation of all law, common and civil—is without a precedent—was a violation of all mining usages, violation of common justice and common sense, and such a conclusion as no Judge could possibly arrive at, except he was a Ditch owner.
>
> Resolved, That the law, or decision, which invests an individual or company who first diverts the water from a stream, with the right of laying the bed dry, and with the right of taking the water to another county, or wherever his fancy or interest may dictate, and giving him an unending right thereto, to the entire exclusion of those who may afterwards live below on said streams, is justly odious, being diametrically opposed to justice and the wants of the community.[33]

The concern these miners were expressing was that ditch owners might obtain a prior right and gain a monopoly over available local water supplies. At least some miners apparently believed that a system that assigned property rights to the first to arrive on the scene could easily benefit ditch companies or other miners at their expense. Indeed, this is not only another manifestation of the tensions between first-comers and newcomers, but also of the tensions between miners and ditch companies, both themes that we saw earlier. The argument found in *Irwin* that respecting senior rights was firmly fixed by "a universal sense of necessity and propriety" has been taken too much at face value by some modern scholars.[34]

An important subsequent case confirmed the primacy of being first and clarified the position of the Court on the relationship between appropriators and riparians. In *Irwin*, the upstream appropriator had come first and the downstream riparian came after. Under these conditions, it was a straightforward application of temporal priority to rule for the appropriator, to the extent of the appropriation. What would happen, however, if the downstream riparian came first? What would be the rights of the appropriator? These questions were presented in 1857 in the case of *Crandall v. Woods*. In a nutshell, this case involved two neighboring tracts of land, where water originated in springs on one tract A and then flowed onto the other tract B. Then, after riparian use had been established on B, the owners of A decided they wanted to sell some of the water to a nearby municipality, thus depriving B of the flow. The Court ruled for the riparian B, on the basis that he was present prior to the diversion by A. In basing its ruling on priority, the *Crandall* court clearly took its lead from *Irwin*:

> If the rule laid down in *Irwin v. Phillips*, is correct as to the location of mining claims and water-ditches, for mining purposes, and *priority* is to determine the rights of the respective parties, it is difficult to see why the rule should not apply to all other cases where land or water had been appropriated. The simple question [in *Irwin*] was, that as between persons appropriating the same land, or land and water both, . . . that the subsequent appropriator takes, subject to the rights of the former.[35] (Emphasis in original)

Crandall thus confirmed and elaborated on the importance of being first in determining, in disputes between riparians and appropriators on public lands, who had the superior right.

In affirming the primacy of the riparian claimant under the circumstances, *Crandall* would have one additional important consequence that distinguished it from *Irwin* in its long-term significance for California water law. Whereas *Irwin* argued in essence that riparian law did not apply in the case at hand because there was no private land ownership, *Crandall* refused to take this absolutist position. Instead, it took the position that locating physically adjacent to a stream did indeed confer riparian status on a claimant, in the sense that the act of appropriating the land itself confers a right to the adjacent water:

> If the owners of the mining-claim, in the case of *Irwin* v. *Phillips*, had first located along the bed of the stream, they would have been entitled, as riparian proprietors, to the free and uninterrupted use of the water, without any other

or direct act of appropriation of the water, as contra-distinguished from the soil. If such is the case, why would not the defendant, who has appropriated land over which a natural stream flowed, be held to have appropriated the water of such stream, as an incident to the soil, as against those who subsequently attempt to divert it from its natural channels for their own purposes.[36]

This odd passage has been interpreted by many scholars as legitimizing riparian rights on public lands, which may have ultimately led to the upholding of riparian rights by the Court in the famous *Lux v. Haggin* ruling in 1886.[37] For our purposes, however, though it uses the language of riparian law, it is not at all clear that what is being referred to here is a riparian right to water. There is no private land ownership, a fact that was crucial to the *Irwin* ruling. And the right to "free and uninterrupted use of the water" by "riparian proprietors" is only enjoyed by claimants who arrive first. In the period considered here, the key to the *Crandall* ruling was temporal priority, which was the conditional upon which all else followed, not riparian status.[38]

If the combined import of *Irwin* and *Crandall* was to promote the importance of temporal priority, then they would also have promoted efficient development of water, to the extent temporal priority supported investment security. However, the efficiency of the temporal priority principle can be questioned on the basis that it may have triggered a resource-wasting competitive scramble to acquire the right, a form of rent dissipation sometimes referred to as *racing dissipation*. This would especially have been the case if potential claimants were broadly homogeneous in terms of their productivity, opportunity costs, and the degree of entrepreneurship they brought to the enterprise of water development.[39] It should be added, however, that the potential for racing dissipation also depends upon the ability to identify and capitalize on an opportunity to gain rents when it appears. The more quickly an opportunity is identified and becomes general public knowledge, the more complete racing dissipation is likely to be. In the gold fields, however, we have seen that the process of gold discovery contained elements of both randomness and scientifically-informed systematic search, though probably more of the former. To the extent that gold discovery was random and therefore unpredictable, water development in support of mining would have followed the discoveries, not anticipated them. Under these conditions, the potential for racing dissipation in the competition to claim prior rights in water would have been reduced.

Within the next two years after *Irwin*, several additional cases involving disputes over diversions of water were brought before the Court.[40] These were not cases to determine whether the principle of first possession was to be controlling: that issue had been settled by *Irwin* and *Crandall*. Rather, the import of the cases was to determine the conditions under which first possession would apply and to refine precisely what first possession meant. As all the disputes occurred on public lands, the courts had to address the looming issue that the federal government could come in and assert its rights to the gold fields at any time. If so, exactly what did a first possession right mean, and how much security did it actually provide?

The answer the courts would give could not have been completely reassuring to many miners and ditch companies, and is another reflection of the influence of English common law on the courts. In *Tartar v. Spring Creek*, it was established that the right based on temporal priority was not a true unconditional private right but rather, a right that could be asserted against all "but the true owner" (namely, the federal government), what it called a quasi private proprietorship.[41] But the courts felt compelled to go further than this and provide some sort of doctrinal justification in English common law for what may have seemed like an illegal occupation of government lands. In *Conger v. Weaver*, it advanced a justification based upon what it termed the "doctrine of presumption of a grant of right." Since it was well known that miners were occupying the gold fields, while at the same time the government was taking no steps to assert its rights, it must be giving its tacit assent to the occupation, which could be construed as conferring on miners a "license to occupy."[42] Together, these two rulings established a doctrinal basis for the miners to continue to mine the gold fields. At the same time, it did not provide a completely secure right, as the government could in principle step in and assert its right at any time.

One might think that miners and ditch companies would be worried at the prospect of remaining in this legal limbo, with all of the uncertainty of rights that entailed. And many of them undoubtedly were, which led to occasional attempts by state legislators to get Congress to renounce its claims to the public lands in the gold fields. In early 1859, for example, one legislator introduced a resolution calling on its Congressional delegation "to use all honorable exertions" to get Congress to pass a law donating all mineral lands in the state to the miners.[43] However, many also worried that the resolution to the situation could be even worse. If the government intervened, at the very least it could mean regulation of the gold fields and at the worst, possible eviction. And even with their most favored option—a no-strings-attached donation of the public lands to the state—a number of miners raised concerns about the danger that the donated lands might wind up being monopolized. Miners were not wholeheartedly in support of the resolution introduced in 1859 but rather, the support of many was conditional on ensuring somehow that the donated lands would not be monopolized by "capitalists and sharpers."[44]

Another issue of practical importance concerned precisely when a right commenced in the process of water development. As we saw in chapter 4, the construction of a ditch system was a time-consuming process. The entire process from initial identification of a suitable source of water for development through to the final delivery of water to miners could take months or even years to complete. The issue of precisely when in the process a priority claim should be dated arose in 1856 in the case of *Conger v. Weaver*. In this case, involving a sawmill company that sued a ditch company for trespass in running a ditch through its property, the defendant ditch company had clearly commenced the survey for its ditch prior to, but not completed construction by, the time the mill was built. Among the arguments of the sawmill company was the fact that the ditch company had not enclosed the ground for the ditch on the sawmill company's property. The ditch company responded that as long as they were the first to locate and commenced in good faith to construct its ditch system, their claim should take precedence. They sarcastically added that they should not be "compelled to run a serpentine fence or enclosure along thirty miles of flume to give them right."[45] The Court sided with the ditch company, arguing that requiring completion of the ditch system would render the initial right "valueless, for after nearly the whole work has been done, any one, actuated by malice or self-interest, may prevent its accomplishment; any small squatter settlement might effectively destroy it." Furthermore, the Court argued:

> a miner, who has a few square feet for his mining claim which he cannot directly occupy, has possession, because he works it, or because he has staked it off to work it, if his acts show no intention to abandon; building a dam, is taking possession of water as a usufruct.
>
> So, in the case of constructing canals, under the license from the State, the

survey of the ground, planting stakes along the line, and actually commencing and diligently pursuing the work, is as much possession as the nature of
the subject will admit, and forms a series of acts of ownership which must be
conclusive of the right.[46]

Thus, *Conger* established the importance of due diligence in prosecuting construction of a ditch to completion, as opposed to the act of
completion itself. In the following year, in *Parke v. Kilham*, the Court
advanced the further notion that the line upon which the ditch will be
dug should be run within a "reasonable time" after the initial survey,
with what is considered reasonable dependent upon the circumstances.[47]
However, the Court ruled, actual acts of diligence were required: mere
intention to appropriate would not be sufficient to stake a claim. Thus,
for example, the Court argued in *Kelly v. Natoma Water Co.* that "it is
not the intention to possess, but the actual possession, which gives the
right," for if appropriation were based on intention, "there would be no
rule to limit or control it."[48]

The Court's decision regarding precisely when actual possession takes
place, when the process of possessing takes time, may be interpreted as
negotiating a tradeoff between encouragement of investment *ex ante* and
avoiding disputes *ex post*. All else equal, a clear act, such as completion
of a ditch, as opposed to "just working on it," helps avoid confusion over
ownership and may help prevent disputes.[49] However, these advantages
of clear acts must be weighed against potentially lost incentives to undertake investments if, after putting in all that work, the investor might
lose his investment at the eleventh hour. The smaller the upfront investment requirements, the more efficient it is to define possession in terms
of a clear act.[50] The Court, by placing the point of actual possession earlier in the process, was acting to preserve incentives to invest under conditions when major investments were required.[51]

The question of how possession was defined raises another question:
possession of what? Exactly how much water did going through the process of investment entitle one to? As we saw in chapter 4, early measurement of water flow was extremely imprecise, and it was only over time
that improved measurement led to reasonably precise quantification of
water claims. A similar trend is evident in disputes over water rights
brought before the local courts. This is seen, for example, in a number of cases brought before the Placer County district court beginning

in 1851. The cases in question all involved complaints regarding an upstream diversion that deprived the plaintiff of water. The common feature of these cases is that parties to the disputes made claims to specific quantities of water but that there was wide variety in the way quantities were described. In the very first such case, the *Yankee Jim's* case, the company made the rather vague claim that the defendant had diverted an amount equal to "about twelve square inches of flowing water," with no reference to water pressure. In *Duell v. Bear River*, brought the following April (1854), water quantities were phrased in *"cubic* inches of water," again with no reference to water pressure. In the following year (1855), the North Shirt Tail Ditch Company dispensed entirely with the geometric modifier and simply described its water entitlement as "1584 inches of water, ditch measure." It was not until December 1855 that a company even mentioned water pressure, in *Maeris v. Bicknell*, where the plaintiff described its water entitlement as "150 inches of water sluice measure under a six inch head."[52]

Indeed, it was not until after 1857 that references to water pressure became regularized in court proceedings. In June 1857, the plaintiff in *Leigh v. Independent Ditch Co.* described its entitlement to 30 inches of water as "running under a six inch water pressure." Cases brought in January 1858 and June 1859 also specify six inches of pressure though in other cases, pressure is measured as little as four inches and as high as three feet. Despite this wide variation, however, water measurement was indeed undergoing standardization, even at this early stage. In one case in early 1857, the court required the plaintiff to amend its complaint by replacing all references to "cubic" inches with "square" inches. Furthermore, in 1858 four-inch pressure started to be referred to as *"usual* ditch measurement" (emphasis added), an indication of movement toward a common standard.[53]

All of this suggests, however, that throughout the 1850s measurement of water was highly imprecise, which confirms our earlier discussion in chapter 4 of vending of water by ditch companies. How, then, did the courts manage to effectively quantify rights to water when deciding water disputes? If a new ditch company claimed the surplus water in a waterway and an older company complained, how did the courts figure out how much water the latter was entitled to and how much was surplus?

Much of the answer appears to be that the courts relied not on direct measurement of the water but rather, on the capacity of the diversion system, which was considerably easier to measure after wooden flumes came into regular use. A flume of certain dimensions set at a certain grade could effectively transport only so much water over a certain period. So, for example, when the North Shirt Tail Ditch Co. sued the Union Canal company to enjoin its diversions in 1855, it was very careful to state the dimensions of its ditch; that is, "5 feet wide at the top, 4 feet wide at the bottom and 2 ½ feet deep; . . . capable of conveying 1584 inches of water, ditch measure." Similarly, later that year in *Maeris v. Bicknell*, the plaintiffs stated in their brief that their main canal was "in dimension 3 feet wide at top, 2 ½ feet wide at bottom and 2 feet deep and has the capacity to carry 300 inches of water sluice measure under a six inch head." They were also careful to specify that they believed themselves entitled to so much water "as may be sufficient to fill their ditch to its full capacity."[54]

In these and other cases, the courts commonly relied upon findings of fact regarding the maximum capacity of the ditch/flume as the measure of the water right. In *Maeris v. Bicknell*, for example, the court awarded the plaintiff 300 inches of water, the full capacity of their canal. Another case brought in 1856 revolved around precisely how much water the plaintiff had title to. In this case, the plaintiff stated the dimensions and grade of its flume—one inch per rod—to support its claim to 120 inches of water, the capacity of its flume. The defendant answered that the grade of the flume was only 2/3 inch per rod and had a capacity of only 100 inches. The jury was left to sort out the truth and ultimately sided with the defendant, and the court ended up awarding the plaintiff 100 inches of water.[55]

None of this fully conveys the difficulty of measuring the capacity of a ditch system, which could be a crazy-quilt of ditches and flumes of various dimensions and grades. Thus, a system's flow capacity and associated water pressure could both vary across various stretches within the system, making it difficult for the courts to determine maximum flow capacity. Consider, for example, the following testimony by an engineer in a dispute between the Tuolumne County Water Company and the Columbia and Stanislaus River Water Company brought before the Tuolumne County district court in 1857:

> The flume on Five Mile Creek is 4 X 2 feet with a grade a little more than 10 ½ feet to the mile—it runs there some 3 to 4 miles per hour—it will carry from 150 to 190 tom streams—190 six inch streams or 150 nine inch streams— that is not the Main ditch—that was originally our Main ditch but it was al-

tered in September 1854—the mouth of our flume where it taps the South Fork is 8 X 2 feet with a fall of 32 feet to the mile—it lessens to six feet and about 20 feet from mouth to 5 feet in width by 2 in depth—its average capacity is from 250 to 270 tom streams of 9 inches—that was finished August 20th 1852—where it empties into the ditch the ditch has a grade of 16 feet to the mile—the original ditch was 4 feet wide at the bottom 2 feet deep and 6 feet wide at top—the grade was 16 feet per mile for 6 miles—then 10 ½ feet for 3 miles—this is along 5 Mile Creek—3 miles of the 5 Mile Creek are on the same grade—that portion of it was cut for 4 feet wide on the bottom 6 feet on the top and 2 feet deep—that portion of it would carry 1/3 more than the 5 Mile Creek flume—the ditch was dug 2 feet below the surface of the ground with an embankment of from 1 to 2 feet above it—the ditch had a heavier grade above and below the flume its object was to enlarge the ditch.[56]

The engineer went on to testify that after the enlargement, the ditch system would carry anywhere from 200 to 300 tom streams. This notably wide range of values gave the Tuolumne County Water Company a good deal of latitude in asserting its water right, which likely formed the basis for its assertion of a water right to 300 tom streams. The jury ended up deciding the case (for the defendant Columbia and Stanislaus River Water Company) on different grounds—namely, what constituted a "reasonable" amount of time for the defendant to begin ditch construction after putting up notices and making surveys—but the point here is that there was probably a very imprecise connection between the capacity of the ditch system and the amount of water actually delivered. The courts indeed adopted the lowest-cost method of quantification available—capacity, not usage—as theory would predict, but even this was highly imperfect.

The fact that quantification was highly imprecise also meant that early water rights were based largely upon possession, not actual use.[57] The dimensions of a ditch system could tell the courts only how much water one had the capacity to use, not how much was actually being used. This fact had extremely important implications for any restrictions or conditions the courts might want to impose on use itself. Let us consider these implications for two key principles of modern appropriative law: *beneficial use*, and the *use requirement* (the *"use-it-or-lose-it"* principle).

The beneficial use principle avers that appropriative rights are valid only if the water is put to some use that is deemed beneficial. It is currently a universal principle of appropriative law, found in all jurisdictions where water rights are based upon prior appropriation.[58] To be clear, the term has been used in two distinct ways, to refer to both a type of use and an amount needed to accomplish a use. It is not considered beneficial either to use water to some inappropriate end or to use too much of it to accomplish an objective.[59] In both cases, however, in economic terms the idea is that a use must have sufficient value to be supported in law.

It is not generally well understood how beneficial use came to be adopted in California. It is sometimes understood as deriving from English common law, and imported at some point into the mining camps.[60] However, there is virtually no evidence that this is true.[61] Not one single mining code in my database contained anything like a requirement that water be devoted to beneficial use. Nor is there any evidence that it was legislated during this early period. In the 1850s, the only possible avenue whereby the notion of beneficial use might have entered into the legal system is through the courts. And there was only case heard by the Supreme Court in the 1850s that decided a case on the basis that a use was not sufficiently valuable or beneficial to be supported by law: *Maeris v. Bicknell* in 1857.

Maeris involved a prior plaintiff who objected to diversions by upstream defendants. The strategy of the defendants was to challenge the prior claim of the plaintiff on the basis that the diversion was merely to drain water from their claims and was not put toward a useful purpose. The Court ruled that since the water had not been used but rather, disposed of, it did not constitute an actual appropriation. On this basis, it ruled for the defendants.[62] Apparently, to be considered a true appropriation, there had to be an actual application of the diverted water toward some valuable end. What speaks volumes here is that this is the only ruling handed down by the Court during the 1850s that denied an appropriative claim on the basis that the use wasn't sufficiently valuable. On reflection, however, the almost total absence of notions of beneficial use in rulings of the Court during the 1850s may not be terribly surprising. Measurement was extremely costly and water rights were basically rights of possession and not rights of use. Thus, the only real way the courts could have determined beneficial use was with extremely crude proxies. It is telling that the only example from the 1850s involved the draining of water from some claims, where absolutely no measurement was involved.

Indeed, the subsequent history of the doctrine of beneficial use suggests that it only became a regular standard of court rulings much later. Prior to 1865, only two other Supreme Court cases—*Weaver v. Eureka Lake* in 1860, and *McKinney v. Smith* in 1863—decided a case on the basis that one of the uses was not sufficiently valuable or beneficial to be supported in law. In both of these cases, measurement was not an issue: *McKinney* involved a drainage issue similar to *Maeris*, and *Weaver* involved the construction of a dam for no specific water use purposes. Every indication is that beneficial use was largely a non-issue throughout the period of this study, perhaps because costly measurement mostly took it out of the picture.

Like beneficial use, the origins of the use requirement for water in California are also not well understood. According to David Schorr, the use requirement with regard to water was present in the mining codes of Colorado after the discovery of gold there in 1859.[63] He argues that the purpose of these use requirements was to prevent speculative appropriations. One might argue that with similar economic currents, one might expect the same thing to have happened in California. However, there is no evidence of a water use requirement in any of my mining codes for California even though, as we have seen, there was almost universal adoption of work requirements for claims in the mining codes after the Early period was over in the early 1850s. But the requirement that miners work their claims is not at all the same thing as losing one's right to water if it is not used. The question is: in the gold fields, where did the water use requirement come from?

The evidence for early California strongly suggests that the use requirement was mandated in the courts, probably with English common-law influence, in the principle of *abandonment*. Under this principle, intentional non-use indicates that one has abandoned the water, which leaves it up for grabs.[64] Practically speaking, since intent is difficult to prove, courts economize on the cost of making a ruling by applying the standard that non-use for an unreasonably long period demonstrates intent to abandon. Unreasonableness is then a question of fact for the jury. Evidence suggests that this principle was present in the gold fields very early on. For example, in the 1853 case of *Heymes v. Kelley*, an early Placer County district court case, the plaintiffs felt compelled to declare, in protesting an upstream diversion, that they had "never at any time by act of either omission or commission forfeited or abandoned the right to said ditches or the use of the water," as if this would be an important fact for the jury to consider.[65] The issue of abandonment came up in a number of cases in Placer County over the next several years.[66]

The early treatment of abandonment was reflected in an issue that the courts would struggle with for several years: Could the use of a natural ravine to convey water as part of a ditch system be construed as abandonment of that water? The difficulty came in a principle of English common law that stated that one has a right to use surface water only during its passage through one's land. After that, it is there for the use of the next person and the first person loses all right. This principle was stated, for example, in *Eddy v. Simpson*:

> The owner of land through which a stream flows, merely transmits the water over its surface, having the right to its reasonable use during its passage. The right is not in the corpus of the water, and only continues with its possession.[67]

The difficulty was experienced, for example, by the defendants in the 1854 Placer County case of *Duell v. Bear River*, which turned in part on the question of whether the defendant had abandoned its right to water that it had developed by turning it into the ravine above the plaintiff's dam.[68] In *Eddy*, as we saw earlier, a company diverted water to the detriment of a downstream user, claiming that an earlier ditch, by recharging the stream, compensated for these diversions. The Court ruled against this company on the grounds that once the water leaves your possession, it is no longer yours. According to the future Chief Justice Lucien Shaw, *Eddy* established the principle that "the mere turning of water" into a stream after having used it was "conclusive evidence of abandonment."[69]

One can immediately sense that adherence to this principle could wreak havoc on water development. Exploiting the naturally occurring contours of terrain would seem to be a logical way to economize on the costs of constructing a ditch system. If ditch companies could not do this without fear of losing their water rights, one can easily envision their making unnecessary expenditures to construct flumes when natural ravines would serve just as well. This principle was, however, subsequently overruled in two subsequent cases: *Hoffman v. Stone*, and *Butte v. Vaughn*.[70] In *Hoffman v. Stone*, a prior plaintiff brought suit against an upstream company for diverting water from a creek feeding its ditch. The defendant argued that the creek was normally dry, and it was merely using it as a connecting link between two of its ditches. The Court overruled a trial court that had found for the plaintiff, arguing in essence that it made no sense to penalize a company for using a natural ravine to conduct water:

> It would be a harsh rule . . . to require those engaged in these enterprises to construct an actual ditch along the whole route through which the waters were carried, and to refuse them the economy that nature occasionally afforded in the shape of a dry ravine, gulch, or canon.[71]

The import of its ruling was that using a natural ravine to convey water did not constitute abandonment. The courts would ultimately see the economic sense of sustaining an appropriation under these conditions, despite the apparent inconsistency with English common law.

Having disposed of this issue, however, another one remained. If using a dry ravine as a connecting link in a ditch system did not constitute abandonment, exactly what did? Ditch companies quickly saw a different threat to their rights, arising from the fact that it was difficult for courts to measure the extent of their right. As we have seen, the early courts relied upon the capacity of ditches to define the extent of a right, because it was extremely costly to measure flow. But capacity indicated nothing about actual use, and it could thus not provide a defense against a charge of abandonment. Because of this, plaintiffs saw the need to speak explicitly to the question of whether they had abandoned their right, above and beyond the question of the capacity of their ditch. We have already seen this in *Heymes v. Kelley*. Consider also the following statement of the plaintiff in another case, *White v. Todd's Valley*:

> Plaintiffs further aver that since spring 1855, they have been owners and possessors of ditch and flume and been entitled to use and enjoyment of ditch and said 120 inches of water; and . . . that *neither they nor those under whom they claim have ever abandoned their right* to [appropriate the water].[72] (emphasis added)

So they apparently considered it insufficient to declare the extent of their right in terms of the capacity of their ditch system: they also had to emphasize that they were actually using the water.[73]

In this way, the issue of non-use would be continually raised in court, even when it was not explicitly the crux of the dispute. It was only a matter of time before cases would arise in which it was. One of the earliest cases involving a specific defense that the plaintiff had abandoned its water right came in the 1858 Placer County case of *Chapman v. Russell*. In this case, the familiar fact pattern was in evidence: an apparently prior plaintiff brought suit against an upstream diverter. In their defense, the defendants argued that when they built their ditch, the plaintiffs had not been using theirs: they had thus abandoned their right to the water. The case was thus specifically about non-use, and the outcome centered on the length of time it had persisted. The judgment ultimately went for the plaintiffs, on the basis that even though there was evidence of non-use, it had not gone on long enough to constitute abandonment.[74]

Some clues as to the thinking of the courts are found in instructions of the *Chapman* judge to the jury as to principles that should govern the outcome. In particular, the judge denied two instructions requested by the plaintiffs: that abandonment does not exist unless non-use has gone on for at least five years; and that it is not abandonment unless plaintiffs made declarations to the effect that they were not going to resume use.[75] In other words, the court viewed a period of five years as inordinately long to constitute legal non-use. And it was not about to set an insurmountable bar for a finding of non-use such as requiring a declaration that an abandonment had occurred. Had it not denied these instructions, water could have remained unused for an excessive amount of time and it would not have been permitted to move expeditiously to new uses. Thus, even though the ruling favored the plaintiff, the principles applied by this judge seemed to be oriented towards the positive objective of promoting greater actual use of water.

The fact that this judge denied a request to require five years for abandonment does not tell us, of course, what the judge thought the standard ought to be. Some additional clues are provided by the case of *Davis v. Gale*, the only other case centrally involving abandonment that made it to the Supreme Court prior to 1870.[76] In *Davis*, we again observe the common fact pattern of prior plaintiffs bringing suit to enjoin diversions by an upstream company. In their defense, the defendants argued that the plaintiffs had worked out their claims and departed the scene over two years before, thereby invalidating their claim to the water. The court sided with the defendants, ruling that the plaintiffs had abandoned their water right. Apparently, two years was sufficient time for non-use to be considered abandonment. But particularly telling was the following statement by the Court:

The fact that the water was appropriated solely for a special and particular purpose, and the further fact that that purpose had been fully accomplished, and the further fact that the parties concerned in it had dispersed to other parts, and that more than two years were allowed to pass without their giving any attention to the ditch, and then only to make a sale of it to others at the nominal sum of twenty-five dollars, all bear directly on that question. In view of those facts, a jury might find abandonment.[77]

This statement speaks to what the Court apparently considered powerful evidence of abandonment. The original purpose had been accomplished and no longer existed, the water no longer had value in that use, and the original right-holders had scattered to parts unknown. Declaring that right abandoned would now free up that water for better, higher-value uses.

In sum, these early abandonment cases seemed to have been designed to promote rational use of water in the gold fields. The courts devised rules that avoided unnecessary expenditures on flumes when natural features would do, and reallocated water reasonably expeditiously when it seemed to be called for.

There was one seemingly curious exception to the temporal priority rule: the rights of agriculturalists (farmers and ranchers) against miners. The early courts consistently ruled that miners were permitted to go onto agricultural lands in search of gold even if farmers and ranchers were there first, as long as the lands were public lands. As we have seen, virtually all of the lands in the mining regions were public lands. Consequently, this set of decisions had enormous implications for land use and the prosecution of mining. Even though the rulings to this effect all governed disputes over lands and not specifically water, closer inspection of this issue provides additional insight into the thinking of the courts.

In 1855, the state Supreme Court considered a dispute from Nevada County in which miners had entered onto public lands to search for gold, where the lands in question were already being used for agricultural purposes. In *Stoakes v. Barrett*, the Court upheld the district court ruling that had sided with the miners. Key to the ruling was an act of the legislature enacted in 1852, the *Possessory Act*, which expressly provided that if the lands contained gold and other precious metals, claims on the lands could be worked "as fully and unreservedly . . . had no possession or claim been made for grazing or agricultural purposes."[78] The Court showed enormous deference to this Act despite the fact that in doing so, it was going against the general pattern of other rulings governing temporal priority:

> The Act . . . is plain, positive, and specific in its terms; and it gives the permission to all persons to work the mines upon public lands, notwithstanding that they may be in the possession and enjoyment of another for agricultural purposes. Nothing can be plainer than the intent of this Act, and nothing more specific than the right which it gives.[79]

The opinion in *Stoakes* is quite terse, providing little rationale for elevating mining other than the Possessory Act. Other early rulings were equally deferential to the Act and to the precedent established in *Stoakes*.[80] In one of these cases, *McClintock v. Bryden*, the Court was considerably more forthcoming in its reasoning. *McClintock* added the twist that the plaintiff farmer had taken possession of his lands prior to passage of the Possessory Act and therefore argued that his possession should not be subject to its provisions. The Court again came down in favor of the miner, arguing in effect that farming and mining were different animals: mining activity on the public lands had been encouraged by the State and acquiesced in by the Federal government, whereas farming had not. Indeed, both the State and Federal governments had imposed restrictions on the right to farm on lands containing minerals. This very point answered the plaintiff's objection that it had settled prior to passage of the Possessory Act, denying that the plaintiff had ever acquired any right:

> The plaintiff never had, from the time of his location, any right, derived from either Government, to the possession of mineral lands inclosed by him, to the exclusion of miners who were in good faith proceeding to extract the gold from the earth.[81]

The Court went on:

> The maxim of the law, "qui prior est in tempore, potior est in jure," cannot be applied in protection of a person who settled upon lands reserved from settlement by the policy of the law, as against one entering for a purpose encouraged wherever minerals may be found.[82]

However, the Court seemed to have some discomfort with its ruling, acknowledging that prior possession of public agricultural lands had been held sufficient in other states "to sustain ejectment" against others invading possession. To this the Court answered, echoing *Irwin*:

> The wants and interests of a country have always had their due weight upon Courts in applying principles of law, which should shape its conditions; and rules must be relaxed, the enforcement of which would be entirely unsuited to the interests of the people they are to govern.[83]

Finally, the Court stated its instrumentalist bottom line:

> If the doctrine were otherwise, it is plain to perceive that persons without any right but that of possession, could, under the pretence of agriculture, invade the mineral districts of the State, and swallow up the entire mineral wealth by settlements upon one hundred and sixty acre tracts of land. It would be using the law to a very bad purpose if we should allow a person who has no evidence of title but his improvements, and no right but that of the naked possession he has usurped, to destroy, for his own benefit, the business of a neighborhood, and put as well the Government, as the mining public at defiance.[84]

The rhetoric of *McClintock* is striking: miners are engaged in a "lawful and honorable pursuit,"[85] whereas farmers who were merely first are potential usurpers who could destroy the business of a neighborhood.

The principle of *Stoakes* and *McClintock* was, however, subsequently reined in, first by the legislature and then by the Court. Shortly after *McClintock*, the legislature enacted the Indemnification Act, which upheld the right of miners to enter onto agricultural lands but required miners to compensate farmers for any improvements made to their lands.[86] In 1860, the Court itself imposed further restrictions on the principle in two cases: *Smith v. Doe* and *Gillan v. Hutchinson*. Both of these cases involved farmers occupying public lands and enclosing tracts of land upon them for agricultural purposes, upon which miners came to dig for gold. Both cases invalidated the Indemnification Act, which they argued unlawfully permitted the legislature "to take the property of one person and give it to another."[87] The rulings served to finally place miners and farmers on equal legal footing with regard to first possession.

What do we make of the courts' initial elevation of mining claims over farming claims, followed by its gradual reversal over time? The initial rulings exemplified by *Stoakes* and *McClintock* appear to reflect the courts bending over backwards to support mining, even at the potential expense of adherence to settled legal principle. It might be reasonable to interpret the movement of the courts away from this extreme position as reflecting the diminished importance of gold mining over time from the early flush days of the early 1850s.[88] However, another thing to note here is the relationship between the courts and the legislature. Both the Possessory Act and the Indemnification Act can be viewed as the legislature taking strongly pro-miner positions, which the courts initially supported but then steadily circumscribed over time. A logical political interpretation is that the legislature was more prone to exhibit "capture" by an extremely powerful interest group—miners—and the courts were often in the position of reining in the legislature when they had flexibility to do so. Consistent with this interpretation, I have recently documented capture of the legislature by miners during most of the 1850s in providing property tax exemptions for the mining industry. However, as mining production fell off and the economy became increasingly diversified, tax exemptions disappeared as mining shrank in importance and legislators began responding to broader economic conditions.[89] In terms of institutional development, there is a suggestion that during this period, the courts may have been more resistant to political pressures, and perhaps more likely to guide the institutions in wealth-supporting, as opposed to redistributive, ways.

7.5. Conclusions

This chapter has painted a complex picture of early appropriative law as it developed in the gold fields. However, despite its complexity, a number of conclusions can be drawn. First and foremost, we have seen a discernible economic logic in the principles that were created that are explicable under the conditions prevailing at the time. The adoption of the principle of first possession did not happen right away. Indeed, it took nearly six years from the start of the Gold Rush before *Irwin* established it as a governing principle, despite the fact that water was being used in mining literally from the very beginning. But there was an economic logic to the length of this transition period. The generalized adoption of first possession could occur only after mining had migrated away from water,

both as a means of supporting investment in dry diggings but also because individualized rights made little economic sense in wet diggings.
And economic pressures for first possession escalated dramatically after
gold separation procedures became heavily water- and capital-intensive,
which occurred with the widespread adoption of hydraulicking after
mid-decade. The timing of the adoption of first possession makes perfect sense when these underlying economic factors are considered.

But the investment security provided by first possession was by no
means perfect, reflecting a number of institutional and technological
factors. We have seen that the fact that the gold fields existed on public
lands was crucial to the adoption of first possession by the courts. However, this very fact lent a certain amount of irreducible uncertainty to
the amount of tenure certainty that first possession could provide. This
was true as long as the issue of government ownership and therefore, the
specter of government assertion of its rights in the gold fields, remained
unresolved. The security provided by first possession was also undermined by the fact that technologies for water measurement remained extremely imprecise throughout this period, which forced the courts to rely
on crude proxies such as ditch capacity instead of actual flow. As a result, miners and ditch companies never really knew for sure how much
water they were actually entitled to. This may have led to excessive investments in ditch capacity in order to ensure that they could claim sufficient volumes of water, which may have compensated to some extent for
lack of complete tenure certainty. Overall, however, it is not possible to
come up any reasonably certain measure of the overall net impact on the
propensity to invest.

The significant costs of measuring flow, and therefore use, also had
important implications for the emergence of effective constraints on actual water use, including two that are widespread today in appropriative
jurisdictions: beneficial use, and use requirements (use-it-or-lose-it). The
fact that actual use was hard to measure meant that courts had to rely on
crude proxies for what constituted beneficial use, which they decided did
not include mere disposal of the water. It also meant that claims of actual
use became part-and-parcel of court arguments, which eventually had
to be ruled upon by courts. Use requirements ultimately derived from
adoption by the courts of the principle of intentional non-use, or abandonment, as a means of facilitating turnover from older, less-valuable
uses to emerging ones.

What was the role of English common law in this process? Certainly the mandate to abide by English common law constrained the judges in adopting principles for creating rights and resolving disputes. This generated initial periods of confusion in deciding important issues such as the basis for diversion of water from surface sources and whether using natural ravines to convey water constituted abandonment. However, the courts readily found ways to adapt the principles to local circumstances in order to support gold mining. The result was a set of reasonably coherent principles that served the needs of water development pretty well.

Ultimately, what the courts came up with was largely a property right that consisted of a right to exclude others once it had been obtained, with much freedom of action in terms of how it could be used. Not only were right-holders largely not held to standards of beneficial use and use requirements, but they were for a time permitted to freely change places of use and purpose of use. This would not be the end of the story, as external impacts from use would become increasingly prominent over time. This trend would give rise to pressures to impose governance constraints on these basic rights, a subject we will now turn to in chapter 8.

CHAPTER EIGHT

Water Quality and the Law of Nuisance

Mining is a necessary art, but it does not tend to beautify the face of nature. On the contrary, earth disfigured into all manner of ungainly heaps and ridges, hills half torn or washed away, and the residue left in as repulsive shape as can well be conceived, roads intersected and often turned to mire by ditches, water-courses torn up and gouged out, and rivers, once pure as crystal, now dense and opaque with pulverized rock—such is the spectacle presented through the mining region. Not a stream of any size is allowed to escape this pollution—even the bountiful and naturally pure Sacramento is yellow with it, and flows turbid and uninviting to the Pacific . . . Despite the intense heat and drought always prevalent at this season, the country is full of springs, which are bright and clear as need be; but wherever three or four of these join to form a little rill, some gold-seeker is sharp on their track, converting them into liquid mud. California in giving up her hoarded wealth, surrenders much of her beauty.—Horace Greeley, 1859[1]

8.1. Introduction

The ruling in *Irwin v. Phillips* and subsequent Gold Rush rulings that upheld the principle of first possession comport well with the prediction that rights would emerge to support investment in water development when water became more valuable as a factor input into gold production. Without the assurance provided by *Irwin* that water developers would retain their right to water if future claimants tried to horn in, gold production could have been severely hampered, especially as investment requirements increased over time. If we leave it at that, the discussion so far suggests that the appropriative right fashioned by the California courts had many of the features of a purely private property right: that first possession was applied by the courts using a strict rule of trespass in order to provide prior claimants with a right to exclude others and to support transfers of water away from surface sources. The analogy to private property was not perfect, because the courts had fashioned only a right to use, not to own, a corpus of water. However, in many ways important to the miners, the basic appropriative right operated much like an ownership right, including the right to buy, sell, and lease, and to be protected in their investments in water development.

It was not long, however, before the courts began to impose various constraints on the free exercise of the appropriative right. As we have seen, in the 1857 case *Maeris v. Bicknell*, the Court drew a sharp distinction between an appropriation and what it termed a "mere" diversion. More generally, the courts began to refine their treatment of externalities far beyond the basic issue of upstream company A depriving downstream company B of water. What if, for example, A had established an appropriative right to divert water prior to B arriving on the scene, but then wanted to divert to a different location? Or what if A wanted to switch to a different use of water, or to move its point of diversion? It turned out that these were important questions for the courts to answer, as it was common for early claimants to want to make these changes. For example, a ditch might be initially extended to placer deposits that did not pay out, or would become depleted over time as they were worked. This would warrant extending the ditch to new deposits, which might entail moving the diversion point as well. The question for the courts was how to treat these changes, in terms of what they meant for the extent of the appropriative right. Should such changes cause the right-holder to lose his priority date?

For the courts, the answer turned out to be "It depended." For changes in place or purpose of use, the courts quickly adopted a policy of permitting such changes without loss of priority. In *Maeris v. Bicknell*, the first case in which the Court addressed these issues, the Court ruled that a ditch company could extend its ditch from one mining locality to another and maintain its priority date. Any other rule, it argued, "would destroy the utility of such works."[2] *Maeris* did not, however, take a position on changes in the purpose of use, as that was not relevant to the case at hand. But in the 1867 case of *Davis v. Gale*, the Court resoundingly decided that changes in both place and purpose of use were to be permitted, arguing that it was "unable to suggest a plausible reason why . . . not." It then concluded by summarizing its view of what the appropriative right consisted of:

Appropriation, use and nonuse are the tests of [the appropriative] right; and place of use and character of use are not. When [a user] has made his appropriation he becomes entitled to the use of the quantity which he has appropriated at any place where he may choose to convey it, and for any useful and beneficial purpose to which he may choose to apply it. Any other rule would lead to endless complications and most materially impair the value of water rights and privileges.[3]

In *Davis*, it is possible to see the logic of the Court in extending the principle from place of use to purpose of use. The Court begins by arguing on grounds reminiscent of *Maeris* in justifying the extension of a ditch to a different mining locality, on the basis that when mining grounds are depleted, it makes sense to permit the water to be supplied to other mines without losing priority. The Court goes on to say:

Or suppose, after working off the surface, he finds quartz, may he not erect a mill and convert the water into a motive power without forfeiting his prior right? Suppose he appropriates the water for the purpose of running a saw mill, and, after the timber is exhausted, he finds that a grist mill will pay— may he not convert the former into the latter without surrendering his priority to some one who may have subsequently and in the meantime tapped the same stream?[4]

Thus, in the view of the Court, there was no qualitative difference between a switch from one mining locality to another and a switch from one use to another. When a new, more valuable opportunity comes along, be it a more productive mine or a more productive other use of the water, why shouldn't water developers be permitted to take advantage of that fact?

On the other hand, the Court treated changes in the point of *diversion* very differently, beginning with the 1860 case of *Kidd v. Laird*. In *Kidd*, the Court cited several common-law authorities in support of the proposition that changes may be made in the point of diversion only if others were not adversely affected by the change. According to the court, these authorities showed conclusively:

In all cases the effect of the change upon the rights of others is the controlling consideration, and that in the absence of injurious consequences to others, any change which the party chooses to make is legal and proper.[5]

Kidd was subsequently affirmed in 1862 in *Butte v. Morgan*, in which the Court called the opinion in *Kidd* "decisive of [the] question."[6] Together, *Kidd* and *Butte* seem to have provided the origin in the California courts of the principle that adverse third-party impacts provided a legal basis for limiting transfers of water.

In principle, why should the courts have treated changes in diversion points differently from changes in the place and purpose of use? One way to understand these court rulings is to recall our earlier discussion of measurement costs and the distinction between exclusion rights and governance restrictions. In effect, what the courts did was to create exclusion rights for individual appropriative rights that conferred considerable leeway on users to use the water wherever they wanted and for whatever purpose. In contrast, changes in diversion points were subject to governance restrictions. Location of use, purpose of use, and point of diversion all seem like attributes which should not be terribly costly to measure. Therefore, all should have been equally subject (or not) to governance restrictions, all else equal. The difference in court treatment probably derived from the greater impact of changes in diversion points on others within the basin. Merely shifting water supply to a new mining location, or using it to power grist mills rather than saw mills, would not have had obvious impacts on other water claimants along the waterway, if the diversion point was not being moved and no more water was being diverted.[7] Changes in diversion points, however—especially moving diversion points upstream—may have generated much more obvious impacts on other users that could be more clearly and convincingly demonstrated in court. These greater external impacts may account for why the courts felt bound to impose governance constraints on changes in diversion points but not changes in place and purpose of use.[8]

A far more serious and wide-ranging set of questions regarding externalities would arise in the effect that mining itself had on the quality of the water that was used for gold separation. In addressing these issues, the courts would struggle to reconcile English common law with the conditions of the gold fields, perhaps even more than they had in affirming the principle of temporal priority. However, the principles that they came up with would again reflect a certain economic logic, just as temporal priority did. Describing the principles they came up with and the thought process they used to formulate them, and interpreting those principles in terms of how well they served efficiency objectives, is the subject of the remainder of this chapter.

8.2. The Environmental Consequences of Technological Advance

From an environmental standpoint, placer mining was largely benign as long as miners used primitive separation technologies. When a miner working by a river swirled gold-bearing debris around in a pan using water from the river, he had minimal impact on other miners working nearby. Similarly, deploying a rocker-and-cradle had little impact on other miners in its effect on the quality of the waste water emerging at the end of the process. The amount of dirt that could be processed using these technologies was simply not enough for any individual company to make much of a difference. It is not surprising, then, that we observe very little evidence of disputes over water quality during 1849 and 1850, when these primitive technologies were dominant.

The emergence of the separation technologies that employed a continuous stream of water would change all this. When water was flumed or piped into and through long toms and sluice boxes, substantial amounts of debris-filled tailings began to be generated. When these tailings were vented back into local rivers and streams, they were carried downstream where they would bury mining claims and fill ditches and reservoirs with dirt and sediment. Similarly, when a ditch company provided water through a ditch or flume, the tailings would commonly be vented back into the ditch. Ground sluicing and hydraulic mining made matters much worse, by magnifying the quantity of debris-filled tailings. The problem was the sheer amount of throughput. At every step along the way, from rockers to long toms to sluice boxes to ground sluicing to hydraulic mining, quantum jumps occurred in both the amount of dirt that could be processed and the amount of tailings that would emerge at the end of the process. Estimates vary regarding how much more productive each of the successive technologies was, but it is likely that miners working a long tom could process anywhere from two to four times as much dirt as miners working a rocker, per man.[9] Similarly, by one estimate, miners working a sluice could roughly double the production of a long tom.[10] In terms of processing dirt, ground sluicing and especially hydraulicking likely dwarfed these earlier technologies.

The impact of reduced water quality on the value of the water for mining purposes was reflected in the prices that ditch companies charged for water. When a ditch was extended into a local diggings, the lucky miners at the head of the ditch would be provided water of relatively high quality. However, through the process of repeated venting of the tailings back into the ditch, successive mining operations would receive increasingly degraded water. Consequently, it was common for ditch companies to employ a sliding scale of water charges, with the highest prices charged to miners located at the head of the ditch. According to one account, ditch companies in Nevada County charged four times as much for the relatively pure water at the head of the ditch as they did for the muddy, turbid water at the bottom of the ditch.[11]

Despite the fact that degraded water quality imposed real costs on miners, there is little evidence that disputes over significantly degraded water quality occurred prior to late 1852. This may seem a bit surprising since as we have seen, long toms and sluice boxes began to be extensively used in the 1851 mining season. One possibility is that water quality issues rose to prominence only after the advent of ground sluicing and hydraulic mining, which did not occur until 1852 and 1853, which is the reason suggested by most histories. A related factor, however, was likely the timing of the development of the ditch industry. A great deal of evidence suggests that much of the dry diggings in the gold fields lacked access to water until well into 1852 and later, especially in the southern diggings. As we saw in chapter 4, in water-scarce areas this would be reflected in the practices of hauling dirt to sources of water, leaving piles of dirt unprocessed in anticipation of rain, or just leaving dry diggings for lack of water.

Figure 8.1 reports the cumulative number of stories in the *Alta Californian* that reported that any of these practices were being employed, for the years 1851 and 1852.[12] The first thing to notice is that hauling dirt and leaving dirt unprocessed were both fairly common occurrences, suggesting that localized lack of water was indeed a general problem during this early period. These data also suggest that hauling dirt was employed fairly continuously throughout the year, whereas leaving dirt unprocessed exhibited a more seasonal pattern, tending to occur more extensively from mid-summer until late in the year. This pattern makes sense, of course, given that the prevailing seasonal pattern of precipitation meant the drying-up of the rivers beginning sometime in the summer. Finally, these data suggest a modest easing of water scarcity in 1852, as all of the practices become less frequently reported in that year.

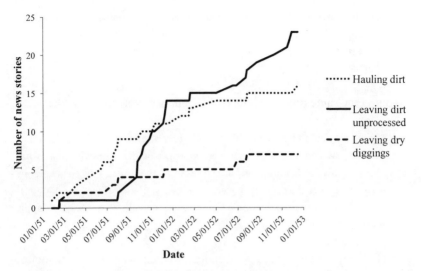

FIGURE 8.1. Miner practices under water scarcity, 1851–1852.

This suggestion of easing water scarcity in 1852 is corroborated by news accounts of developments in the ditching industry that suggest that significant water development occurred beginning in the 1851 mining season, but accelerated noticeably in 1852. Figure 8.2 graphs the cumulative number of stories appearing in the *Alta Californian* that reported new ditches were either completed or near completion for the years 1851 and 1852.[13] In 1851, there were several reports of new ditches that were in the planning stages, but I could find only one report of a ditch company—the Rock Creek Company in Nevada County—that was actively supplying water to miners. By contrast, in 1852 there were seventeen reports of ditches that were completed or nearly completed. It seems, then, that ditch construction to completion advanced considerably in 1852. This impression is corroborated by items that appeared in the *Alta Californian* toward the end of 1852. In December, a correspondent from Sonora described the great strides that had been taken in water development in Tuolumne County that year:

> The principal cause of success this year above that of former years, may be traced to the various water companies. Formerly the miners, except in a very few choice localities, were compelled by scarcity of water to use the rocker, or else to cart away the dirt to a stream sufficiently large to run a long tom.

Now the water is coursing down almost every gulch, and toms are stationed on every claim. The labor and expense of mining are thereby reduced at least one-half, and the quantity of gold collected is nearly twice as great to every laborer.[14]

Around the same time, the *Alta Californian* was able to report that:

A great revolution has occurred in the system of mining during the past few months. The completion of the gigantic works of the water companies has placed numerous facilities within the reach of the miner, and consequently has given a more permanent character to the population. They can now, during both the winter and summer months, be certain of a constant supply of water.[15]

The rapid growth of the ditch industry, along with the technological advances that were occurring in gold separation, meant that it was only a matter of time before disputes over degraded water quality would begin to occur. Perhaps the first account of a dispute over water quality to appear in the *Alta Californian* occurred in December 1852, when a news item described a dispute between two mining companies in Tuolumne County. In this case, a mining company was charged with diverting water from Sullivan's Creek, a small tributary of the Tuolumne River,

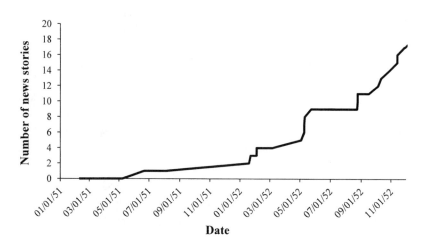

FIGURE 8.2. New ditch construction, 1851–1852

and returning water to the creek "turbid and muddy."[16] In the following month, a dispute broke out between two mining companies in Placer County when one allegedly diverted water from the Bear River and

> greatly injured, altered, changed, and impaired the value of the remainder of the water, . . . by rendering the same muddy, turbid, and mixing the same with soil, dirt and sediment, thereby rendering the same much less valuable to said plaintiffs for mining purposes; . . . and thereby causing the said ditch of said plaintiffs to become filled with soil, dirt, and sediment.[17]

In October 1854, a mining company in Tuolumne County brought suit against the Tuolumne County Water Company for flooding its claims with degraded water. In late 1855, we begin to see a series of disputes involving degraded water quality being brought to the Placer County district court, beginning with *Bear River and Auburn Water and Mining Company vs. New York Mining Company. Bear River* was followed by no fewer than four similar cases in Placer County within a few short months.[18]

8.3. Economic Considerations in Assessing Water Quality Impacts

It will be useful to revisit the model presented in chapter 2, which was used to answer the question: given use and reuse along a surface waterway, what definition of water rights would promote total rent-maximization? The basic result presented then was that under conditions of constant water quality, efficient use of a river requires that rights be defined in terms of consumptive use; that is, only that portion of a diversion that is physically consumptive of the river.[19] We have already seen an important implication of this model for appropriative rights: that defining individual rights to the quantity diverted supports rent-maximization within a watershed when use is associated with no recharge to the waterway. During the 1850s, especially as water came to be used more and more for dry diggings remote from their water sources, it made efficiency sense to define water rights in terms of diversion amounts with few restrictions on use.

A somewhat different implication for rent-maximization arises, however, when consumption degrades water quality. In this case, upstream diversions inflict negative externalities on downstream companies, which subtract from total rents by reducing the extra rents that recharge confers on downstream companies. According to the model, efficient rights definition then requires, relative to the constant water quality case, higher marginal value upstream and thus, restricted upstream diversions, to offset the costs inflicted on downstream companies.[20] If the impacts on downstream companies are not too large, a balancing rule that does not prohibit upstream diversions but imposes some governance restrictions on free exercise of that right would move in this direction.

The picture is, however, quite different if diversions by the upstream company severely degrade water quality in the river. To see this, consider an extreme situation where diversions by an upstream company render the waters in the river completely valueless for downstream uses. If diversions by A completely destroy the value of the river for B, total combined rents reduce to the rents enjoyed by A. In this case, a first possession trespass rule may be more efficient as long as it is accompanied by low transaction costs in trading rights. If A is awarded a first possession right by virtue of being first, this maximizes overall rents if the value of his operation exceeds that of B. If B's operation is more valuable, this can still maximize rents as long as the transaction costs of B buying off A are low. A similar argument obviously holds if B is present first. The courts, in promoting transfers of rights, would have been supporting these sorts of Pareto-improving transactions.[21]

This argument yields the following implication for situations involving degraded water quality: governance restrictions on use may make efficiency sense when those impacts are relatively small, but an exclusion right may make efficiency sense when those impacts are large. With this in mind, let us turn to what the courts actually did.

8.4. "Clear as Mud?": The Initial Adoption of Reasonable Use

As it turned out, the issue of water quality presented some major doctrinal challenges, perhaps even more perplexing to the courts than those posed by first possession. As we have seen, in the 1850s the California courts were staunchly committed to supporting the burgeoning mining industry. At the same time, they labored under a legislative mandate to apply English common-law principles to decide legal disputes, which led them to search for strategies that could be pursued under the circum-

stances in order to get the outcomes they desired.[22] Having settled the issue of primacy to a given corpus of water on public lands with the notion
of temporal priority, however, the issue of water quality degradation introduced a new wrinkle: suddenly, given corpuses of water of different
qualities could not be considered the same. The question would then become: If a particular claimant enjoyed a first possession right to a certain
amount of water, exactly what was it that he enjoyed a right to?

It is fair to say that most English common-law authorities and the vast
majority of English common-law cases involving riparian rights were
concerned not so much with water quality but rather, deprivation or irregularity of flow. The older cases involving principles of ancient/prior
use or natural flow could be, and sometimes were, interpreted as including the right to a stream of water not degraded in quality. However, they
were typically silent on, or sometimes did not seem to be speaking to,
this issue. And even as reasonable use principles slowly spread through
the rulings in the early nineteenth century, the relevant passages were
typically worded without explicit reference to water quality. The landmark riparian law case *Tyler v. Wilkinson*, though it speaks to injury,
goes on to clarify that it is referring to diminution of quantity, or changes
in the speed of the current:

> There may be, and there must be allowed of that, which is common to all, a
> reasonable use. The true test of the principle and extent of the use is, whether
> it is to the injury of the other proprietors or not. There may be a diminution
> in quantity, or a retardation or acceleration of the natural current indispens-
> able for the general and valuable use of the water, perfectly consistent with
> the existence of the common right. The *diminution, retardation, or acceler-*
> *ation*, not positively and sensibly injurious by diminishing the value of the
> common right, is an implied element in the right of using the stream at all.[23]
> (emphasis added)

Thus, Judge Story, who penned the *Tyler* ruling, seems to be speaking
exclusively to the circumstances of the eastern United States, where the
disputes over riparian use that entered into case law were largely about
activities that did not degrade the quality of the water in the waterways,
such as mill dams.[24] Subsequent eastern cases into the early 1850s would
continue the rhetorical pattern of speaking in most cases in terms of diversion and obstruction of river flows.[25]

Not that there were no English common-law cases involving damages to water quality. It is well known that in England, the onset of industrialization in the late eighteenth and early nineteenth centuries associated with the British industrial revolution brought with it all sorts of environmental damages. Not the least of these were to English waterways, into which all sorts of industrial and domestic wastes were vented. The response of the English courts was to treat pollution as subject to a trespass rule: any significant pollution would be enjoined, regardless of the social benefit of the activity.[26] Angell put the principle as follows in *Watercourses*:

> It is clearly the duty of riparian proprietors, upon a watercourse, to refrain from erecting upon its banks any works which render the water unwholesome or offensive.[27]

Angell, however, goes on to cite mostly cases involving waste disposal from activities not having to do with the extraction and use of the water, such as dumping chemicals, or erecting a cesspool or tanyard that leaches noxious materials into the river.[28] As we shall see shortly, such cases would not be considered by judges to provide meaningful analogies to most water quality cases that were emerging in the gold fields.

It is perhaps not surprising, then, that the courts would go through an initial period of doctrinal uncertainty when attempting to apply English common-law principles to conditions in the gold fields. This is clearly seen in considering two of the very first cases directly involving water quality that came before the courts: *Bear River and Auburn Water and Mining Co.* and *Hill v. King*.[29] Both of these cases originated in the Placer County district court and were appealed to the state Supreme Court, which heard the cases in rapid succession in late 1857. Both involved essentially the same fact pattern: a prior plaintiff brought suit to enjoin the diversions of a newcomer upstream company. In both cases it was shown that the actions of the upstream company were degrading the quality of the water to the detriment of the downstream company. Yet in *Hill v. King*, the Court sided with the downstream plaintiffs on the issue of water quality, while in *Bear River* the Court sided with the upstream defendants. Indeed, the two cases are generally viewed as laying down different rules for adjudging cases involving degraded water quality.[30] It would take several years, in a series of further rulings, for the Court to set out a consistent principle for judging these sorts of cases.

To make sense of the Court treatment of the issues, let us consider the two cases in more detail. In *Hill v. King*, the plaintiff owned two ditches that were conveying water from Indian Canon, a tributary of the American River, for sale to miners. The ditches had been constructed in 1852, well before the defendants came on the scene in late 1855. The defendants took up some mining claims above the ditches of the plaintiff and began working them with sluices, and the tail waters flowed into Indian Canon, into which was deposited dirt and sediment. The muddy water then flowed down into the ditches of the plaintiff, who lost customers and revenues from water sales. The defendants did not deny that they were responsible for generating the tailings that damaged the downstream company. However, in their defense they said they worked their claim in a careful manner, using no more water than was absolutely necessary to process the gold, and that there was no other way to work the claims. Finally, in order to add the standard imprimatur of legitimacy to their case, they argued that all of their work had been done in accordance with "the customs and usages of miners" in the local mining district.[31] A jury was apparently convinced by these arguments, and found for the defendants.

A key issue during the trial centered upon a decision made by the district judge to deny a request by the plaintiff for a particular instruction to the jury. This instruction read as follows:

> That if plaintiff had constructed his ditches, and appropriated the waters of Indian Canon, and was using said water, for sale for mining purposes, and defendants subsequently located mining claims near the bank of said canon, and above the head of plaintiff's ditches, and in working said claims, they, the defendants, occasioned a material and essential injury to the waters of said canon, so that their value was materially and essentially impaired for the mining uses to which they were being put by plaintiff, such acts are sufficient to entitle the plaintiff to his action. *And although defendants may have worked their claims in the most practicable and reasonable manner, and may have done no more damage than it was necessary to do, in order to work their claims, yet the plaintiff was entitled to recover from them to the extent of the damage done by them.* (emphasis added)

The last sentence indicates that the district court judge denied a request by the plaintiff to apply what was in effect a rule of trespass: that a mere finding of damage, regardless of how reasonably the defendant had behaved, be considered sufficient to find in their favor. In the opinion of

the Court, written by Chief Justice Murray, it should have been controlling that the plaintiff enjoyed a prior right, which should have entitled
him to "exclusive enjoyment of the [water], pure and undiminished." The
Court held that the trial court had erred by refusing to instruct the jury
that a mere finding of damage would be controlling. This became the basis for the Court to overturn the district court ruling. The case was re-
manded back to district court, and upon rehearing, the judge promptly
ruled for the plaintiff.

In *Bear River*, the dispute was between two ditch companies, with
the plaintiff's claim to waters of the Bear River dating from spring of
1851, for the purpose of supplying miners in the vicinity of the town of
Auburn. The defendant came along in 1853 and constructed a dam and
ditch above the plaintiff's ditch and diverted water and as in *Hill*, then
returned it to the river filled with dirt and sediment. In contrast to *Hill*,
the plaintiff brought three charges: that it had been deprived of water,
that the flow in the river had become irregular, and that the quality of
the water had been degraded. In the trial court, the plaintiff prevailed on
all three charges. But upon appeal, the Court reversed the ruling on the
third charge of diminished water quality, arguing that the degradation
of water quality should be considered "injury without consequent damage."[32] This ruling turned out to be a major victory of sorts for the defendant, as the jury had concluded that alleged damages from degraded
water quality were large and were in fact well in excess of the damages
from water deprivation and irregularity combined. The *Bear River* ruling meant a dramatically reduced damage award to the plaintiff.[33]

It should be mentioned that the Court struggled mightily in coming
to this ruling, because of what it perceived as lack of doctrinal guidance
in the English common-law authorities. Apparently considering the old
English pollution cases irrelevant, the Court focused on eastern riparian
cases, which were painfully devoid of precedent regarding water quality for what was in its view a very good reason. Existing uses of surface
water that dominated in the eastern United States, the Court argued,
did not present water quality issues because some uses such as domestic
use and watering of stock (what the Court termed "preferred uses") consumed water entirely, whereas other uses such as powering mills by their
nature did not degrade water quality. The Court went on to say:

> But in our mineral region we have a novel use of water, that cannot be classed
> with the preferred uses; but still a use that deteriorates the quality of the ele-

ment itself, when wanted a second time for the same purposes. In cases here-
tofore known, either the element was entirely consumed, or else its use did
not impair its quality, when wanted again for the same purpose. And this fact
constitutes the great difficulty in this, and other like cases. If the use of water for mining purposes did not deteriorate the quality of the element itself,
then the only injury that could be complained of, would be the diminution in
the quantity, and the interruption in the flow. *It is this novel use of water, and
its effects upon the fluid itself, that constitute the main difficulty in this case.*[34]
(emphasis added)

Because of this, the Court considered itself left "without any direct precedent" to guide it in its rule-making, characterizing the issue of water
quality degradation as "one of the most difficult of that most perplexing
class of cases [i.e., disputes over water among miners]."[35]

What it came up with, of course, was something that was for all intents and purposes the reasonable use doctrine as applied to water quality. What was needed was a balancing of needs, for if no significant degradation by any operation was permitted, the Court argued, this would
paralyze a mining industry heavily dependent on water-intensive gold
separation technologies.

As a number of scholars have noted, the purported rationale for the
ruling was an essentially pragmatic one, that if the Court enjoined diversions that degraded water quality, this would make it virtually impossible to prosecute mining:

> *If, then, we lay down the doctrine as true, that the ditch owner is entitled to the
> water in as pure a state as it was at the time he constructed his ditch, the result
> must be that those locating above him can never use the water at all, . . .* For as
> the streams are rapid, the sediment must, in greater or less quantities, come
> down to his ditch. The inevitable practical result must be, that the water can-
> not be used so often, and the general usefulness of this element for mining
> purposes must be greatly impaired, and the leading intention of the superior
> proprietor be thus far defeated.[36] (emphasis added)

It is useful to notice the orientation of the *Bear River* ruling, with its focus on water remaining in its pure state. It makes no sense, the Court is
arguing, to enjoin every single activity that degrades the water so that
it is left in its pure state. Given the reality that the new gold separation
technologies must degrade the water, it is far better to balance the needs

of upstream and downstream companies in order to permit greater prosecution of mining. *Bear River*, then, may be interpreted as consistent
with the basin rent-maximization model presented earlier when water
quality effects are modest in magnitude.

We may now see what was apparently the crux of the matter, concerning why the two rulings came down on opposite sides. The ruling in *Hill
v. King* may be seen in essence as an application of the natural flow principle referred to in the previous chapter. Recall that in *Hill*, the Court
had ruled that the instructions to the jury that had been improperly denied were in effect that reasonableness was not a valid defense for having caused damage to the plaintiffs. In other words, the Court wanted
the jury to decide on the basis that any damages were actionable, which
is roughly equivalent to mandating a natural flow right. *Bear River*, as
we have just seen, for all intents and purposes adopted a reasonableness
standard. Thus, the seemingly contradictory rulings in *Bear River* and
Hill were the result of one standard being applied in one case and the
other standard being applied in the other case. It is thus not at all surprising that the plaintiff in *Hill* prevailed when the natural flow standard
was applied and the defendant in *Bear River* prevailed when the reasonableness standard was applied.

Why would the same Court, in two back-to-back cases involving virtually identical fact patterns, end up taking doctrinally opposing positions on the issue of water quality? I believe this can be explained in
part by the existing doctrinal void in English common law with regard to
water quality, especially as the Court tried to formulate doctrine under
the new circumstances of the gold fields. The Court was grappling with
a difficult issue that had major implications for the most economically
important industry in the state. The last thing it wanted to do was to
hand down rulings that would damage that industry. But if it believed it
was protecting the industry by mandating reasonable use, certainly there
were others who believed it was doing the exact opposite. In late December 1857, a miner, who probably spoke for many, wrote an extended
letter to the *Alta Californian*, excoriating the *Bear River* ruling. Referring to the recent rulings upholding first possession, the miner argued:
no sooner had the Court protected water rights then what does it do? It
permits others to "injure it by mud, as to render it valueless to the original appropriator." The *Bear River* ruling, in his opinion, had made the
doctrine regarding water rights "as clear as mud."[37] It is easy to envision such a struggle between incompatible positions playing out in the

minds of the Court justices. It is telling, for example, that one justice, Peter Burnett, was in the majority opinion in both cases. But while he sided with the reasonable use position in *Bear River*, he used *Hill* to voice his concerns about that very doctrine, saying that "(u)pon more full and mature consideration, I think the former opinion of the Court [Bear River] should receive some qualification."[38]

Burnett's statement in *Hill* cannot be interpreted as a repudiation of *Bear River*, however. As we will see below, Burnett would continue to ascribe to the *Bear River* principle for the rest of his term on the Court. But in any case, the coexistence of the two seemingly incompatible rulings reflected, or perhaps produced, a great deal of ambivalence in the late 1850s on the part of judges regarding how to treat water quality. In another case, tried in the Placer County district court at about the same time as *Hill* and *Bear River*, the Bear River Company appeared as defendants against another ditch company, the Oakland Ditch Company. As in all these water quality cases, the plaintiffs claimed a prior right which the defendants were alleged to have violated by adulterating the water. However, some additional issues arose that had not appeared in other cases, such as whether the plaintiffs had given their consent to the actions of the defendants, and who was liable: the defendants or the miners to whom the water was sold. Regarding the issue of water quality, the judge gave the following instructions to the jury:

> Defendants would have no right in order to consult their own convenience, to hold up the water, and then let it off, mixed with the accumulated mud, in large and unreasonable quantities to the injuries of the plaintiffs below. It is not every slight injury of this character that will entitle plaintiffs to recover: it must be a substantial material injury to authorize a recovery.[39]

What is interesting here is the standard set by the judge: the defendants were not permitted to release "large and unreasonable quantities" that would inflict "substantial material injury" on the plaintiffs. If it did, the result would presumably be an injunction and award of damages, which is consistent with the ruling in *Bear River*, the difference being the magnitude of the damages. Large damages, apparently, would be sufficient to merit an injunction.

The doctrine in *Bear River* was also sustained in another case brought before the Court in the late 1850s, this time by the Mokelumne Hill Canal and Mining Company, a ditch company operating in Calaveras

County. This company claimed a prior right and brought suit against another ditch company requesting damages and an injunction for degrading the waters of the Mokelumne River. In the district court, the judge, at the request of the plaintiffs, gave the following instruction to the jury:

> In order to recover, it is only necessary for the plaintiffs to prove that they first appropriated the waters of the South Fork of the Mokelumne River, for the purpose indicated in their complaint, and that the defendant has diverted and lessened the quantity, or impaired the quality thereof materially, as averred in the complaint, and that plaintiffs have been injured thereby.

Thus, the jury had been instructed that as long as the plaintiffs were there first, a mere finding of damage would be controlling in their favor, meriting an injunction and full damages: clearly a trespass rule. Since the plaintiff's prior right was unquestioned, the jury found for the plaintiff. However, upon appeal the Court reversed the district court ruling on the basis that the instructions were "erroneous," and it went on to cite the *Bear River* ruling as controlling, having been "rendered after the most mature and anxious consideration."[40] It should be added that Burnett, who had authored *Bear River*, wrote the opinion for this ruling as well.

A third case, however, raised some doubts regarding the position of the courts on the *Bear River* doctrine. In 1858, the Court decided a case involving a ditch company operating in El Dorado County, which brought a complaint against some miners for damaging the water quality in its ditch. Though the ruling in favor of the ditch company was largely on technical grounds, the Court revealed its ambivalence about the *Bear River* ruling in concluding that:

> It has nowhere been held that a defendant is not responsible for injuries done the ditch of another by the deposit of mud and sediment in it. The doctrine of the *Bear River Company v. York Mining Company* probably went quite as far as it ought to have gone.[41]

Unfortunately, the Court did not elaborate on precisely what its reservations were about *Bear River*, and the wording of this brief passage could be interpreted either as supporting a trespass rule or a reasonable use rule. But in any case, it does suggest some concern that *Bear River* might have overreached in applying the reasonable use standard.

8.5. The Move to a Rule of Trespass

Beginning in the early 1860s, however, the courts would do an about-face in its treatment of water quality, moving from the reasonable use principle in *Bear River* to the trespass rule in *Hill*. The first case occurred in 1863, in *Phoenix Water Company v. Fletcher*. In *Phoenix*, a previously-located ditch company in Tuolumne County sued a sawmill company for degrading the waters of a local creek that it had been tapping to supply water to miners. As the sawmill was charged with throwing bark and sawdust into the creek, it resembled in its particulars some of the early English pollution cases we saw earlier. The defendant sawmill company did not deny it had come later but echoing *Bear River*, argued that it was entitled to use the water if it used it in a "reasonable manner"; that is, in such a way as to not inflict "material injury" to the plaintiff. On the issue of water quality, the Court found for the plaintiff, citing the following principle

> As prior appropriators the plaintiffs are entitled to damages for such injuries, and to be protected from future loss. The prior appropriator is clearly entitled to protection against acts which materially diminish the quantity of water to which he is entitled, or deteriorate its quality, for the uses to which he wishes to apply it. (*Phoenix v. Fletcher*, p. 487)

Thus, *Phoenix* provided a clear enunciation of the strict liability rule, a clear move away from the principle of *Bear River*.[42] However, since the case involved the discarding of wastes into the canal, it was straightforward to apply the strict liability rules from the old English cases. Indeed, the opinion cited a number of the same cases that Angell had cited to support strict liability. As a result, the case did not provide clear guidance on the canonical gold fields fact pattern involving the venting of tail waters from mining operations.

However, two years later, in *Hill v. Smith*, the Court considered a dispute that did involve a mining company that generated tail waters that damaged water quality to a previously-situated downstream ditch company. In *Hill v. Smith*, the court again found for the plaintiff and gave a more complete explication of its new position with regard to water quality:

There seems to have been a successful effort made on the part of the defense to prove that the defendant had studiously conducted his mining operations in such a manner as to cause the least possible injury to the water rights of the plaintiff. It is probable that the jury supposed that, having thus worked, the defendant was not responsible for injuries unavoidably resulting from his work, upon the vague notion that everybody has a right to mine at such points as he may choose, provided he causes as little injury to others as is possible under all the circumstances. . . . *How cautiously or carefully the defendant worked was a matter of no consequence, for if his work in fact injured the plaintiff, he was none the less liable to an action.*[43] (emphasis added)

Thus, *Hill v. Smith* made it clear that the Court had in effect retreated from its previous balancing rule to what was for all intents and purposes a strict rule of trespass.

It is important to note that by the 1860s, the courts were beginning to believe that the problem of degraded water quality was becoming more serious, inflicting greater costs on downstream companies. Consider, for example, the following passage from *Phoenix*:

This kind of injury to water [referring to sawdust and refuse bark being deposited into the stream by the upstream mill] is a peculiar one, as, while the actual quantity of the water in the stream is not thereby materially diminished, yet these acts so affect the water as to materially diminish the quantity the plaintiffs are able to take from the stream and use for mining purposes. Practically, it is well known to be a serious injury, very materially diminishing the value and profits of the ditch property.[44]

Perhaps even more telling is the following passage from *Hill v. Smith*:

Where [the plaintiff] had previously sold only sixty inches of water she was compelled to sell a hundred and a hundred and twenty at the same price in consequence of the deterioration of its solvent capacity by reason of the sediment and mud from defendant's claim. It further appears that on one or two occasions the miners, or some of them, who purchased water from the plaintiff, quit work entirely, because the water was so thick with sediment that it could not be used with any reasonable success in hydraulic mining.[45]

Thus, in *Hill*, the damages are apparent to the Court because they are easily seen as a 50 percent reduction in revenues from water sales.[46] The marketing and selling of water may have made it easier for the courts to quantify damages and, perhaps, may have impressed upon them the magnitude of the costs inflicted on downstream companies.

The story suggests that only after a period of confusion did the Court settle down into a consistent application of the rule of trespass to all cases involving damages to water quality from upstream diversions. A stronger normative version of this interpretation might argue that the Court overreached in *Bear River* (as some subsequent rulings suggested) in terms of being overly solicitous of the needs of the mining industry. However, as I argued earlier, I believe a stronger case can be made that it was not the courts but rather, the legislature that tended to exhibit "capture" by the mining industry during this period, and the courts— especially the higher courts—were often in the position of reining in the legislature, to the extent they had flexibility to do so. This arguably occurred, as we saw in the last chapter, in mining vs. agriculture disputes, where the legislature had mandated in 1852 that miners could invade previously settled agricultural lands in search of gold and the courts, after going along for a while, gradually circumscribed this policy. But these political factors were likely dominated by a more important economic reality: that the courts responded to certain important economic factors, especially transaction costs, in crafting their rulings regarding water quality. And we should not lose sight of the fact that ultimately, the courts moved to the English common-law position of strict liability as a means of dealing more efficiently with disputes over water quality.

8.6. Conclusions

After some initial confusion caused in part by English common law, the California courts settled on a rule of strict liability in cases regarding degradation of water quality. The evidence most strongly suggests the importance of economic factors in shaping court doctrine regarding water quality. The ultimate emergence of a liability rule makes economic sense under conditions of low transaction costs, when it would be easy for the affected parties to negotiate to a mutually agreeable settlement. And though one might think transaction costs would be high with regard to water quality because of measurement costs, in fact there is reason to believe transaction costs were often reasonably low. During this early period, disputes over water quality typically involved small numbers of parties on moderate-sized waterways, where it was apparent how the pollution was being generated, and who was doing it. And the (Type II) transaction costs arising from strategic behavior by parties who found themselves in a bilateral bargaining situation were likely limited by the challenges of concealing public information concerning both damages suffered and the behavior that inflicted those damages. The evidence also suggests that the thinking of the courts was influenced by the magnitude of the damages: that they were more likely to make polluters strictly liable when damages were larger. This is also suggestive of efficiency, as larger, more salient damages would have accompanied situations of more complete information regarding the generation of damages, supporting private negotiations. Furthermore, under these conditions, trespass rules would have dominated nuisance rules by economizing on transaction costs. All of this is consistent with our model of rent maximization within a watershed.

As it turned out, there would be another type of externality that miners would have to regularly contend with during this period: damages from collapsing dams. These periodic incidents, which actually happened quite often, would afford judges the opportunity to develop a different aspect of the law of torts. Let us now turn to this issue, which will provide still more complementary insights into the doctrinal thinking of the courts, and the economic currents that influenced that thinking.

Appendix A

Rent-Maximization in a Simple River System with Water Quality Impacts

Consider again the model of rent maximization subject to a riverflow constraint that was contained in the Lagrangean in equation (2.2), reproduced here:

(2.2)
$$L = \text{Max} \sum_i \left\{ \int_0^{D_i} [f_i(\theta_i)] d\theta \right\} + \lambda[X - \sum D_i(1 - R_i)]$$

To allow this model to capture diminished water quantity and degraded water quality, define a water quality parameter α, which takes on negative values and is a function of both total upstream diversions and the total volume of water in the river. In the simple two-party case, for the downstream company B, this parameter is:

(8.1)
$$\alpha_B = \alpha(D_A, X_B)$$

where $X_B = X - D_A(1 - R_A)$. It is assumed that water quality is positively affected by the volume of water in the river and negatively affected by total upstream diversions. As before, each claimant derives productive value from water use, which is assumed to increase in both water use and water quality. Expressed in marginal terms, we assume the following marginal value function:

(8.2) $MV_j = f(D_j) + \alpha(D_i, X_j)$

Substituting into equation (2.2), we derive the following modified Lagrangean:

(8.3) $L = \text{Max } \Sigma \int [f_i(\theta_i)]d\theta + \alpha[\Sigma D_j, X - \Sigma D_j (1 - Rj)]$
               $+ \lambda[X - \Sigma D_i(1 - R_i)]$

Maximizing (8.3) now leaves us with the following result:

(8.4) $f_i/(1 - R_i) > f_j/(1 - R_j)$

Intuitively, equation (8.4) says that when consumption degrades water quality, efficient rights definition requires higher marginal value upstream, to offset the additional costs inflicted on downstream users. This implies that reducing upstream rights allocations would serve to promote efficient use of the river. For moderate damages, a governance rule that does not prohibit upstream diversions but imposes some restrictions on free exercise of that right, such as reasonable use, would move in this direction. In measurement cost terms, this superimposition of a governance rule upon the basic exclusion right serves to preserve the efficiency-enhancing power of market exchanges, while moderating them to account for the externality associated with use.

The prescription, however, may be somewhat different if diversions by the upstream firm result in severe degradation of the water quality in the river. Under these conditions, a governance rule like reasonable use makes less sense. If diversions by A, for example, completely destroy the value of the river for B, total combined rents reduce to the rents enjoyed by A. In this case, a first possession trespass rule may be more efficient as long as it is accompanied by low transaction costs in trading rights. If A is awarded a first possession right by virtue of being first, this maximizes rents if the value of his operation exceeds that of B. If B's operation is more valuable, this can still maximize rents as long as the transaction cost of B buying off A are low. A similar argument obviously holds if B is present first. The courts, in promoting transfers of rights, would have been supporting these sorts of Pareto-improving transactions.

CHAPTER NINE

Bursting Dams and the Law of Torts

This morning—Sept. 24th—the water was rising in its might. Notwithstanding our aqueduct and canal, the bed of the river was nearly full. We hastened to remove all our mining implements. Slowly, but surely, the freshet came, till the destruction of all our works seemed inevitable.

We thought not of hunger, though we had been laboring hard much of the night and all the morning. About ten o'clock there was a pause of fearful suspense. The rising seemed arrested—might it not be on the turn? For a short time there was hope; the pendulum vibrated each moment between our hopes and our fears. We hastened up the hill side—after all had been done which could be—to a spot commanding a view of the whole, to see our hopes and not our fears realized. We perceived at once that the existence of all our works depended upon the Paine's Bar dam above us. Would that stand the torrent? Should that maintain its position, we were safe; let that go, all would be swept away!

As we kept our eyes fixed upon this—it was a quarter of a mile above us—the black line of wall was suddenly broken, and the torrent poured through a small opening forced in the dam, and in a few seconds the river ran foaming over the entire length of the wall, which bowed and sank before the irresistible force. Then and there was heard a sound new and strangely startling to me. It was caused by large stones rushing and grinding under water, borne on by the tremendous power of the current. It might be imagined that the thousand submerged chariots and cars of Pharaoh's host were driving impetuously over that river channel. As soon as the dam above us gave way, the water rose with great rapidity—two, three, four, six, eight feet—till it poured over the top of the aqueduct. Still it nobly stood, held in its place by the immense weight of the water which poured through it from the canal above. It was indeed surprising to see a thing so light resisting that mad and mighty force. It was but a moment! Gently and gracefully it yielded, swayed forward, and moved with the ease and rapidity of a thing of life. Thus, in one moment, we saw the work of one thousand and twenty-nine days done by the company swept away and rendered useless.
—Daniel Woods, 9/24/1850

9.1. Introduction

So Daniel Woods, a clergyman originally from Philadelphia, described the destruction of his river mining company's diversion aqueduct by a collapsing dam in 1850. Indeed, incidents like this occurred with alarming frequency in early California and sometimes with more tragic consequences than experienced by Woods. Not surprisingly, a number of these cases wound up in court as aggrieved downstream companies would sue for damages, and the Gold Rush courts spent a great deal of time sorting out the rights of the conflicting parties. The doctrinal result was Gold Rush California's contribution to the evolving nineteenth-century law of tort.

At first blush, one might expect these cases to be fairly cut-and-dried. After all, in Woods' case it had been obvious whose dam had collapsed and who had been the unlucky recipient of the escaped water and debris. However, Gold Rush mining and ditch companies were constantly in danger of being flooded out by freshets and rapidly rising river currents. For those working near sources of water, flooding was a regular occupational hazard. The courts were willing, generally speaking, to provide relief to downstream companies when it was clear that a ditch company was to blame. However, it was not always easy to know how much the ditch companies were to blame when their dams collapsed. A key issue was whether they had been negligent in the construction and maintenance of their dam, but defining negligence would turn out to be no easy thing.

A close examination of this particular set of tort cases reveals that the California courts quickly adopted a rule based on negligence: damming companies were responsible for damages to downstream companies only if it could be shown that they had been negligent in dam construction. The question ultimately became whether dam builders had taken sufficient precautions in the construction process, though as we shall see, the standards of negligence varied nontrivially. In addition, however, judges regularly conjoined application of the negligence rule with the principle of first possession that we have seen came to govern water disputes during this period. That is, damming companies who perfected their water right prior in time to allegedly damaged plaintiffs were consistently held to a lower standard of precaution than those who perfected their right afterwards.

One interesting question is how to interpret this judicial practice, as it is not clear that efficient investment is necessarily promoted by protecting earlier investors from tort claims, where there is the likelihood of significant external costs being inflicted when dams collapse. The answer comes from the modern theoretical literature on negligence. Specifically, the efficiency of the negligence standard depends upon, among other things, the latitude/capacity/ incentives of the plaintiff to avoid the alleged harm. Under plausible conditions, the ability to avoid harm is greater *ex ante* to the location decision than it is *ex post*. Application of the first possession principle served the function of providing the California courts with a workable decision rule to distinguish between those plaintiffs better able and those less able to avoid harm. This would tend to promote efficient allocations of liability, especially in cases when the damming companies were generating significant societal rents through, for example, providing water supply to large numbers of miners.

9.2. The Problem of Dam Failures

As we have seen, from the very beginning of the Gold Rush much early mining occurred in wet diggings at or near the beds of rivers and streams. The first dams constructed were little more than logs and dirt thrown into a river to block the flow and permit river mining companies to divert the water out of the river through an earthen diversion channel. The miner Edwin Morse describes the primitive process he and his company used to dam the Yuba River near Marysville in summer of 1850:

> I worked like a good fellow on the dam. First we felled logs and laid them across the river, and then cut smaller poles or pilings, as they were called, and placed them at an angle with one end resting against the dam and the other embedded in the river bottom. Against this barrier we dumped dirt which we brought from the bank in hand barrows made by stretching a raw hide over two poles. Thus we banked up the earth until no water could seep through. Then we turned the river into the race and proceeded to wash the bed.[1]

Rather than dam an entire river, early miners often built *wing dams*, which were water-tight structures made of rocks or boulders that extended from the bank out into the river and then angled downstream. Though this process only laid bare a portion of the river, it was some-

times preferred because it eliminated the need to dig a race through
which to divert the river. Even so, it was no easy task. Daniel Woods
provides another vivid description, this time of the monumental effort it
took for his company to build a wing dam to clear a portion of the bed of
the Tuolumne River:

> A line was formed, extending out to the middle of the river, those at the end
> of the line working in four feet water, where the current was so strong that
> our feet would often be forced from under us, and we would be whirled away
> down the current, to scrabble on shore as we could . . . The whole force of the
> company, aided by some thirty Mexicans we have employed to work for us, is
> concentrated upon the wall which is to be the head of the dam. This is to run
> from the shore out to the middle of the river, or about forty feet. Two walls
> are thrown up parallel to each other, and about two feet apart. The difficulty
> of this is almost inconceivable. We must roll the stones and adjust them where
> there is a rapid current four feet in depth. Sometimes a whole section of this
> will be swept off at once, and must be done all over again. After the walls
> are completed, strong cloth is spread down against the whole wall, and over
> its whole surface. The space is then filled up with small twigs, sand, and clay.
> After the wall is carried thus to the middle of the river, it must turn, forming
> a right angle, and run down through the middle of the river, parallel to the
> shore, a distance of two hundred and fifty feet, till it passes over some falls,
> by which means the water is partially drained from a portion of the channel.
> This portion so drained is then divided off into pens, which are surrounded
> by small walls, so made as to exclude the water, which is then bailed out, and
> all the space within the walls of the pens is just worked.[2]

As a rule, early dams were not constructed for permanence and usu-
ally lasted only until the fall rains swelled the river and caused the dams
to be swept away.[3] Indeed, many were undoubtedly quite flimsy and fell
victim to summer freshets or spontaneous collapse at any time.[4] But
their generally small scale also meant that damages inflicted on others
when they collapsed were typically pretty limited. And when dam failures did occur, early miners were more likely to attribute any associated
damages to rising river waters rather than upstream miners who had
somehow been remiss.

It was not long, however, before companies began to build larger and
more substantial dams. As early as the summer of 1851, the *Alta Cali-*

FIGURE 9.1. River operations at Murderer's Bar. Mining camp in Eldorado County on Middle Fork of American River

fornian was reporting on plans to build a "permanent structure" to dam the South Yuba River with capital of $200,000.[5] In summer of 1854, the *Sacramento Union* reported that the Murderer's Bar Company had succeeded in building a dam on the American River that had "withstood all the freshets of the last winter" and was considered "the firmest structure of its kind in the State."[6] (See Figure 9.1). Over time, dams became wider, taller, and stronger. By July 1853, the *Alta Californian* reported that a company was about to complete its dam up in the mountains, which was eighty-five feet wide and twenty-five feet high. By December 1856, another company was reportedly in process of building a dam two hundred sixty feet in length, strong enough to contain water in a reservoir nearly one square mile in area to the depth of twenty feet.[7]

Impetus for stronger, more permanent structures was provided by the discovery of gold at dry diggings, which encouraged the construction of ditches and canals to transport water to the claims. The dams needed to be large, permanent structures in order to create reservoirs that regulated the flow of water into these ditches and canals, thus providing for a more certain, regular water supply. The challenge of constructing these more substantial structures required greater care in construction and new design methods. When the Tuolumne County Water Company erected its dam above Pine Log Crossing in 1856, it made sure to dig all the way down to a layer of solid granite, which it thoroughly sluiced off to dislodge loose stone. It then erected timbers on top of the firm base, supporting these timbers with gravel. Dams also began to be made with built-in escape-gates, which were opened by on-duty attendants if water levels rose too high.[8] Dams continued to become increasingly durable through improved construction and design methods that rendered them both stronger and more integrated, as one observer noted, for example, in 1857:

> So sudden and destructive a freshet [as the one resulting from the recent rains], and one more destructive to property generally, has seldom been seen on this river . . . The Eureka Ditch Company's dam, however, sustained no material injury by the rise in the waters. The principle upon which this dam is constructed is now being generally adopted, on the river, by companies wishing to build permanent dams. It is composed entirely of rock, thickly mixed with large, heavy brush—the whole being thrown loosely together in one heavy breastwork across the river, with a gradual curve up the stream. The rock give it the necessary weight and durability; while the brush, mixed promiscuously, in large quantities, through it, lends strength and tension to the whole, and renders it impossible for a portion to give way without all of it moving bodily.[9]

Such advances did not, of course, completely eliminate the problem of breaking dams, which occurred with some regularity in Tuolumne, Placer, and Nevada counties in the mid- to late 1850s. Furthermore, as dams became larger over time, the downstream consequences of breaking dams became increasingly serious. In 1859 two stories appeared in the *Alta Californian* that strongly suggest that dams had become large enough to wreak enormous havoc on downstream companies when they failed. The first one occurred in the southern mines, in Tuolumne County:

> Last Friday night a large reservoir, belonging to the Shaw's Flat Ditch Company, gave way, and an immense body of water was precipitated into Sullivan's Creek, and swept the Tuolumne with resistless force, devastating the creek for many miles. This catastrophe has caused great injury to the miners, for, not anticipating such an event, their sluices were carried down by the current, their races filled up, and all their work, within reach of the devouring element, destroyed in a moment. It will be a hard blow upon the company, for many will sue them for damages.[10]

The other occurred in the northern mines and resulted in not only destruction of property but also a number of lives being lost.

> On Monday last, the dam of the Eureka Ditch Company gave way, and . . . water rushed dywn [sic] into the Yuba and flooded it. The flood wave varied in height from 6 to 8 feet, according to the width of the channel . . . This terrible wave made a clean sweep of everything before it; logs, boards, sluice boxes, tools and human traps, formed a common brotherhood in the foaming chaos. Many are supposed to have lost their lives. Opposite this place, which is two miles from the river, four men were at work in the bank some eight feet below the bed of the stream, and three were drowned—the fourth escaped; and a few miles further up, five Chinese were also drowned.[11]

Just how common were collapsing dams? Table 9.1 reports a number of cases involving bursting dams and ditches that were presented to the district courts of three key Gold Rush counties: Placer County from 1851 to 1859, Tuolumne County from 1851 to 1859, and Nevada County from 1856 to 1860. One of the dam failures—the 1857 case involving the Tuolumne County Water Company at Pine Log—involved at least eighteen separate lawsuits. It should be added that these cases do not include disputes where companies were damaged by more-or-less intentional releases of water by upstream companies. Nor do they include an undoubtedly large number of cases that were settled out of court and thus

TABLE 9.1. **District court cases involving bursting dams or ditches, Placer County (1851–1859), Tuolumne County (1853–1859), and Nevada County (1857–1860)**

Plaintiff	Defendant	Date	County
Eberhart	Tuolumne County Water Co.	1853	Tuolumne
Haskett et al.	Bear and Auburn Water and Mining Co.	1854	Placer
Graham	Tuolumne County Water Co.	1856	Tuolumne
Tuolumne County Water Co.	Columbia and Stanislaus River Water Co.	1856	Tuolumne
Kidd	Laird	1857	Nevada
Evans et al.	Hill	1857	Placer
Vass and Smith	Brophy and Phelan	1857	Nevada
Butler et al.	Laird et al.	1857	Nevada
Walker et al.	Rock Creek, Deer Creek and South Yuba Canal Co.	1857	Nevada
Howe et al.	Jennings et al.	1857	Nevada
Numerous plaintiffs	Tuolumne County Water Co. (Pine Log)	1857	Tuolumne
Green et al.	Williams et al.	1858	Nevada
Reilly et al.	Independent Ditch Co.	1859	Placer

never appeared in district court records. The evidence strongly suggests that dam failures were a serious cause for concern in the gold fields in the 1850s.

9.3. An Illustrative Incident: Pine Log

A closer look at the incident at Pine Log provides some useful insights into the challenges facing damming companies, and it will help us better interpret the legal issues that arose in court rulings as the judges were formulating doctrine regarding dam failures. Pine Log was a mining camp located on the south fork of the Stanislaus River two miles north of Columbia, where gold had been discovered possibly as early as summer of 1848. It thrived during the early 1850s owing to extremely rich placer deposits that provided occupation for hundreds of miners, and new rich strikes were being made as late as 1857. The Tuolumne County Water Company was formed in 1851 to supply water to miners in Columbia, and by 1857 it had constructed three large reservoirs upstream from Pine Log. In July of 1857, one of its dams collapsed and sent a torrent of water down onto Pine Log and a neighboring camp, Italian Bar. The flood resulted in a great deal of property damage and the loss of sixteen lives, and unleashed at least eighteen separate lawsuits brought before the Tuolumne County district court by various residents of Pine Log and Italian Bar.[12]

The Company's board of trustees proceeded with caution, appointing a committee to "repair to the damaged locality" to investigate damage claims and hiring an attorney to provide legal advice. At the same time, it immediately authorized the ditch manager to repair the breach, and to "exercise his discretion to mode of operations," seemingly anxious to be back in business. When it became clear the Company might be at fault, the board appropriated $5,000 for the purpose of paying damages in settlements with other companies, while making it clear that it considered itself under no legal obligation to pay.[13] It spent the next few months settling a number of claims for damages, while spending a great deal of time in court fighting lawsuits from those who refused to settle.

All of the lawsuits centered on the key legal point: had the Company been negligent in constructing its dam? The court made clear its position that negligence was controlling in one of the cases, *Hoffman v. Tuolumne County Water Company*, when it instructed the jury:

> That if they believed the break was caused by the carelessness or negligence
> of defendants they were liable in damages.[14]

It is not surprising that the thrust of the plaintiffs' strategies was precisely to establish that the Company had been negligent. In one of the
cases, the plaintiffs brought in a witness who testified:

> I noticed the point of the break. The soil presented a loose gravelly appear-
> ance—looked almost like sand in a solid state—the poorest quantity [sic] of
> decomposed granite—it broke on the south bank—the dam was constructed
> of timbers run into the soil on each side—water has the effect of dissolving
> that formation of soil—the dam was about 30 feet high backed water ½ a mile
> average width 300 or 400 yards—dam was pretty near full—never saw it so
> full before.[15]

Another witness testified that the foundation of the dam was "decomposed granite—the action of water would tear it out."[16] So apparently,
negligence was to be proven by calling into question the Company's diligence in ensuring a solid foundation for its dam and inadequately an-
choring the dam to the foundation.

The Company's defense strategy, on the other hand, was essentially to try to establish that it did what it reasonably could to make
the dam solid, on the basis of the information available to it. Upon
cross-examination, one of the witnesses who had testified to decomposed granite was forced to admit that the decomposed granite "presents a solid appearance externally." The other admitted that the Company went about sluicing "from ten days to three weeks endeavoring to
get an abutment." The thrust of the defenses to this seemingly damn-
ing charge of erecting its dam on a defective foundation thus amounted
to this: the Company did what it could to ensure the foundation was
solid, and to all external appearances, it was. Furthermore, the defense
brought a battery of witnesses on its own behalf, who testified to the diligence of the Company in digging down deep to find the granite, sluicing it down to where it was solid, and checking as carefully as they could
that it provided a solid foundation. They also spoke to their own years
of experience in assessing dam strength and safety.[17] Read: they thought
the Company practices were sound, and they knew what they were talk-
ing about.

On the face of it, the Company would end up faring poorly in the lawsuits: in every case, either the jury found for the plaintiffs or after the Company was found guilty, the two sides ended up settling. However, the Company was also often able to get awards reduced by employing various strategies such as moving for a new trial or appealing to a higher court, on the grounds of some irregularity in court proceedings. It also lodged what smacked of nuisance defenses "worth a shot," such as invoking an 1807 act of Congress that had attempted to prevent settlements on public lands, to argue that as illegal trespassers, the plaintiffs were not entitled to redress.[18] Nevertheless, the Company undoubtedly incurred substantial costs as a result of this unfortunate incident, in terms of court awards of damages, settlement payouts, lawyer's fees, and time and energy devoted to defending its actions.

But aside from the bottom line disposition of the disputes, there is an important message here regarding the effort expended by the Company to ensure its dams would not collapse. The case files strongly suggest that there was private information that only the Company itself had about its own level of effort, which was captured only imperfectly with external signals such as the solidity of the granite foundation, the way the dam was anchored to the foundation, or whether the dam leaked water. Under cross examination, one witness for the plaintiffs reluctantly confirmed the imperfectness of one of these signals when he admitted that he couldn't tell what kind of soil the supporting timbers had been anchored to because "it was washed away."[19] Another admitted that he: "Never saw a dam that didn't leak—that doesn't take any of its strength away."[20] Private information about effort expended to make dams strong would have been endemic to dam construction generally in the gold fields. This fact will help explain court doctrine, to which we now turn.

9.4. The Courts and Dam Failures

The experiences of the Tuolumne County Water Company in the Pine Log case is anecdotally suggestive of the courts' thinking on dam failures, but a compelling case requires a broader examination of all of the dam failure cases that arose during this period. At this point, therefore, let us turn to a broader discussion of cases brought in Nevada, Placer, and Tuolumne counties in the mid-1850s for evidence on the position of

the Gold Rush courts on liability for dam breaks. Perhaps most strik-
ingly, the district courts consistently held that defendants were not
strictly liable for damages: negligence had to be shown. This is clearly
seen, for example, in the Placer County case of *Evans v. Hill*.[21] In *Evans*,
the defendant had constructed a reservoir upstream from a company of
miners that allegedly broke and washed away several thousand dollars
worth of gold from the miners' claims. The plaintiffs asked the court to
instruct the jury that the breaking of the reservoir was *prima facie* evidence that it was "insecurely and carelessly built or kept in repair" and
rendered the defendant liable for damages. This request was refused. Instead, the judge accepted a request by the defendant to instruct the jury
that the plaintiff not be allowed to recover damages:

> without showing some negligence on the part of the defendant either in the
> construction or maintenance of the reservoir or in the filling of the same,
> with water at the time of the break.

In a similar case the Nevada County district court accepted, in *Green
et al. v. Williams et al.*, a request by the defendants to instruct the jury
that even if the evidence clearly showed the plaintiff had suffered loss,
that they not be allowed to recover damages "until shown that the defendants were negligent, lacking in reasonable and proper precaution, or
wrong in the use or maintenance of their property."[22] Juries took such instructions to heart in awarding verdicts: in *Evans* the jury found in favor
of the defendant despite the damage inflicted. Similarly, in 1854 a jury
found, in *Haskett v. Bear River and Auburn Water and Mining Company*, that the defendant's reservoir did in fact break and damage the
plaintiff, but ruled for the defendant on the grounds that "said breach
and escape was not occasioned through any fault or negligence, or want
of care or diligence" on the part of the defendants.[23]

The question remained, of course, of what constituted negligent behavior: how much precaution would be considered "reasonable and
proper"? Some contingencies the courts disposed of quickly. Dam
breaks that were shown to be accidental, for example, were not considered the result of negligent behavior, nor were breaks caused by burrow-
ing squirrels or gophers. The courts also held that defendants were not
absolved of blame if they contracted out the entire construction of a dam
to a third party. Nor could defendants take refuge in a finding that the
plaintiff knew a structure was weak and did not inform the defendants.[24]

More challenging for the courts, however, was filling in the remaining large gray area regarding precisely what did constitute negligent behavior. Here the courts were remarkably inconsistent. Much of the time, they invoked some variant of the common "reasonable care" standard: the care that a reasonable person would have taken under similar conditions.[25] For example, in *Walker v. Rock Creek et al.*, the judge of the Nevada County district court gave instructions to the jury that the standard for negligence was behavior expected of a man of "ordinary prudence":

> If the defendants have used the same degree of prudence and care in the construction and management of their flume or ditch that a man of ordinary prudence would use under similar circumstances then . . . the defendants are entitled to a verdict.[26]

On the other hand, the defendant in *Evans v. Hill* was denied the following instruction, which seems to instruct the jury to hold him to a very similar standard:

> If he built his reservoir and maintained it in the usual manner such as was customary in the section of the country where the reservoir was situated and in the construction and maintenance *used such care as prudent and careful men engaged in the same business were accustomed to use* and the reservoir thus made and maintained broke and did damage to the plaintiff it would not be an injury for which the plaintiff could recover.[27] (emphasis added)

It is telling what the court did end up instructing the jury: namely, to take into account the extent of the project and require the defendant to "exercise an amount of diligence in proportion to the danger incurred by the magnitude of his reservoir." If reasonable behavior was tied to the extent of the damages, this comes closer to a Learned Hand-type rule that weighs expected benefits against expected costs. The judge in this case may have been reacting to the magnitude of the tort, a factor emphasized by some scholars.[28]

One possibility is that judges were idiosyncratic—that different judges applied different standards. In this particular example, perhaps the Nevada County judge simply took a different position than the Placer County judge. However, in some cases, the same judge seemed to be applying different standards simultaneously. For ex-

ample, in one of the Pine Log cases—*Liss v. TCWC*—the judge gave
what seem to be contradictory instructions to the jury. On the one
hand, it instructed:

> That if the P's have satisfied the jury that they have suffered damage in con-
> sequence of the freshet produced by the defendants dam breaking they will
> find for the amount of damages so suffered unless the defendants show the
> damage was caused by some act of God or some overwhelming force against
> which *ordinary prudence* could not have guarded. (emphasis added)

And then it turned around and gave the following instruction to the
same jury:

> That if one builds a dam by which a large quantity of water is accumulated
> and by the breakage of the dam causes the neighbor below to be injured by
> its flood, the injury is presumptuous proof of insufficient and inartificial con-
> struction which can only be excused by showing that the breakage was pro-
> duced by some cause against which the *utmost vigilance and care* could not
> have guarded.[29] (emphasis added)

This evidence certainly suggests some confusion by this particular judge
over what a constituted a reasonableness standard. But combined with
the previous evidence, it also suggests that judges may have not felt particularly constrained to consistently apply particular standards mandated by precedent or general common expectations of what was considered reasonable.

The fact that the courts did not constrain themselves to consistently apply a standard of customary and prudent business practice left them with
greater flexibility to base a negligence standard on other factors. One
factor that came up frequently in the court arguments was the question of who had arrived on the scene first, the plaintiff or the defendant.
Both sides tried to use temporal priority to their advantage when the
facts were on their side. In *Evans*, for example, the plaintiff, who enjoyed a prior claim, asked the court to instruct the jury that the liability rule depended upon whether "the plaintiff or defendant was first in
point of time in making the location of their respective possessions." It
also asked that the burden of proof lay on the defendant to show it had
not been negligent in constructing and maintaining its reservoir.[30] Simi-

larly, in *Howe v. Jennings*, the plaintiff tried to exploit its temporal priority by requesting the court to instruct the jury:

> That if the jury believe from the evidence . . . , that the plaintiff located the line of their proposed tail sluice before the erection of the defendant's reservoir, then . . . they are held to an *extraordinary degree of prudence* for the purpose of preventing injury to the plaintiff.[31] (emphasis added)

Defendants also tried to exploit their temporal priority with equal vigor, though the nature of their arguments was slightly different. They typically did not use their status as prior claimant to completely absolve themselves of responsibility but rather, either to bolster the legitimacy of their claim or to request they be held to a lower standard of precaution. In *Darst v. Bush*, for example, the defendants asked the court to instruct the jury:

> that if the defendants hold this mining ground under a location prior to that of the plaintiff—then they have a right to work their said mining ground in the most usual and convenient manner and are not liable to the plaintiff for any injury not caused by their negligence.[32]

And in *Green et al. v. Williams et al.*, the defendant explicitly requested that the jury be instructed to hold him to a lower level of precaution because he was there first:

> Where a company constructs an embankment for a reservoir upon a proper model and the work is well and strongly done, such company is not responsible for damages occasioned by any breakage occurring without negligence on the part of the owner, and where both parties are located upon the public land or mineral region within this state and the reservoir is older in point of time than the rights of the damaged party, a less degree of care and precaution is required on the part of the owners of the reservoir.[33]

The response of the courts was to be broadly sympathetic to arguments that temporal priority should be considered. Each of the requests just mentioned in the cases of *Evans*, *Oakland Ditch Co.*, *Howe*, *Darst*, and *Green* was granted by the presiding judge and the jury was directed to consider who enjoyed the temporally prior right. Practically speaking, these cases taken together reflected the principle that when the plaintiff enjoyed temporal priority, the defendant both was required to take greater precautions to avoid inflicting harm and shouldered the burden of proving that it had not acted negligently. None of this meant, of course, that the first possessor necessarily prevailed because other factors could still trump first possession under a negligence rule. In *Evans*, the defendant prevailed despite having a subsequent claim because he was able to convince the jury it had not been negligent.

None of these district court holdings, of course, are conclusive in defining the broad parameters of negligence law in California during this period because they could be overturned on appeal to the state Supreme Court. However, in 1857 the Court handed down a ruling in *Tenney v. Miners' Ditch Co.* that confirmed, for all practical purposes, the holdings of the district courts with regard to first possession and provided an extended doctrinal justification for basing negligence rulings in part on first possession.[34] *Tenney* involved a classic tort dispute over a ditch that had broken and flooded the mining claims of some downstream mining companies. Both the ditch and the mining claims were on public lands. In the district court, a question of fact was put to a jury as to whether the ditch company had been guilty of negligence in the construction and operation of its ditch. The jury decided it had not been negligent and ruled in its favor. The plaintiffs appealed to the Supreme Court on the basis that the district judge had improperly excluded a jury instruction requested by the plaintiffs that a ditch break carries a presumption of negligence by the defendant. The Court ruled that the district court had acted properly and affirmed its ruling.

The *Tenney* ruling is striking in the importance it ascribed to temporal priority. After noting that the defendant had constructed its ditch prior to the location of the claims by the plaintiff, it said that the central question was "to ascertain what rights the plaintiffs, who were subsequent locators, acquired against the defendants."[35] Its answer was that the defendant, by virtue of its prior location, was entitled to "a reasonable exercise" of its right:

> Any other rule would allow a malevolent person to make a trespass whenever he pleased, by settling along the line of a water ditch or canal where he supposed from its location, or construction, it was most likely to give way.[36]

By acknowledging the possibility of this particular type of strategic behavior by the plaintiff, the *Tenney* court implies that its ruling might well
have been different had the temporal roles of the plaintiff and defendant
been reversed. Apparently, by virtue of being first, dam builders were entitled to protection from tort lawsuits that they might not otherwise enjoy.

But *Tenney* was not an entirely pragmatic ruling. The Court sought a
way to base the ruling in English common-law doctrine, ultimately settling on the same principle it applied in diversion disputes: *first-in-time
is first-in-right*. The Court argued that the principle applied in this case
because the dispute took place on public lands and neither party owned
the land they were on. After dismissing an alternative principle for resolving the dispute based on land ownership, the Court went on:

> but in a case like the present, where neither party claims an ownership in the
> soil, and all the rights they possess relate back, or are acquired at the date of
> their respective locations, the reason of the rule ceases, and the maxim, "*qui
> prior est in tempore, potior est in jure*," as applied by this Court to cases in-
> volving disputes growing out of mining claims, would seem more applicable.[37]

Thus, it seems, the public lands status of the gold fields provided yet another opportunity for the courts to mold the common law to their liking
in spite of their legislative mandate.

9.5. Coming to the Tort

Two things are striking about the courts' treatment of liability for dam
failures: their consistent reliance on a negligence rule and their consistent holding that upstream companies need not exercise as much precaution in dam construction when there was no downstream company present. The consistent application of a negligence rule can, I
think, be readily explained as the courts responding to a high transaction cost situation by applying not a strict rule of trespass that awards
a clear-cut property right but rather, a balancing rule of nuisance. As
we saw earlier in our discussion of Pine Log, companies building dams,
particularly large ones, would have been privy to much private information about how much effort they had expended to make the dam
strong and resistant to collapse. Much of this information would not
have been known to downstream parties afflicted by collapsing dams,

making it difficult to prove that the dam company had been negligent. This situation of asymmetric information would have generated significant transaction costs in negotiations between the company and downstream parties over how strong to build the dam. Under these conditions, courts would have been prone to apply a balancing rule of nuisance such as negligence rather than a trespass-like standard of strict liability.[38]

The perhaps more interesting question is how we understand the general policy of the courts to reduce the required level of precaution under the negligence standard when the upstream company was present first. I believe there are multiple complementary ways to make sense of this legal principle. The first relates to our earlier discussion of efficient standard-setting by courts in situations of bilateral precaution. In situations where both parties to a tort can exercise precaution, the prediction is that courts interested in minimizing costs will tend to impose greater liability on whichever party can more easily exercise precaution to avoid the occurrence of the tort. In the context of application of a negligence rule, this would be accomplished by the stringency of the negligence standard. For example, a standard that required the dam builder to exercise "the utmost vigilance and care" or "an extraordinary degree of prudence" would be more stringent than a standard that merely required "ordinary prudence." Thus, if it was relatively costless for the dam building company to exercise precaution to build a "safe" dam, then one might predict that the courts would hold the company to a stringent standard of negligence.

Conversely, if it was relatively costless for the downstream parties to exercise precaution, the prediction is that courts interested in minimizing costs would have held the damming company to a less stringent negligence standard. When a dam fails, a downstream company that is already present has little scope of action to take precautions to avoid damages, aside from moving away. However, if the company is not present downstream, in a real sense it is easy for it to take precautions to avoid damages. Imposing a less stringent negligence standard on a company that arrives on the scene first would have reflected that fact.[39]

The second way to think about the policy is in terms of the findings of the scholarly literature on the legal principle called *coming to the nuisance*, in which there are obvious parallels to the issue at hand.[40] Under the coming to the nuisance principle, a company A that generates a nuisance is not held liable for damages to a newcomer B who arrives on the scene after A has already started operations. The implicit assumption is that the holding would be quite different if the roles of A and B were temporally reversed. Indeed, this could make all the difference between a finding of liability or not. So under the coming to the nuisance principle, A is held to a less stringent legal standard when he was already operating when B came on the scene. The same thing is true under the *Tenney* principle, where the negligence standard for a dam failure is lowered by the dam company if the downstream companies moved in after.

The question a number of economists and legal scholars have asked is this: Is the coming to the nuisance rule efficient? The answer seems to be that it depends on the circumstances. Donald Wittman has, for example, modeled the problem as sequential investment in which the generator of the nuisance A exists for two periods of time and can choose two locations: either the one she is currently located at, or a different location with a lower (reservation) value.[41] In the second period, another company B can then choose to move within nuisance range, or not, and also has a possible alternative location. In Wittman's model, the efficient outcome depends crucially on the relative values of the alternative locations of both companies. Importantly for our purposes, the coming to the nuisance standard will be efficient if the location is (relatively) more valuable for A than it is for B. This will obviously not always be the case, but we can envision many cases in the gold fields in which it would. Key among these would be where a ditch company builds a large dam to provide water to a number of localities, which under many conditions would be likely to dominate in value any river diggings down below.

Rohan Pitchford and Christopher Snyder have extended Wittman's model to consider situations where courts have imperfect information regarding the rents of the different parties and must apply a general rule that applies across all disputes.[42] The question is whether the coming to the nuisance rule would be efficient in this case. They use a sequential model similar to Wittman's in basic structure, but are more explicit about the nature of transaction costs that lead to potentially inefficient outcomes. In their model, the company A that generates the nuisance goes first and must make an investment without being able to negotiate with a newcomer B who might come afterwards. This limited ability to negotiate *ex ante* is the source of inefficiency of rules designed to address the nuisance.

For our purposes, their key finding is that a coming to the nuisance principle will tend to lead to overinvestment by A, intuitively because greater investment improves the bargaining position of A toward B with regard to the nuisance. However, the tendency toward overinvestment will be moderated to the extent that A's activity generates greater rents than B's activity, which is consistent with Wittman's findings. In this case, the coming to the nuisance rule tends to dominate rules that favor the newcomer downstream company B. Again, within our context this would tend to be the case if A is a ditch company supplying many miners with water. The tendency toward overinvestment is also likely moderated to the extent that racing dissipation is limited, as for example in our case by random discoveries of gold, as was argued earlier. Finally, the tendency toward overinvestment is based in part on an assumption of their model that there are zero transaction costs in the second stage negotiations over the nuisance. As we have seen, in fact there were probably large transaction costs in negotiating over the safety of a dam. The structure of their model suggests that this, too, may limit overinvestment by making it more difficult for A to realize extra rents in those negotiations.

To summarize, we have analyzed the *Tenney* principle from two complementary viewpoints: as a rule governing torts under conditions of bilateral precaution and as a variant of rules governing nuisance that favor first-comers, the so-called coming to the nuisance principle. Both viewpoints generate similar results under conditions likely to have obtained in many contexts in the gold fields. The *Tenney* principle would have tended to promote efficiency by economizing on costs of precaution under general conditions, and when the generator of the nuisance also generates significant rents in the operation of its business. As applied to ditch companies constructing large dams for their water supply systems, the *Tenney* principle had much to recommend it.

9.6. Conclusions

This chapter has illustrated the economic logic of the courts' treatment of dam failures on two levels. The first is the application of a rule of negligence, which reflected the existence of large transaction costs arising from private information on dam construction effort. When one considers the fact that some of these dam failures were quite destructive, including resulting in significant loss of life, one might be surprised that the courts did not move to a rule of strict liability. As we saw in chapter 2, one consistent pattern in the history of the English common law of torts has been the application of trespass rules such as strict liability in cases of large, direct, visible damages inflicted on others.[43] This would seem to describe collapsing dams quite aptly. The answer may well be a question of degree. Though the dam failures of 1850s California were often quite spectacularly destructive, they paled in comparison with later dam failures that could result in hundreds, or even thousands, of lives lost. In some sense, the dam failures considered in this book may simply have been not destructive enough, in the eyes of the courts.

The second level of economic logic in the courts' treatment of dam failures observed here has to do with yet another application of the rule of first possession, this time within the context of torts resulting from dam failures. The economic logic in this case is not centered on first possession as a means of providing investment security, or as a response to large nuisances, as we observed in the previous two chapters. Rather, it likely reflected the ability of parties to a dam failure to take precautions to avoid damages, which was considerably easier for parties to do *ex ante* than *ex post*. And it likely promoted efficient outcomes by encouraging appropriate investments by large ditch companies providing water service to large numbers of miners. As a result, first possession provided yet another way for the courts to promote efficient resource allocation, this time in terms of economizing on the resources brought by companies to a potential tort situation.

Appendix B

Bilateral Precaution in Dam Failures

Consider our prototypical surface waterway with two possible locations for mining companies A and B to locate—upstream or downstream—and consider an alternative parameterization suitable to the probabilistic nature of the tort. We will assume that when either company takes one of the sites, this co-opts the other from claiming that site, leaving him either to take the other site or locate elsewhere. Assuming that these sites are more valuable than claims located elsewhere, there are two possible sequences of location: either the upstream site is taken first, or the downstream site is taken first. In order for mining to be successfully prosecuted at either site, a dam must be constructed with expenditures of E. Building a dam permits each company to earn a stream of revenues. At the upstream location, assume this revenue stream is Z and at the downstream location, assume this revenue stream is Y. For each company there is a non-zero probability that the dam will collapse, which would wipe out the company's revenue stream and if the upstream dam collapses would also wipe out the downstream company's revenue stream, if present. Assume for simplicity that in the event of a dam failure, both revenue streams become zero. For the purpose of understanding the application of first possession to the negligence rule, let us focus our attention on the upstream dam.

The upstream company may choose to spend more money to build a stronger dam, which reduces the probability of a dam failure. We will assume a probability function with construction expenditures as the argument: $P = P(E)$ where $P' < 0$ and $P'' > 0$. That is, extra expenditures decrease the probability of dam failure, but at a decreasing rate. At any point in time, there exists a court-mandated standard of negligence. This may be thought of as a requirement for the upstream company to take sufficient precaution in constructing its dam. I will assume that there is a one-to-one correspondence between the level of precaution and the amount spent on dam construction, so that any particular negligence standard is modeled as a requirement to spend so much on dam construction E. If the upstream company's dam collapses and it is found to be negligent, the downstream company is awarded his full damages, here assumed to be equal to his revenue stream Y, if he is present. Both companies are assumed to be risk neutral, and therefore act in order to maximize expected income.

A. Downstream Miner Present First

Consider the situation where a mining company locates downstream first, and suppose there is an existing negligence standard set at E_0. The upstream company will spend E_0, or just enough to avoid being liable for negligence and having to pay damages to the downstream company. It would not spend more because doing so would yield no expected benefits. If the upstream company's dam collapses, it completely wipes out both companies' revenue streams, in which case total rents are $-E_0$, or the lost expenditures of the upstream company. If the upstream dam does not collapse, both revenue streams are preserved and total rents are $(Z + Y - E_0)$. Since the probability of a dam failure is P, we can calculate the total combined expected rent stream as $P(-E_0) + (1 - P)[Z + Y - E_0]$, which simplifies to $(1 - P)(Z + Y) - E_0$. This makes intuitive sense, as it can be interpreted as total combined expected revenues minus construction expenditures E_0.[1]

The question is: where would a court interested in promoting efficient precaution set the negligence standard E_0? Generally speaking, such a court will balance the social cost of extra precaution taken by the upstream company against the social benefit of taking extra precaution. When a downstream company is already present, total societal rents are $(1 - P(E))[Z + Y] - E$, and the first order condition for efficient precaution is $-P'[Z + Y] = 1$. The upstream company will, of course, have incentive to maximize private rents of $(1 - P(E))Z - E$, setting $-P'Z = 1$.

This implies directly that the upstream company will generally exercise insufficient precaution, because it does not fully internalize the social benefits of exercising precaution. Setting the negligence standard at the level $E^*(> E_0)$ consistent with $-P'[Z + Y] = 1$ will encourage the upstream company to choose that level in order to avoid liability. And of course, given that the upstream company is avoiding liability, the downstream company is provided incentive to exercise efficient precaution as well, because it is bearing all of the costs (and reaping all the benefits) of any precautionary measures it might take, including locating elsewhere.

B. Upstream Miner Present First

Now consider the situation where the upstream company is present first. The question is where would the efficient negligence standard be set in this case, and how does it compare to the standard in the previous case where the downstream company was present first. Here, with no downstream company, societal rents would appear to be: $(1 - P(E))Z - E$ and the upstream company would seem to have incentive to exercise efficient precaution. This in turn would seem to make a negligence standard of any kind unnecessary. All of this ignores, however, the possibility that a company might subsequently move in downstream, at which point it would be subject to the dangers associated with a collapsing dam. Whether or not it would do so would depend upon the value of the opportunities available elsewhere.

To incorporate this possibility into the analysis, I define a weighting parameter W that reflects the probability that in general, companies will move in downstream to an established upstream operation. One might think of this parameter W as reflecting the value of the downstream location compared with the value of the next-best alternative for the downstream company. Denoting this latter value as X, then W will be an increasing function of the additional value of mining downstream as opposed to locating elsewhere, or $W = W(Y - X)$, where $W' > 0$ and W is between zero and one. The expected societal rent function becomes: $(1 - P(E))[Z + W(Y - X)Y] - E$, and the first order condition becomes: $-P'[Z + WY] = 1$. Given this condition, the court would set a lower standard of negligence (less required precaution) than in the previous case where the downstream company was present first, which as we have seen is precisely what we observed in the Gold Rush mining cases involving collapsed dams. Notice that whenever $W > 0$, the courts would have wanted to set a negligence standard rather than relying on companies to take sufficient precautions themselves. All of this is consistent with the previous description of the judicial treatment of collapsing dams during the Gold Rush.

CHAPTER TEN

Conclusions

The picture that has been painted in this narrative has been detailed for a reason: the development of appropriative law in early California was highly complex. Indeed, it was a good deal more complex than it is commonly thought to be. The current standard explanation of the emergence of appropriative law in California is a simple story that combines elements of scarcity and necessity: that it emerged to support valuable gold mining where rivers were few and far between. Because the standard story is seductively simple and intuitively plausible, everyone seems to know and believe it. And when we all know what happened, and there is no need to look further.

Though plausible, the standard story leaves a great deal unexplained. It was not the case that first possession was immediately adopted in the mining camps because miners wanted it to support their mining efforts. For a time, miners were of mixed minds about the desirability, or even the necessity, of first possession. During the Early period, there was very little demand in general for secure water rights, when miners were still primarily using pans and rockers-and-cradles. Even well into the Middle period, after miners had begun to migrate to dry diggings, there was little demand until at least 1852, when ditch companies began to make significant inroads in supplying water to dry diggings. It was only after that, but increasingly so as ditch systems became larger and the demand for water grew, that there was broad-based demand for the water rights security provided by first possession.

Even then, however, miners were deeply divided over first possession. When *Irwin v. Phillips* was handed down, it was excoriated by many miners. We have seen two reasons why this was so. First and perhaps foremost, newcomers believed it would favor those who had arrived earlier. The reason must be stressed, however: *it was not that they worried that they would get no water.* Throughout this period, leases and sales of water were easy and supported by the courts. Under these conditions, one would expect the water to end up in the hands of whoever valued it the most. For newcomers, the problem with first possession was that they would have to pay for water if they wanted it. It was not the size of the pie that was at stake: it was how it was sliced up.

The second and related reason is that ditch companies who vended water were often able to exploit their local market power to charge monopoly prices to miners. The entire decade of the 1850s witnessed a vigorous struggle between miners and ditch companies over the quasi-rents from development of water supplies. It was an extremely common pattern for miners in dry localities to beg and plead for companies to come along and develop water supplies, and then quickly bristle at the terms at which the water was offered once it was there. First possession, by giving ditch companies a firm legal right to the water, also provided legal support for their pricing practices.

So why did first possession become the law of the land? We must attribute a great deal of importance to a fundamental economic reality: secure water rights were needed to support investments in water development. This was not a serious issue as long as mining was largely prosecuted in wet diggings, where little investment in water supply was needed. In the wet diggings, it was thus considerably less costly for miners to mandate sharing arrangements rather than temporal priority. When you add the fact that water use in the wet diggings largely flowed back and recharged the surface source, it is not at all surprising that no species of private right to water occurred there. But with the discovery of gold in locations remote from surface water, and with the tremendous value-added of water in gold separation, it is impossible to imagine legal principles not emerging to support the enormous investments that would be required. Facing the prospect of large expenditures on dams, ditches, and flumes, the last thing that a potential investor in a ditch company would have wanted was an uncertain right to the water it was considering developing.

As we have seen, a potential obstacle for the courts in fashioning its first possession principle to support mining was the inconvenient fact that the legislature had adopted English common law as the standard for deciding disputes over water rights. Fortuitously, the fact that the gold fields were located on the public lands provided the courts a doctrinal basis for creating a right to divert based on first possession. I believe, however, that a case could be made that even without this convenient pretext, the courts would have found some other basis to support investments in water to be taken away from surface sources to remote locations. The stakes were simply too high. I do not believe they would have simply ignored English common law, but English common law has proved in general to be sufficiently flexible and elastic to be able to accommodate dramatic changes in economic conditions. Surely it could have accommodated the conveying of water to dry diggings, the traditional precepts of riparian law notwithstanding.

However, there were limits to the amount of rights security that first possession could provide. Ideally, a prospective water developer would want to know with some precision the quantity of water that a given investment was going to give it a legal right to. We have seen, however, that measurement of water flow was extremely imprecise throughout this entire period. This technological fact was reflected in adjustments made both in water markets and in court rulings that defined rights to water. Miners generally did not contract with ditch companies for specific quantities of water but rather, for times of service. Courts typically did not base water rights on amounts used but rather, on the capacity of ditch systems. Both of these developments reflected an attempt to economize on measurement costs under the circumstances. At the same time, they also reflected the fact that there was a certain amount of irreducible uncertainty with regard to how precisely an effective right to water could be defined.

The fact that water rights were based on capacity rather than use presents an important interpretive point, in terms of the efficiency of the definition of an individual water right. Basing a right on the capacity of a ditch system meant that the right was defined to the amount capable of being diverted. As we saw in chapter 2, generally speaking a right based on diversion is a second-best right definition when water use also generates recharge back into the local source of water. Here, defining the right to consumptive use (diversion net of recharge) is the efficient standard. However, the efficiency of the diversion right and the consumptive right converge as recharge decreases, which happens when water is diverted well away from the source of water. Thus, defining the water right on the basis of ditch capacity would have had the fortuitous consequence of promoting water basin rent-maximization, given the possibility of easy water transfers. I say "fortuitous" because the definition of water right as

ditch capacity was not a conscious decision of the courts to promote efficient water use, but a necessity thrust upon them by the fact of costly
measurement.

The fact that measurement costs were considerable also imposed certain limits on judicial attempts to create governance provisions to regulate actual use. This was reflected, for example, in the fact that we observed very few judicial attempts to ensure that water was being put to
beneficial use during this period, and what attempts there were relied
on extremely crude proxies, such as drainage, or indeed, no dedicated
uses at all. Use requirements, which were enforced through the principle of abandonment, also relied on crude proxies, such as evidence that
mining claims had paid out and miners had moved away. Changes in use
and purpose of use were, on the other hand, more readily measured and
thus, it is not surprising that the courts addressed these sorts of disputes.
Just because it was difficult to measure use in general did not, of course,
mean that water was not used. Hence, margins for expropriating rents,
such as challenging priority dates, ditch expansions, challenges to using
natural ravines as components of ditch systems, compromising on dam
safety, and a whole slew of other issues remained open and exploitable.
This meant that when the transaction costs of contracting over the open
margins were considerable, costly measurement likely presented major challenges to courts in any attempts they might have made to limit
dissipation.

Some uses, however, presented clear enough evidence of rent dissipation that the courts did attempt to impose governance restrictions on
use. This occurred especially with regard to degradation of water quality, which could occur only through actual use and everyone knew it.
The initial approach of the courts was to impose a reasonableness standard, which they did when the imposed damages were only moderate in
size. However, as damages increased in magnitude, the courts adopted
a standard of strict liability, thus moving from a nuisance rule to a rule
of trespass. Such a progression is broadly consistent with maximization
of basin rents because it imposed restrictions on upstream users who
were inflicting negative externalities on downstream users. It also economized on both transaction costs of negotiating over the externality and
measurement costs in enforcing governance restrictions on the various
margins for rent dissipation.

The way the courts treated dam failures is also broadly consistent
with attempts to minimize the costs of precaution in the presence of sig-

nificant transaction costs, particularly in the choice of negligence as the legal standard for determining liability. The application of a less stringent negligence standard for dam builders who came first is also consistent with a "coming to the nuisance" rule that is efficient if the dam builder confers large rents on society. This rule would have supported the construction of larger ditch projects that provided water supply to larger numbers of miners.

In sum, the legal rules that emerged from the gold fields in early California had much to commend them on efficiency grounds. The rules certainly were not perfect, but given the constraints of measurement technologies and the unresolved issue of federal ownership of the public lands, they could have been a lot worse.

So what are the lessons of the early California experience for current water policy? When you fast-forward to the present, it is very easy to find staunch critics of the current system of California water law, including many of the principles that emerged from the gold fields. Some argue that the principle of first possession, though it encouraged and facilitated the development of the American West, inefficiently favors the first uses of water, regardless of how valuable those uses are today.[1] Others have argued that first possession is inefficient in imposing excessive risk on newcomers, who bear the brunt of water deficiencies in times of drought.[2] The use requirement principle is commonly thought to encourage overuse of water because of the incentives for continued use merely in order to hold onto the right.[3] It also disfavors certain valuable non-use purposes like maintaining instream flows for wildlife habitat. The beneficial use principle fares somewhat better. Some argue that beneficial use requirements are a good thing because they limit waste of water, and they may discourage sitting on unused rights now in hopes of obtaining greater value in the future.[4] Others argue that they can provide a legal basis for managing water in the public interest.[5] Critics, however, argue that the requirement instills rigidity into the rights structure by locking water into uses historically considered beneficial and discouraging new emerging beneficial uses, such as instream flow for wildlife habitat.[6]

When one considers these critiques of current California law, many of them are based on the implicit assumption that the opportunity cost to a right-holder of keeping her appropriative right is small, which could be the case for a number of different reasons. It may be that there are legal obstacles to selling water, such as legislative restrictions on out-of-basin exports. Or there may be no local institutional mechanisms and/or infrastructure that would support active water markets. Or it may be that a proposed alternative use, such as maintaining instream flow for wildlife habitat, is not recognized by existing water codes to be a legitimate use of water.[7] In each of these cases, significant transaction costs exist in some form, which impede a potential Pareto-improving transfer. Otherwise, one might not expect, for example, maximizing right-holders to use water just to retain a right. More generally, water would not remain in low-valued uses when higher-valued uses are available.

One message of the early California experience is that there is nothing in appropriative law that necessarily imposes restrictions on the transfer, and therefore the reallocation to higher-value uses, of water. As we have seen, the early judges were quite liberal in permitting transfers of rights to different uses and places of use, and they even facilitated the retirement of existing uses in favor of new, higher-valued uses. Even today, however, some scholars argue that in many contexts, legal restrictions on water transfers are neither numerous nor strongly limiting under current appropriative law.[8] Indeed, the fundamental principle of first possession in appropriative law provides the tenure security necessary to support exchanges of rights. It seems clear that at the most fundamental level, appropriative law can provide doctrinal and practical support for the reallocations of water, including through water markets, which are likely to be called-for in the future.[9]

Current appropriative law does not, of course, craft individual, secure rights to water that may be transferred around freely like cars and television sets. Over time, a variety of governance mechanisms have emerged that effectively restrict transfers under certain conditions. These include limitations imposed by states and localities on out-of-basin transfers and various restrictions imposed on water supplied to farmers both by the Bureau of Reclamation and by local irrigation districts.[10] In addition, federal legislation in the form of the Wild and Scenic Rivers Act and the Endangered Species Act have also been used to impose limitations on exports of water from various river basins. Yet another example is the application of the public trust doctrine by various courts in order to limit water exports. All of these restrictions generate what one economist has termed *policy-induced transactions costs*.[11]

In terms of our theoretical framework, these restrictions may all be thought of as governance restrictions that various entities have imposed on the basic appropriative right, which in its original form in early California was a simple exclusion right. As governance restrictions, they address externalities that are generated in the development and use of local water supplies, when the relevant attributes are not subject to insuperable measurement costs. These governance restrictions largely target externalities that occur within the exporting basin, and are designed to prevent the loss of benefits to users within that basin. Since the days of early California, the set of externalities they target has been considerably broadened to include regional economic impacts, community cohesion, concerns over access to water, and a variety of environmental impacts, including endangered species habitat and unique water resources that are considered to be part of the "common heritage" of the public.[12] This broadened set of concerns has made it more challenging to consider both reallocations of water among users within a basin and reallocations of water to potentially higher-valued uses in other basins. Going forward in the twenty-first century, addressing third party impacts may be the single most important issue that impinges on the ability of the western economy to reallocate water to higher-valued uses.[13]

As we have seen, another message of the early California experience is that both mining camps and courts, each in their own way, were reasonably effective in addressing various issues involving third-party impacts associated with the development and use of available water supplies. The rules created by the mining camps reflected the political pressures internal to the camps while taking into account a variety of important economic factors. The rules created by the courts systematically reflected the transaction costs associated with the various kinds of disputes over water that could and did arise. Both worked within the basic framework of rights based upon first possession, which proved to be remarkably resilient and adaptable in servicing the economic needs of miners in the gold fields. All of this suggests that the system of prior appropriation may well be able to service present-day needs if it can be modified to address current conditions in the water policy arena, especially the reallocation of water to higher-value uses.

One obvious difference between early California and the present day is that we now face a tremendously expanded universe of potential ways to use water, including irrigated agriculture, municipal use, industrial use, and power production, not to mention environmental protection, recreation, and habitat protection. Within our measurement cost framework, the expanded universe of uses implies that given sources of water have an expanded set of potentially valuable attributes and therefore, a greater number of margins for expropriating value. For example, an appropriative right currently being used for irrigation is subject to challenge by various parties such as environmental groups and Indian tribes seeking to maintain instream flows, in ways never dreamed of by Gold Rush miners or later nineteenth-century irrigation colonizers. The *in situ* uses of the water have emerged as valuable attributes of an increasingly complex resource.

Much of the economic debate surrounding sectoral reallocations of water away from existing uses, especially interbasin transfers, has focused on the tradeoff between the higher value of new uses and the loss of external amenities in the exporting basin, including loss of in situ uses.[14] For example, opponents of rural-urban transfers concede that cities may well value the water more highly in economic terms. However, they argue, the cost of a transfer to urban areas is not merely the relatively low value of the water for irrigation or fish habitat, but all of the external benefits of keeping the water for those in the basin of origin. These external benefits are thus viewed as providing an economically supportable rationale for not exporting water to the cities.

What is less often heard, however, is the argument that the value of leaving water in a basin also depends upon the use and reuse of water within the basin, as use generates return flow. As we have seen, the larger is the return flow, the more the water takes on the characteristics of a public good. Aside from its implications for how best to define the water right, there is the added implication that all else being equal, greater return flow implies greater value, in terms of rents, to the watershed. The more water can be used and reused in the exporting basin, the greater the loss of rents within that basin when the water is exported. This is in no way to deny that there may be a similar dynamic in the *importing* basin, to the extent that water can be used and reused there. However, as we have also seen, this depends totally upon the uses to which the water is put once it is there. If we acknowledge that the nature of the uses matters explicitly in terms of their implications for return flow, this will permit a more reasoned weighing of the costs and benefits of a proposed transfer. It may also permit us to avoid the unfortunate asymmetry sometimes observed in policy discussions of considering only the loss of external benefits in the exporting basin, while ignoring the potential gain of external benefits in the importing one.[15]

But if transfers are going to be an important component of water policy moving forward, and third-party impacts are going to remain an important objection to transfers, what lessons remain for property rights solutions toward improved water allocation? Are there feasible ways to economize on transaction costs to permit a fuller consideration of all the costs and benefits associated with improved allocations of water, including water conservation and management?

One influential argument maintains that appropriative rights should be defined not to the amount one diverts but rather, only to the portion of that diversion that is actually consumed.[16] The difference is, of course, the return flow from one's diversion. In terms of addressing third-party impacts, one can immediately see the appeal of this idea. If individual right-holders are entitled only to the amount they actually consume, then any export of their right will have no impact on other claimants in the watershed.[17] The practicality of this idea, however, depends upon the cost of measuring return flows, which are nontrivial and likely quite significant in many circumstances. Others have argued that even if it were feasible to measure return flows, such a modified system would be more costly to administer, especially given the actual hydrologic complexity of a river.[18] The proposal encounters even stiffer challenges when we consider the possibilities that water in the river might hold in situ value, or that use could degrade the quality of the water in the river, as we have seen.[19] Though this proposal holds great appeal in theory, the sheer complexity of the resource, resulting in sizable measurement costs, likely makes it infeasible in practice.

Short of redefining the appropriative right itself, what can be done to improve the operation of the appropriative system? Some evidence is provided by the state of our knowledge of the magnitude of transaction costs associated with water transfers. Though economists vary in their assessment of the current magnitude of transaction costs, the weight of evidence appears to indicate transaction costs that are commonly large enough to significantly impede water transfers.[20] Large transaction costs may occur when there are many potential uses of water and when more user groups enjoy legal, administrative, political, or ethical standing in how that water is allocated. Multiple parties enjoying standing to participate in the resolution of an issue can create a situation where it becomes costly to take positive action, because anyone may resist an outcome not to their benefit.[21]

At the same time, however, transaction costs are subject to sizable variation both cross-sectionally and under different conditions of use and scarcity. For example, according to one calculation, policy-induced transaction costs vary dramatically across different western states, being considerably higher in Colorado than in either New Mexico or Utah.[22] It might be fruitful to examine more closely the sources of those differences, in order to gain insight into ways we might be able to economize on transaction costs in order to promote reallocation. Some existing evidence for certain western states, for example, suggests that policy-induced transaction costs are higher when water is scarcer and more valuable, when proposed transfers involve larger quantities of water, and when a proposed transfer is from agriculture to another sector, as opposed to within the agricultural sector.[23] Some of these cross-sectional differences seem to stem from different policy decisions made by different jurisdictions, regarding such matters as burdens of proof regarding third-party injury, and legislative bans on transfers of agricultural water.[24] However, clearly more systematic research is warranted to better understand not only when, but also why, policy-induced transaction costs vary across institutional contexts.

In pursuing this path, we should consider carefully the locus of policy-making power, as well as how different institutional entities interact with each other. In current policy discussions, every single one of the governmental entities responsible for promulgating and implementing water policy—the courts, the legislatures, and water management agencies—has had their detractors. Water management agencies have been criticized for being hidebound, and for being overly focused on narrow technical or engineering issues and not sufficiently considering broader social objectives.[25] On the other hand, some have envisioned an important role for them to play in generating information on transfer impacts, so that individual transferors do not have to do it themselves.[26] The courts have been criticized for lacking sufficient scientific knowledge to make informed decisions on third-party impacts, and also for constituting an adversarial venue, prompting "overinvestment in attorneys and other experts."[27] Legislators have been criticized for pursuing special interest, rather than public interest, goals, or for merely pursuing their own personal objectives.[28] On the other hand, some have viewed legislative participation as crucial in establishing guidelines for water management agencies for the broad social goals that water policy should support.[29]

The evidence from early California mainly concerns the relationship between the courts and the legislature, which was a complex one. On the one hand, the courts seemed to strongly defer to the legislature on a number of issues, such as the adoption of English common law. And they also deferred to many statutes that seemed to bend over backwards to support the burgeoning mining industry. However, the early California courts also showed they had minds of their own as seen, for example, when they reined in the legislature in favoring miners over agriculturalists, and also in their own attempts to minimize any adverse impact on water use that adherence to English common law might impose on miners. They also strongly deferred to the miners' codes, which were obviously not legislatively enacted. In many ways, the objectives of the courts and legislature were consonant in desiring to promote mining as much as possible. However, I believe the main lesson of the 1850s regarding the locus of policy making is that the courts largely served as impartial arbiters in water disputes: certainly more than the legislature, which exhibited legislative capture until mining started to wane in the early 1860s. And in dealing with transaction costs in its various guises, the courts exhibited remarkable ingenuity and resourcefulness.

In the present-day considerably more complex world, courts, legislatures, and administrative agencies will all play important roles in promulgating water policy. At the state level, courts will continue to defer to legislatures on many water issues.[30] However, courts will play an important independent role as well, in interpreting statutes while considering broad economic, social, and environmental objectives, and in deciding the occasional constitutional issue. How well the courts service improved water allocation will depend in part on their ability to master and adequately address the scientific complexities surrounding many water issues, which was largely a non-issue in the 1850s. Legislatures will have an important positive role to play in guiding water management agencies by setting coherent, inclusive economic and social goals for water policy to promote.[31] However, their ability to accomplish this will depend upon the complexities of interest group politics, and the extent to which resulting political outcomes are able to promote and sustain rationalized water policies. Finally, water management agencies will have an important role to play, by providing technical assistance in support of water transfers, and generating information on the third-party impacts of transfers.[32]

The other lesson from the 1850s regarding policy making concerns the operation of the mining camps, in their attempts to rationally allocate the available gold and water. This lesson is especially relevant currently, with growing academic interest in managing natural resources through self-organizing local entities, inspired by the important work of Elinor Ostrom. The local exercises in collective action that resulted in the mining codes exhibited the unquestionable influence of powerful economic pressures stemming from technological advance, economies of scale, the location of a mining camp relative to sources of water, and local hydrological conditions. At the same time, the camps struggled with certain inherent sources of instability characteristic of many common-property resources, including open access conditions, lack of repeated interaction among miners, and the fact that most individual miners were not invested in the long-term management of the resource. Many present-day local entities attempting to manage common-property resources are likely to face similar opportunities and challenges.

The main lessons from the mining camp experience concern the factors that made these local exercises in collective action either more or less successful. The factors that tended to promote the stability of the codes included common interests among miners in the peaceful resolution of disputes over gold and water; norms and customs held in common among miners, such as interest in fairness; and face-to-face communication among miners when they were writing the rules. Mining camps probably did well by establishing procedures for writing their codes that were inclusive and considered fair in many respects. Doing so likely enhanced the legitimacy of the codes in the eyes of miners, making them less costly to enforce. The factors that tended to promote instability included various sources of heterogeneity across miners, including ethnicity and national origins; evenly divided coalitions with opposing objectives; and difficulty in monitoring adherence to camp rules. Current scholars working in the area of common-property resource management should take special heed of the complex combination of factors that influence the ability of a self-organizing entity to enforce its own rules, under a variety of conditions.

Finally, I believe the narrative of 1850s California provides us a sense for why water management reform is so difficult and controversial today. We have seen how water rights principles can have significant distributional consequences; for example, in favoring first-comers over newcomers, or ditch companies over miners. Sometimes, the economic justification for certain principles can be so compelling as to overwhelm the opposition of those who harbor concerns about the distributional consequences. But this will not always be the case and then, reforms may be slow, halting, and ultimately ineffective. Current efforts to reform water management practices should firmly keep in mind their distributional implications and in particular, the sources of distributional impacts. Understanding what those distributional impacts are and what causes them may help to devise preemptive ways to mitigate those impacts in order to defuse opposition and make meaningful reform more likely.

One question left open by the parable of the elephant and the blind men concerns what happened afterwards. After each one drew his own unique conclusion about the nature of the elephant, did they sit down and compare notes? Did they try to reconcile their different findings? Or did each one simply walk away, confident in the rightness of his own opinion and the wrongness of everyone else's? I like to think that they put their heads together and ultimately came up with an understanding that was greater than the sum of the parts. But I have no evidence that this occurred. The danger that they did not is the reason that it may be useful for research on events of such great complexity as the California Gold Rush and its aftermath to draw upon a wide range of sources of information, of which there are many. That is, the strategy is to sample all parts of the elephant. This is what I have tried to do here, in my attempt to draw a picture that is balanced and comprehensive. It will be noticed that, in considering as much evidence as I could, I have eschewed the purely quantitative approach that is normally the province of economists, while presenting quantitative evidence when it was available and when it spoke to the argument. The available qualitative evidence is also extremely rich and detailed, and it tells a story that complements and fills in the gaps left by the quantitative picture. The danger, as always, is to try to say too much with the information one has. I cannot say that I have definitively described the nature of the elephant. But I believe the picture that has emerged advances in key ways our understanding of its fundamental nature.

Notes

Chapter One

1. On the notion of path dependence generally, see David, "Clio and the Economics of QWERTY". Regarding path dependence in water resources development, see, for example, Carey and Sunding, "Emerging Markets in Water"; Brewer, Glennon, Ker, and Libecap, "Water Markets in the West"; Libecap, "Institutional Path Dependence." For evidence of path dependence in other natural resources, see Libecap and Lueck, "Demarcation of Land"; Wilkinson, Crossing the Next Meridian. The notion of path dependence is implicit in Charles Wilkinson's colorful notion: the "Lords of Yesterday."

2. See, for example, Simmons, "Indian Peoples," on the history of native Americans in California. For statistics on agricultural production under Mexican rule, see Archibald, *Economic Aspects*. Early histories strongly emphasize the pastoral nature of the pre-statehood Mexican era as one dominated by large ranchos, with Robert Glass Cleland comparing the ranchos with medieval manors and the rancheros with feudal lords. See Cleland, *Cattle on a Thousand Hills*, p. 30. See also Cleland, *From Wilderness to Empire*, pp. 125–42; Robinson, *Land in California*, pp. 59–72. This characterization is sustained by standard general histories of California. (See, for example, Bean, *California: An Interpretive History*, pp. 70–72.) Though recent scholarship is providing a more nuanced picture of the pre-statehood economy in terms of trade, commerce, and life in the pueblos, the overall picture remains one of a heavily agriculturally-based economy. See, for example, Hackel, "Land, Labor and Production."

3. See, for example, Paul, *California Gold*, pp. 23–25.

4. See, for example, Zerbe and Anderson, "Culture and Fairness"; Schorr, "Appropriation as Agrarianism"; Schorr, *Colorado Doctrine*; McDowell, "From Commons to Claims."

5. Kinney, *Law of Irrigation and Water Rights*; Wiel, "'Priority' in Western Water Law"; Wiel, "Theories of Water Law." See also Shaw, "Development of the Law of Waters in the West."

6. Webb, *Great Plains*, p. 439. See also Worster, *Rivers of Empire*, p. 89.

7. Dunbar, "Adaptation of Groundwater-Control Institutions"; Dunbar, *Forging New Rights*; Dunbar, "Adaptability of Water Law"; Bakken, "English Common Law"; Bakken, "Influence of the West," p. 67.

8. Worster, *Rivers of Empire*; Pisani, *From the Family Farm to Agribusiness*; Pisani, *To Reclaim a Divided West*; Littlefield, "Water Rights during the California Gold Rush," pp. 424–25.

9. Demsetz, "Toward a Theory of Property Rights"; Anderson and Hill, "Evolution of Property Rights," p. 177.

10. Rose, "Energy and Efficiency." See also Rose, "Crystals and Mud."

11. See, for example, Anderson and Hill, "Race for Property Rights"; Lueck, "Rule of First Possession."

12. Schorr, "Appropriation as Agrarianism"; Schorr, *Colorado Doctrine*.

13. See especially Schorr, "Appropriation as Agrarianism," pp. 30–31.

14. On institutions and institutional change generally, see North, *Institutions*; North, *Structure and Change*; North, *Understanding the Process*; the readings in Drobak and Nye, *Frontiers of the New Institutional Economics*.

15. The literature on this point is vast. In the context of water, see, for example, Ostrom, *Governing the Commons*; Blomquist, *Dividing the Waters*.

16. Posner, *Economic Analysis of Law*. Economists have been long interested in the question why a common-law regime would tend toward efficiency. An influential view is that inefficient rulings tend to be superseded by more efficient ones as the former are more likely to be challenged in subsequent cases. See, for example, Rubin, "Why Is the Common Law Efficient?"; Priest, "Common Law Process." This tendency toward efficiency is promoted when judges use information gathered at trial to adjust standards of culpability. See Cooter, Kornhauser, and Lane, "Liability Rules." On the other hand, this tendency may be counteracted to some extent by biases against efficiency held by judges. See Gennaioli and Shleifer, "Evolution of Common Law"; Miceli, "Legal Change."

17. This basic idea has been advanced and developed by a number of economists, especially over the past thirty years or so. See, for example, Buchanan, Tollison, and Tullock, *Toward a Theory of the Rent-Seeking Society*; Tollison, "Rent Seeking"; Eggertsson, *Economic Behavior and Institutions*.

18. See, for example, Olson, *Logic of Collective Action*; Noll, "Economic Perspectives."

19. Beard, *Economic Interpretation*; McGuire and Ohsfeldt, "Economic Interests"; McGuire and Ohsfeldt, "Self-Interest."

20. See Schauer, "Precedent."

21. Rose, "Energy and Efficiency."

22. Idaho Legislature, *Section XV, Water Rights, Idaho Constitution.*

23. "Is It a Water-Rights Fee or a Backdoor Tax? Calif.'s High Court Will Decide," *New York Times*, December 2, 2010; "Washington's Municipal Water Law Challenged as Unconstitutional," *Marten Law*, October 11, 2006.

24. William Landes and Richard Posner, for example, treat precedents embodied in a set of court rulings as analogous to a capital stock that depreciates over time as conditions change, with new precedents acting as investments added to the existing stock. See Landes and Posner, "Legal Precedent." Benjamin Klein comments on the imperfectness of this analogy, but concurs with the usefulness of the notion of legal capital. See Klein, "Legal Precedent . . . Comment," p. 312. The treatment of judges as being constrained by precedent is consistent with many scholarly treatments of the behavior of judges. See, for example, Landes and Posner, "Legal Precedent"; Schauer, "Precedent"; Segal and Spaeth, "Influence of Stare Decisis"; Knight and Epstein, "Norm of Stare Decisis."

25. See also Pisani, "Enterprise and Equity"; Littlefield, "Water Rights during the California Gold Rush."

26. The available first-hand accounts are way too numerous to do justice to here. A famous example of an outright fictionalized account dressed up as real is J. Tyrwhitt Brooks, *Four Months among the Gold-Finders in Alta California*, which was so masterfully done that it was used as evidence regarding Gold Rush life by both Hubert Howe Bancroft and Charles Shinn. On the other hand, the authentic miner's accounts I have found particularly useful are by J. D. Borthwick, *Three Years in California*; Edward Buffum, *Six Months in the Gold Mines*; Peter Burnett, *Recollections and Opinions of an Old Pioneer*; Enos Christman, *One Man's Gold*; Alonzo Delano, *Across the Plains*; Howard Gardiner and Dale L. Morgan, *In Pursuit of the Golden Dream*; William Graham Johnston, *Experiences of a forty-niner*; Albert Lyman, *Journal of a voyage*; Frank Marryat, *Mountains and Molehills*; A. J. McCall, *Pick and pan*; Samuel McNeil, *McNeil's travels in 1849*; William Redmond Ryan, *Personal adventures in Upper and Lower California*; Riley Senter, *Crossing the continent*; and Daniel Woods, *Sixteen months at the gold diggings.* J. S. Holliday, in *World Rushed In*, has done a masterful job of compiling, annotating, and contextualizing the journal and letters of the forty-niner William Swain. Also of note is the annotated journal of Elisha Perkins by Thomas Clark, *Gold Rush Diary.* Particularly useful contemporary accounts by nonminers are Colton, *Three Years in California*; Moerenhout, *Inside Story of the Gold Rush*; Taylor, *El Dorado*; and Wierzbicki, *California as It Is and as It May Be.* Other useful sources from a woman's perspective are Sarah Royce, *Across the Plains*, and Louise Clappe, *Shirley Letters*, whose account was written under the pseudonym Dame Shirley.

27. See also James Rawls, "Introduction," p. 11.

28. Several good general book-length histories of the Gold Rush have been published in the past twenty years. These include works by Paula Mitchell Marks,

Precious Dust; Malcolm Rohrbough, *Days of Gold*; and H. W. Brands, *The Age of Gold*. Rohrbough and Brands focus exclusively on the California Gold Rush, while Marks usefully contextualizes the California experience within the other gold and silver rushes of the nineteenth century. Also worthy of note are several excellent Gold Rush compendiums that came out around the time of the sesqui-centennial. These include Burns and Orsi, *Taming the Elephant*; Gutierrez and Orsi, *Contested Eden*; Starr and Orsi, *Rooted in Barbarous Soil*; and Rawls and Orsi, *A Golden State*.

29. David Rich Lewis uses content analysis of emigrant journals to charac-terize the overland experience as centrally one of "aggression and social con-flict" (Lewis, "Argonauts," p. 304). On quantifying the incidence of violence, see McGrath, *Gunfighters, Highwaymen, and Vigilantes*; McKanna, "Enclaves of Violence." For an excellent survey of frontier opportunities and the new so-cial history, see Mann, "Frontier Opportunities." On the frontier opportunities in commerce afforded by the Gold Rush, see Decker, *Fortunes and Failures*. See Ferrie, "Up and Out or Down and Out?" on social mobility in nineteenth-century America.

30. See, for example, Zerbe and Anderson, "Culture and Fairness," p. 119 and the sources cited there. Using detailed micro-census data, Karen Clay and Randall Jones confirm that the emigrants tended to enjoy relatively high literacy rates. See Clay and Jones, "Migrating to Riches?," p. 1010.

31. Clay and Jones, "Migrating to Riches?," p. 1022.

32. See, for example, Jung, "Capitalism Comes to the Diggings"; St. Clair, "Beginnings."

33. Margo, "Wages in California."

34. Kanazawa, "Immigration, Exclusion, and Taxation"; Kanazawa, "Taxa-tion with(?) Representation."

35. Umbeck, *Theory of Property Rights*, p. 4.

36. Umbeck, "California Gold Rush"; Umbeck, *Theory of Property Rights*. See also Barzel, *Economic Analysis of Property Rights*, pp. 62–63. Ford Runge has added that the absence of existing property rights helped move to the new regime, both by increasing the value of defining new rights to increase predict-ability of outcomes, and by the implied absence of entrenched interests who might want to block the move. See Runge, "Strategic Interdependence," p. 811.

37. Anderson and Hill have argued that other aspects of the miners' laws also acted to promote efficiency. For example, contracts that contained work require-ments while not specifying what work needed to be done operated to effectively enforce rights to claims, while minimizing dissipation of rents due to enforce-ment costs. See Anderson and Hill, "Privatizing the Commons," p. 445.

38. Clay and Wright, "Order without Law?"

39. Zerbe and Anderson, "Culture and Fairness."

40. Reid, "Binding the Elephant," p. 285.

41. Reid documents these results in a series of articles and books. See, for example, Reid, *Law for the Elephant*; Reid, "Binding the Elephant"; Reid, "Replenishing the Elephant"; Reid, "Governance of the Elephant."

42. Reid, "Replenishing the Elephant," p. 65. It should be mentioned that Reid's basic thesis that the overland trail was mostly characterized by cooperation and nonaggression is not accepted by all historians. For a contrary view, see David Rich Lewis, "Argonauts."

43. McDowell, "From Commons to Claims"; McDowell, "Real Property, Spontaneous Order, and Norms."

Chapter Two

1. A fourth type of dispute may arise if A and B are situated sufficiently close together: the reservoir created by B's dam may effectively obstruct the flow of water to A. This type of dispute had a rich history in eastern riparian law in cases involving mill dams, which required a head of water to effectively power water wheels. See Rose, "Energy and Efficiency." Though we shall occasionally see such cases in California, these types of disputes were not as common and did not play much of a role in shaping the evolution of appropriative law.

2. See also Allen, "Rhino's Horn."

3. Anderson and Hill, "Evolution of Property Rights."

4. See Allen, "Transaction Costs"; Eggertsson, *Economic Behavior*, pp. 13–20.

5. See Gordon, "Economic Theory"; Scott, "Fishery." See also Feeny, Hanna, and McEvoy, "Questioning the Assumptions"; Johnson and Libecap, "Contracting Problems and Regulation."

6. The importance of open access is stressed in a vast scholarly literature. On the importance of homogeneity, see Johnson and Libecap, "Contracting Problems and Regulation"; Anderson and Hill, "Cowboys and Contracts"; Ostrom and Gardner, "Coping with Asymmetries." For general statements of the conditions likely to give rise to complete rents dissipation in a tragedy of the commons, see Feeny et al., "Twenty-Two Years Later"; Feeny, Hanna, and McEvoy, "Questioning the Assumptions."

7. See Olson, *Power and Prosperity*.

8. See, for example, Feeny, Hanna, and McEvoy, "Questioning the Assumptions," pp. 189–95; Feeny et al, "Twenty-Two Years Later," pp. 9–12.

9. This will not be strictly true if A's diversion reduces the water quality of the river. This case will be addressed later.

10. See Johnson, Gisser, and Werner, "Definition of a Surface Water Right." To be clear, here I am abstracting away from their assumption that there is a reason, such as a river compact, that a minimum flow of water needs to be left in the river at the end. This model is a variation of models employed by Hartman and

Seastone, *Water Transfers*. Anderson and Johnson extend the model in a different direction, adding an in situ value parameter to model instream flows; Anderson and Johnson, "Problem of Instream Flows." Kanazawa extends the model to
include water quality. See Kanazawa, "Water Quality."

11. See also Johnson, Gisser, and Werner, "Definition of a Surface Water
Right." One important caveat here, emphasized by Johnson et al., concerns any
impacts on the flow of water at points along the river, resulting from use, that
keep users from realizing their optimal amounts (that "bind" on those users).
Such binding flow constraints may reduce the efficiency of this particular definition of rights.

12. To be clear, one should think of the definition of transaction costs employed here as including the costs of enforcement (see Allen, "Transaction
Costs"). I am separating out enforcement costs in the discussion here to draw the
link to Anderson and Hill's earlier contribution.

13. See Barzel, "Measurement Cost"; Barzel, *Economic Analysis of Property
Rights*.

14. See, Barzel, "Measurement Cost," pp. 35–37.

15. Kanazawa, "Origins of Common-Law Restrictions."

16. See, for example, Smith, "Exclusion vs. Governance."

17. In Henry Smith's view, a key determinant of the form taken by property
rights is the cost of measuring the attributes of a resource, and exclusion and
governance emerge as measurement cost-minimizing responses to varying demand for precision in the definition of property rights. See Smith, "Exclusion vs.
Governance"; Smith, "Governing Water."

18. Pejovich, "Towards an Economic Theory"; North, *Structure and Change*;
Field, "Evolution of Property Rights," pp. 319–20; Libecap, "Economic Variables and the Development of the Law"; Demsetz, "Toward a Theory of Property Rights"; McManus, "Economic Analysis of Indian Behavior"; Dean Lueck,
"Extermination"; Umbeck, *Theory of Property Rights*; Rose, "Energy and Efficiency"; Ramseyer, "Water Law in Imperial Japan."

19. Pejovich, "Towards an Economic Theory"; North, *Structure and Change*;
Libecap, "Economic Variables and the Development of the Law"; Demsetz, "Toward a Theory of Property Rights"; Ramseyer, "Water Law in Imperial Japan."

20. McManus, "Economic Analysis of Indian Behavior"; Field, "Evolution
of Property Rights," pp. 319–20; Lueck, "Extermination"; Rose, "Energy and
Efficiency."

See also Henry Smith, who notes that early English land law moved from a
regime of roughly individual holdings to a commons-like open field system during a period of rising scarcity, before the famous Enclosure movement eventually restored a modified system of private holdings. Smith, "Exclusion vs. Governance," pp. S458–62.

21. See, for example, Field, "Evolution of Property Rights"; Umbeck, *The-*

ory of Property Rights; Lueck, "Extermination"; Barzel, *Economic Analysis of Property Rights*; Allen, "Rhino's Horn."

22. Lueck, "Extermination."

23. See also Allen, "Rhino's Horn."

24. Demsetz, "Toward a Theory of Property Rights."

25. Umbeck, *Theory of Property Rights*, pp. 60–63.

26. McManus, "Economic Analysis of Indian Behavior."

27. Henry Smith has argued that the conditions for shifting enforcement costs are quite strong, too strong for this phenomenon to be of general concern. See Smith, "Exclusion vs. Governance." However, I would argue that the possibility is more likely with complex resources with multiple margins. See also Allen, "Rhino's Horn."

28. See, for example, Kinney, *Law of Irrigation and Water Rights*; Wiel, "'Priority' in Western Water Law"; Wiel, "Theories of Water Law"; Webb, *Great Plains*, p. 439; Dunbar, *Forging New Rights*; Dunbar, "Adaptability of Water Law"; Bakken, "Influence of the West," p. 67.

29. Anderson and Hill, "Evolution of Property Rights," p. 177.

30. Mark Ramseyer's study of Imperial water law in Japan is largely consonant with this general view. See Ramseyer, "Water Law in Imperial Japan."

31. Hart, "Property Rights, Costs, and Welfare."

32. Rose, "Energy and Efficiency."

33. Kanazawa, "Efficiency in Western Water Law."

34. Smith, "Exclusion and Property Rules"; Smith, "Governing Water."

35. Smith, "Governing Water."

36. The literature on legal remedies for infringements on property rights is vast. Some particularly useful studies are Epstein, "Nuisance Law"; Merrill, "Trespass"; Landes and Posner, *Economic Structure*; Merrill and Smith, "What Happened to Property"; Smith, "Exclusion vs. Governance"; Smith, "Exclusion and Property Rules."

37. See Merrill, "Trespass"; Landes and Posner, *Economic Structure*.

38. Merrill, "Trespass," pp. 26–35. See also Merrill and Smith, "What Happened to Property," p. 395.

39. Smith, "Exclusion and Property Rules," p. 996–98. See also Merrill and Smith, "What Happened to Property," p. 396.

40. See Merrill and Smith, "What Happened to Property," p. 396.

41. See, for example, Landes and Posner, *Economic Structure*.

42. This is not to argue that precautionary behavior was necessarily absent from our previous discussion. It was implicit, for example, in the strategies of parties to disputes over water quality where a reasonableness rule was being applied, to the extent that they modified their behavior in conscious recognition of some sort of reasonableness standard.

43. It is a common presumption that the magnitude of transaction costs is key

to the application of tort law rather than contract law. See Cooter and Ulen, *Law and Economics*, p. 325.

44. The issues of measurement and strategic bargaining, though related under many conditions, are not the same. Measurement costs can create impediments to exchanges even in the absence of strategic bargaining considerations. See, for example, Libecap, *Contracting for Property Rights*, pp. 23–24. However, strategic bargaining can exacerbate the difficulties of effecting an exchange.

45. See Barzel, "Measurement Cost"; Allen, "Transaction Costs," especially pp. 906–7. Allen stresses that the presence of information costs does not necessarily imply transaction costs, because zero transaction costs would imply that contingent claims contracts could be written over all possible contingencies, eliminating the problem of costly information.

46. See Merrill and Smith, "What Happened to Property," pp. 376–78. The scholarly literature on contracting and transaction costs is enormous. For examples related to natural resources see, for example, Libecap, *Contracting for Property Rights*.

47. Merrill and Smith, "What Happened to Property," pp. 379–83.

48. Calabresi and Melamed, "Property Rules, Liability Rules, and Inalienability."

49. Ayres and Talley, "Solomonic Bargaining."

50. Kaplow and Shavell, "Do Liability Rules Facilitate Bargaining?"; Kaplow and Shavell, "Property Rules vs. Liability Rules."

51. Rose, "Shadow of the Cathedral."

52. See, for example, Merrill, "Trespass."

Chapter Three

1. DeGroot, *Recollections*, pp. 3–4. See also Bancroft, *History*, p. 36; Hittell, *Mining in the Pacific States*, pp. 9–11.

2. This is the consensus version of the story taken from a number of different sources. See DeGroot, *Recollections*, pp. 6–8; Bancroft, *History*, pp. 38–45; Caughey, *Gold Is the Cornerstone*, p. 17; Hittell, *Mining in the Pacific States*, pp. 14–15; Bigler, *Diary of a Mormon*, in Paul, *California Gold Discovery*, p. 158; Bean, *California: An Interpretive History*, pp. 109–10.

3. Gudde, *Bigler's Chronicle*, pp. 104–11; Gudde, *California Gold Camps*, p. 225; Castro, *Carson's California*, pp. 5–6; Moerenhout, *Inside Story of the Gold Rush*, p. 17.

4. *Californian*, 3/15/1848; Bieber, "California Gold Mania," p. 9; Bean, *California: An Interpretive History*, pp. 110–11; *Californian*, 5/17/1848; Teggart and Lyman, "Diary of C. S. Lyman," p. 182; *California Star*, 5/27/1848; Colton, *Three Years in California*, pp. 242–49. Moerenhout, *Inside Story of the Gold Rush*,

6/10/1848; Caughey, *Gold Is the Cornerstone*, p. 21; Hussey, in Swan, *A trip to the gold mines*, p. x; Buffum, *Six Months in the Gold Mines*, p. 83.

5. Hussey, in Swan, *A trip to the gold mines*, p. xi; Bieber, "California Gold Mania," p. 12; Caughey, *Gold Is the Cornerstone*, pp. 23–24; *Californian*, 9/9/1848; Sherman, *California gold fields*, 10/28/1848. See *Star and Californian*, 12/2/1848; Paul, *California Gold*, pp. 23–24.

6. Gudde, *California Gold Camps*, p. 33; *History of Butte County*, p. 209. See also Bancroft, *History*, pp. 71–72.

7. This may have been one of the richest bars in the state. According to Erwin Gudde, David Parks, whom the bar was named after, ultimately left for New Orleans with $85,000 in his pocket. See Gudde, *California Gold Camps*, p. 259.

8. Bancroft, *History*, pp. 361–62.

9. Gudde, *California Gold Camps*, p. 100.

10. Ibid., p. 237.

11. Bancroft, *History*, p. 77; Gudde, *California Gold Camps*, p. 220.

12. Bancroft, *History*, p. 77; Heckendorn and Wilson, *Miners and Businessmen's Directory*, pp. 6, 80; *History of Tuolumne County*, pp. 3–4; Stoddart, *Annals of Tuolumne County*, pp. 53–58, including De Ferrari's excellent annotation.

13. Larkin letter, dated 6/1/1848, in *California gold regions*, p. 13; Hussey, in Swan, *A trip to the gold mines*, pp. x–xi. See also *Alta Californian*, 5/3/1848, 5/17/1848.

14. Moerenhout, *Inside Story of the Gold Rush*, 7/25/1848, pp. 25–26.

15. See, for example, Gardiner and Morgan, *In Pursuit of the Golden Dream*, p. 102. See also Baker, June 1850, in Holliday, *World Rushed In*, pp. 332–33; *Miners' Own Book*, p. 15; Morse, "Story of a Gold Miner," p. 216. On auxiliary technologies to drain the river bed, see *Alta Californian*, 7/22/1851, 7/29/1851, 9/22/1851. On wing-damming, see Stephens, *Life sketches*, p. 29; Morse, "Story of a Gold Miner," pp. 218–19.

16. *Star and Californian*, 12/2/1848. The timing of the introduction of river mining has been a source of confusion among gold rush historians, who sometimes suggest that river mining did not start until 1849. See Holliday, *World Rushed In*, p. 307; Littlefield, "Water Rights during the California Gold Rush," p. 420; Rohe, "Origins and Diffusion," p. 140. Rohe refers to an abortive attempt to drain the American River near Mormon Island in fall of 1848, in support of his conclusion that the true beginning of river mining was 1849. This event, however, was reported in the *Alta Californian* in September of 1850, nearly two years later. I find it unlikely that a contemporary report citing a "usual" practice would be less reliable than a retrospective account two years later.

17. *Alta Californian*, 3/29/1849; Holliday, *World Rushed In*, p. 307; Delano, *Across the Plains*, p. 122; *Alta Californian*, 8/5/1850; *Alta Californian*, 7/12/1852.

18. *Alta Californian*, 4/24/1850, 5/24/1850.

19. Buffum, *Six Months in the Gold Mines*, p. 99; Taylor, *El Dorado*, pp. 84–

85; Woods, *Sixteen months at the gold diggings*, p. 64. See also Stephens, *Life sketches*, p. 28; Lyman, *Journal of a voyage*, p. 113.

20. Gardiner and Morgan, *In Pursuit of the Golden Dream*, p. 102; *Alta Californian*, 4/12/1849; *Alta Californian*, 8/2/1849. The wage calculation assumes Rodman Paul's estimate of $16 per day in 1849. See Paul, *California Gold*, p. 120; Delano, *Across the Plains*, p. 122.

21. Baker, in Holliday, *World Rushed In*, pp. 332–33.

22. Woods, *Sixteen months at the gold diggings*, pp. 149–50.

23. Derbec, *A French journalist in the California Gold Rush*, 7/25/1850, p. 109.

24. Buffum, *Six Months in the Gold Mines*, p. 100.

25. For the effect of low precipitation on river mining in 1855 and 1856, see *Alta Californian*, 11/12/1855, 8/20/1856, 9/5/1856, 9/10/1856, 9/11/1856. For river mining operations in the southern mines, see *Alta Californian*, 2/26/1855, 3/6/1855, 5/15/1855, 7/18/1855, 9/13/1856. For river mining operations on the Feather, see *Alta Californian*, 7/7/1856, 9/24/1856.

26. See, for example, Caughey, *Gold Is the Cornerstone*, p. 251.

27. Letter from Colonel Mason (8/30/1848), in Kells, *California, from its discovery*, pp. 26–27; Burnett, *Recollections and Opinions of an Old Pioneer*, p. 273; Lyman, *Journal of a voyage*, pp. 267–68; *Californian*, 9/5/1848; Moerenhout, *Inside Story of the Gold Rush*, 7/24/1848, p. 24. See Gudde for a discussion of the pursuit hypothesis and Paul for a discussion of the Cornish miner hypothesis. Gudde, *California Gold Camps*, p. 238; Paul, *California Gold*, p. 147. For a good general description of the early coyoteing process, see Sawyer, *Way sketches*, 11/25/1850, p. 118. Rohe concurs that drifting likely originated near Nevada City in 1850. See Rohe, "Origins and Diffusion," p. 146. On use of windlasses, see Borthwick, *Three Years in California*, p. 113; *Miners' Own Book*, p. 8.

28. *Alta Californian*, 5/1/1850, 7/20/1850, 3/13/1851, 9/28/1851, 5/22/1852, 10/23/1855, 5/7/1856, 11/8/1857.

29. *Alta Californian*, 12/8/1851, 6/27/1852, 7/3/1852, 3/24/1857.

30. *Alta Californian*, 6/14/1858, 1/28/1856, 3/1/1857.

31. *Alta Californian*, 5/19/1857.

32. Clappe, *Shirley Letters*, p. 136. See also Holliday, *World Rushed In*, p. 353, for another characterization of the Gold Rush as a great lottery.

33. Shinn, *Mining Camps*, p. 104. See also Colton, *Three Years in California*, pp. 310–11; Woods, *Sixteen months at the diggings*, pp. 56–57.

34. Brands, *Age of Gold*, p. 198.

35. For a contemporary view similar to Shinn's, see Bruce, *Launching of Modern American Science*, p. 140. See also Spence, *Mining Engineers and the American West*, p. 4. Nor was this view confined to the gold rush in California. Williams quotes a veteran of the Georgia gold rush: "It's just like gambling—all luck." See Williams, *Georgia Gold Rush*, p. 65.

36. On the rumors of the gold lake, see Delano, *Across the Plains*, p. 145. For the volcano theory, see Buffum, *Six Months in the Gold Mines*, pp. 111–12; Colton, *Three Years in California*, pp. 310–11. Colton says: "The deposits here baffle all the pretensions of science. The volcanoes did their work by no uniform geological law; they burst out at random, and scattered their gold in wanton caprice."

37. Paul, *California Gold Discovery*, pp. 203–4.

38. See Williams, who quotes one nineteenth-century mining engineer as referring to the gold fields of the American south as "the cradle . . . in which the California '49-er was born." Williams, *Georgia Gold Rush*, p. 118.

39. According to Rodman Paul, "In forty-nine and the early fifties it was considered a great advantage to have a Georgian, Carolinian, or Cornishman in one's party." Paul, *California Gold*, p. 48.

40. See, for example, Read, *Development of Mineral Industry Education*, p. 15, on the importance of Agricola's work. See also Paul, *California Gold*, p. 45.

41. See Phillips, "Essay on the Georgia Gold Mines," especially pp. 1–3.

42. Dana, *Manual of Mineralogy*, p. iii.

43. Ibid., p. 316.

44. Wierzbicki, *California as It Is and as It May Be*, p. 56.

45. See Stillson, *Spreading the Word*, p. 136.

46. *Alta Californian*, 10/4/1849.

47. Delano, *Across the Plains*, p. 163. See also the suggestive remarks in Lyman, *Journal of a voyage*, pp. 267–68, 271, 283; McNeil, *McNeil's travels in 1849*, p. 22.

48. Paul, *California Gold Discovery*, p. 170.

49. See, for example, Paul, *California Gold*, pp. 51–52.

50. Wooden pans, or bateas, tended to be used by Mexican or South American miners and thus, were observed more frequently in the southern mines. See Rohe, "Origins and Diffusion," pp. 129–30.

51. See, for example, Colton, *Three Years in California*, p. 275.

52. As shall be developed shortly, this fact largely reflects a growing segmentation of the labor market in the 1850s between small-scale independent miners and wage laborers working for large-scale mining businesses.

53. *Alta Californian*, 7/4/1856.

54. For good general descriptions of the rocker-and-cradle technology, see *Miners' Own Book*, pp. 3–4; Moerenhout, *Inside Story of the Gold Rush*, 7/17/1848, pp. 17–19; on team production, see Swan, *A trip to the gold mines*, p. 33; Moerenhout, *Inside Story of the Gold Rush*, 7/17/1848, pp. 17–19; Paul, *California Gold*, p. 53; Burnett, *Recollections and Opinions of an Old Pioneer*, p. 274. On the timing of the introduction of the rocker-and-cradle into California, see also Rohe, "Origins and Diffusion," p. 131.

55. Buffum, *Six Months in the Gold Mines*, p. 57–58; Wierzbicki, *California*

as It Is and as It May Be, pp. 45–46; Rohe, "Origins and Diffusion," pp. 131–32; *Alta Californian*, 4/15/1850.

56. The precise timing of the introduction of long toms in California has been subject to dispute. Rodman Paul asserts that long toms were introduced into California in the winter of 1849–50. See Paul, *California Gold*, p. 61. This timing is corroborated by Bancroft, who argues that long toms were beginning to be in use in California in 1850, and had previously existed as a technology in Georgia. See Bancroft, *History*, p. 410. See also Hittell, *Mining in the Pacific States*, p. 22; May, *Origins of Hydraulic Mining*, pp. 32, 36. For a contemporary account, see J. B. Hill, *In the gold mines*, p. 15. Randall Rohe asserts that long toms were introduced "as early as May 1849." See Rohe, "Origins and Diffusion," p. 135, and sources cited therein. However, at least some of the sources Rohe cites, such as Paul and Hittell, do not support his claim. And my newspaper database contains absolutely no evidence of the existence of long toms in early 1849. I must conclude that long toms were not available in any numbers prior to the 1850 mining season, and only began to achieve widespread use in 1851.

57. *Alta Californian*, 2/8/1851. See also Borthwick, *Three Years in California*, p. 101.

58. *Alta Californian*, 6/9/1851, 8/4/1852; Borthwick, *Three Years in California*, p. 99. See also Rohe, "Origins and Diffusion," p. 136.

59. Paul, *California Gold*, p. 63. See also Hittell, *Mining in the Pacific States*, p. 22.

60. *Marysville Herald*, 4/26/1851.

61. *Calaveras Chronicle*, as reported in the *Alta Californian*, 12/22/1851.

62. *Alta Californian*, 3/24/1853.

63. *Miners' Own Book*, p. 6. See also Rohe, "Origins and Diffusion," p. 137.

64. Paul, *California Gold*, pp. 62–63.

65. The first mention of the sluicing technology in the *Alta Californian* was likely on 7/16/1851. See also *Alta Californian*, 12/22/1851, 3/24/1853. On the lag in adoption of sluices in the southern mines, see, for example: *Alta Californian*, 4/30/1854.

66. Thompson and West's *History of Nevada County*, p. 179, asserts that ground sluicing "came into general use" in Nevada County near Nevada City in early 1852. For the progression of its adoption over time, see *Alta Californian*, 6/20/1853, 6/10/1857.

67. Though there is some controversy over who first invented this process, most histories credit it to Matteson. See, for example, Paul, *California Gold*; Kelley, *Gold vs. Grain*; May, *Origins of Hydraulic Mining*. For an excellent brief summary of the controversy over its origins, see Greenland, *Hydraulic Mining in California*, pp. 32–35.

68. *Alta Californian*, 6/7/1853.

69. Paul, *California Gold*, p. 156; *Alta Californian*, 5/21/1854; Greenland, *Hy-*

draulic Mining in California, pp. 44–45; *North San Juan Press*, reported in *Alta Californian*, 10/9/1858; Rohe, "Hydraulicking," p. 22.

70. See also Rohe, "Hydraulicking," p. 20.

71. This database was constructed by going chronologically through the *Daily Alta Californian* issues beginning in January 1849, and noting (virtually) every story that appeared regarding the mining industry for the next eleven years. Though scholars have noted certain political leanings of the newspaper, it is hard to see how these could have biased the basic reporting of technological conditions in the goldfields.

72. A wide range of periodizations of the California Gold Rush can be observed in existing studies, which mark it as ending anywhere from as early as 1851 to sometime in the mid-1850s. To the extent that gold rushes are considered to be associated with extremely simple, labor-intensive mining (see, for example, McDowell, *Gold Rushes Are All the Same*), this evidence indicates that the Gold Rush was briefer than suggested by many studies.

73. Like panning, this technology was an ancient one, also found in the works of Agricola. See, for example, Paul, *California Gold*, p. 138.

74. A common problem was that the stamping process was extremely imprecise, often crushing the quartz rock either too coarsely or too finely. As a result, much gold was lost: perhaps as much as 80 percent. Furthermore, when gold was chemically encased in sulphides, it would not amalgamate with quicksilver in order to increase gold recovery. See Caughey, *Gold Is the Cornerstone*, pp. 255–56; Paul, *California Gold*, pp. 139–41.

75. See, for example, Allsop, *California and its Gold Mines*, p. 43; Spence, *British Investments and the American Mining Frontier*, p. 3; Jenks, *Migration of British Capital*, p. 161; Jung, "Capitalism Comes to the Diggings," p. 67.

76. See Caughey, *Gold Is the Cornerstone*, p. 257. See also Paul, *California Gold*, pp. 145–46.

77. Lyman, *Journal of a voyage*, p. 103; Jung, "Capitalism Comes to the Diggings," p. 59.

78. See, for example, Woods, *Sixteen months at the gold diggings*, pp. 170, 181; Shinn, *Mining Camps*, p. 105.

79. References to miners hiring out for wage labor are quite common. See, for example Stoddart, *Annals of Tuolumne County*. p. 61; Wyman, "California Emigrant Letters," p. 19; Hill, *Letters of a young miner*, pp. 37–38; Senter, *Crossing the continent*, 3/30/1851; Christman, *One Man's Gold*, p. 143. See also Jung, "Capitalism Comes to the Diggings," p. 59.

80. Paul, *California Gold*, p. 118.

81. Senter, *Crossing the continent*, 3/30/1851.

82. Hill, *Letters of a young miner*, 5/13/1850, pp. 37–38.

83. For another example of the difficulty of such transaction costs, see *Alta Californian*, 7/31/1851. The argument is similar to that of Alston, and Alston and

Higgs, who have investigated the importance of both enforcement costs and supervisory costs in explaining the type of labor contracts that emerged in southern agriculture after the Civil War. See Alston, "Tenure Choice"; Alston and Higgs, "Contractual Mix." A third hypothesis—that partnerships might have been formed to share risk—has a difficult time explaining the dominance of partnerships over wage labor because that would require the assumption that miners as employees were more risk-averse than miners as employers (see, for example, Higgs, "Race, Tenure, and Resource Allocation"). It is difficult to see why this would be true.

84. *An Act concerning corporations*, enacted 4/22/1850.

85. See Paul, *California Gold*, p. 122. See Odell, "Integration of Regional and Interregional Capital Markets," for a discussion of financial markets on the Pacific Coast at the time of the gold rush, and the emergence of San Francisco as the financial center of the region.

86. See Schweikart and Doty, "From Hard Money to Branch Banking," p. 221.

Chapter Four

1. Woods, *Sixteen months at the gold diggings*, p. 68. See also Johnston, *Experiences of a forty-niner*, p. 274; Hill, *Letters of a young miner*, pp. 86–87.

2. *Alta Californian*, 8/23/1850; 1/25/1851; 6/21/1851; 7/29/1851; 5/10/1852.

3. *Alta Californian*, 2/19/1851.

4. *Alta Californian*, 10/5/1851, 1/6/1852, 6/26/1854.

5. *Alta Californian*, 6/26/1854.

6. *Alta Californian*, 8/1/1851.

7. Buffum, *Six Months in the Gold Mines*, p. 64.

8. On the water-driven seasonality of mining generally, see Huntley, *Adventures in California*, vol. 2, p. 13. See also Woods, *Sixteen months at the diggings*, p. 69; *Alta Californian*, 2/8/1851. On the strategy of accumulating dirt piles, see *Alta Californian*, 12/4/1850, 10/10/1851, 11/18/1851, 2/18/1859, 2/23/1859.

9. *Alta Californian*, 4/4/1851.

10. See Thompson and West, *History of Nevada County*, p. 171; Lardner and Brock, *History of Placer and Nevada Counties*, p. 322; May, *Origins of Hydraulic Mining*, pp. 34–36. Gudde cites a source that claims this was the first (obviously non-river) mining ditch in the state. See Gudde, *California Gold Camps*, p. 86.

11. The information here has been taken from multiple sources. See Thompson and West, *History of Nevada County*, p. 171; Lardner and Brock, *History of Placer and Nevada Counties*, pp. 322–23; *History of Yuba County*, p. 136; *Historical Souvenir of El Dorado County*, p. 104; *Alta Californian*, 5/8/1851; *History of Amador County*, pp. 262, 265; *Directory of the County of Placer*, p. 46.

12. These companies were the Seco Water Company, the Sonora Water Company, the Sullivan's Creek Company, and the Woods Diggings Company, all of which tapped Woods Creek and Sullivan's Creek, two tributaries of the Tuolumne River, to supply water to miners at Campo Seco, Sonora, Shaw's Flat, and Montezuma. Evidently, none of these ditches were very extensive nor did they carry much water, at most enough to service twenty or thirty long toms. See *Alta Californian*, 8/4/1852. See also Witness Testimony, *Woods Diggings Company v. Tuolumne County Water Company*, Tuolumne County Court (1852).

13. See Borthwick, *Three Years in California*, p. 246.

14. *Alta Californian*, 10/1/1855, 4/14/1859, 7/31/1859.

15. *Records of Incorporation and Articles of Incorporation, 1850–1862.*

16. *Alta Californian*, 5/23/1852, 11/13/1852.

17. *Alta Californian*, 12/10/1853, 12/26/1853.

18. *Historical Souvenir of El Dorado County*, p. 106; *Sacramento Daily Union*, 4/29/1856.

19. *Alta Californian*, 4/29/1853.

20. The counties are Nevada, Amador, Placer, El Dorado, Tuolumne, Butte, and Calaveras.

21. See *History of Amador County*, p. 267.

22. Paul, *California Gold*, p. 164.

23. *Alta Californian*, 8/8/1853.

24. *San Joaquin Republican*, as reported in the *Alta Californian*, 12/3/1852. See also Mann, *After the Gold Rush*, p. 24.

25. These data were collected annually by the office of the state Surveyor-General beginning in 1855. See *Annual Report of the Surveyor-General*, various years, 1855–1866.

26. The mileage figure for 1855 is almost certainly a gross understatement, because of missing data for certain counties. Therefore, Figure 4.1 understates the amount of ditching activity that occurred prior to that year.

27. These fourteen counties were Amador, Butte, Calaveras, El Dorado, Nevada, Placer, Plumas, Sacramento, Shasta, Sierra, Siskiyou, Trinity, Tuolumne, and Yuba.

28. Borthwick, *Three Years in California*, p. 246.

29. See *Alta Californian*, 8/3/1851: the report on the "permanent" dam structure probably refers to the newly incorporated South Yuba Mining and Sacramento Canal Company. For reports on these particular dams, see *Alta Californian*, 7/14/1853 (Tuolumne Hydraulic Association), 5/1/1855 (Mississippi Bar). For other early reports on "substantial" dams, see also *Alta Californian*, 11/13/1852 (Placer County); 11/15/1853 (El Dorado County).

30. *Alta Californian*, 11/30/1857.

31. *Alta Californian*, 8/4/1852.

32. Gardiner and Morgan, *In Pursuit of the Golden Dream*, pp. 240–41.

33. Eastman, "John Wallace and the Tuolumne County Water Company," p. 299.

34. *Alta Californian*, 7/3/1852, 11/15/1853.

35. *Alta Californian*, 8/23/1852, 7/6/1854.

36. One of the earliest such elevated flumes was built by the Bear River Water and Mining Company. By fall of 1852, this company had constructed such a flume 850 feet in length and 147 feet high. See *Placer Herald*, 9/25/1852.

37. *Alta Californian*, 11/16/1857. See also the following February, for a story about a similar suspension flume structure being planned at Jenny Lind, in Calaveras County. *San Andreas Independent*, 2/1/1858.

38. *Alta Californian*, 8/23/1852.

39. Marryat, *Mountains and Molehills*, 10/1851, p. 158.

40. Letter from Pusey Graves, *Correspondence*, Georgetown, 11/28/1852; Senter, *Crossing the continent*, Murphy's,1853. See also Pisani, "Origins of Western Water Law," p. 243.

41. *An Act concerning Corporations*, enacted 4/22/1850, pp. 365–66.

42. *Alta Californian*, 3/1/1853, 12/10/1853.

43. When, for example, the Bear River and Auburn Water and Mining Company incorporated in May of 1851, its initial subscribers almost entirely resided in Nevada City. By July 1852, the vast majority of subscribers resided in San Francisco. See *List of Names of Stockholders in the Bear River and Auburn Water and Mining Company*. See also Pisani, "Origins of Western Water Law," p. 244.

44. *An Act to provide for the Formation of Corporations for certain purposes*, enacted 4/14/1853, pp. 89–90.

45. *Minutes, Board of Trustees of Tuolumne County Water Company from September 6 1852 to November 4, 1853 inclusive*; *Minute Book, Tuolumne Redemption Company, 1859–1860*; *Minutes of Board of Trustees, Columbia and Stanislaus River Water Company, 1856–1859*.

46. Black, *Report on Middle Yuba Canal*, pp. 5–6; Pagenhart, *Water Use in the Yuba and Bear River Basins*, p. 90.

47. Pagenhart, *Water Use in the Yuba and Bear River Basins*, p. 90.

48. Ibid., p. 90.

49. Defendant's Answer, *Duell v. Bear River and Auburn Water and Mining Company*, Placer Co. District Ct. #173.

50. See also May, *Origins of Hydraulic Mining*, p. 49.

51. *Alta Californian*, 2/11/1853.

52. *Alta Californian*, 2/25/1856, 3/7/1856, 5/27/1856, 12/28/1856, 4/28/1857, 1/26/1858, 2/1/1858, 2/22/1858.

53. Pisani, "Origins of Western Water Law," p. 244.

54. Eastman, "John Wallace and the Tuolumne County Water Company," p. 310.

55. *Alta Californian*, 11/7/1853.

56. See, for example, Letter, Columbia Businessmen. To Tuolumne County Water Company, March 18, 1855. *Minutes, Board of Trustees of Tuolumne County Water Company, March 7, 1859, August 22, 1859. Minute Book, Tuolumne Redemption Company, February 3, 1860.*

57. *History of Tuolumne County*, pp. 166–68; *Alta Californian*, 3/31/1855, 11/29/1855, 2/25/1856, 3/7/1856, 3/25/1856, 3/31/1856, 9/30/1857, 10/14/1857.

58. *Alta Californian*, 3/25/1856, 9/30/1857, 10/14/1857.

59. *History of Tuolumne County*, pp. 166–67.

60. *Alta Californian*, 2/11/1853, 3/25/1856. *History of Tuolumne County*, pp. 162–78.

61. *Minutes, Board of Trustees of Tuolumne County Water Company*, February 27, 1857.

62. *Letter, Gale and Elliot. To Tuolumne County Water Company, March 4, 1857.*

63. *Minutes, Board of Trustees of Tuolumne County Water Company*, December 5, 1856, June 18, 1858, February 14, 1859. *Minutes, Board of Trustees of Columbia and Stanislaus River Water Company*, March 6, 1856.

64. Lardner and Brock, *History of Placer and Nevada Counties*, p. 323. Greenland, *Hydraulic Mining in California*, p. 82.

65. *Yreka Herald*, in *Alta Californian*, 2/10/1855. See also the *Columbia Gazette*, 1/22/1853, as quoted in Rensch, *Columbia: A Gold Camp of Old Tuolumne*, p. 69; Pisani, "Origins of Western Water Law".

66. Hill, *Letters of a young miner*, 6/12/1851, p. 66.

67. *Alta Californian*, 12/4/1852.

68. See, for example, *Alta Californian*, 11/1/1857, 11/15/1857, 12/27/1857. See also the series of district court cases for Nevada and Placer counties in chapter 8.

69. *Alta Californian*, 7/15/1851.

70. See, for example, *Alta Californian*, 11/15/1853, and the district court cases in chapter 9.

Chapter Five

1. The ceded lands also included all of Nevada, Utah, and Texas, and parts of Wyoming, Colorado, Arizona, New Mexico, and Oklahoma.

2. See, for example, Umbeck, who points out that at the time, the federal government had no laws regulating the acquisition of mining rights, and even if it had, it is doubtful they could have been enforced. See Umbeck, "Theory of Contract Choice," p. 429. See also Scott, *Evolution of Resource Property Rights*, p. 219.

3. Letter from Mason dated 9/10/1848, in Kells, *California, from its discovery*, p. 25.

4. Ibid., pp. 27–28.

5. *Alta Californian*, 5/24/1848.

6. Letter from Mason dated 9/10/1848, in Kells, *California, from its discovery*, p. 28–29.

7. Sherman, *California gold fields*, 10/29/1848.

8. Swan, *A trip to the gold mines*, p. 11.

9. The early Gold Rush is a good example of how the cost of enforcing exclusion rights can increase as the value of a resource goes up, the argument made by a number of economists, including Field, "Evolution of Property Rights," Barzel, *Economic Analysis of Property Rights*, and Allen, "Rhino's Horn."

10. See, for example, Caughey, *Gold Is the Cornerstone*, p. 4.

11. Lyman, *Journal of a voyage*, 12/3/1849, p. 133.

12. Ibid., p. 135.

13. Kanazawa, "Taxation with(?) Representation."

14. Castro, *Carson's California*, p. 16.

15. Ibid., p. 3.

16. Colton, *Three Years in California*, pp. 309–10. See also p. 291.

17. Lienhard, *A pioneer at Sutter's fort*, p. 144–45; Ryan, *Personal adventures in Upper and Lower California*, vol. 2, p. 37.

18. Buffum, *Six Months in the Gold Mines*, p. 60.

19. McDowell, "From Commons to Claims," pp. 13–15.

20. Kells, *California, from its discovery*, p. 29.

21. Ryan, *Personal adventures in Upper and Lower California*, pp. 21–22.

22. Hussey, in Swan, *A trip to the gold mines*, p. xii.

23. See, for example, Stephens, *Life sketches*, p. 30; Taylor, *El Dorado*, p. 101; Woods, *Sixteen months at the gold diggings*, p. 115; Christman, *One Man's Gold*, p. 129; Marryat, *Mountains and Molehills*, p. 124; Borthwick, *Three Years in California*, p. 102.

24. Woods, *Sixteen months at the gold diggings*, p. 57.

25. Marryat, *Mountains and Molehills*, p. 124. See also Shaw, who in the fall of 1849 describes "the laws of the placers with respect to land occupation" as "very undefined." (Shaw, *Golden Dreams*, p. 84.)

26. See, for example, Christman, *One Man's Gold*, pp. 135–36; Woods, *Sixteen months at the gold diggings*, p. 115.

27. Burnett, *Recollections and Opinions of an Old Pioneer*, pp. 273–74. See also Stephens, *Life sketches*, p. 30; Christman, *One Man's Gold*, p. 273; Borthwick, *Three Years in California*, pp. 102, 129.

28. For an example of salting claims with gold, see Woods, *Sixteen months at the gold diggings*, pp. 89–90.

29. Borthwick, *Three Years in California*, p. 129.

30. Stephens, *Life sketches*, p. 30.

31. Lynch law fascinated many observers and thus, it is easy to find references to it and often, vivid descriptions. See, for example, Taylor, *El Dorado*, p. 99; Castro, *Carson's California*, p. 13; Clappe, *Shirley Letters*, pp. 93–96; Buffum, *Six Months in the Gold Mines*, pp. 107–10; Lyman, *Journal of a voyage*, pp. 121–22; Ryan, *Personal adventures in Upper and Lower California*, pp. 51–54, 62–64; McCall, *Pick and pan*, p. 22.

32. Delano, *Across the Plains*, p. 157.

33. Castro, *Carson's California*, p. 19.

34. Holliday, *World Rushed In*, p. 317.

35. Ibid., p. 317.

36. Ostrom and Gardner, "Coping with Asymmetries," p. 93.

37. One way to think about this is that each miner in a camp potentially wore two hats. On the one hand, he went about his day-to-day business of working his claim. On the other hand, he participated in a process of crafting rules to govern mining activity, recognizing that those rules would apply to himself if he continued to mine. Schlager and Ostrom, for example, term these *operational* and *collective-choice* levels of action. See Schlager and Ostrom, "Property-Rights Regimes and Natural Resources," p. 249.

38. See Clay and Wright regarding universal participation, though it should be mentioned that when present as a minority in a camp, foreign miners were often excluded from these meetings. See Clay and Wright, "Order without Law?" On fairness as an important factor, see Zerbe and Anderson, "Culture and Fairness"; Schorr, "Appropriation as Agrarianism." For the importance of communication, see Ostrom, "A Diagnostic Approach for Going beyond Panaceas," p. 15183. For the importance of legitimacy, see Schlager and Ostrom, "Property-Rights Regimes and Natural Resources," p. 250.

39. See Smith, "Governing Water," for the argument that both of these systems of allocating water rights involve exclusion, albeit in different ways and to differing degrees.

40. See, for example, Schorr, "Appropriation as Agrarianism"; Schorr, *Colorado Doctrine*.

41. Clay and Wright, "Order without Law?" See Anderson and Snyder for the same argument in relation to water. Anderson and Snyder, *Water Markets*, p. 59.

42. See, for example, Zerbe and Anderson, "Culture and Fairness," for a forceful statement of this position. See Rose, "Possession as the Origin of Property," for a discussion of the Lockean position more generally.

43. *Alta Californian*, 5/24/1850.

44. Accounts of these two meetings may be found in *Alta Californian*, 7/27/1851; *Alta Californian*, 8/2/1851.

45. This situation should be distinguished from one of bilateral monopoly

with much private information about, say, how much care was exercised in building and maintaining a dam. The dispute described here would have involved relatively little private information.

46. *US Mining Laws*, p. 284.

47. The standard efficiency interpretation is bolstered by the fact that defining exclusion rights in this manner would have served the additional economizing function of minimizing measurement costs associated with measuring the various attributes of a property right. See Smith, "Exclusion vs. Governance"; Smith, "Governing Water."

48. See Schorr, "Appropriation as Agrarianism"; Schorr, *Colorado Doctrine*.

49. For a discussion of measurement costs as permitting exploitation of margins of effort, see Barzel, "Measurement Cost"; Barzel, *Economic Analysis of Property Rights*. Most Gold Rush scholars emphasize the joint stock association model of mining companies, which was probably the dominant company model, especially early on. However, we saw in chapter 3 that there is also much evidence of an active wage labor market at the time. See, for example, Wyman, "California Emigrant Letters," p. 19; Hill, *In the gold mines*, pp. 37–38; Christman, *One Man's Gold*, pp. 143–45; Senter, *Crossing the continent*, 3/30/1851; Stoddart, *Annals of Tuolumne County*, p. 61. In addition, a number of scholars have remarked on the use of Indian labor, as well as the use of slaves by transported southerners. See Brands, *Age of Gold*, p. 198; Rohrbough, *Days of Gold*, p. 125.

50. Heckendorn and Wilson, *Miners and Businessmen's Directory*, p. 83; *US Mining Laws*, p. 331.

51. *US Mining Laws*, p. 333.

52. Heckendorn and Wilson, *Miners and Businessmen's Directory*, p. 83.

53. Delano, *Across the Plains*, p. 121. See also Gudde, *California Gold Camps*, p. 91

54. Zerbe and Anderson, "Culture and Fairness"; Clay and Wright, "Order without Law?"; McDowell, "From Commons to Claims"; McDowell, "Real Property, Spontaneous Order, and Norms."

55. (1) *US Mining Laws*: p. 342 (Constitution Hill, Washington Hill), p. 277 (Weaver Creek), p. 337 (Rockwell Hill), pp. 276–77 (Upper Yuba, East Fork of North Trinity); (2) Heckendorn and Wilson, *Miners & Businessmen's Directory*, p. 80 (Jackass Gulch); (3) *Earl v. George*, Placer County District Ct. #125 (Volcano Hill). For the first time, we also began to observe refinement of the maximum claims provision to allow for special circumstances. The Upper Yuba code specified that miners could successfully bid for the claims of deceased miners, even if they already held other claims.

56. The notion that miners were limited to one claim is common in existing studies. See Schorr, "Appropriation as Agrarianism"; Schorr, *Colorado Doc-*

trine; Scott, *Evolution of Resource Property Rights*, p. 220; Clay and Wright, "Order without Law."

57. (1) *Earl v. George*, Placer County District Ct. #125 (Volcano Hill); (2) Columbia: *Alta Californian*, 10/12/1853; (3) Vallecito: Document, Bancroft Library [pfF869 V17V3 1853]; (4) *US Mining Laws*, pp. 276–77 (East Fork of North Trinity).

58. (1) *US Mining Laws*, p. 342 (Constitution Hill), p. 337 (Rockwell Hill), p. 277 (Weaver Creek), p. 298 (Warren Hill); (2) *Herrick v. Davis*, Placer County Co. Ct. #37 (Empire, New York City Diggings); Heckendorn and Wilson, *Miners and Businessmen's Directory*, p. 80 (Jackass Gulch), pp. 54–55 (Jamestown). The 1852 code of Volcano Hill contained the unusual provision that claims could be held if miners put in more than $25 worth of labor, "provided it be practicable so to do," not being explicit about the period within which the work needed to be done.

59. Clay and Wright, "Order without Law?"

60. *Rice v. Emmons*, Placer Co. County Ct. #103. See also Warren Hill, *US Mining Laws*, p. 298.

61. Columbia: *Alta Californian*, 10/12/1853. See also *US Mining Laws*, pp. 297–98 (Murphy's).

62. (1) *US Mining Laws*, pp. 283–84 (Smith's Flat), p. 281 (French Creek), p. 289 (Ohio Flat), p. 286 (Oregon Gulch); (2) Heckendorn and Wilson, *Miners and Businessmen's Directory*, p. 91 (Garote), p. 76 (Saw Mill Flat).

63. Marryat, *Mountains and Molehills*, p. 120.

64. Heckendorn and Wilson, *Miners and Businessmen's Directory*, p. 87 (Poverty Hill, Yorktown and Chili Camp). See also McDowell, "From Commons to Claims," p. 43.

65. This latter interpretation of fairness is not in the egalitarian sense but rather, in the sense supported in the positive justice literature, that individuals perceive non-egalitarian outcomes to be fair if individuals have "earned" larger rewards through greater effort, a Lockean notion, but also, that fairness demands that individuals not be penalized for circumstances beyond their control. See Hoffman and Spitzer, "Entitlements, Rights, and Fairness"; Konow, "Which Is the Fairest," pp. 1209–11.

66. The seminal economic scholarship that study the mining codes is by Umbeck, *California Gold Rush*; Umbeck, *Theory of Property Rights*. For more recent studies, see Clay and Wright, "Order without Law?," and Stewart, "Cooperation when N is Large."

67. (1) *US Mining Laws*, p. 288 (Oro Fino Diggings); (2) Heckendorn and Wilson, *Miners and Businessmen's Directory*, p. 81 (Montezuma), pp. 54–55 (Jamestown), p. 87 (Poverty Hill, Yorktown and Chili Camp), pp. 65–66 (Springfield), pp. 60–61 (Shaw's Flat); (3) *Herrick v. Davis*, Placer County Co. Ct. #37 (Em-

pire, New York City Diggings); (4) Rice v. Emmons, Placer County Co. Ct. #103 (Brushey Canyon); (5) Ricketts v. Tubbs, Placer County Co. Ct. #123 (Wisconsin Hill); (6) Bancroft Library (Irish Hill).

68. (1) *US Mining Laws*, p. 280 (Lower Calaveritas), p. 298 (Warren Hill); (2) *Herrick v. Davis*, Placer County Co. Ct. #37 (New York City Diggings).

69. Codes that require "sufficient" water to work a claim but which do not quantify sufficiency include Jackass Gulch, in Heckendorn and Wilson, *Miners and Businessmen's Directory*, p. 80. See also Warren Hill, Ohio Flat, and Odd Fellows, all in *US Mining Laws*, p. 280 (Warren Hill), pp. 289–90 (Ohio Flat), p. 291 (Odd Fellows).

70. (1) US *Mining Laws*, p. 284 (Smith's Flat), p. 286 (Oregon Gulch), p. 301 (Bodie). (2) Heckendorn and Wilson, *Miners and Businessmen's Directory*, p. 91 (Garote). In some cases, district bylaws specified that claims were not forfeited if not worked on account of too *much* water. This latter category included districts such as Weaver Creek, Upper Yuba, and Rockwell Hill, where mining took place in the beds of rivers and creeks. See *US Mining Laws*, p. 277 (Upper Yuba, Weaver Creek), p. 337 (Rockwell Hill).

71. (1) *US Mining Laws*, p. 278 (Weaverville), p. 291 (Little Humbug Creek), p. 293 (Main Little Humbug Creek), p. 286 (Oregon Gulch); (2) Heckendorn and Wilson, *Miners and Businessmen's Directory*, p. 78 (Brown's Flat); (3) *Rice v. Emmons*, Placer County Co. Court #103 (Brushey Canyon); (4) *Alta Californian*, 10/12/1853 (Columbia).

72. *US Mining Laws*, p. 284. See also *US Mining Laws*, p. 291 (Little Humbug Creek), p. 293 (Maine Little Humbug Creek).

73. *US Mining Laws*, p. 284.

74. Ibid., p. 291. See also *US Mining Laws*, p. 293 (Maine Little Humbug Creek).

75. Heckendorn and Wilson, *Miners and Businessmen's Directory*, p. 55.

76. *US Mining Laws*, p. 318. See also the codes of Con Cow (1851), Rich Gulch (1852), Centreville and Helltown (1857), and Hungry Creek Diggings (1857) for similar statements of first possession acquisition rights. *US Mining Laws*, p. 273 (Con Cow), p. 273 (Rich Gulch), p. 296 (Centreville and Helltown), and p. 297 (Hungry Creek Diggings).

77. Ibid., p. 278. (Weaverville).

78. *US Mining Laws*, p. 277. See also *US Mining Laws*, p. 297 (Hungry Creek), p. 289 (Ohio Flat).

79. (1) Heckendorn and Wilson, *Miners and Businessmen's Directory*, p. 78 (Brown's Flat), p. 76 (Saw Mill Flat), pp. 65–66 (Springfield); (2) *US Mining Laws*, pp. 289–90 (Ohio Flat), p. 291 (Little Humbug Creek), p. 293 (Maine Little Humbug Creek).

80. Heckendorn and Wilson, *Miners and Businessmen's Directory*, p. 91.

81. *US Mining Laws*, p. 301.

82. Ibid., pp. 283–84.

83. Ibid., p. 286.

84. Ibid., p. 278.

85. These characterizations are broadly consistent with those of Umbeck, *Theory of Property Rights*, pp. 104–7, with attempts made to fill in the gaps in Umbeck's account using supplemental material.

86. Pisani, "Origins of Western Water Law," attributes the rise of prior appropriation in the mining camps to technological advance and changes in the industrial organization of mining. This explanation is incomplete because it does not consider the heterogeneity in mining water use practices discussed here.

87. See also Rose, "Energy and Efficiency."

88. See, for example, Meyers and Posner, *Market Transfers of Water Rights*; Epstein, "Why Restrain Alienation?"; Gould, "Transfer of Water Rights"; Lueck, "Rule of First Possession."

89. Kanazawa, "Origins of Common-Law Restrictions."

Chapter Six

1. California never attained territorial status, moving directly from military control to statehood in 1850.

2. Hunt, "Legal Status of California," p. 66.

3. A number of private land grants that had been acquired under Spanish and Mexican rule were retained as private property after statehood after being validated by a judicial commission under the California Land Act of 1851. See, for example, Gates, "California Land Act," for a thorough description of the confirmation process under the Land Act. See also Robinson, *Land in California*, pp. 68, 91–109; Clay, "Property Rights and Institutions," pp. 124–27.

4. For a discussion of the alcalde system, see Langum, *Law and Community*, pp. 30–33; see also Shinn, *Mining Camps*, pp. 80–82; Zentner, "Positive and Natural Law"; Grivas, "Alcalde Rule."

5. Field, *Personal reminiscences*, pp. 26–41.

6. See, for example, Grivas, "Alcalde Rule," p. 24.

7. A surviving record of alcalde proceedings from June 1849 to April 1850 for Woods Diggings and Jamestown in Tuolumne County provides a revealing look at the operation of these courts during the transitional period. By this time, jury trials had become common in this alcalde's court, as well as other elements of the formal civil and criminal court procedures that would be followed after statehood in the official court system, including arrest warrants, setting bail, sworn depositions, jury verdicts, and awards of damages. See *Alcalde Record, Woods Diggins and Jamestown.*

8. Zentner, "Positive and Natural Law," p. 62.

9. *California Star*, 1/23/1847, quoted in Zentner, "Positive and Natural Law," p. 63.

10. Grivas, "Alcalde Rule," p. 24.

11. Article VI, California Constitution (1849), in *Appendix, Statutes of California, First Session*, pp. viii–ix. San Jose: Winchester, 1850.

12. *An Act to organize the Supreme Court of California*, Chapter 14, Laws of the State of California, First Session, enacted February 14, 1850; *An Act to organize the District Courts of the State of California*, Chapter 33, Laws of the State of California, First Session, enacted March 16, 1850; *An Act to regulate proceedings in Civil Cases in the District Court, the Superior Court of the City of San Francisco, and Supreme Court*, Chapter 142, Laws of the State of California, First Session, enacted April 22, 1850.

13. *An Act to supersede certain Courts, and to regulate Appeals therefrom to the Supreme Court*, Chapter 23, Laws of the State of California, First Session, enacted February 28, 1850.

14. *Gay, Daggett and Myers v. Auburn and Bear River Mining Co.*, Placer Co. Dist. Ct. #1.

15. *Lundy v. Gold Hill and Bear River Water Co.*, Placer Co. Dist. Ct. #18; *Albion v. McDonald*, Placer Co. Dist. Ct. #580; *Roberts v. Pea Vine Ditch Company*, Placer Co. Dist. Ct. #786.

16. *Yankee Jim's Union Water Co. v. Moss*, Placer Co. Dist. Ct. #131.

17. *Von Schmidt v. Huntington*, 1 Cal 55; *People v. Naglee*, 1 Cal 232.

18. Paul, *California Gold*, p. 223, 225.

19. McCurdy, "Stephen J. Field and Public Land Law Development," p. 237–38.

20. *Alta Californian*, 8/5/1851.

21. *Alta Californian*, 1/3/1853.

22. *Alta Californian*, 1/11/1853.

23. Pisani, "Origins of Western Water Law," pp. 252–54.

24. This is a variant of the argument made by Steven Cheung, Yoram Barzel, and others that we encountered earlier: when it is costly to measure all attributes of a resource, the result is imperfectly delineated rights and an opportunity for individuals to capture rents along unmeasured margins. See Cheung, "Structure of a Contract"; Cheung, "Why Are Better Seats Underpriced?"; Barzel, "Measurement Cost"; Barzel, *Economic Analysis of Property Rights*.

25. These are standard results from the positive political theory literature. See, for example, Noll, "Economic Perspectives." The last condition of homogeneity within coalitions relates to the transaction cost of creating an effective coalition.

26. Shinn, *Land Laws of Mining Districts*, pp. 563–64, quoted in Drummond and Martinez, *Popular and Legal Tribunals*, p. 47.

27. Drummond and Martinez, *Popular and Legal Tribunals*, p. 32.

28. See also Paul, *California Gold*, p. 224.

29. These data are from Umbeck, *Theory of Property Rights*, pp. 121–23.

30. See, for example, Woods, *Sixteen months at the gold diggings*, p. 115, 2/21/1850; Christman, *One Man's Gold*, p. 129 (3/31/1850), pp. 135–36; Stephens, *Life sketches*, p. 60.

31. Drummond and Martinez, *Popular and Legal Tribunals*, pp. 32–33.

32. Clay and Wright, "Order without Law?"

33. See, for example, Castro, *Carson's California*, p. 190.

34. Charles Shinn observes that first-comers "readily yielded" when new miners arrived. Shinn, *Mining Camps*, p. 166. Charles McCurdy concludes that newcomers "readily mustered new majorities to alter the local regulations." McCurdy, "Stephen J. Field and Public Land Law Development," p. 240. For contemporary evidence on this point, see *Alta Californian*, 12/22/1851; Hill, *In the gold mines*, p. 298–99.

35. Hill, *In the gold mines*, p. 298.

36. Ibid., p. 299.

37. See, for example, the codes of Rich Gulch, French Creek, Oregon Gulch, and Ohio Flat, all contained in *US Mining Laws*, pp. 273–74(Rich Gulch); 281(French Creek); 286–87(Oregon Gulch); 289–90(Ohio Flat).

38. In late 1851, the *Alta Californian* reported that miners at Mokelumne Hill were agitating for larger claim sizes because the existing limits of fifteen feet square were too small to "pay for the labor of working it." See *Alta Californian*, 11/28/1851. See also David Schorr, "Appropriation as Agrarianism," who makes a similar argument regarding early mining in Colorado.

39. Paul, *California Gold*, pp. 223–25.

40. Caughey, *Gold Is the Cornerstone*, p. 238; Bakken, "Courts, the Legal Profession, and the Development of Law," pp. 82–84.

41. See, for example, Pisani, "Gold Rush and American Resource Law," p. 141.

42. *Alta Californian*, 7/14/1851.

43. *Alta Californian*, 2/22/1854. See also *Calaveras Chronicle*, in *Alta Californian*, 8/4/1853.

44. *Alta Californian*, 1/16/1853.

45. See Caughey, *Gold Is the Cornerstone*, p. 232; Woods, *Sixteen months at the gold diggings*, pp. 115–171; Stoddart, *Annals of Tuolumne County*, pp. 124–25; *Alta Californian*, 1/3/1853.

46. *Alta Californian*, 1/3/1854.

47. Ibid.

48. Good anecdotal evidence is available that miners took advantage of local rules to amass a large number of claims. Writing in 1852, for example, the miner James Carson spoke of one individual who owned fifty claims at Vallecita, which

he boasted he had "bought and paid for 'like a man.'" See Castro, *Carson's California*, p. 188. Even alcaldes got in on the action, as the miner Daniel Woods found out when he was prospecting around Mormon Gulch in 1850, and found out that the local alcalde held thirty claims. See Woods, *Sixteen months at the gold diggings*, p. 115.

49. *Alta Californian*, 4/22/1852.

50. See also the miner James Carson, who observed that unlimited-purchase provisions were contained in the "grand majority" of camp codes. See Castro, *Carson's California*, p. 188.

51. *Alta Californian*, 1/14/1853.

52. *Alta Californian*, 1/25/1853.

53. Rule 5th, Mining Laws of Mississippi Valley mining district, *Records of the Mississippi Valley*, pp. 1–2; Article 4, Mining Laws of Junction Bluff mining district, *Records of the Mississippi Valley*, pp. 4–5. Neither district code contained any explicit provision regarding miners working in association.

54. The numbers are probably a bit higher because of some missing pages from the records.

55. This figure is a rough approximation of the area of Junction Bluff, taken from a crude map found in *Records of the Mississippi Valley*.

56. These reported numbers of claims for the first and second largest companies were not generally held at the same time.

57. Clappe, *Shirley Letters*, p. 132.

58. *An Act to regulate Proceedings in Civil Cases in the Courts of Justice of this State*, Chapter 5, Laws of the State of California, Second Session, enacted May 1, 1850, p. 149.

59. McCurdy, "Stephen J. Field and Public Land Law Development," p. 241.

60. *Moran v. Driskill*, Nevada Co. Dist. Ct. #1118 (1859); *Turner et al. v. Morrison and Company*, Nevada Co. Dist. Ct. #782 (1858); *Gray et al. v. Johnson et al.*, Nevada Co. Dist. Ct. #953 (1858); *Bear River and Auburn Water and Mining Company v. New York Mining Company*, Placer Co. Dist. Ct. #384 (1855).

61. *Truxal et al. v. Grant et al.*, Nevada Co. Dist. Ct. #315 (1857); *Gray et al. v. Johnson et al.*, Nevada Co. Dist. Ct. #953 (1858); *Lampman v. Gray et al.*, Nevada Co. Dist. Ct. #1047 (1859).

62. *Hicks v. Bell*, 3 Cal 219 (1853); *McClintock v. Bryden*, 5 Cal 97 (1855); *Smith v. Doe*, 15 Cal 100 (1860); *Gillan v. Hutchinson*, 16 Cal 153 (1860).

63. *Herrick v. Davis*, Placer Co. Co. Ct. #37 (1853); *Gray et al. v. Johnson et al.*, Nevada Co. Dist. Ct. #953 (1858); *Turner et al. v. Morrison and Company*, Nevada Co. Dist. Ct. #782 (1858). For the ruling in *McDonald vs. Vandeling*, see *Alta Californian*, 5/20/1859.

Chapter Seven

1. Data for this figure are from Berry, *Early California*, p. 84.

2. Claim, Camp Seco Watering Co., William W. Traylor, 1851.

3. Water Privilege, Thomas C. Brunton and James Parsons, 1857.

4. Placer Co. Dist. Ct. #131 (1853).

5. Both of the following instructions were requested by the plaintiff, and both were denied by the judge: (a) That the right to the use of the water in question can only result from the ownership of the soil through or by which its natural channel runs, or from its prior appropriation. In this case the land in question belongs to neither party, but is public land—and therefore the parties can claim no right to the use of the water as incident to their ownership of the soil. The prior appropriation of the water must therefore determine the rights of the parties—and if the jury find from the evidence that the plaintiff was first in his possession and use of said water, then by virtue of such prior possession and use . . . plaintiff became entitled thereto as against the defendants, and the verdict should be for the plaintiff accordingly. (b) None ought to complain but those who had been in such prior use or were owners. If therefore the jury find that the defendants had not been in such prior use, then in this respect the finding ought to be for the plaintiff. See Plaintiff Instructions, *Yankee Jim's v. Moss*.

6. Defendant Instructions, *Yankee Jim's v. Moss*.

7. Plaintiff Instructions, *Yankee Jim's v. Moss*. The second sentence is found almost verbatim in the classic riparian case of *Tyler v. Wilkinson*, 24 Fed. Cas. 472 (1827).

8. "*An Act adopting the Common Law*," Chapter 95, Laws of the State of California, First Session, enacted April 13, 1850, p. 219.

9. *Eddy v. Simpson*, 3 Cal 249 (1853).

10. Ibid., at 250.

11. McCurdy, "Stephen J. Field and Public Land Law Development," p. 254.

12. Littlefield, "Water Rights during the California Gold Rush," pp. 428–29.

13. *Heymes v. Kelley*, Placer Co. Dist. Ct. #146 (1853); *Duell v. Bear River and Auburn Water and Mining Co.*, Placer Co. Dist. Ct. #173 (1854); *Bennet et al. v. Dingman and Randall*, Placer Co. Dist. Ct. #205 (1854); *North Shirt Tail Ditch Co. v. Union Canal Co.*, Placer Co. Dist. Ct. #333 (1855).

14. *Bennet et al. v. Dingman and Randall*, Placer Co. Dist. Ct. #205 (1854).

15. *Duell v. Bear River and Auburn Water and Mining Co.*, Placer Co. Dist. Ct. #173 (1854).

16. *North Shirt Tail Ditch Co. v. Union Canal Co.*, Placer Co. Dist. Ct. #333 (1855).

17. *Taylor v. Gorman*, Placer Co. Dist. Ct. #387 (1855).

18. See, for example, Priest, "Selective Characteristics"; Priest, "Measuring Legal Change"; Priest and Klein, "Selection of Disputes."

19. For powering a sawmill, see *Tartar v. Spring Creek*, 5 Cal 395 (1855); *Conger v. Weaver*, 6 Cal 548 (1856). For municipal use, see *Crandall v. Woods*, 8 Cal 136 (1857).

20. See, for example, Horwitz, *Transformation*, p. 35; Rose, "Energy and Efficiency"; Getzler, *History of Water Rights*, p. 272.

21. This view has commonly been termed the *formalist* view. For discussions of the formalist view, see Quevedo, "Formalist and Instrumentalist Legal Reasoning"; Stephenson, "Legal Realism." Joshua Getzler is a proponent of this view within the context of water rights specifically. See Getzler, *History of Water Rights*, p. 3.

22. See, for example, Gray, "'In Search of Bigfoot,'" for a statement of the pragmatic position within the context of California water law.

23. Horwitz, "Rise of Legal Formalism"; Horwitz, *Transformation*. As another example, the legal realist movement of the early twentieth century is generally viewed as a reaction against nineteenth-century formalism, which was viewed as hidebound and overly conservative. This gave rise to what became known as the *instrumentalist* view that judges consider economic and social objectives in creating legal rules. See Quevedo, *Formalist and Instrumentalist Legal Reasoning*.

24. Horwitz's thesis have given rise to a sizable literature, which demonstrates its influence. For critical accounts, see Simpson, "Horwitz Thesis"; Kalman, "Transformations." See also Scheiber, "Regulation, Property Rights" within the context of law in the western United States, and Schwartz, "Tort Law and the Economy" for specific evidence on tort law in California.

25. See Stephenson, "Legal Realism," pp. 200–202. For other conceptions of the objective functions of judges, see, for example, Higgins and Rubin, "Judicial Discretion"; Posner, "What Do Judges and Justices Maximize?"; Posner, *How Judges Think*.

26. See, for example, Landes and Posner, "Legal Precedent"; Schauer, "Precedent"; Schwartz, "Policy, Precedent, and Power."

27. This argument follows Landes and Posner, "Legal Precedent," who liken a body of legal doctrine to a stock of capital, with each ruling regarded as an investment in that capital stock. Similarly to capital, a body of legal doctrine may depreciate over time, particularly as economic conditions change. See also Klein, "Legal Precedent . . . Comment." Martin Shapiro has modeled precedent using communications theory and in particular, the notion of redundancy in repeated messaging (Shapiro, "Toward a Theory of 'Stare Decisis'"). More recent work by Bueno de Mesquita and Stephenson also models legal doctrine in terms of information content (Bueno de Mesquita and Stephenson, "Informative Precedent"). Along similar lines, Ronald Heiner has argued that the inherent complexity of many economic contexts leads to the adoption of satisficing decision-

making rules that manage and reflect the associated uncertainty. See Heiner, "Origin of Predictable Behavior."

28. *Irwin v. Phillips*, 5 Cal 140 (1855).

29. Ibid., p. 147.

30. Ibid., p. 145.

31. Ibid., p. 146.

32. *Hoffman v. Stone*, 7 Cal 46 (1857), at 49. See also *Conger v. Weaver*, 6 Cal 548 (1856), at 558; *Merced Mining Co. v. Fremont*, 7 Cal 317 (1857), at 326; *Crandall v. Woods*, 8 Cal 136 (1857), at 141.

33. *Alta Californian*, 12/12/1857. See also Pisani, "Origins of Western Water Law", p. 251.

34. See, Wilkinson, "Western Water Law," p. 36; Wilkinson, *Crossing the Next Meridian*, p. 234. See also Gould, "Water Rights Transfers," p. 8.

35. *Crandall v. Woods*, 8 Cal 136 (1857), at 143.

36. Ibid., at 143.

37. See, for example, Wiel, "Public Policy," p. 14; Miller, "Shaping California Water Law," p. 20; Pisani, *From the Family Farm to Agribusiness*, p. 35; Gray, "'In Search of Bigfoot,'" p. 242. Charles McCurdy is one of the few who stress the instrumentalist nature of the ruling (McCurdy, "Stephen J. Field and Public Land Law Development," p. 255).

38. See also Lucien Shaw, who has argued that during this early period, the Court paid lip service to riparian rights, but the fact that a party to a dispute claimed riparian status was never determinative of a ruling on a water dispute (Shaw, "Development of the Law of Waters in the West," p. 451). This conclusion goes counter to that of Samuel Wiel, who stressed the upholding of riparian rights as the true import of Crandall, while its ruling on priority was merely "dictum" (Wiel, "Public Policy," p. 14).

39. See, for example, Lueck, "Rule of First Possession"; Anderson and Hill, "Cowboys and Contracts."

40. *Tartar v. Spring Creek*, 5 Cal 395 (1855); *Hill v. Newman*, 5 Cal 451 (1855); *Kelly v. Natoma Water Co.*, 6 Cal 105 (1856); *Conger v. Weaver*, 6 Cal 548 (1856); *Hoffman v. Stone*, 7 Cal 46 (1857); *Maeris v. Bicknell*, 7 Cal 261 (1857); *Crandall v. Woods*, 8 Cal 136 (1857); *Thompson v. Lee*, 8 Cal 275 (1857).

41. *Tartar v. Spring Creek*, 5 Cal 395 (1855), at 406. See also *Crandall v. Woods*, 8 Cal 136 (1857), at 143.

42. *Conger v. Weaver*, 6 Cal 548 (1856), at 557. The wording of *Conger* is a bit imprecise here. Though the language "doctrine of presumption of a grant of right" is used in the opinion, it subsequently goes on to say that what is being presumed to have been granted is a "license to occupy." Thus, the actual right was not an outright grant but rather, took more the form of an easement.

43. *Alta Californian*, 1/14/1859.

44. *Alta Californian*, 1/24/1859.

45. *Conger v. Weaver*, 6 Cal 548 (1856), at 555.

46. Ibid., at 558.

47. *Parke v. Kilham* 8 Cal 77 (1857), at 79.

48. *Kelly v. Natoma Water Co.* 6 Cal 105 (1856), at 108. See also *Maeris v. Bicknell* 7 Cal 261 (1857), *Thompson v. Lee* 8 Cal 275 (1857).

49. See, for example, Rose, "Possession as the Origin of Property," p. 76.

50. See Dharmapala and Pitchford, "Economic Analysis of 'Riding to Hounds.'" This distinction is what makes the present case different from the famous *Pierson v. Post* case, which ruled against a fox hunter in hot pursuit, because he did not have the fox in actual possession. See Rose, "Possession as the Origin of Property," pp. 76–77.

51. It seems apparent that going even further back in the process and basing possession on intention to possess would have been completely impractical, for informational reasons.

52. Complaint, *Yankee Jim's Union Water Co. v. Moss et al.*, Placer Co. Dist. Ct. #131 (1853); Answer, *Duell v. Bear River and Auburn Water and Mining Co.*, Placer Co. Dist. Ct. #173 (1854); Complaint, *North Shirt Tail Ditch Co. v. Union Canal Co.*, Placer Co. Dist. Ct. #333 (1855); Complaint, *Maeris v. Bicknell*, Placer Co. Dist. Ct. #401 (1855).

53. Complaint, *Leigh v. Independent Ditch Co.*, Placer Co. Dist. Ct. #718 (1857); Verdict, *Chapman et al. v. Russell*, Placer County Dist. Ct. #868 (1858); Complaint, *Bear River and Auburn Water and Mining Co. v. New York Mining Co.*, Placer County Dist. Ct. #828 (1858); Amended Complaint, *Gold Hill and Bear River Water Co. v. Bear River and Auburn Water and Mining Company*, Placer County Dist. Ct. #622 (1857).

54. Complaint, *North Shirt Tail Ditch Co. v. Union Canal Co.*, Placer Co. Dist. Ct. #333 (1855); Complaint, *Maeris v. Bicknell*, Placer Co. Dist. Ct. #401 (1855).

55. Court Findings, *Maeris v. Bicknell*, Placer Co. Dist. Ct. #401 (1855); Complaint, Answer, *White and Brown v. Todd's Valley Water Company*, Placer County Dist. Ct. #489 (1856).

56. Deposition, Bernard, *Tuolumne County Water Company v. Columbia and Stanislaus River Water Company*, Tuolumne Co. Dist. Ct., 2/1859.

57. See also, Wiel, *What Is Beneficial Use of Water?*, pp. 461–62. The decline over time of measurements costs has altered this situation dramatically, even though significant issues in measurement remain. See Smith, "Governing Water," pp. 469–70.

58. Getches, *Water Law*, pp. 97–100.

59. Beneficial use is "the measure, the basis and the limit of the appropriator's right to use water." See ibid., p. 122.

60. See, for example, Anderson and Snyder, *Water Markets*, p. 79.

61. See also Schorr, *Colorado Doctrine*, p. 45.

62. There is a parallel here to the English common law notion that a riparian water right, being a use (usufructuary) right, is lost once the water passes from possession. See Angell, *Treatise*, pp. 94–95; *Eddy v. Simpson*, 3 Cal 249 (1853), at 252; *Kelly v. Natoma Water Company*, 6 Cal 105 (1856).

63. Schorr, *Colorado Doctrine*, pp. 19–22.

64. It is this intentionality that distinguishes abandonment from the related principle of *forfeiture*, where intention is not a condition for losing a water right. See, for example, Getches, *Water Law*, pp. 178–79.

65. Complaint, *Heymes v. Kelley*, Placer Co. Dist. Ct. #146 (1853).

66. *Duell v. Bear River and Auburn Water and Mining Co.*, Placer Co. Dist. Ct. #173 (1854); *Maeris v. Bicknell*, Placer Co. Dist. Ct. #401 (1855); *White and Brown v. Todd's Valley Water Company*, Placer Co. Dist. Ct. #489 (1856); *El Dorado Water Co. v. Johnson*, Placer Co. Dist. Ct. #507 (1856); *Oakland Ditch Company v. Bear River and Auburn Water and Mining Company*, Placer Co. Dist. Ct. #529 (1856).

67. *Eddy v. Simpson*, 3 Cal 249, at 252, citing Angell, *Treatise*.

68. *Duell v. Bear River and Auburn Water and Mining Co.*, Placer Co. Dist. Ct. #173 (1854).

69. Shaw, "Development of the Law of Waters in the West," p. 448. See also *Kelly v. Natoma Water Company*, 6 Cal 105 (1856).

70. *Hoffman v. Stone*, 7 Cal 46 (1857); *Butte Canal and Ditch Company v. Vaughn*, 11 Cal 143 (1858). See also, Shaw, "Development of the Law of Waters in the West," p. 448.

71. *Hoffman v. Stone*, 7 Cal 46 (1857), at 49.

72. Complaint, *White and Brown v. Todd's Valley Water Company*, Placer Co. Dist. Ct. #489 (1856).

73. See also Complaint, *American River Water and Mining Company v. Bear River and Auburn Water and Mining Company*, Placer Co. Dist. Ct. #621 (1856); Complaint, *Gold Hill and Bear River Water Co. v. Bear River and Auburn Water and Mining Company*, Placer Co. Dist. Ct. #622.

74. *Chapman et al. v. Russell*, Placer Co. Dist. Ct. #868 (1858).

75. Plaintiff Instructions, *Chapman et al. v. Russell*, Placer Co. Dist. Ct. #868 (1858).

76. *Davis v. Gale*, 32 Cal 26 (1867).

77. Ibid., at 34–35.

78. *Stoakes v. Barrett*, 5 Cal 37, at 39. The Possessory Act is found at *3 Cal Stats. 158*.

79. *Stoakes v. Barrett*, 5 Cal 37, at 39.

80. *Fitzgerald v. Urton*, 5 Cal 308 (1855); *Tartar v. Spring Creek*, 5 Cal 395 (1855); *McClintock v. Bryden*, 5 Cal 97 (1855).

81. *McClintock v. Bryden*, 5 Cal 97 (1855), at 100–101.

82. Ibid., at 101.

83. Ibid., at 101.

84. Ibid., at 102.

85. Ibid., at 102.

86. *6 Cal Stats. 145.*

87. *Gillan v. Hutchinson*, 16 Cal 153 (1860); *Smith v. Doe*, 15 Cal 100 (1860).

88. Some legal scholars emphasize factors such as the preferences of judges for doctrinal consistency and issues of fairness. McCurdy emphasizes, for example, the influence of a single judge—Stephen J. Field—on the development of the law and upholding of private property. See McCurdy, "Stephen J. Field and Public Land Law Development."

89. Kanazawa, "Taxation with(?) Representation."

Chapter Eight

1. *Alta Californian*, 10/28/1859. For more on Greeley's trip, see Paul, *Far West and the Great Plains*, pp. 7–25.

2. *Maeris v. Bicknell*, 7 Cal 261 (1860), p. 263.

3. *Davis v. Gale*, 32 Cal 26 (1867), p. 34.

4. Ibid., p. 34.

5. *Kidd et al. v. Laird et al.*, 15 Cal 161 (1860), p. 181.

6. *Butte T. M. Company v. Morgan*, 19 Cal 609 (1862), p. 616.

7. This is not to argue, of course, that there would be no differences in impacts on other users. For example, moving to a different mining location would have affected the location of local return flows, including the venting of the tailwaters from mining operations.

8. The doctrinal treatment of these three issues would converge later in the century to the position that none of these three types of changes were permissible if they inflicted external injuries on other users. This subsequent evolution could reflect increasing recognition and frequency of external impacts on others and possibly, better understanding of external hydrologic impacts that became increasingly compelling to judges. This would be consistent with my earlier findings with regard to the evolution of groundwater law (Kanazawa, "Origins of Common-Law Restrictions").

9. Borthwick, *Three Years in California*, p. 101; Greenland, *Hydraulic Mining in California*, p. 22. See also *Alta Californian*, 2/8/1851.

10. Greenland, *Hydraulic Mining in California*, p. 22.

11. Thompson and West, *History of Nevada County*, p. 172.

12. (a) Hauling dirt to water: *Alta Californian* 1/25/1851 (southern dry diggings), 2/13/1851 (hill near Mokelumne river, 4/4/1851 (Jamestown), 5/8/1851 (Placerville), 6/12/1851 (Volcano Diggings), 6/21/1851 (near Placerville);

7/18/1851 (Chinese diggings), 7/29/1851 (Wood's Creek), 8/1/1851 (Jamestown and Camp Seco), 10/5/1851 (Big Oak Flat), 11/10/1851 (Douglas Flats), 1/22/1852 (dry diggings), 2/21/1852 (Jackson), 5/1/1852 (Spanish Bar, Short's Bar), 7/26/1852 (Sonora Gulch), 12/15/1852 (Kincaid's Flat).

(b) Leaving dirt unprocessed: *Alta Californian* 2/15/1851 (Yankee Hill), 8/1/1851 (Mormon Gulch, Sullivan's Creek, Curtisville, Chinese Camp), 9/21/1851 (general, gulch miners), 9/21/1851 (Mokelumne Hill), 9/22/1851 (Mormon Creek), 9/23/1851 (Camp Guadaloupe), 10/5/1851 (Big Oak Flat), 10/10/1851 (dry diggings, Middle and North Forks, American river), 10/27/1851 (general), 11/3/1851 (Tuttletown), 12/4/1851 (general), 12/8/1851 (general), 12/14/1851 (Calaveras), 2/14/1852 (San Joaquin), 2/18/1852 (Carson's Creek, Murphy's), 6/17/1852 (Columbia); 7/22/1852 (southern diggings); 7/25/1852 (Coon Hollow), 8/22/1852 (Columbia); 10/8/1852 (Murphy's); 11/15/1852 (Sonora, Columbia, Shaw's Flat, Chinese Camp, Camp Seco); 11/22/1852 (North Yuba); 11/28/1852 (dry diggings, El Dorado county).

(c) Leaving dry diggings for lack of water: *Alta Californian* 2/16/1851 (Auburn), 3/17/1851 (near Castoria), 7/16/1851 (Grass Valley), 8/1/1851 (Sonora), 12/8/1851 (general), 6/26/1852 (Mariposa), 7/25/1852 (Mokelumne).

13. There were thirty-four news items in total about ditch construction for the two years, which were divided into four categories: Being planned, In progress, Almost Completed, and Completed.

14. *Alta Californian*, 12/4/1852.

15. *Alta Californian*, 12/3/1852.

16. *Alta Californian*, 12/4/1852.

17. Placer County District Court #384.

18. *Hill v. Vaughn*, Placer Co. Dist. Ct. #524; *Hill v. King*, Placer Co. Dist. Ct. #526; *Oakland Ditch Company v. Bear River and Auburn Water and Mining Co.*, Placer Co. Dist. Ct. #529; *Ross/Wade and Co. v. Sill/Bradley et al.*, Placer Co. Dist. Ct. #540.

19. Recall that this was a necessary but not sufficient condition for rent-maximization, because of the possibility of flow constraints. See Johnson, Gisser, and Werner, "Definition of a Surface Water Right"; Gould, "Water Rights Transfers."

20. This result was originally derived in Kanazawa, "Water Quality." For details, see Appendix A.

21. Recall also our earlier discussion of application of the trespass rule when damages are large, which may be interpreted using the measurement cost approach as inflicting major damages on various attributes of the resource. This may tip the scale in favor of applying a rule of trespass rather than a rule of nuisance. See Smith, "Exclusion and Property Rules," pp. 996–98.

22. In the last chapter, we discussed the question of how binding precedent actually is on judges. See Scott and Coustalin, "Evolution of Water Rights," pp. 863–65, for a useful discussion of this issue specifically with regard to water.

23. *Tyler v. Wilkinson*, 24 Fed. Cas. 472 (1827), at 474.

24. See Horwitz, *Transformation*; Rose, "Energy and Efficiency"; Hart, "Property Rights, Costs, and Welfare"; Scott and Coustalin, "Evolution of Water Rights," pp. 871–74.

25. See, for example, *Webb v. Portland Manufacturing*, 29 F. Cas 506 (1838); *Cary v. Daniels*, 49 Mass. 466 (1844); *Elliot v. Fitchburg Railroad Company*, 64 Mass. 191 (1852).

26. Scott and Coustalin, "Evolution of Water Rights," pp. 876–77.

27. Angell, *Treatise*, p. 155.

28. This manner of treating practices that render water "unwholesome and offensive" appears to follow the pattern of most English common law authority that subjected nuisances that were clear, visible, and large to a rule of trespass. See Merrill, "Trespass."

29. *Bear River and Auburn Water and Mining Co. v. New York Mining Co.*, 8 Cal 327 (1857); *Hill v. King*, 8 Cal. 337 (1857).

30. See Shaw, "Development of the Law of Waters in the West," p. 450; Wiel, "'Priority' in Western Water Law," p. 191.

31. Complaint, Answer, *Hill v. King*, Placer County Dist. Ct. #526.

32. This wording is odd, because it seems to confound two English common law principles: *damnum absque injuria (damnum)*, and *injuria absque damno (injuria)*. *Damnum* generally refers to cases where there are damages which are not actionable because there is no legally recognized injury. Such a principle is consistent with the reasonable use principle, that some actions (reasonable ones) are permissible even if they inflict damages. *Injuria*, on the other hand, refers to actionable wrongs even if there are no damages, such as might be treated under a trespass rule. The wording in *Bear River* is phrased as *injuria* when it seems to be invoking *damnum*.

33. Finding and Opinion, *Bear River and Auburn Water and Mining Company v. New York Mining Company*, Placer County Dist. Ct. #384, 9/4/1856.

34. *Bear River and Auburn Water and Mining Company v. New York Mining Company*, 8 Cal 327 (1857), at 333.

35. Ibid., at 332.

36. Ibid., at 335.

37. *Daily Alta Californian*, 12/27/1857.

38. *Hill v. King*, 8 Cal 337 (1857), at 339.

39. Judge's Instructions to Jury, *Oakland Ditch Company v. Bear River and Auburn Water and Mining Company*, Placer County Dist. Ct. #529.

40. *Mokelumne Hill Canal and Mining Company v. Woodbury*, 10 Cal 185 (1858).

41. *Pilot Rock Creek Canal Co. v. Chapman*, 11 Cal 161 (1858).

42. Scholars have been confused or unclear on this issue. Samuel Wiel has suggested that *Phoenix* enunciated a reasonableness rule but in fact, it only did

so for a different issue: irregularity of flow. See Wiel, "'Priority' in Western Water Law." Similarly, Charles McCurdy suggests that water pollution was subject to reasonable use during this period, at least during the tenure of Justice Field. See McCurdy, "Stephen J. Field and Public Land Law Development," p. 261. Neither *Phoenix* nor the next case, *Hill v. Smith*, can be reasonably interpreted in this way.

43. *Hill v. Smith*, 27 Cal 475 (1865), p. 481.

44. *Phoenix Water Company v. Fletcher*, 23 Cal 482 (1863), p. 487.

45. *Hill v. Smith*, 27 Cal 475 (1865), p. 481.

46. See also *Natoma Water and Mining Company v. McCoy*, 23 Cal 491 (1863), p. 491, also describing "serious" damages to the plaintiff due to loss of water sales.

Chapter Nine

1. Morse, "Story of a Gold Miner," p. 216. But depending upon local conditions, anything that effectively obstructed the flow of river could be used, including boulders and bags filled with earth. See *Stockton Journal*, reported in *Alta Californian*, 7/25/1852.

2. Woods, *Sixteen months in the gold diggings*, pp. 153–54. See also Stephens, *Life sketches*, p. 29.

3. Paul, *California Gold*, p. 125. See also Pagenhart, *Water Use in the Yuba and Bear River Basins*, p. 112; *Alta Californian*, 1/17/1851, 5/16/1851, 9/12/1851, 2/5/1852, 9/23/1852.

4. See *Alta Californian*, 9/12/1851.

5. *Alta Californian*, 8/3/1851.

6. *Sacramento Union*, reported in *Alta Californian*, 7/6/1854.

7. *Alta Californian*, 7/14/1853. *Union Democrat*, reported in *Alta Californian*, 12/30/1856. See also *Alta Californian*, 9/26/1855, for plans for another dam that was intended to be seventy-five feet high and three hundred feet wide.

8. *San Andreas Independent*, reported in *Alta Californian*, 1/25/1858.

9. *Alta Californian*, 11/30/1857.

10. *Alta Californian*, 5/13/1859.

11. *Alta Californian*, 7/8/1859.

12. See, for example, Young, "Pine Log," pp. 281–83.

13. Tuolumne County Water Company *Records, 1853–1904, Volume 2.* Minutes, 1856–1859, July 17, 1857, July 30, 1857. Five thousand dollars was not a trivial amount to this company, representing roughly three to four months of salary for all company officers.

14. *Hoffman v. Tuolumne County Water Company*, Tuolumne Co. Dist. Ct. (1857).

15. Witness statement, Wilson: *Crawford et al. v. Tuolumne County Water Company*, Tuolumne Co. Dist. Ct. (1857).

16. Witness statement, Fletcher: ibid. See also Witness statement, Wilson: *Fox v. Tuolumne County Water Company*, Tuolumne Co. Dist. Ct. (1857).

17. Witness statements, Bernard, Kendall, Stewart, Fletcher: *Crawford et al. v. Tuolumne County Water Company*, Tuolumne Co. Dist. Ct. (1857). *Fox v. Tuolumne County Water Company*, Tuolumne Co. Dist. Ct. (1857).

18. For example, *Crawford et al. v. Tuolumne County Water Company*, Tuolumne Co. Dist. Ct. (1857). For more on the 1807 congressional act, see Kanazawa, "Possession Is Nine Points of the Law."

19. Witness statement, Wilson: *Fox v. Tuolumne County Water Company*, Tuolumne Co. Dist. Ct. (1857).

20. Witness statement, Fletcher: *Crawford et al. v. Tuolumne County Water Company*, Tuolumne Co. Dist. Ct. (1857).

21. *Evans v. Hill*, Placer County District Court File #645 (1857).

22. *Green et al. v. Williams et al.*, Nevada County District Court File #798 (1858).

23. *Haskett v. Bear River and Auburn Water and Mining Company*, Placer County District Court #197 (1854).

24. *Kidd v. Laird*, Nevada County District Court File #226 (1857); *Walker et al. v. Rock Creek, Deer Creek and South Yuba Canal Co.*, Nevada County District Court #308 (1857); *Green et al. v. Williams et al.*, Nevada County District Court File #798 (1858).

25. Reasonable care is commonly described as the tort standard emphasized in English common law jurisdictions. See Cooter and Ulen, *Law and Economics*, p. 333.

26. *Walker et al. v. Rock Creek, Deer Creek and South Yuba Canal Co.*, Nevada County District Court #308 (1857).

27. *Evans et al. v. Hill*, Placer County District Court File #645 (1857).

28. See, for example, Shugerman, "Floodgates of Strict Liability"; Merrill, "Trespass."

29. Court instructions, *Liss v. Tuolumne County Water Company*, Tuolumne Co. Dist. Ct. (1857).

30. Plaintiff Instructions, *Evans et al. v. Hill*, Placer County District Court File #645 (1857). See also Plaintiff Instructions, *Oakland Ditch Co. v. Bear River and Auburn Water and Mining Co.*, Placer County District Court File #529 (1857); *Darst v. Bush*, Nevada County District Court #795 (1858).

31. Plaintiff Instructions, *Howe et al. v. Jennings et al.*, Nevada County Court #713 (1857).

32. *Darst v. Bush*, Nevada County District Court #795 (1858).

33. *Green et al. v. Williams et al.*, Nevada County District Court File #798 (1858).

34. *Tenney v. Miners' Ditch Company*, 7 Cal 335 (1858).

35. Ibid., at 339.

36. Ibid., at 340.

37. Ibid., at 340.

38. See Merrill, "Trespass"; Landes and Posner, *Economic Structure.*

39. This intuitive result is derived rigorously in the appendix to chapter 9.

40. The literature on the coming to the nuisance rule is considerable. See Wittman, "First Come, First Served"; Wittman, "Optimal Pricing of Sequential Inputs"; Pitchford and Snyder, "Coming to the Nuisance" for economic treatments of the rule. See Epstein, "Clear View of the Cathedral," especially pp. 2104–5 for a forceful critique of the coming to the nuisance rule as tending to destabilize private property rights. See also Epstein, "Nuisance Law."

41. Wittman, "First Come, First Served." See also Wittman, "Optimal Pricing of Sequential Inputs."

42. Pitchford and Snyder, "Coming to the Nuisance."

43. Merrill, "Trespass"; Merrill and Smith, "What Happened to Property"; Smith, "Exclusion and Property Rules."

Appendix B

1. B's dam construction expenditures are assumed for simplicity to be subsumed in Y. This assumption has no effect on the fundamental results.

Chapter Ten

1. Milliman, "Water Law," pp. 51–52; Whittlesey and Huffaker, "Water Policy Issues," p. 1199; Wilkinson, *Crossing the Next Meridian*, pp. 287–89; Stevens, "Recreational Land Use," p. 153.

2. See, for example, Burness and Quirk, "Appropriative Water Rights," pp. 25–26.

3. Anderson and Snyder, *Water Markets*, pp. 87–88; Scott, *Evolution of Resource Property Rights*, pp. 108–9.

4. See, for example, Burness and Quirk, "Appropriative Water Rights," pp. 25–26; Reisner and Bates, *Overtapped Oasis*, p. 66.

5. Getches, "Water Resources," p. 128; Getches, *Water Law*, pp. 128–29.

6. Anderson and Snyder, *Water Markets*, pp. 80–81; Newman, "Beneficial Use, Waste, and Forfeiture," p. 996.

7. Colby, "Transactions Costs," p. 1186.

8. Gould, for example, argues that legal restrictions on water rights transfers are "not numerous" except for regulations imposed by the Bureau of Reclama-

tion and by irrigation districts (Gould, "Water Rights Transfers," pp. 4–5); Colby argues that there is "no convincing evidence" that western states overregulate water transfers (Colby, "Transactions Costs," p. 1190). According to Tarlock, the only binding restriction imposed in most jurisdictions has been limitations on out-of-basin transfers (Tarlock, "New Water Transfer Restrictions," p. 987).

9. The scholarly literature on water markets is vast, with most economically oriented treatments either coming down in support, or grudgingly viewing them as inevitable. See, for example, Anderson and Snyder, *Water Markets*; Kline, "Water Transfers," pp. 254–57; Morriss, "Real People, Real Resources"; Glennon, "Water Scarcity"; Carey and Sunding, "Emerging Markets in Water"; Sax, "Understanding Transfers."

10. See, for example, Gould, "Water Rights Transfers," pp. 4–5; Tarlock, "New Water Transfer Restrictions," p. 987. See also Hanak, "Stopping the Drain," for local legislative restrictions on exports of groundwater.

11. Colby, "Transactions Costs." More specifically, Colby defines these policy-induced transaction costs as the cost of obtaining "legal approval for the proposed change in water use." In her analysis, Colby focuses on state water transfer policies, but the idea appears to apply more broadly.

12. See Young, "Why Are There So Few Transactions," pp. 1147–50. This "common heritage" terminology was used, for example, in the famous 1983 case of *National Audubon Society vs. Superior Court*, which protected the water resources of Mono Lake. See *National Audubon Society*, 33 Cal 3rd 419.

13. See Gould, "Water Rights Transfers," pp. 6–12; Huffaker, Whittlesey, and Hamilton, "Role of Prior Appropriation," p. 266; Sax, "Understanding Transfers," p. 33, 38. George Gould has argued that addressing water transfers is the main concern with modern appropriative law, which otherwise possesses a number of desirable properties, including fairness, ease of administration, and support for investment in development of water resources both by junior and senior appropriators. See Huffaker et al. for a view that the costs of administering the appropriative system are increasing in recent days (Huffaker, Whittlesey, and Hamilton, "Role of Prior Appropriation," p. 269).

14. See Colby, "Transactions Costs"; Young, "Why Are There So Few Transactions," pp. 1147–49.

15. See Kline, however, for a discussion of the *costs* of water transfers to importing communities, which includes supporting unsustainable growth and incurring various social, economic, and environmental costs. Kline, "Water Transfers." To the extent these costs are real and significant, they should of course be factored in as well.

16. Johnson, Gisser, and Werner, "Definition of a Surface Water Right."

17. Ibid. Johnson et al. stress that this is true only in the absence of binding flow constraints along the waterway. However, granting this, the appeal of the idea remains, in terms of addressing third-party impacts.

18. Gould, "Water Rights Transfers"; Tarlock, "New Water Transfer Restrictions."

19. For a discussion of in situ value, see Anderson and Johnson, "Problem of Instream Flows."

20. See Lawrence MacDonnell for a pessimistic assessment of the magnitude of transaction costs with regard to water transfers (MacDonnell, "Water Transfer Process"). See also Tarlock, "New Water Transfer Restrictions." See Colby for a more positive view (Colby, "Transactions Costs").

21. Bretsen and Hill, "Water Markets as a Tragedy of the Anticommons."

22. Colby, "Transactions Costs," p. 1188.

23. Colby, "Transactions Costs"; MacDonnell, "Water Transfer Process."

24. Huffaker, Whittlesey, and Hamilton, "Role of Prior Appropriation," p. 267.

25. Young, "Why Are There So Few Transactions," p. 1148; Gould, "Water Rights Transfers," pp. 32–35.

26. Colby, "Transactions Costs," p. 1191.

27. Ibid. On the scientific shortcomings of judges in water cases, see Huffaker, Whittlesey, and Hamilton, "Role of Prior Appropriation," p. 268. See also Glennon, *Water Follies*.

28. Young, "Why Are There So Few Transactions," p. 1148.

29. Gould, "Water Rights Transfers," pp. 32–35.

30. Ibid., p. 32. George Gould has noted, for example, a similar deference adopted by the Colorado Supreme Court to a decision by the Colorado legislature in the 1960s to adopt a policy of "maximum utilization" of the water resources of the state. See Gould, "Water Rights Transfers," p. 32.

31. Gould, "Water Rights Transfers," pp. 32–35.

32. Ibid., p. 35–40. See also Colby, "Transactions Costs," p. 1191.

References

A. Legal Material

1. Court Cases

a. California Supreme Court

Bear River and Auburn Water and Mining Co. v. New York Mining Co., 8 Cal
    327 (1857)
Butte Canal and Ditch Company v. Vaughn, 11 Cal 143 (1858)
Butte T. M. Company v. Morgan, 19 Cal 609 (1862)
Conger v. Weaver, 6 Cal 548 (1856)
Crandall v. Woods, 8 Cal 136 (1857)
Davis v. Gale, 32 Cal 26 (1867)
Eddy v. Simpson, 3 Cal 249 (1853)
Fitzgerald v. Urton, 5 Cal 308 (1855)
Gillan v. Hutchinson, 16 Cal 153 (1860)
Hicks v. Bell, 3 Cal 219 (1853)
Hill v. King, 8 Cal 337 (1857)
Hill v. Newman, 5 Cal 451 (1855)
Hill v. Smith, 27 Cal 475 (1865)
Hoffman v. Stone, 7 Cal 46 (1857)
Irwin v. Phillips, 5 Cal 140 (1855)
Kelly v. Natoma Water Company, 6 Cal 105 (1856)
Kidd et al. v. Laird et al., 15 Cal 161 (1860)
Lux v. Haggin, 69 Cal 255 (1886)
Maeris v. Bicknell, 7 Cal 261 (1857)
McClintock v. Bryden, 5 Cal 97 (1855)
McKinney v. Smith, 21 Cal 374 (1863)
Merced Mining Co. v. Fremont, 7 Cal 317 (1857)

Mokelumne Hill Canal & Mining Company v. Woodbury, 10 Cal 185 (1858)
Natoma Water & Mining Company v. McCoy, 23 Cal 491 (1863)
Parke v. Kilham, 8 Cal 77 (1857)
People, ex rel. the Attorney-General v. Naglee, 1 Cal 232 (1850)
Phoenix Water Company v. Fletcher, 23 Cal 482 (1863)
Pilot Rock Creek Canal Company v. Chapman, 11 Cal 161 (1858)
Smith v. Doe, 15 Cal 100 (1860)
Stoakes v. Barrett, 5 Cal 37 (1855)
Tartar v. Spring Creek Water and Mining Co., 5 Cal 395 (1855)
Tenney v. Miners' Ditch Company, 7 Cal 335 (1857)
Thompson v. Lee, 8 Cal 275 (1857)
Von Schmidt et al. v. Huntington et al., 1 Cal 55 (1850)

b. Nevada County

Butler et al. v. Laird et al., Nevada Co. Dist. Ct. #288 (1857)
Darst v. Bush, Nevada Co. Dist. Ct. #795 (1858)
Gray et al. v. Johnson et al., Nevada Co. Dist. Ct. #953 (1858)
Green et al. v. Williams et al., Nevada Co. Dist. Ct. #798 (1858)
Howe et al. v. Jennings et al., Nevada Co. Dist. Ct. #713 (1857)
Kidd v. Laird, Nevada Co. Dist. Ct #226 (1857)
Lampman v. Gray et al., Nevada Co. Dist. Ct. #1047 (1859)
Moran v. Driskill, Nevada Co. Dist. Ct. #1118 (1859)
Truxal et al. v. Grant et al., Nevada Co. Dist. Ct. #315 (1857)
Turner et al. v. Morrison & Company, Nevada Co. Dist. Ct. #782 (1858)
Vass & Smith v. Brophy & Phelan, Nevada Co. Dist. Ct. #277 (1857)
Walker et al. v. Rock Creek, Deer Creek and South Yuba Canal Co., Nevada Co.
    Dist. Ct. #308 (1857)

c. Placer County

Albion Co. v. McDonald & Co., Placer Co. Dist. Ct. #580 (1856)
*American River Water & Mining Company v. Bear River & Auburn Water &
    Mining Company,* Placer Co. Dist. Ct. #621 (1856)
*Bear River and Auburn Water & Mining Company v. New York Mining Com-
    pany,* Placer Co. Dist. Ct. #384 (1855)
*Bear River and Auburn Water & Mining Company v. New York Mining Com-
    pany,* Placer Co. Dist. Ct. #828 (1858)
Bennet et al. v. Dingman & Randall, Placer Co. Dist. Ct. #205 (1854)
Chapman et al. v. Russell, Placer Co. Dist. Ct. #868 (1858)

Duell v. Bear River & Auburn Water & Mining Company, Placer Co. Dist. Ct. #173 (1854)

Earl v. George, Placer Co. Dist. Ct. #125 (1855)

El Dorado Water Co. v. Johnson, Placer Co. Dist. Ct. #507 (1856)

Evans et al. v. Hill, Placer Co. Dist. Ct. #645 (1857)

Gay, Daggett and Myers v. Auburn & Bear River Mining Co., Placer Co. Dist. Ct. #1 (1851)

Gold Hill & Bear River Water Co. v. Bear River & Auburn Water & Mining Co., Placer Co. Dist. Ct. #622 (1857)

Haskett v. Bear River & Auburn Water & Mining Co., Placer Co. Dist. Ct. #197 (1854)

Herrick v. Davis, Placer Co. Co. Ct. #37 (1853)

Heymes v. Kelley, Placer Co. Dist. Ct. #146 (1853)

Hill v. King, Placer Co. Dist. Ct. #526 (1856)

Hill v. Vaughn, Placer Co. Dist. Ct. #524 (1856)

Leigh v. Independent Ditch Company, Placer Co. Dist. Ct. #718 (1857)

Lundy v. Gold Hill & Bear River Water Co. and the Ridge Mining Co., Placer Co. Dist. Ct. #18 (1852)

Maeris v. Bicknell, Placer Co. Dist. Ct. #401 (1855)

North Shirt Tail Ditch Co. v. Union Canal Co., Placer Co. Dist. Ct. #333 (1855)

Oakland Ditch Company v. Bear River & Auburn Water & Mining Company, Placer Co. Dist. Ct. #529 (1856)

Reilly et al. v. Independent Ditch Company, Placer Co. Dist. Ct. #1013 (1859)

Rice v. Emmons, Placer Co. Co. Ct. #103 (1855)

Ricketts v. Tubbs, Placer County Co. Ct. #123 (1855)

Roberts et al. v. Pea Vine Ditch Company, Placer Co. Dist. Ct. #786 (1857)

Ross/Wade and Co. v. Sill/Bradley et al., Placer Co. Dist. Ct. #540 (1856)

Taylor v. Gorman, Placer Co. Dist. Ct. #387 (1855)

White & Brown v. Todd's Valley Water Company, Placer Co. Dist. Ct. #489 (1856)

Yankee Jim's Union Water Company v. Moss et al., Placer Co. Dist. Ct. #131 (1853)

d. Tuolumne County

Collins v. Tuolumne County Water Company, Tuolumne Co. Dist. Ct. (1856)

Eberhart v. Tuolumne County Water Company, Tuolumne Co. Dist. Ct. (1853)

Gale and Elliott v. Tuolumne County Water Company, Tuolumne Co. Dist. Ct. (1857)

Graham v. Tuolumne County Water Company, Tuolumne Co. Dist. Ct. (1856)

Hoffman v. Tuolumne County Water Company, Tuolumne Co. Dist. Ct. (1857)

(Numerous plaintiffs) v. Tuolumne County Water Company, Tuolumne Co. Dist. Ct. (1857)

Shay v. Tuolumne County Water Company, Tuolumne Co. Dist. Ct. (1854)

Tuolumne County Water Company v. Columbia and Stanislaus River Water Company, Tuolumne Co. Dist. Ct. (1856)

Tuolumne County Water Company v. Columbia and Stanislaus River Water Company, Tuolumne Co. Dist. Ct. (1859)

Woods Diggings Company v. Tuolumne County Water Company, Tuolumne Co. Co. Ct. (1852)

e. Other

Cary v. Daniels, 49 Mass. 466 (1844)

Elliot v. Fitchburg Railroad Company, 64 Mass. 191 (1852)

McDonald v. Vandeling, Mokelumne Hill (1859)

Tyler v. Wilkinson, 24 Fed. Cas. 472 (1827)

Webb v. Portland Manufacturing, 29 Fed. Cas. 506 (1838)

2. *Other Legal Material*

Alcalde Record, 1849–1850 of Woods Diggins and Jamestown. Transcribed by Edward M. Nissen, October 16, 2002. Carlo De Ferrari Archive, Sonora, CA.

California gold regions: with a full account of their mineral resources; how to get there, and what to take; the expenses, the time, and the various routes. With sketches of California; an account of the life, manners, and customs of the inhabitants, its history, climate, soil, productions, &c. New York: Pratt, 1849.

California. Secretary of State. *Record of Incorporations*, 1850–1862. California State Archives, Sacramento, CA.

California. Statutes, Appendix. *Article VI, Constitution of the State of California.* San Jose: Winchester, 1850.

California. Statutes, passed at the First Session of the Legislature, Chapter 14. "An Act to organize the Supreme Court of California," enacted February 14, 1850, San Jose: Winchester, 1850.

California. Statutes, passed at the First Session of the Legislature, Chapter 23. "An Act to supersede certain Courts, and to regulate Appeals therefrom to the Supreme Court," enacted February 28, 1850, San Jose: Winchester, 1850.

California. Statutes, passed at the First Session of the Legislature, Chapter 33. "An Act to organize the District Courts of the State of California," enacted March 16, 1850, San Jose: Winchester, 1850.

California. Statutes, passed at the First Session of the Legislature, Chapter 95.

"An Act adopting the Common Law," enacted April 13, 1850, San Jose: Winchester, 1850.

California. Statutes, passed at the First Session of the Legislature, Chapter 128. "An Act concerning Corporations," enacted April 22, 1850, San Jose: Winchester, 1850.

California. Statutes, passed at the First Session of the Legislature, Chapter 142. "An Act to regulate proceedings in Civil Cases in the District Court, the Superior Court of the City of San Francisco, and Supreme Court," enacted April 22, 1850, San Jose: Winchester, 1850.

California. Statutes, passed at the Second Session of the Legislature, Chapter 5. "An Act to regulate Proceedings in Civil Cases in the Courts of Justice of this State," enacted May 1, 1850, Casserly, 1851.

California. Statutes, passed at the Fourth Session of the Legislature, Chapter 65. "An Act to provide for the Formation of Corporations for certain purposes," enacted April 14, 1853, San Francisco: Kerr, 1853.

California. Surveyor General. Annual Report, 1856. Sacramento: Allen, 1856.

California. Surveyor General. Annual Report, 1857. Sacramento: O'Meara, 1857.

California. Surveyor General. Annual Report, 1858. Sacramento: O'Meara, 1858.

California. Surveyor General. Annual Report, 1859. Sacramento: Botts, 1859.

California. Surveyor General. Annual Report, 1860. Sacramento: O'Meara, 1860.

California. Surveyor General. Annual Report, 1862. Sacramento: Avery, 1862.

California. Surveyor General. Annual Report, 1863. Sacramento: Clayes, 1863.

California. Surveyor General. Annual Report, 1864. Sacramento: Clayes, 1864.

Claim, Camp Seco Watering Co., William W. Traylor. *Deeds*, Vol. 1, pp. 237–38, Tuolumne County Recorder, Sonora.

Historical Background of Pacific Gas and Electric Company's Ditch System in Tuolumne County. Tuolumne County Water Company Collection. State Historic Park Archives, Columbia, CA.

Idaho. Legislature. *Constitution of the State of Idaho*. www.legislature.idaho.gov /idstat/IC/Title003.htm.

Letter, Columbia Businessmen. To Tuolumne County Water Company, March 18, 1855. Joseph Pownall Papers, P229, Huntington Library.

Letter, Gale & Elliot. To Tuolumne County Water Company, March 4, 1857. Joseph Pownall Papers, PW 314, Huntington Library.

List of Names of Stockholders in the Bear River and Auburn Water and Mining Company, Incorporated May 1, 1851.

Marten Law. "Washington's Municipal Water Law Challenged as Unconstitutional," October 11, 2006. www.martenlaw.com/newsletter/20061011-water -law-challenged.

Minute Book, Tuolumne Redemption Company, 1859–1860. Joseph Pownall Papers, PW 976, Huntington Library.

Minutes of Board of Trustees, Columbia and Stanislaus River Water Company, 1856–1859. Joseph Pownall Papers, PW 234, Huntington Library.

Minutes, Board of Trustees of Tuolumne County Water Company from September 6 1852 to November 4, 1853 inclusive. Joseph Pownall Papers, PW 973, Huntington Library.

Records of the Mississippi Valley, Junction Bluff, and North San Juan Mining Districts in Bridgeport, 1854–1859. Bancroft Library, University of California, Berkeley.

Thom, Robert. *Mining Report of Tuolumne County California.* Board of Supervisors, Tuolumne County, 1913.

Tuolumne County. *Secured Property Assessment Roll, 1856.* Carlo de Ferrari Archive, Sonora, CA.

Tuolumne County Water Company. *Records, 1853–1904, Volume 2.* Minutes, 1853–1904. Bancroft Library, University of California, Berkeley.

United States. Bureau of Mines. *Mines of the southern Mother Lode Region. Part II: Tuolumne and Mariposa Counties.* By C. E. Julihn and F. W. Horton. Washington, DC, 1940.

United States. Department of the Interior. Census Office. *The United States Mining Laws and Regulations Thereunder, and State and Territorial Mining Law, to which are appended Local Mining Rules and Regulations.* Washington, DC: Government Printing Office, 1885.

Water Privilege, Thomas C. Brunton and James Parsons. Recorded 3/5/1857, *Claims Book*, Vol. 1–7, pp. 502–3, Tuolumne County Recorder, Sonora.

B. General Material

Allen, Douglas W. "Transaction Costs." *The History and Methodology of Law and Economics.* Vol. 1 of *Encyclopedia of Law and Economics*, edited by Boudewijn Bouckaert and Gerrit De Geest, 893–926. Cheltenham: Edward Elgar Press, 2000.

Allen, Douglas W. "The Rhino's Horn: Incomplete Property Rights and the Optimal Value of an Asset." *Journal of Legal Studies* 31 (June 2002): S339–S358.

Allsop, Thomas, ed. *California and its Gold Mines: Being a Series of Recent Communications from the Mining Districts, upon the Present Condition and Future Prospects of Quartz Mining; with an Account of the Richer Deposits, and Incidental Notices of the Climate, Scenery, and Mode of Life in California.* London: Groombridge & Sons, 1853.

Alston, Lee J. "Tenure Choice in Southern Agriculture, 1930–1960." *Explorations in Economic History*, 18 (July 1981): 211–32.

Alston, Lee J., and Robert Higgs. "Contractual Mix in Southern Agriculture since the Civil War: Facts, Hypotheses, and Tests." *Journal of Economic History* 42 (June 1982): 327–53.

Anderson, Terry L., and Peter J. Hill. "The Evolution of Property Rights: A Study of the American West." *Journal of Law and Economics* 18 (1975): 163–79.

Anderson, Terry L., and Peter J. Hill. "Privatizing the Commons: An Improvement?" *Southern Economic Journal* 50 (October 1983): 438–50.

Anderson, Terry L., and Peter J. Hill. "The Race for Property Rights." *Journal of Law and Economics* 33 (1990): 177–98.

Anderson, Terry L., and Peter J. Hill. "Cowboys and Contracts." *Journal of Legal Studies* 31 (June 2002): S489–S514.

Anderson, Terry L., and Ronald N. Johnson. "The Problem of Instream Flows." *Economic Inquiry* 24 (October 1986): 535–54.

Anderson, Terry L., and Pamela Snyder. *Water Markets: Priming the Invisible Pump*. Washington: Cato, 1997.

Angell, Joseph K. *A Treatise on the Common Law in Relation to Watercourses*. Boston, 1824.

Archibald, Robert. *The Economic Aspects of the California Missions*. Washington: Academy of American Franciscan History, 1978.

Ayres, Ian, and Eric Talley. "Solomonic Bargaining: Dividing a Legal Entitlement to Facilitate Coasean Trade." *Yale Law Journal* 104, no. 5 (March 1995): 1027–117.

Bakken, Gordon M. "The English Common Law in the Rocky Mountain West." *Arizona and the West* 11 (Summer 1969): 109–28.

Bakken, Gordon M. "The Influence of the West on the Development of Law." *Journal of the West* 24 (1985): 66–72.

Bakken, Gordon M. *Practicing Law in Frontier California*. Lincoln: University of Nebraska Press, 1991.

Bakken, Gordon M. "The Courts, the Legal Profession, and the Development of Law in Early California," in *Taming the Elephant: Politics, Government and Law in Pioneer California*, edited by John F. Burns and Richard J. Orsi, 74–95. Berkeley: University of California Press, 2003.

Bancroft, Hubert H. *History of California, Vol. VI: 1848–1859*. San Francisco: History Company, 1888.

Barzel, Yoram. *Economic Analysis of Property Rights*. Cambridge: Cambridge University Press, 1989.

Barzel, Yoram. "Measurement Cost and the Organization of Markets." *Journal of Law and Economics* 25 (1982): 27–48.

Bean, Walton. *California: An Interpretive History*. New York: McGraw-Hill, 1968.

Beard, Charles. *An Economic Interpretation of the Constitution of the United States*. New York, 1913.

Berry, Thomas Senior. *Early California: Gold, Prices, Trade*. Richmond: Bostwick Press, 1984.

Bieber, Ralph P. "California Gold Mania." *Mississippi Valley Historical Review* 35 (June 1948): 3–28.

Black, George. *Report on Middle Yuba Canal*. San Francisco: Towne, Bacon, Book and Job, 1864.

Blackstone, William. *Commentaries on the Laws of England*. Facsimile of the first edition of 1765–1769. Chicago: University of Chicago Press, 1971.

Blomquist, William. *Dividing the Waters: Governing Groundwater in Southern California*. San Francisco: ICS, 1992.

Borthwick, J. D. *Three Years in California*. Oakland: Biobooks, 1948.

Brands, H. W. *The Age of Gold*. New York: Doubleday, 2002.

Bretsen, Stephen N., and Peter J. Hill. "Water Markets as a Tragedy of the Anticommons." *William and Mary Environmental Law and Policy Review* 33 (2009): 723–83.

Brewer, Jedidiah, Robert Glennon, Alan Ker, and Gary Libecap. "Water Markets in the West: Prices, Trading, and Contractual Forms." *Economic Inquiry* 46 (April 2008): 91–112.

Brooks, J. Tyrwhitt. *Four Months among the Gold Finders in Alta California*. London, 1849.

Bruce, Robert B. *The Launching of Modern American Science*. New York: Knopf, 1987.

Buchanan, James M., Robert D. Tollison, and Gordon Tullock, eds. *Toward a Theory of the Rent-Seeking Society*. College Station: Texas A&M University Press, 1980.

Bueno de Mesquita, Ethan, and Matthew Stephenson. "Informative Precedent and Intrajudicial Communication." *American Political Science Review* 96 (December 2002): 755–66.

Buffum, Edward G. *Six Months in the Gold Mines*. Ann Arbor: University Microfilms, 1966.

Burness, H. Stuart, and James P. Quirk. "Appropriative Water Rights and the Efficient Allocation of Resources." *American Economic Review* 69 (March 1979): 25–37.

Burnett, Peter H. *Recollections and Opinions of an Old Pioneer*. New York, 1880.

Burns, John F., and Richard J. Orsi, eds. *Taming the Elephant: Politics, Government, and Law in Pioneer California*. Berkeley: University of California Press, 2003.

Calabresi, Guido, and A. Douglas Melamed. "Property Rules, Liability Rules, and Inalienability: One View of the Cathedral." *Harvard Law Review* 85 (1972): 1089.

Carey, Janis M., and David L. Sunding. "Emerging Markets in Water: A Comparative Institutional Analysis of the Central Valley and Colorado-Big Thompson Projects." *Natural Resources Journal* 41 (Spring 2001): 283–328.

Castro, Doris Shaw. *James H. Carson's California, 1847–1853.* Bloomington: AuthorHouse, 2006.

Caughey, John Walton. *Gold Is the Cornerstone.* Berkeley: University of California Press, 1948.

Cheung, Steven. "The Structure of a Contract and the Theory of a Non-Exclusive Resource." *Journal of Law and Economics* 13, no. 1 (1970): 49–70.

Cheung, Steven. "Why Are Better Seats Underpriced?" *Economic Inquiry* 15 (1977): 513–22.

Christman, Enos. *One Man's Gold: The Letters & Journals of a Forty-Niner.* New York: McGraw-Hill, 1930.

Clappe, Louisa. *The Shirley Letters from the California Mines, 1851–1852.* New York: Knopf, 1949.

Clark, Thomas D. *Gold Rush Diary.* Lexington: University of Kentucky Press, 1967.

Clay, Karen B. "Property Rights and Institutions: Congress and the California Land Act of 1851." *Journal of Economic History* 59 (March 1999): 122–42.

Clay, Karen B., and Randall Jones. "Migrating to Riches? Evidence from the California Gold Rush." *Journal of Economic History* 68 (2008): 997–1027.

Clay, Karen B., and Gavin Wright. "Order without Law? Property Rights during the California Gold Rush." *Explorations in Economic History* 42 (April 2005): 155–83.

Cleland, Robert Glass. *The Cattle on a Thousand Hills.* San Marino: Huntington Press, 1975 (orig. 1941).

Cleland, Robert Glass. *From Wilderness to Empire: A History of California, 1542–1900.* New York: Knopf, 1949.

Colby, Bonnie G. "Transactions Costs and Efficiency in Western Water Allocation." *American Journal of Agricultural Economics* 72 (December 1990): 1184–92.

Colton, Walter. *Three Years in California.* Stanford: Stanford University Press, 1949.

Cooter, Robert D., Lewis Kornhauser, and David Lane. "Liability Rules, Limited Information, and the Role of Precedent." *Bell Journal of Economics* 10 (Spring 1979): 366–73.

Cooter, Robert D., and Thomas Ulen. *Law and Economics.* Boston: Addison-Wesley, 2008.

Daily Alta Californian, Various issues, 1849–1860.

Dana, James D. *Manual of Mineralogy including Observations on mines, rocks, reduction of ores, and the Application of the Science to the Arts.* 4th ed. New Haven: Durrie & Peck, 1851.

David, Paul A. "Clio and the Economics of QWERTY." *American Economic Review* 75 (May 1985): 332–37.

Decker, Peter R. *Fortunes and Failures: White Collar Mobility in Nineteenth Century San Francisco.* Cambridge: Harvard University Press, 1978.

DeGroot, Henry. *Recollections of California mining life.* San Francisco: Dewey, 1884.

Delano, Alonzo. *Across the Plains and Among the Diggings.* New York: Wilson-Erickson, 1936.

Demsetz, Harold. "Toward a Theory of Property Rights." *American Economic Review* 57 (1967): 347–59.

Derbec, Etienne. *A French journalist in the California gold rush: the letters of Etienne Derbec.* Edited by A. P. Nasatir. Georgetown: Talisman, 1964.

Dharmapala, Dhammika, and Rohan Pitchford. "An Economic Analysis of 'Riding to Hounds': Pierson v. Post Revisited." *Journal of Law, Economics and Organization* 18 (April 2002): 39–66.

Directory of the County of Placer. San Francisco: Robbins, 1861.

Drobak, John N., and John V. C. Nye. *The Frontiers of the New Institutional Economics.* San Diego: Academic Press, 1997.

Drummond, Frank J., and Tyrrell Martinez. *The Popular and Legal Tribunals of Tuolumne County, 1849–1867.* Berkeley, 1936.

Dunbar, Robert G. "The Adaptation of Groundwater-Control Institutions to the Arid West." *Agricultural History* 51 (October 1977): 662–80.

Dunbar, Robert G. *Forging New Rights in Western Waters.* Lincoln: University of Nebraska Press, 1983.

Dunbar, Robert G. "The Adaptability of Water Law to the Aridity of the West." *Journal of the West* 24 (1985): 57–65.

Eastman, Barbara. "John Wallace and the Tuolumne Water Company." *CHISPA* 9 (Oct–Dec, 1969): 297–99.

Eastman, Barbara. "John Wallace and the Tuolumne Water Company." *CHISPA* 9 (Jan–Mar, 1970): 308–12.

Eggertsson, Thrainn. *Economic Behavior and Institutions.* Cambridge: Cambridge University Press, 1990.

Epstein, Richard A. "Nuisance Law: Corrective Justice and Its Utilitarian Constraints." *Journal of Legal Studies* 8 (January 1979): 49–102.

Epstein, Richard A. "Why Restrain Alienation?" *Columbia Law Review* 85 (1985): 970–90.

Epstein, Richard A. "A Clear View of the Cathedral: The Dominance of Property Rules." *Yale Law Journal* 106 (May 1997): 2091–120.

Feeny, David, Susan Hanna, and Arthur F. McEvoy. "Questioning the Assumptions of the 'Tragedy of the Commons' Model of Fisheries." *Land Economics* 72 (May 1996): 187–205.

Feeny, David, Fikret Berkes, Bonnie J. McCay, and James M. Acheson. "The

Tragedy of the Commons: Twenty-Two Years Later." *Human Ecology* 18 (March 1990): 1–19.

Ferrie, Joseph P. "Up and Out or Down and Out? Immigrant Mobility in the Antebellum United States." *Journal of Interdisciplinary History* 26 (Summer 1995): 33–55.

Field, Barry C. "The Evolution of Property Rights." *Kyklos* 42 (1989): 319–345.

Field, Stephen Johnson. *Personal reminiscences of early days in California.* [San Francisco?] c.1880.

Gardiner, Howard C., and Dale L. Morgan. *In Pursuit of the Golden Dream.* Stoughton: Western Hemisphere, 1970.

Gates, Paul. "The California Land Act of 1851." *California Historical Quarterly* 50 (December 1971): 395–430.

Gennaioli, Nicola, and Andrei Shleifer. "The Evolution of Common Law." *Journal of Political Economy* 115 (2007): 43–68.

Getches, David H. *Water Law in a Nutshell.* St. Paul: West, 1990.

Getches, David H. "Water Resources: A Wider World," in *Natural Resources Policy and Law: Trends and Directions*, edited by Lawrence J. MacDonnell and Sarah F. Bates, 124–47. Washington: Island Press, 1993.

Getzler, Joshua. *A History of Water Rights at Common Law.* Oxford: Oxford University Press, 2004.

Glennon, Robert. *Water Follies.* Washington: Island, 2002.

Glennon, Robert. "Water Scarcity, Marketing, and Privatization." *Texas Law Review* 83 (2005): 1874–1902.

Gordon, H. Scott. "The Economic Theory of a Common Property Resource: The Fishery." *Journal of Political Economy* 62 (1954): 124–42.

Gould, George A. "Water Rights Transfers and Third-Party Effects." *Land and Water Law Review* 23 (1988): 1–41.

Gould, George A. "Transfer of Water Rights." *Natural Resources Journal* 29 (1989): 457–78.

Graves, Pusey. *Correspondence of Pusey Graves, 1850–1852.* Huntington Library, mccFAC 1615-1646.

Gray, B. E. "'In Search of Bigfoot': The Common Law Origins of Article X , Section 2 of the California Constitution." *Hastings Constitutional Law Quarterly* 17 (1989): 225–73.

Greenland, Powell. *Hydraulic Mining in California: A Tarnished Legacy.* Spokane: Clark, 2001.

Grivas, Theodore. "Alcalde Rule: The Nature of Local Government in Spanish and Mexican California." *California Historical Society Quarterly* 40 (March 1961): 11–32.

Gudde, Erwin G. *Bigler's Chronicle of the West.* Berkeley: University of California Press, 1962.

Gudde, Erwin G. *California Gold Camps*. Berkeley: University of California Press, 1975.

Gutierrez, Ramon A., and Richard J. Orsi, eds. *Contested Eden: California before the Gold Rush*. Berkeley: University of California Press, 1998.

Hackel, Steven W. "Land, Labor, and Production: The Colonial Economy of Spanish and Mexican California," in *Contested Eden: California Before the Gold Rush*, edited by Ramon A. Gutierrez and Richard J. Orsi, 111–46. Berkeley: University of California Press, 1998.

Hanak, Ellen. "Stopping the Drain: Third-Party Responses to California's Water Market." *Contemporary Economic Policy* 23 (January 2005): 59–77.

Hart, John F. "Property Rights, Costs, and Welfare: Delaware Water Mill Legislation, 1719–1859." *Journal of Legal Studies* 27 (1998): 455–71.

Hartman, L.M., and D. Seastone. *Water Transfers: Economic Efficiency and Alternative Institutions*. Baltimore: Johns Hopkins University Press, 1970.

Heckendorn, John, and W. A. Wilson. *Miners & Businessmen's Directory*. Columbia: Heckendorn & Wilson, 1856.

Heiner, Ronald A. "The Origin of Predictable Behavior." *American Economic Review* 73 (September 1983): 560–95.

Higgins, Richard S., and Paul H. Rubin. "Judicial Discretion." *Journal of Legal Studies* 9 (1980): 129–38.

Higgs, Robert. "Race, Tenure, and Resource Allocation in Southern Agriculture, 1910." *Journal of Economic History* 33 (March 1973): 149–69.

Hill, Jasper Smith. *Letters of a young miner*. San Francisco: Howell-Books, 1964.

Hill, John Berry. *In the gold mines in '50, '51 and '52*. Coloma: El Dorado County Historical Society, 1966.

Historical Souvenir of El Dorado County California with Illustrations and Biographical Sketches of its Prominent Men and Pioneers. Oakland: Sioli, 1883.

History of Amador County. Oakland: Thompson & West, 1881.

History of Butte County. Berkeley: Howell-North, 1973.

History of Tuolumne County. San Francisco: Alley, 1882.

History of Yuba County. Oakland: Thompson & West, 1879.

Hittell, John S. *Mining in the Pacific States of North America*. San Francisco: Bancroft, 1861.

Hoffman, Elizabeth, and Matthew L. Spitzer. "Entitlements, Rights, and Fairness: An Experimental Examination of Subjects' Concepts of Distributive Justice." *Journal of Legal Studies* 14 (1985): 259–97.

Holliday, J. S. *The World Rushed In: The California Gold Rush Experience*. New York: Simon & Schuster, 1981.

Horwitz, Morton J. "The Rise of Legal Formalism." *American Journal of Legal History* 18 (1975): 251–64.

Horwitz, Morton J. *The Transformation of American Law, 1780–1860*. Cambridge: Harvard University Press, 1977.

Huffaker, Ray, Norman Whittlesey, and Joel R. Hamilton. "The Role of Prior Appropriation in Allocating Water Resources into the 21st Century." *International Journal of Water Resources Development* 16 (2000): 265–73.

Hunt, Rockwell D. "Legal Status of California, 1846–49." *Annals of the American Academy of Political and Social Science* 12 (November 1898): 63–84.

Huntley, Henry Vere. *Adventures in California: Its gold fields, and its inhabitants.* London: Dean and Son, 1856, v. 1–2.

Jenks, Leland H. *The Migration of British Capital to 1875.* New York, 1927.

Johnson, Ronald N., Micha Gisser, and Michael Werner. "The Definition of a Surface Water Right and Transferability." *Journal of Law and Economics* 24 (1981): 273–88.

Johnson, Ronald N., and Gary Libecap. "Contracting Problems and Regulation: The Case of the Fishery." *American Economic Review* 72 (1982): 1005–22.

Johnston, William Graham. *Experiences of a forty-niner.* Pittsburgh, 1892.

Jung, Maureen A. "Capitalism Comes to the Diggings: From Gold-Rush Adventure to Corporate Enterprise," in *A Golden State: Mining and Economic Development in Gold Rush California*, edited by James J. Rawls and Richard J. Orsi, 52–77. Berkeley: University of California Press, 1999.

Kalman, Laura. "Transformations." *Law and Social Inquiry* 28 (Autumn 2003): 1149–55.

Kanazawa, Mark T. "Water Quality and the Economic Efficiency of Appropriative Water Rights," in *The Economics of Management of Water and Drainage in Agriculture*, edited by A. Dinar and D. Zilberman, 821–39. Boston: Kluwer, 1991.

Kanazawa, Mark T. "Possession Is Nine Points of the Law." *Explorations in Economic History* 33 (1994): 227–49.

Kanazawa, Mark T. "Efficiency in Western Water Law: The Development of the California Doctrine, 1850–1911." *Journal of Legal Studies* 27 (January 1998): 159–85.

Kanazawa, Mark T. "Origins of Common-Law Restrictions on Water Transfers: Groundwater Law in Early California." *Journal of Legal Studies* 32 (January 2003); 153–80.

Kanazawa, Mark T. "Immigration, Exclusion, and Taxation: Anti-Chinese Legislation in Gold Rush California." *Journal of Economic History* 65 (September 2005): 779–805.

Kanazawa, Mark T. "Taxation with(?) Representation: The Political Economy of Public Finance in Antebellum California." *Research in Economic History* (2008): 205–33.

Kaplow, Louis, and Steven Shavell. "Do Liability Rules Facilitate Bargaining? A Reply to Ayres and Talley." *Yale Law Journal* 105, no. 1 (October 1995): 221–33.

Kaplow, Louis, and Steven Shavell. "Property Rules vs. Liability Rules: An Economic Analysis." *Harvard Law Review* 109 (1996): 713.

Kelley, Robert. *Gold vs. Grain: The Hydraulic Mining Controversy in California's Sacramento Valley.* Glendale: Clark, 1959.

Kells, Charles E. *California, from its discovery by the Spaniards, to the present time, with a brief description of the gold region, its present position; together with a few hints to 'gold hunters,' and a guide to those about to visit that country. By a traveler.* New York, 1848.

Kinney, Clesson S. *A Treatise on the Law of Irrigation and Water Rights and the Arid Region Doctrine of Appropriation of Waters.* San Francisco: Bender-Moss, 1912.

Klein, Benjamin. "Legal Precedent: A Theoretical and Empirical Analysis: Comment." *Journal of Law and Economics* 19 (August 1976): 309–13.

Kline, Christine A. "Water Transfers: The Case against Transbasin Diversions in the Eastern States." *UCLA Journal of Environmental Law and Policy* 25 (2008): 249–82.

Knight, Jack, and Lee Epstein. "The Norm of Stare Decisis." *American Journal of Political Science* 40(1996): 1018–35.

Konow, James. "Which Is the Fairest One of All? A Positive Analysis of Justice Theories." *Journal of Economic Literature* 41 (December 2003): 1188–239.

Landes, William M., and Richard A. Posner. "Legal Precedent: A Theoretical and Empirical Analysis." *Journal of Law and Economics* 19 (August 1976): 249–307.

Landes, William M., and Richard A. Posner. *The Economic Structure of Tort Law.* Cambridge: Harvard University Press: 1987.

Langum, David J. *Law and Community on the Mexican California Frontier.* Norman: University of Oklahoma Press, 1987.

Lardner, W. B., and M. J. Brock. *History of Placer and Nevada Counties.* Los Angeles: Historic Record Company, 1924.

Lewis, David Rich. "Argonauts and the Overland Trail Experience: Method and Theory." *Western Historical Quarterly* 16 (July 1985): 285–305.

Libecap, Gary D. *Contracting for Property Rights.* Cambridge: Cambridge University Press, 1993.

Libecap, Gary D. "Economic Variables and the Development of the Law: The Case of Western Mineral Rights." *Journal of Economic History* 38, no. 2 (June 1978): 338–62.

Libecap, Gary D. "Institutional Path Dependence in Climate Adaptation: Conan's 'Some Unsettled Problems of Irrigation.'" *American Economic Review* 101 (February 2011): 64–80.

Libecap, Gary D., and Dean Lueck. "The Demarcation of Land and the Role of Coordinating Property Institutions." *Journal of Political Economy* 119 (June 2011): 426–67.

Lienhard, Heinrich. *A pioneer at Sutter's fort, 1846–1850.* Los Angeles: Calafia, 1941.

Littlefield, Douglas R. "Water Rights during the California Gold Rush: Conflicts over Economic Points of View." *Western Historical Quarterly* 14 (October 1983): 415–34.

Lueck, Dean. "The Rule of First Possession and the Design of the Law." *Journal of Law and Economics* 38 (1995): 393–436.

Lueck, Dean. "The Extermination and Conservation of the American Bison." *Journal of Legal Studies* 31 (June 2002): S609–52.

Lyman, Albert. *Journal of a voyage to California, and life in the gold diggings . . .* Hartford: Pease, 1852.

MacDonnell, Lawrence. "The Water Transfer Process as a Management Option for Meeting Changing Water Demands." Boulder: Natural Resources Law Center, 1990.

Mann, Ralph. *After the Gold Rush: Society in Grass Valley and Nevada City, California, 1849–1870.* Stanford: Stanford University Press, 1982.

Mann, Ralph. "Frontier Opportunities and the New Social History." *Pacific Historical Review* 53 (November 1984): 463–91.

Margo, Robert A. "Wages in California during the Gold Rush." NBER Working Paper No. H0101. Cambridge, MA: National Bureau of Economic Research, June 1997.

Marks, Paula Mitchell. *Precious Dust.* New York: Morrow, 1994.

Marryat, Frank. *Mountains and Molehills; or Recollections of a Burnt Journal.* Philadelphia: Lippincott, 1962.

May, Philip R. *Origins of Hydraulic Mining in California.* Oakland: Holmes, 1970.

McCall, A. J. *Pick and pan: trip to the diggings in 1849.* Bath: Steuben Courier, 1883.

McCurdy, Charles. "Stephen J. Field and Public Land Law Development in California, 1850–1866: A Case Study of Judicial Resource Allocation in Nineteenth-Century America." *Law and Society Review* 10 (1976): 235–66.

McDowell, Andrea. "From Commons to Claims: Property Rights in the California Gold Rush." *Yale Journal of Law and Humanities* 14 (2002): 1–72.

McDowell, Andrea. "Real Property, Spontaneous Order, and Norms in the Gold Mines." *Law & Social Inquiry* 29, no. 4 (Autumn 2004): 771–818.

McDowell, Andrea. "Gold Rushes Are All the Same: Labor Rules the Diggings," in *Property in Land and Other Resources,* edited by Daniel H. Cole and Elinor Ostrom. Cambridge: Lincoln Institute, 2012.

McGrath, Roger. *Gunfighters, Highwaymen, and Vigilantes: Violence on the Frontier.* Berkeley: University of California Press, 1984.

McGuire, Robert A., and Robert L. Ohsfeldt. "Economic Interests and the American Constitution: A Quantitative Rehabilitation of Charles A. Beard." *Journal of Economic History* 44 (June 1984): 509–19.

McGuire, Robert A., and Robert L. Ohsfeldt. "Self-Interest, Agency Theory, and Political Voting Behavior: The Ratification of the United States Constitution." *American Economic Review* 79 (March 1989): 219–34.

McKanna, C. V. "Enclaves of Violence in Nineteenth-Century California." *Pacific Historical Review* 73 (August 2004): 391–424.

McManus, John C. "An Economic Analysis of Indian Behavior in the North American Fur Trade." *Journal of Economic History* 32 (March 1972): 36–53.

McNeil, Samuel. *McNeil's travels in 1849, to, through and from the gold regions, in California*. Columbus: Scott & Bascom, 1850.

Merrill, Thomas W. "Trespass, Nuisance, and the Costs of Determining Property Rights." *Journal of Legal Studies* 14 (January 1985): 13–48.

Merrill, Thomas W., and Henry E. Smith. "What Happened to Property in Law and Economics?" *Yale Law Journal* 111 (November 2001): 357–98.

Meyers, Charles, and Richard Posner. *Market Transfers of Water Rights: Towards an Improved Market in Water Resources*. National Water Commission Legal Study No. 4, 1971.

Miceli, Thomas J. "Legal Change: Selective Litigation, Judicial Bias, and Precedent." *Journal of Legal Studies* (2009): 157–68.

Miller, Gordon R. "Shaping California Water Law, 1781 to 1928." *Southern California Quarterly* 55 (Spring 1973): 9–42.

The Miners' Own Book. San Francisco: Book Club of California, 1949 (reprint of 1858 edition).

Moerenhout, Jacques Antoine. *The Inside Story of the Gold Rush*. San Francisco: California Historical Society, 1935.

Morriss, Andrew P. "Real People, Real Resources, and Real Choices: The Case for Market Valuation of Water." *Texas Tech Law Review* 38 (2006): 973–1009.

Morse, Edwin F. "The Story of a Gold Miner: Reminiscences of Edwin Franklin Morse." *California Historical Society Quarterly* 6 (September 1927): 205–37.

Newman, Janet C. "Beneficial Use, Waste, and Forfeiture: The Inefficient Search for Efficiency in Western Water Use." *Environmental Law Review* 29 (1998): 919–95.

New York Times. "Is It a Water-Rights Fee or a Backdoor Tax? Calif.'s High Court Will Decide," December 2, 2010.

Noll, Roger G. "Economic Perspectives on the Politics of Regulation," in *Handbook of Industrial Organization*, vol. 2, edited by R. Schmalensee and R. Willig, 1253–87. New York: North-Holland, 1989.

North, Douglass C. *Institutions, Institutional Change, and Economic Performance*. Cambridge: Cambridge University Press, 1990.

North, Douglass C. *Structure and Change in Economic History*. New York: Norton, 1981.

North, Douglass C. *Understanding the Process of Economic Change*. Princeton: Princeton University Press, 2005.

Odell, Kerry A. "The Integration of Regional and Interregional Capital Markets: Evidence from the Pacific Coast, 1883–1913." *Journal of Economic History* 49 (June 1989): 297–310.

Olson, Mancur. *The Logic of Collective Action*. Cambridge, MA: Harvard University Press, 1971.

Olson, Mancur. *Power and Prosperity*. New York: Basic Books, 2000.

Ostrom, Elinor. "A Diagnostic Approach for Going beyond Panaceas." *PNAS* 104 (September 25, 2007): 15181–87.

Ostrom, Elinor. *Governing the Commons: The Evolution of Institutions for Collective Action*. Cambridge: Cambridge University Press, 1990.

Ostrom, Elinor, and Roy Gardner. "Coping with Asymmetries in the Commons: Self-Governing Irrigation Systems Can Work." *Journal of Economic Perspectives* 7 (Autumn 1993): 93–112.

Pagenhart, Thomas H. *Water Use in the Yuba and Bear River Basins, California*. PhD diss., University of California Berkeley, 1969.

Paul, Rodman W. *California Gold: The Beginning of Mining in the Far West*. Lincoln: University of Nebraska Press, 1947.

Paul, Rodman W. *The California Gold Discovery*. Georgetown: Talisman Press, 1966.

Paul, Rodman W. *Far West and the Great Plains in Transition, 1859–1900*. New York: Harper & Row, 1988.

Pejovich, Svetovar. "Towards an Economic Theory of Creation and Specification of Property Rights." *Review of Social Economy* 30 (1972): 309–25.

Phillips, William. "Essay on the Georgia Gold Mines." *American Journal of Science and Arts* 24 (July 1833): 1–18.

Pisani, Donald J. "Enterprise and Equity: A Critique of Western Water Law in the Nineteenth Century." *Western Historical Quarterly* 18 (1987): 15–37.

Pisani, Donald J. *From the Family Farm to Agribusiness*. Berkeley: University of California Press, 1984.

Pisani, Donald J. "The Origins of Western Water Law: Case Studies from Two California Mining Districts." *California History* (Fall 1991): 242–57.

Pisani, Donald J. *To Reclaim a Divided West: Water, Law, and Public Policy, 1848–1902*. Albuquerque: University of New Mexico Press, 1992.

Pisani, Donald J. "'I am resolved not to interfere, but permit all to work freely': The Gold Rush and American Resource Law," in *A Golden State: Mining and Economic Development in Gold Rush California*, edited by James J. Rawls and Richard J. Orsi. Berkeley: University of California Press, 1999: 123–48.

Pitchford, Rohan, and Christopher M. Snyder. "Coming to the Nuisance: An Economic Analysis from an Incomplete Contracts Perspective." *Journal of Law, Economics, and Organization* 19 (October 2003): 491–516.

Posner, Richard A. *Economic Analysis of Law*. 3rd ed. Little, Brown: Boston: 1986.

Posner, Richard A. *How Judges Think*. Cambridge: Harvard University Press, 2009.

Posner, Richard A. "What Do Judges and Justices Maximize? (The Same Thing Everybody Else Does)." *Supreme Court Economic Review* 3 (1993): 1–41.

Priest, George L. "The Common Law Process and the Selection of Efficient Rules." *Journal of Legal Studies* 6 (1977): 65–82.

Priest, George L. "Selective Characteristics of Litigation." *Journal of Legal Studies* 9 (March 1980): 399–421.

Priest, George L. "Measuring Legal Change." *Journal of Law, Economics and Organization* 3 (Autumn 1987): 193–225.

Priest, George L., and Benjamin Klein. "The Selection of Disputes for Litigation." *Journal of Legal Studies* 13 (January 1984): 1–55.

Quevedo, Steven M. "Formalist and Instrumentalist Legal Reasoning and Legal Theory." *California Law Review* 73 (January 1985): 119–57.

Ramseyer, J. Mark. "Water Law in Imperial Japan: Public Goods, Private Claims, and Legal Convergence." *Journal of Legal Studies* 18 (1989): 51–77.

Rawls, James J. "Introduction," in *A Golden State*, edited by James J. Rawls and Richard J. Orsi. Berkeley: University of California Press, 1999.

Rawls, James J., and Richard J. Orsi, eds. *A Golden State: Mining and Economic Development in Gold Rush California*. Berkeley: University of California Press, 1999.

Read, Thomas Thornton. *The Development of Mineral Industry Education in the United States*. New York: American Institute of Mining and Metallurgical Engineers, 1941.

Reid, John Phillip. "Binding the Elephant: Contracts and Legal Obligations on the Overland Trail." *American Journal of Legal History* 21 (October 1977): 285–315.

Reid, John Phillip. "Governance of the Elephant: Constitutional Theory on the Overland Trail." *Hastings Constitutional Law Quarterly* 5 (Winter 1978): 421–43.

Reid, John Phillip. "Replenishing the Elephant: Property and Survival on the Overland Trail." *Oregon Historical Quarterly* 79 (Spring 1978): 64–90.

Reid, John Phillip. *Law for the Elephant*. San Marino: Huntington Library, 1980.

Reisner, Marc, and Sarah Bates. *Overtapped Oasis: Reform or Revolution for Western Water*. Washington: Island, 1990.

Rensch, Hero E. *Columbia, A Gold Camp of Old Tuolumne: Her Rise and Decline*, Together with some mention of her social life and cultural strivings. History of Mining Districts of California Columbia Series. Berkeley: 1936.

Robinson, W. W. *Land in California*. Berkeley: University of California Press, 1979 (reprint of 1948 edition).

Rohe, Randall E. "Hydraulicking in the American West: The Development and

Diffusion of a Mining Technique." *Montana: Magazine of Western History* 35 (Spring 1985): 18–35.

Rohe, Randall E. "Origins and Diffusion of Traditional Placer Mining in the West." *Material Culture* 18 (Fall 1986): 127–66.

Rohrbough, Malcolm J. *Days of Gold: The California Gold Rush and the American Nation.* Berkeley: University of California Press, 1997.

Rose, Carol M. "Possession as the Origin of Property." *University of Chicago Law Review* 52, no. 1 (Winter 1985): 73–88.

Rose, Carol M. "Crystals and Mud in Property Law." *Stanford Law Review* 40 (February 1988): 577–610.

Rose, Carol M. "Energy and Efficiency in the Realignment of Common-Law Water Rights." *Journal of Legal Studies* 19 (1990): 261–94.

Rose, Carol M. "The Shadow of the Cathedral." *Yale Law Journal* 106, no. 7 (May 1997): 2175–200.

Royce, Josiah. *California from the Conquest in 1846 to the Second Vigilance Committee in San Francisco: A Study of American Character.* Boston: Houghton-Mifflin, 1886.

Royce, Sarah. *Across the Plains.* Edited by J. D. Adkison. Tucson: University of Arizona, 2009.

Rubin, Paul. "Why Is the Common Law Efficient?" *Journal of Legal Studies* 6 (1977): 51–63.

Runge, C. Ford. "Strategic Interdependence in Models of Property Rights." *American Journal of Agricultural Economics* 66 (December 1984): 807–13.

Ryan, William Redmond. *Personal adventures in Upper and Lower California, in 1848–49; with the author's experience at the mines.* London: Shoberl, 1850.

St. Clair, David J. "The Gold Rush and the Beginnings of California Industry," in *A Golden State: Mining and Economic Development in Gold Rush California,* edited by James J. Rawls and Richard J. Orsi, 185–208. Berkeley: University of California Press, 1999.

Sawyer, Lorenzo. *Way sketches.* New York: Eberhardt, 1926. Huntington Library Rare Books 86469.

Sax, Joseph L. "Understanding Transfers: Community Rights and the Privatization of Water." *West-Northwest Journal of Environmental Law and Policy* 14 (Winter 2008): 33–39.

Schauer, Frederick. "Precedent." *Stanford Law Review* 39 (February 1987): 571–605.

Scheiber, Harry N. "Regulation, Property Rights, and the Definition of 'The Market': Law and the American Economy." *Journal of Economic History* 41 (March 1981): 103–9.

Schlager, Edella, and Elinor Ostrom. "Property-Rights Regimes and Natural Resources: A Conceptual Analysis." *Land Economics* 68 (August 1992): 249–62.

Schorr, David B. "Appropriation as Agrarianism: Distributive Justice in the Creation of Property Rights." *Ecology Law Quarterly* 32 (2005): 3–71.

Schorr, David B. *The Colorado Doctrine*. New Haven: Yale University Press, 2012.

Schwartz, Edward P. "Policy, Precedent, and Power: A Positive Theory of Supreme Court Decision-Making." *Journal of Law, Economics, and Organization* 8 (April 1992): 219–52.

Schwartz, Gary T. "Tort Law and the Economy in Nineteenth-Century America: A Reinterpretation." *Yale Law Journal* 90 (July 1981): 1717–75.

Schweikart, Larry, and Lynne Pierson Doty. "From Hard Money to Branch Banking: California Banking in the Gold-Rush Economy," in *A Golden State: Mining and Economic Development in Gold Rush California*, edited by James J. Rawls and Richard J. Orsi, 209–232. Berkeley: University of California Press, 1999.

Scott, Anthony. "The Fishery: The Objectives of Sole Ownership." *Journal of Political Economy* 63 (1955): 116–24.

Scott, Anthony, and Georgina Coustalin. "The Evolution of Water Rights." *Natural Resources Journal* (Fall 1995): 821–979.

Segal, Jeffrey A., and Harold J. Spaeth. "The Influence of Stare Decisis on the Votes of United States Supreme Court Justices." *American Journal of Political Science* 40 (1996): 971–1003.

Senter, Riley. *Crossing the continent to California gold fields*. Lemon Cove: Senter, 1938.

Shapiro, Martin. "Toward a Theory of 'Stare Decisis.'" *Journal of Legal Studies* 1 (January 1972): 125–34.

Shavell, Steven. "Strict Liability versus Negligence." *Journal of Legal Studies* 9 (January 1980): 1–25.

Shavell, Steven. "Torts in Which Victim and Injurer Act Sequentially." *Journal of Law and Economics* 26 (1983): 589–612.

Shaw, Lucien. "The Development of the Law of Waters in the West." *California Law Review* 10 (1922): 443–60.

Shaw, William. *Golden Dreams and Waking Realities*. London: Smith, 1851.

Sherman, William Tecumseh. *The California gold fields in 1848: two letters*. Huntington Library.

Shinn, Charles H. *Mining Camps: A Study in American Frontier Government*. New York: Knopf, 1948.

Shugerman, Jed Handelsman. "The Floodgates of Strict Liability: Bursting Reservoirs and the Adoption of Fletcher v. Rylands in the Gilded Age." *Yale Law Journal* (November 2000): 333–77.

Simmons, William S. "Indian Peoples of California," in *Contested Eden: California before the Gold Rush*, edited by Ramon A. Gutierrez and Richard J. Orsi, 48–77. Berkeley: University of California Press, 1998.

Simpson, A. W. B. "The Horwitz Thesis and the History of Contracts." *University of Chicago Law Review* 46 (1979): 533–601.

Smith, Henry E. "Exclusion vs. Governance: Two Strategies for Delineating Property Rights." *Journal of Legal Studies* 31 (2002): S453–87.

Smith, Henry E. "Exclusion and Property Rules in the Law of Nuisance." *Virginia Law Review* 90, no. 4 (2004): 965–1049.

Smith, Henry E. "Governing Water: The Semicommons of Fluid Property Rights." Arizona Law Review 50, no. 2 (2008): 445–78.

Spence, Clark C. *Mining Engineers and the American West: The Lace-Boot Brigade, 1849–1933.* New Haven: Yale University Press, 1970.

Spence, Clark C. *British Investments and the American Mining Frontier, 1860–1901.* Moscow: University of Idaho Press, 1995.

Starr, Kevin, and Richard J. Orsi, eds. *Rooted in Barbarous Soil: People, Culture and Community in Gold Rush California.* Berkeley: University of California Press, 2000.

Stephens, Lorenzo Dow. *Life sketches of a jayhawker of '49.* San Jose: Nolta, 1916.

Stephenson, Matthew C. "Legal Realism for Economists." *Journal of Economic Perspectives* 23 (Spring 2009): 191–211.

Stewart, James. "Cooperation when N is Large: Evidence from the Mining Camps of the American West." *Journal of Economic Behavior and Organization* 69 (2009): 213–25.

Stillson, Richard T. *Spreading the Word: A History of Information in the California Gold Rush.* Lincoln: University of Nebraska Press, 2006.

Stoddart, Thomas Robertson. *Annals of Tuolumne County.* Clovis: Word Dancer Press, 1963.

Swan, John Alfred. *A trip to the gold mines of California in 1848*, edited by John A. Hussey. San Francisco: Book Club of California, 1960.

Tarlock, Dan. "New Water Transfer Restrictions—The West Returns to Riparianism." *Water Resources Research* 27 (June 1991): 987–94.

Taylor, Bayard. *El Dorado, or Adventure in the Path of Empire.* Glorieta: Rio Grande Press, 1967.

Teggart, Frederick J., and C. S. Lyman. "The Gold Rush: Extracts from the Diary of C. S. Lyman 1848–1849." *California Historical Society Quarterly* 2 (October 1923): 181–202.

Thompson, Thomas Hinckley, and Albert Augustus West. *History of Nevada County, California.* Berkeley: Howell-North Books, 1970 (reprint of 1880 edition).

Tollison, Robert D. "Rent-Seeking: A Survey." *Kyklos* 35 (1982): 575–602.

Umbeck, John R. "The California Gold Rush: A Study of Emerging Property Rights." *Explorations in Economic History* 14 (1977): 197–226.

Umbeck, John R. "A Theory of Contract Choice and the California Gold Rush." *Journal of Law and Economics* 20 (October 1977): 421–37.

Umbeck, John R. *A Theory of Property Rights with Application to the California Gold Rush.* Ames: Iowa State University Press, 1981.

Webb, Walter Prescott. *The Great Plains.* Boston: Ginn, 1931.

Whittlesey, Norman K., and Ray G. Huffaker. "Water Policy Issues for the Twenty-First Century." *American Journal of Agricultural Economics* 77 (December 1995): 1199–203.

Wiel, Samuel C. "'Priority' in Western Water Law." *Yale Law Journal* 18 (January 1909): 189–98.

Wiel, Samuel C. "Public Policy in Western Water Decisions." *California Law Review* 1 (1912): 11–31.

Wiel, Samuel C. "What Is Beneficial Use of Water?" *California Law Review* 3 (September 1915): 460–75.

Wiel, Samuel C. "Theories of Water Law." *Harvard Law Review* 27 (April 1914): 530–44.

Wierzbicki, Felix P. *California as It Is and as It May Be.* San Francisco: Grabhorn, 1933.

Wilkinson, Charles F. "Western Water Law in Transition." *Journal of the American Water Works Association* 78 (October 1986): 34–47.

Wilkinson, Charles F. *Crossing the Next Meridian: Land, Water, and the Future of the West.* Washington: Island, 1992.

Williams, David. *The Georgia Gold Rush: Twenty-Niners, Cherokees, and Gold Fever.* Columbia: University of South Carolina Press, 1993.

Wittman, Donald. "Optimal Pricing of Sequential Inputs: Last Clear Chance, Mitigation of Damages, and Related Doctrines in the Law." *Journal of Legal Studies* 10 (1981): 65–91.

Wittman, Donald. "First Come, First Served: An Economic Analysis of 'Coming to the Nuisance.'" *Journal of Legal Studies* 9 (1980): 557–68.

Woods, Daniel B. *Sixteen months at the gold diggings.* New York: Harper & Brothers, 1851.

Worster, Donald J. *Rivers of Empire: Water, Aridity and the Growth of the American West.* New York: Pantheon, 1985.

Wyman, Walker D. "California Emigrant Letters." *California Historical Society Quarterly* 24 (March 1945): 17–46.

Young, Jim. "Pine Log." *CHISPA* 8 (April–June, 1969): 281–84.

Young, Robert A. "Why Are There So Few Transactions among Water Users?" *American Journal of Agricultural Economics* 68 (December 1986): 1143–51.

Zentner, Rene D. "Positive and Natural Law in California, 1846–1849." *California Law Review* 45 (March 1957): 59–65.

Zerbe, R. O., and Anderson, C.L. "Culture and Fairness in the Development of Institutions in the California Gold Fields." *Journal of Economic History* 61 (2001): 114–43.

Index

Page numbers in italics refer to figures.